UNDERSTANDING GAṆAPATI

Insights into the Dynamics of a Cult

UNDERSTANDING GAṆAPATI

Insights into the Dynamics of a Cult

ANITA RAINA THAPAN

MANOHAR
1997

First published 1997

ISBN 81-7304-195-4

Published by
Ajay Kumar Jain for
Manohar Publishers & Distributors
2/6 Ansari Road, Daryaganj
New Delhi 110 002

Lasertypeset by
A J Software Publishing Co. Pvt. Ltd.
305 Durga Chambers
1333 D.B. Gupta Road
Karol Bagh, New Delhi 110 005

Printed at
Rajkamal Electric Press
B-35/9, G.T. Karnal Road Indl. Area
Delhi 110033

For Arjun, Gaurav and Madhav

Contents

Acknowledgements

This book is based on my Ph.D dissertation completed in 1993 at the University of Delhi. There are many who have shared in my endeavour from the conception of the idea in 1988 to the writing of the thesis and to its subsequent appearance as a book. I am happy to be able to finally express my appreciation to them for having helped make this such a rich learning experience.

The many thought-provoking interventions of my supervisor, Professor K.M. Shrimali, helped sustain the excitement and enthusiasm with which this work was undertaken. I am deeply grateful to him for his considerable patience and intellectual generosity. The comments of my examiners enabled me to refine many ideas and acquire fresh insights into the subject. Professor François Grimal generously provided me every facility I needed at the French Institute of Pondicherry and the help of his staff at the Sanskrit Department. To Dr. Surya Narayan Bhatt I am especially grateful for the many hours he spent with me going through transcripts and esoteric texts. His fluency in spoken Sanskrit was sheer delight. Shereen Ratnagar has, at various stages, provided encouragement and assistance with her criticial and incisive comments as also with her useful suggestions in matters related to archaeology. Only I know how much I have benefited from our meetings. Professor N.N. Bhattacharya was good enough to read and comment on some of my final drafts. Several lengthy discussions with Dr. Marta Vannucci, as also her scientific and logical approach to all study, have been a stimulating influence.

To *Studies in History* I am grateful for permission to use material in Chapter III from my article which was originally published in their journal (Vol. X, No. 1, 1994, pp. 1-22) and to *Social Science Probings*, too, for permission to give a new *avatāra* in Chapter II to my article originally published by them (Vol. 9, Nos. 1-4, Mar.-Dec. 1992, pp. 31-41). Raveendranath Rajan was generous in his assistance with the maps. More recently, I have appreciated the punctuality and efficiency with which my publishers, Messrs Ramesh and Ajay Jain, have processed every stage in the bringing out of this book.

Many friends have provided support of various kinds. Amita Satyal has, on several occasions, checked things out for me in the libraries in Delhi and sent me material I needed at short notice. Viru and Gita Acharya offered me their home as a base for my field work in Karnataka and, on occasion, also acted as interpreters when the only language the *pujārī* could speak was Kannada. Snimer Sahni and K. Srinivas helped with the logistics of field-work in Maharashtra. Jyotsna Sekhar provided me the base for my visits in and around Madras and Kerala and has, through the years, shared in the joys and frustrations of my work.

The most rewarding experience has been the interaction with the numerous *pujārīs* at the several temples that I visited. It is not possible to name them all. However, special mention must be made of some who were generous with their time: Shri V. Gururaja Dikshit, the *pradhān arcak* of the Mahagaṇapati Temple, Mallesvaram Circle, Bangalore; Shri Moreshwar Dinkar Pendse, the *mukhya pujārī* of the Gaṇapati temple at Theur; Shri Tryambaka Narain Joshi, head trustee and *pujārī* at the temple at Titwala; Shri Narayana Upadhyaya and Shri Gopala Mahadev of the main temple at Gokarna. I am also grateful to Vani and Purnima the two daughters of Shri Gopala Mahadev. They were my very able guides to all the lesser known shrines in and around Gokarna. Shrimati Vighnahari Deo at Cincvad (whose husband is the eleventh descendant of Morayā Gosāvī, believed to be the first of a dynasty of eight incarnations of Gaṇapati) and her daughter Shrimati Bhakti Bhate provided me with some insights into the life of a family which has constituted the core of the Gāṇapatya tradition in Maharashtra over so many generations. Shri Rajabhau Deodhar and several artisan families at Pen, Maharashtra, welcomed me into their homes and patiently answered my numerous queries.

Invaluable assistance was provided by my mother who cheerfully took over many of my domestic responsibilities enabling me to spend long hours at work. My sons, Gaurav and Madhav, were little boys when I began working on the thesis. Their numerous questions along the years provided both motivation and inspiration. Now, as adolescents, they have offered useful advice on the finer points of wordprocessing. I hope that when they read this book they will appreciate the study that engaged their mother's mind during their formative years.

Finally, I am indebted to my husband, Arjun, for his constant support and understanding through the ups and downs of this work. He has been subjected to numerous discussions, readings and interpretations and has, involuntarily and despite any inclination, become quite knowledgeable about Gaṇapati. I have specially valued his sense of humour and editorial comments.

Manila, Philippines ANITA RAINA THAPAN
April 1996

Abbreviations

ABORI	*Annals of the Bhandarkar Oriental Research Institute*
ASIAR	*Archaeological Survey of India Annual Report*
ASI	Archaeological Survey of India
BBMPG	*Bulletin of the Baroda Museum and Picture Gallery*
BHU	Banaras Hindu University
BMFA	*Bulletin of the Museum of Fine Arts (Boston)*
CII	*Corpus Inscriptionum Indicarum*
EA	*Epigraphia Andhrica*
EC	*Epigraphia Carnatica*
EI	*Epigraphia Indica*
EW	*East and West*
FIP	French Institute of Pondicherry
IHQ	*Indian Historical Quarterly*
IO	*Inscriptions of Orissa*
JBBRAS	*Journal of the Bombay Branch of the Royal Asiatic Society*
JBORS	*Journal of the Bihar and Orissa Research Society*
JBRS	*Journal of the Bihar Research Society*
JESHO	*Journal of the Economic and Social History of the Orient*
JGJhRI	*Journal of the Ganganatha Jha Research Institute*
JOIB	*Journal of the Oriental Institute of Baroda*
JRAS	*Journal of the Royal Asiatic Society of Great Britain and Ireland*
JUPHS	*Journal of the UP Historical Society*
PIHC	*Proceedings of the Indian History Congress*
SAA	*South Asian Archaeology*
SII	*South Indian Inscriptions*

List of Maps and Plates

Transliteration of Sanskrit Letters

अ	आ	इ
a	ā	i
ई	उ	ऊ
ī	u	ū
ऋ	ॠ	ळ
ṛ	ṝ	ḷ
ए	ऐ	ओ
e	ai	o
औ	अं	अः
au	aṃ	aḥ

Anusvāra ˙ ṃ
Visarga : ḥ

क	ख	ग	घ	ङ
ka	kha	ga	gha	ṅ
च	छ	ज	झ	ञ
ca	cha	ja	jha	ña
ट	ठ	ड	ढ	ण
ṭa	ṭha	ḍ	ḍha	ṇa
त	थ	द	ध	न
ta	tha	da	dha	na
प	फ	ब	भ	म
pa	pha	ba	bha	ma
य	र	ल	व	श
ya	ra	la	va	śa
ष	स	ह	क्ष	
ṣa	sa	ḥa	kṣa	

CHAPTER I

Introduction

Gaṇapati is best understood when situated in a broad historical context. From his obscure origins in antiquity he gradually rose to find a permanent place in the pantheons of the three major religious systems of ancient India—Brahmanism, Buddhism and Jainism. Over time, he came to be associated with various castes and occupational groups in towns and villages and acquired manifold powers and functions. This evolution culminated in his becoming one of the most popular and well-loved deities in India.

The purpose of this study is to map the dynamic process of the development of the cult of Gaṇapati and analyse the compulsions behind it. Since society is constantly evolving, so also are religious needs and attitudes and, thereby, the perception of deities. In fact, the whole body of living and practised beliefs of the Hindus are essentially dynamic, adaptable and transformable to suit the needs of men and the times. This is not, however, how Brahmanism views itself. In fact, there is a tendency in the Brahmanical texts to obliterate historical time and facts. It is considered that historical accounts are misleading, since they reduce the eternal to the temporal and that gods and their powers are universal and, therefore, do not belong to the profane which is limited in time and space and which alone can be understood by modern academic disciplines. At several old Gaṇapati temples which I visited, whenever I asked how old the temple or the site was, I was informed by the priest that it belonged to another *yuga*. According to Hinduism, there are four *yugas* or ages called Kṛta, Tretā, Dvāpara and Kali. To quote Basham 'their lengths are respectively 4,800, 3,600, 2,400 and 1,200 "years of gods" each of which equals 360 human years. Each *yuga* represents a progressive decline in piety, morality, strength, stature, longevity and happiness. We are at present in the *Kali yuga* which began, according to tradition, in 3120 BC, believed to be the year of the Mahābhārata war.'[1] These four *yugas* form part of each of the seventy-one *mahā-yugas* or aeons which in turn form part of each of the fourteen *manvantaras* or secondary cycles. Finally, these *manvantaras* are part of the basic cycle, the *kalpa,* which constitutes a day of Brahmā or 4,320 million earthly years. Brahmā's nights are of equal length while his total life span is of 100 years, or 311,040,000 million earthly years, after which the whole universe returns to the ineffable world spirit until another creator god is evolved.[2] With such a concept it is easy to understand how insignificant man's life is in the Brahmanical perception and how great the gulf is between the time frame of the sacred and that of the profane. The historic world is unreal, because, in comparison with the cosmic rythm it lasts only for an instant and is, therefore, *māyā* or illusion. From this knowledge stems the desire to renounce this world and seek the *Brahman* (Absolute Reality) which alone enables one to pierce the veil of *māyā.* Buddhism and Jainism also accept the same doctrine of cyclic time, in its general outlines.

However, even if man's existence on this earth is insignificant in terms of time, while he is alive his needs are very material and most of the religious texts describe rituals, fasts, pilgrimages and prayers to be performed for material benefits. As material conditions change so do human needs and, consequently, certain gods rise or decline in importance. A study of changing material conditions and their effects on the religious life of people necessitates a vast time frame. Religious phenomena have to be viewed over an extended duration of time since religious evolution and transformation is slow both in the case of religious habits and the vision of the world. Social changes cause men to develop new ideas and aspirations and this results in the gradual modification of various aspects of the religious system. Today, when the discoveries and inventions in the realm of science and technology appear to be unlimited, many people feel that miracles and religious phenomena can be explained scientifically and that there is an insurmountable contradiction between religious faith and scientific thought. It is also in the developed societies where religious fervour appears to have declined the most. The religious sentiments of individuals or particular castes or sub-castes are also determined by their position within a society. As individuals or groups rise higher or descend lower in the social hierarchy their mentalities undergo a change. Similarly, social changes can lead one group to demand the religious rights and privileges of other groups. Emancipation of women in western society has led them to demand admission to the clergy, traditionally reserved only for men.

In this modern day at least one new goddess, Santoṣī Mā, has emerged in India. She has certain characteristics that are lacking in the goddesses of the Sanskritic tradition or the folk tradition. She is specifically suited to the needs of the urban woman in the lower and middle class income groups. At the same time, with the development of medicine and faith in doctors, particularly in the urban areas, many traditional goddesses of various diseases have lost their popularity. One such example is Śītalā, the smallpox goddess, who has declined in importance in several regions with the eradication of small pox or in the absence of epidemics since many years. Therefore, the functions deities are believed to perform correspond to the needs of their worshippers and since these are constantly evolving so are the deities that fulfill them.

My intention is to examine, within a chronological framework, the process by which Gaṇapati evolves and why he is gradually accommodated in different religious contexts; how he is Brahmanized; how the syncretic religious texts, the Purāṇas, evolving out of a necessity to create a wider social base and reach out to a greater number of people in the face of competition from Buddhism, Jainism and other religious sects, manipulate this deity; how the cult of the Puranic Gaṇapati spreading from the *madhyadeśa* region (Indo-Gangetic divide and the Ganga-Yamuna Doab and its environs) reaches the peripheral areas, comes in contact with local beliefs and associations and further undergoes a change; when and why Gaṇapati becomes associated with the trading community; why the Gāṇapatya sects come into being and the significance Gaṇapati acquires within different religious groups—Buddhist, Śaivas and Smārtas; and, finally, which of these several layers of Gāṇapatya tradition continue to be relevant and what are the modern facets of Gaṇapati worship which are not mentioned in ancient texts.

Such an analysis highlights both the regional variations in beliefs and practices as also those elements that retain a common symbolism nation wide. Similarly, it also permits an understanding of those aspects of the deity that remain constant over a prolonged period of time and those that have evolved or are in the process of evolving. These differences and similarities are best understood when the canvas on which they are unfolding is large. While I accept the importance and necessity of regional studies because of the deep insights they provide into the workings of local processes, I have deliberately chosen, instead, to undertake a more broad-based analysis in order to fully appreciate the dynamics of a cult over a large area, much of which constitutes modern India. It is in India that the deity represents a continuing tradition and where he enjoys an important position in the religious life of millions. My thrust, therefore, is on the evolution of an Indian god with all the regional diversities that it implies. The most significant developments in the forms and roles of Gaṇapati occur in the peripheral regions. It is in western India that he first becomes the deity of traders. In the south he acquires a variety of forms each recommended for installation in a specific category of town or village. Similarly, it is mainly in the south and in the Deccan area that the various sects of the Gāṇapatyas emerge. Even the ambiguities in his personality, or in his relationships with other deities, may vary between regions. In fact, the ambivalence of many aspects of his personality and role may be understood as being the result of the coalescence of the Sanskritic and non-Sanskritic traditions which results in a character that is full of dichotomies.

Against this background, it is possible to rationalize to some extent the modern trends in the beliefs associated with Gaṇapati. A recent dimension to the personality of Gaṇapati is that of paternity of the newly invented goddess Santoṣī Mā. Until then, Gaṇapati's relationship with the goddess was that of son, husband, brother and consort. What is significant in this development of his acquiring a daughter is not just the fact that he is associated with a new goddess, thereby asserting his own popularity in the modern context, but of his constant and manifold relationship with the goddess in general. The film *Jai Santoshi Ma* is responsible for popularizing the cult of this goddess. The story is based on a Hindi *Kathā* with some modifications. The *Kathā*, for example, does not mention that Santoṣī Mā is the daughter of Gaṇapati. Santoṣī Mā is essentially a north Indian goddess who has not found a place in the Gaṇapati temples south of the Vindhyas, at least not in the several temples that I visited. This fact is best understood against a background of the varying perceptions of Gaṇapati's marital status in the northern and southern regions.

Recently, Gaṇapati images accepting milk from devotees

all over the world has generated considerable awe and excitement. Although this phenomenon is associated with Nandi, Śiva's *vāhana* (vehicle) and the Goddess as well, Gaṇapati is believed to have accepted the greatest quantity of milk and from the largest number of people. Whatever be the interpretations of this event, the sacred texts have not prescribed milk as a favourite food of the deity. Henceforth, however, I have no doubt that it will be included in the daily offerings, for who knows when Gaṇapati will decide to accept it again.

Several scholars have contributed to an understanding of this deity. Some consider him to have been derived from the totem of a Dravidian tribe[3], or, at least, from some pre-Aryan tradition.[4] Others consider that it was the early Aryan settlers themselves who, out of fear or desire to acquire the strength of the elephant, began to worship the animal. The latter, gradually came to be looked upon as a guardian deity.[5] There are scholars who maintain that Gaṇapati evolved from within the Brahmanical fold, being present in concept in the Vedas.[6] According to some, Gaṇapati, both in concept and form, is the product of popular imagination and certainly not of Vedic origin.[7] Przyluski believes that Śiva and Gaṇapati were originally one and the same god.[8] Others, like Heras, consider that Skanda and Gaṇapati were originally synonymous.[9] Whereas these scholars discuss the diverse possible sources of his origin as also the stages that mark his development, none describes the actual process by which this deity emerges.

Some of the important studies on Gaṇapati analyse the cult not only in India but in several parts of Asia. Getty's pioneering work, first published in 1936, focuses on an analysis of the deity as described and depicted in literature, iconography, sculpture and painting in Hinduism and Buddhism in India, Nepal, Chinese Turkestan, and Tibet, and of the introduction of his image and worship in Java, Bali, Borneo, China and Japan. The most recent, comprehensive study of Gaṇapati is the one edited by Robert L. Brown[10] which contains articles on wide-ranging aspects of Gaṇapati in Asia by several scholars. Some of these are based on literary texts that have recently been translated and on fresh sculptural data. This book provides some original insights into the cult of Gaṇapati in several countries.

A.K. Narain's article in the book edited by Brown discusses

the protohistory of the idea and icon of Gaṇapati.[11] His detailed and informative analysis still leaves some questions unanswered. Who were the people who worshipped the sacred elephant and with which specific regions were they associated? Why is the elephant associated with mountains and with snakes? Is there any connection between Airāvata, Indra's elephant mount, and Gaṇapati? Why are the evil spirits, that had been ritually placated from the earliest of times, suddenly referred to as Vināyakas? Why do the Vināyakas and the elephant deity find mention in only a limited number of Brahmanical texts and, essentially, within one particular school of the Vedas, namely, the *Kṛṣṇa Yajur Veda*? What is the process by which the syncretism between them takes place, by whom is it brought about and in which region? I have attempted to answer some of these questions as they help provide a deeper insight into Gaṇapati's origins.

Gaṇapati's role and significance within the Brahmanical framework is reflected essentially in the Mahāpurāṇas. Courtright has given a detailed analysis of the Puranic myths pertaining to Gaṇapati, as also his ritual and worship based on these texts.[12] The myths explain neither his origin nor his nature, for the Purāṇas depict only an aspect of his personality. Nor do they throw light on the reasons for the contradictions and the many facets that exist in his Puranic personality and which are not quite apparent in the Buddhist, Jaina or Tantric contexts. Often, psychoanalytic readings of the myths of Gaṇapati obscure as much as they reveal. The role of the Puranic Gaṇapati is better understood when compared to that of other secondary deities of Puranic pantheon.

Gaṇapati is the favourite deity of traders and merchants in contemporary India. His image, along with that of Lakṣmī, adorns even the humblest of shops and market places. Both are worshipped for prosperity. Yet, Lakṣmī is the consort of Viṣṇu and is not really associated with Gaṇapati in Puranic mythology. A study of the Brahmanical texts alone does not allow an understanding of how and why this happens. From at least one or two centuries before the Christian era, Kubera was accepted as the lord of wealth and Maṇibhadra was popular with traders in the region of the upper and middle Ganga plain. This study highlights how and why Gaṇapati comes to be associated with these two deities and eventually takes over their role and significance. It shows how Gaṇapati's growing importance with the trading community initially begins with non-Brahmanical communities in those very regions where trade continues to flourish inspite of a general decline in trading activity over most of the country in the post-Gupta period. This association spreads to other regions where trade picks up from about the tenth century onwards and where non-Brahmanical communities are also present. Gradually, the Brahmanical Gaṇapati is also identified with this activity which was, initially, looked down upon in the Purāṇas. This aspect of Gaṇapati has not been analysed in previous studies of the deity. Situating the deity in the context of a specific category of society can reveal some lesser known facets of his personality and role.

There have been a few regional studies of the Gaṇapati cult but they are essentially focussed on Maharashtra. Preston discusses the sites sacred to Gaṇapati in Maharashtra from about AD 1300 to the nineteenth century.[13] Courtright devotes part of his book to an analysis of Gaṇapati worship and the celebration of the Gaṇeśa *caturthī* festival by a particular community of *brāhmaṇas* in Maharashtra. Richard Cashman discusses the political recruitment of Gaṇapati by Bal Gangadhar Tilak in Maharashtra in order to forge a united Hindu front during the freedom struggle at the end of the nineteenth century and in the early years of the twentieth century. Perhaps, one reason for a paucity of regional data is because a detailed historical study of the deity in the subcontinent as a whole has been lacking. Since I associate different stages in the development of the cult with specific geographical areas, this study may offer a background of information on various regions and could provide some clue to the areas which offer scope for a detailed study. An analysis of the regional variations of the cult could then be related to the trans-regional cult as a whole.

The Gāṇapatyas remain a little known sect. Although mentioned by nearly all the scholars who have worked on Gaṇapati, we know little about who they were, where and when they emerged and what the differences between the various sub-sects were. The development of this sect represents the culmination of a process which had been developing during several preceding centuries. I have associated the various sub-sects with different geographical locations and have attempted to understand the differences between them. Since Gaṇapati is part of a living tradition, a historical enquiry of this nature would remain incomplete if it did not make some attempt to relate historical data to the existing trends in regions where these sects flourished. An understanding of the contemporary perceptions of Gaṇapati brings out the elements of continuity as well as disjunctions in the tradition of Gaṇapati worship. While my analysis is far from exhaustive, considering the size of India and the existence of innumerable temples and traditions, it does permit some pertinent conclusions.

My assessment of the influence of the Gāṇapatya sects in the regions with which they were associated is based on field-work. Visits to about forty Gaṇapati temples in these regions permitted me to gain a deeper insight into some aspects of contemporary religious beliefs. Understanding the present, puts much of the past in perspective. Texts alone are insufficient for the understanding of a culture where the oral tradition has always remained very rich and important. Texts only provide us with what has been considered worth recording by the literate classes. The actual practice of religion in India is a mixture of both the oral and written traditions. Each region has a variety of traditions and what is striking is the extreme plasticity of religious beliefs and practices. The data that I collected, based on field-work, enabled me to gain a deeper insight into some of the religious phenomena that I have described in Chapter VI. Details of my field-work are given in the next section devoted to sources.

I should explain why I refer to this deity as Gaṇapati, rather than as Gaṇeśa. Both Alice Getty and Courtright chose to refer to him as Gaṇeśa. Haridas Mitra and Heras prefer the epithet Gaṇapati. From the sources that I have consulted, it is apparent that this deity is referred to most frequently as Gaṇapati. In the Buddhist Tantras he is either Vināyaka or Gaṇapati. Other epithets are less often used. In the Purāṇas, he is referred to as Gaṇa, Vināyaka or by other epithets, of which Gaṇeśa is only rarely used. As Mahāgaṇapati, he figures as a deity in his own right, worthy of worship. Likewise, in inscriptions, or in the Āgamas and Tantras, he is not referred to as Gaṇeśa very often. The sect which chose him as the supreme deity is named after Gaṇapati. Even the eight famous Gaṇapati temples, the *aṣṭavināyakas* in Maharashtra, are named Śrī Mayureśvara, Śrī Siddhi Vināyaka, Śrī Bāllaleśvara, Śrī Varada Vināyaka, Śrī Cintāmaṇi, Śrī Girijātmaja, Śrī Vighneśvara and Śrī Mahāgaṇapati. It, therefore, seems appropriate to refer to him as Gaṇapati. The epithet Gaṇeśa appears to have been popularized by the *Gaṇeśa Purāṇa* which is associated with the region of modern Maharashtra, Varanasi, Karnataka and perhaps some parts of Andhra Pradesh. Possibly, the sectarian devotees of the deity sought to give him a distinct name. Today the epithet Gaṇapati is popular in the south while Gaṇeśa is more frequently used in Maharashtra and the north.

It is also necessary to clarify some of the terms that I have used in the text. These terms are used more for the sake of convenience and do not represent any definite and unanimously accepted categories or distinctions. By Vedic religion is meant the religion based on the Vedas, the Brāhmaṇas which are looked on as appendices to the Vedas, and the mystical Āraṇyakas and Upaniṣads which are, in turn, appendices to the Brāhmaṇas. Of the four Vedas, the *Ṛg Veda* is the oldest religious text in the world which is still looked upon as sacred and it was probably composed between 1500-1000 BC. The *Yajur, Sāma* and *Atharva Vedas* are later than the *Ṛg Veda,* about 1000-800 BC, although the *Atharva Veda* may be even a little later. The *Brāhmaṇas* are situated between *c.* 800-600 BC and while some of the Upaniṣads overlap with the latest Brāhmaṇas, some are certainly of a later date. By Brahmanism I mean the religion based on the *Dharma Sūtras* or the Sacred Books of Law, the *Gṛhya Sūtras* or the manuals for simple everyday domestic ceremonies and rituals, the epics (the *Rāmāyaṇa* and the *Mahābhārata*), and the Purāṇas. The *Dharma Sūtras* and *Gṛhya Sūtras* have originated from one or other of the four Vedic schools but, unlike the Vedas, they are not considered as divine revelation or *Sruti.* They are considered to be *Smṛti,* a term which literally means 'memory' and which constitutes Tradition, as opposed to *Sruti* or Revelation. *Smṛti* also includes the two epics and the Purāṇas.

The epics and Purāṇas were available to all castes, yet they were the product of *brāhmaṇas* and portrayed the world-view of Brahmanical society with its insistence on *varṇa* (caste) and *āśrama* (the four stages of life). Most Brahmanical literature, in its present form, belongs to the Christian era although some of the law-books and domestic manuals as also the core of the epics, existed in the two or three centuries before the Christian era. The principal Brahmanical deities are Śiva, Viṣṇu and the Goddess who were all relatively minor figures in the Vedic pantheon. There are also many other deities who are not mentioned in the Vedic texts. However, the authority and sanctity of the Vedas is upheld by Brahmanism even though many new beliefs and attitudes, sometimes contrary to the Vedas, are reflected by it. By Hinduism

I mean the sum-total of the traditions mentioned above, i.e. Vedic texts, Brahmanical texts and, in addition, the Tantras and Āgamas and various texts of the Bhakti tradition both from the south and the north many of them in the vernaculars and sometimes composed by non-*brāhmaṇas;* various *Sthala Purāṇas* (collection of myths about specific sites or places) many of which are post fifteenth century; *Māhātmyas* (texts glorifying a particular place or deity); poems such as the *Gīta Govinda*; and many folk rituals which have become a part of contemporary religious practice and which, in some cases, found their way into the older texts, and, in other cases, remained part of the oral tradition.

Various sects existed within the framework of Brahmanism and some continue to exist in modern Hinduism. The three well-known sects are the Śaivas, the Smārtas and the Vaiṣṇavas. The Śaivas and the Vaiṣṇavas have, traditionally, been divided into various subsects many of which do not exist today. The Śaivas believe only in one god, Śiva, who is self-existent. The Smārtas worship the five deities of the *pañcāyatana,* i.e. Śiva, Viṣṇu, the Sun, Gaṇapati and the Goddess. They may choose any one of these as their personal and principal god but that does not exclude the worship of the four others. They consider all five as manifestations of the supreme spirit and who, in the end, are to be absorbed into the infinite sprit. The word *Smārta* derives from the term *Smṛti* or Tradition on which this group bases its beliefs and rituals. The Vaiṣṇavas, in general, are followers of either of the three Vaiṣṇava reformers, Caitanya (in Bengal), Rāmānuja (Tamil Nadu) and Mādhava (Karnataka). They consider Viṣṇu to be the chief god. Similarly, the Śāktas worship Śakti or the goddess as the principal deity. Other well known sects in the past were the Gāṇapatyas and the Sauras who looked upon Gaṇapati and the Sun, respectively, as their supreme deities. Many modern Hindus are not part of any sect and worship all or any of the deities. At other times, even when they are part of a sect they feel free to worship other deities as well.

SOURCES

The time frame of this study is wide. The sources, therefore, are numerous and varied. Since most aspects of Gaṇapati's personality, as we know it, emerge by about the fifteenth century, a large part of sources used cover the period from the time of the Harappan civilization until about AD 1500. Where required, I have used sources of a later date because Gaṇapati is part of a continuing tradition. The final chapter is based on field work in those regions where the Gāṇapatya sects evolved and established a tradition of their own. It analyses the relevance of that tradition in the modern context.

Whereas the archaeological, numismatic, epigraphical and iconographical sources do not pose a problem, the same cannot be said for the literary sources. These are often hard to date. Scholars attribute different dates to the same text. Besides, there are so many texts that I have had to be selective because it is not possible to cover all of them. Certain texts such as the eighteen Mahāpurāṇas and the Gāṇapatya Upapurāṇas are indispensable for a discussion on Gaṇapati. The Tantric texts have been selected because they reflect some regional diversities, being from Kashmir, Bengal and the south. The Āgamas are essentially those that have been published or that were available in transcript form in the library of the French Institute of Pondichery (FIP). The inscriptions number several thousand and, besides those in Sanskrit, there is a vast collection in the many regional languages. To examine them all is beyond the scope of most scholars as it implies a knowledge of several languages. Therefore, I have restricted myself to those published in the *EI, CII* and to those inscriptions from Andhra Pradesh, Karnataka, Bengal, Orissa, and south India that have been translated into English.

Since some texts have been crucial for determining the chronological framework, a preliminary discussion on them appears essential. Among the early Buddhist texts that I have relied on to reconstruct certain traditions and beliefs in the lifetime of, or shortly after the death of the Buddha, are the Niddesa Commentary of the *Suttanipāta* and the Jātakas. According to Winternitz, some of the poetical Suttas of the *Suttanipāta* reach back to the time of the beginning of Buddhism. Many would have probably originated, at least, in the circles of the first disciples of the Buddha, not long after his death.[14] It is significant that this text mentions the elephant among several animal deities worthy of worship, since Buddhist iconography of the second century BC depicts these animals as the Buddha in his previous life, or as symbols representing some aspect of the Buddha's life. This suggests that this part of the *Suttanipāta*, which refers to the animal cults, is perhaps older than the third-second century BC, when in the early stages of Buddhism, the Buddha was not deified and did not have a mythology. The Niddesa Commentary upon these verses of the *Suttanipāta* is fairly old, since it is included in the canon.[15] It is possibly earlier than the time of the third council during the reign of Aśoka (269/268 BC–232 BC), and some of the explanations given in it go back to the time of the Buddha and were perhaps compiled by his disciple Sāriputta.[16]

The Jātakas, a collection of about 550 stories about the Buddha's former births, constitute an important part of the Buddhist tradition. These stories, which are difficult to date, grew over several hundred years until the sixth century AD or so when they acquired the form that we know today. It is generally accepted that the core of the narratives was widely known by the third century BC. Several Jātakas carry echoes of a pre-Buddhist period even though they may have been compiled a few centuries after the Buddha's birth. Some probably acquired their present form in the early centuries of the Christian era. Rhys Davids considers that some of the Jātakas, when they were first incorporated into the Buddhist tradition, were already old.[17] By about the middle of the third century AD some of them had been translated into Chinese.[18] Representations of a few Jātaka stories are found on reliefs of the Bharhut *stūpa* showing that they had already become popular by the second century BC.[19] The scene of Buddha entering the womb of his mother in the form of a six-tusked elephant is depicted on a relief at the *stūpa* at Bharhut. However, in the *Alīnacitta Jātaka*,[20] the *Susīma Jataka*,[21] or the *Kurudhamma Jātaka*,[22] for example, there are references to a sacred elephant or the elephant festival in which the elephant is quite distinct to the Buddha. These were probably older stories for eventually the 'good' elephant became the symbol of the Buddha's conception or the Buddha in a previous incarnation. Although the *Susīma Jātaka* refers to the elephant festival it gives no description of the event. Yet the fact that such a ritual did exist is confirmed by the *Hastyāyurveda*, a text which also describes this festival. This brings us to the problem of dating the *Hastyāyurveda*[23] and the *Mātaṅgalīlā*.[24]

Both the *Mātaṅgalīlā* and the *Hastyāyurveda* are texts that are not very well known. Winternitz, Macdonell and Sukumari

Bhattacharji make no reference to them. Keith erroneously gives the author of the *Mātaṅgalīlā* as Nārāyaṇa instead of Nīlakaṇṭha. Apart from the fact that he regards it as more modern than the *Hastyāyurveda,* he gives no other information on these two texts.[25] The manuscript of the *Mātaṅgalīlā* gives no indication of its date. Nothing is known of Nīlkaṇṭha who is mentioned as its author. The editor, Gaṇapati Śāstri, states that the three manuscripts he used are about three hundred years old. He suggests that the author was from Kerala since the work was well known there.[26]

An analysis of the contents of these two texts, however, makes it possible to get an idea of the age of the rituals and mythology they reflect, as also their place of origin. The *Hastyāyurveda* refers to an annual festival where the elephant was worshipped. There are some parallels between this ritual and that of the *aśvamedha* (horse sacrifice), which suggest an early date for the ritual of the elephant festival. There is another text called the *Hasti Ratna Dhanamyeti Upadeśa* (The Instructions for Acquiring Wealth through the Precious Elephant), preserved in the Tibetan Buddhist canon[27] which refers to a more evolved version of this ritual. The author is stated to be Ārya Nāgārjuna of Nālandā (seventh or eighth century AD). Wilkinson states that there is no certainty that Nāgārjuna was indeed the real author. It may well be a later text legitimized with the name of an earlier famous author. However, the essential point is that such a tradition came from India, since elephants were not native to Tibet.[28] Most of the Indian texts in the Tibetan Buddhist canon were brought into Tibet or translated into Tibetan between the seventh and the eleventh centuries AD.[29] Since the ritual described in this text appears to be more recent than the version described in the *Hastyāyurveda,* the latter is evidently considerably older. The *Mātaṅgalīlā* and the *Hastyāyurveda* probably originated in the *madhyadeśa* where evidence of the cult of a sacred elephant exists from an early period. Even if the texts were compiled at a later period, the traditions they describe appear to belong to the pre-Christian era.

The *Hastyāyurveda* essentially contains two kinds of information, the mythology of the elephant and the management and treatment of elephants (*gaja śāstra*).[30] Whereas it is not known how old the mythology is, the tradition of *gaja śāstra* goes back, at least, to the time of the *Arthaśāstra*.[31] Although the more recent texts may contain some new material or variations on old themes the ancient tradition of *gaja śāstra* itself has persisted through the centuries until modern times. Take the example of the rite known as the *Gajasampādana* described in the *Prapañcasāra Tantra* (ninth/tenth centuries AD).[32] It is a ritual performed for capturing a large number of wild elephants to replenish the King's stables. The *Gajasampādana* described in the *Prāṇatoṣiṇī*,[33] a nineteenth century text, is virtually a replica of that described in the *Prapañcasāra Tantra*. Therefore, the problem relating to literary sources is two-fold: on the one hand the date of the text itself, and on the other hand, the date of the rituals reflected in the text. A ritual text does not necessarily reflect existing practices. Often a manuscript may be nothing more than the faithful copy of a much older work preserved because of the sanctity it once enjoyed. It may or may not have relevance during the period when it was recopied. Newer developments are merely added to the text. Large scale revisions of the older sections rarely take place. This is evident in the Purāṇas, for instance, where much of the contradictory material in a text can be explained as being associated with differences in time and space.

Chapter III of this study is based on the *Mānava Gṛhya Sūtra* which can only be tentatively dated. Kane assigns the *Gṛhya Sūtras* to a period prior to 600-300 BC and considers that they had attained a position of supreme authority in the second century BC.[34] Sukumari Bhattacharji situates them generally in the period between 600-200 BC and Macdonell between 500-200 BC.[35] Gonda does not commit himself to a date but states that "the structure of the *Gṛhya Sūtras* presented no difficulties to the individual compilers when they wished to insert or omit certain ceremonies even in those cases in which these were obviously of 'popular' or 'non-Vedic' origin or belonged to the traditions of particular religious communities".[36] Whatever be the date of this text, I am more specifically concerned with the dating of the section pertaining to the Vināyaka rites.

The Vināyakas first find mention in the *Mānava Gṛhya Sūtra* where they appear as four demonic creatures. Among the list of beings associated with them, figure three of the four Buddhist *lokapālas* (guardians of the quarters), as also Mahādeva and Mahāsena. This implies that not only was Buddhism viewed inimically by the *brāhmaṇa* authors of this text (since it is indirectly associated with the demons), but so were Mahādeva and Mahāsena. The Buddhist *lokapālas* seem to have been an established part of Buddhist mythology in the second century BC since they are depicted at the Bharhut *stūpa* at Amarāvatī. They are also mentioned in texts such as the Mahāvagga portion of the *Dīgha Nikāya,* the *Mahāvastu* and the *Lalitavistara.* Whereas the *Dīgha Nikāya* contains some very old material, probably older then the schism between the two sects (fourth century BC), it is a compilation of material from different sources and the *lokapālas* are, perhaps, amongst the later additions. The *Mahāvastu* has certain Mahayanic features which point to the early centuries of the Christian era. But the nucleus of the work is old and had originated already in the second century BC.[37] The *Lalitavistara* is mainly assigned to about AD 200.[38] This would imply that the concept of *lokapālas* evolved along with other aspects of Buddhist mythology and probably came into being sometime before the second century BC when they are depicted at Bharhut.

Mahādeva and Mahāsena were popular gods during the Aśokan period, as brought out by the *Arthaśāstra.* They had not yet acquired a high status within the Brahmanical framework. It is also in Aśoka's time that a strong impetus was given to Buddhism and its propagation, which must have posed a threat to adherents of the Vedic tradition. A detailed analysis of the Vināyakas in Chapter III, leads me to believe that this is the period reflected in the Vināyaka section of the *Mānava Gṛhya Sūtra,* i.e. between the end of the third and early second century BC.

The Vināyakas also find mention as evil beings in the Śānti Parva of the *Mahābhārata* where they are mentioned along with *bhūtas* and *piśācas.* This portion of the Śānti Parva is likely to correspond to a period shortly after that of the composition of the Vināyaka section in the *Mānava Gṛhya Sūtra.* The *Mahābhārata* as we know it was probably compiled between approximately the second century BC and the second century AD although the kernel of the text is much older, and interpolations must have been made until about the fourth century or so. In the Anuśāsana Parva the Gaṇeśvara-Vināyakas are described as being worshipped along with the Rudragaṇa. No longer are they depicted as evil beings. This portion certainly belongs to the first one or two centuries of the Christian era. To this period would also belong the passage in the Sabhā Parva which mentions Danti. The latter appears to be synonymous with the Mahākāya (one having a huge body) who is named along with the Gaṇesavara-Vināyakas as part of the entourage of Śiva in the Anuśāsana Parva. The didactic portions of Viṣṇu and Mahādeva in the Anuśāsana and Śānti Parvas correspond to a still later stage (third or fourth centuries AD) when these two deities were in the process of becoming the major gods of the Puranic pantheon.

In addition to the critical edition of the *Mahābhārata*, I have consulted the Geeta Press edition, and the volumes translated by Van Buitenen. Unless specifically stated, the references are to the critical edition alone. Material relevant to this discussion is found in the Āraṇyaka, the Sabhā, the Śānti and the Anuśāsana Parvas. It is significant that almost all references to the Vināyakas, their related beings and to the elephant deity, do not figure in the main body of the critical edition but are only mentioned in the Appendices. They do, however, form part of the Geeta Press edition. This shows that the tradition associated with the Vināyakas and the elephant deity was limited to a few versions which must have been associated only with specific regions.

The *Yājñavalkya Smṛti* is another important text for my discussion. Kane places it between AD 100-300.[39] Macdonell considers AD 350 as a reasonable date[40] and Winternitz situates it not earlier than the third or fourth centuries of the Christian era.[41] I am concerned with the section on Vināyaka worship, and the end of the second century/early third century AD appears to be the most reasonable period for this portion of the text. Here, the four Vināyakas of the *Mānava Gṛhya Sūtra* have evolved into one single Vināyaka with four names. His worship is associated with that of Ambikā, Śiva and Skanda. Yet he is neither Śiva's son nor his *gaṇa*. Hence this portion is earlier than the Purāṇas.

The *Taittirīya Āraṇyaka* and the *Maitrāyaṇī Saṃhitā* contain *gāyatrīs* (sacred verses) to the elephant deity named Danti and to several other Puranic deities such as Narasiṃha and Durgā. In the case of the *Taittirīya Āraṇyaka* the two *gāyatrīs* belong to the *Nārāyaṇopaniṣad* which is an appendix of the *Taittirīya Āraṇyaka* and belongs to a later date than the main body of the text. Although both these texts belong to the pre-Christian era, many of these *gāyatrīs* were obviously added to it in the early centuries of the Christian era. Farquhar situates the *Nārāyaṇopaniṣad* in the period between AD 550 and 900[42] but it is possible that some portions were interpolated earlier than that. Narasiṃha and Durgā were acknowledged by the Brahmanical religion from about the Gupta period (fourth to sixth century AD) onwards. The Narasiṃha *avatāra* of Viṣṇu had became popular in the Gupta period when it is alluded to in some coin legends of Kumāra Gupta.[43] However, the different *gāyatrīs* were not necessarily interpolated at the same time and by the same person. The portions of these two texts, relating to Danti, belong to approximately the second century of the Christian era, since Danti is also mentioned in those portions of the *Mahābhārata* which appear to belong to the second century AD. After the fourth century when the elephant headed deity begins to evolve within the framework of the Purāṇas the epithet Danti is hardly ever used.

The eighteen Mahāpurāṇas have formed an integral part of this study. The Purāṇas (literally meaning 'ancient') are a compendia of legends and religious instructions. They are supposed to deal with five themes: creation, re-creation, genealogies of the gods, ages of Manus and the genealogies and histories of royal lineages. In fact, they often do not strictly adhere to these criteria. The Purāṇas are complex and multi-layered works and this makes it difficult to establish any precise chronology in their development or to relate them to specific geographical regions. Even if a text is generally considered to belong to a certain epoch, elements of it are borrowed from older traditions, and interpolations continue to be added up to a later date. Broadly, the Purāṇas were compiled from approximately the third century until about the fourteenth century of the Christian era. Accepting that wide timeframe, I have discussed how the mythology of Gaṇapati develops and how he comes to acquire a particular kind of personality in the Puranic Śaiva pantheon. I am concerned with the evolution of concepts. It is in the Purāṇas that Gaṇapati acquires a mythology, a role in the Śaiva pantheon and eventually in the pantheons of Viṣṇu and the Goddess as well. However, because the Purāṇas cannot be situated in a definite geographical or chronological context, souces such as sculpture and epigraphy become indispensable for establishing the approximate dates at which Puranic beliefs pertaining to Gaṇapati are accepted in different parts of the country. These sources permit an assessment of the extent of the deity's popularity; the period when he acquires temples of his own; his association with other deities; the common features of his cult in different parts of the sub-continent and the regional particularities. Sculptures and inscriptions also make it possible to ascertain whether certain myths are more popular in some regions than others.

The *Mudgala Purāṇa* and the *Gaṇeśa Purāṇa* are two sectarian Upapurāṇas central to my discussion on the Gāṇapatyas. The Upapurāṇas are also eighteen in number and are written in the same style as the Mahāpurāṇas. However, they deal with local cults and sects and are, by and large, later than most of the Mahāpurāṇas. There is no unanimous agreement about the names of the eighteen Upapurāṇas especially since there are a large number of texts, many of them fairly recent, which claim to be Purāṇas or Upapurānas. The *Mudgala Purāṇa* has been published by the Śrī Mudgala Prakashan Mandalam, Bombay, and the *Gaṇeśa Purāṇa* by the Śrī Yogīndra Maṭha at Moregaon, Maharashtra (the site of one of the *aṣṭavināyaka* temples).[44] The edition of the *Mudgala Purāṇa* is claimed to be based on a handwritten copy of a text which, in turn, was based on the version of the Purāṇa revealed to Śrī Yogindra at Moregaon in the sixteenth century. This sixteenth century version, according to the *maṭha,* was 'revealed' to Śrī Yogīndra since an earlier version of the Purāṇa had been lost.[45] Granoff refers to an edition that was published with an anonymous commentary in 1822 Sarvari from Kurundavada.[46] As far as I know, the *Mudgala* is otherwise available only in manuscript form.

Various authorities date the *Mudgala Purāṇa* before or after the *Gaṇeśa Purāṇa.* Hazra situates this text somewhere between AD 1100 and 1400 and considers that it is earlier than the *Gaṇeśa Purāṇa.*[47] Farquhar, too, considers the *Mudgala Purāṇa* to be earlier than the *Gaṇeśa Purāṇa.*[48] Preston simply states that the date of the *Mudgala Purāṇa* is unknown.[49] Kane considers that the dates of these two Purāṇas are uncertain.[50] Courtright places the *Mudgala Purāṇa* between the fourteenth and sixteenth century.[51] Granoff believes that, on the basis of internal evidence alone, it is difficult to arrive at an absolute date for the text. According to her it is possible to suggest a relative chronology of Gaṇeśa texts and she places the *Mudgala Purāṇa* as the last of the philosophical works that treat of Gaṇapati.[52] She bases her conclusion on the fact that the *Mudgala* refers to the *Gaṇeśa Purāṇa;* that there is a degree of convergence in their contents, particularly in their stories; and that the *Mudgala* repeatedly mentions the *Śrī Atharvaśiras,* a text which is accepted as being a late composition.[53] Courtright suggests the sixteenth and seventeenth century for the *Śrī Atharvśiras,* which, incidentally, has also been translated by him.[54]

It is true that there are portions of the *Mudgala Purāṇa* that are late. However, on the basis of these late portions alone can one consider the entire text to be a late one? Does textual comparison alone make it possible to come to a definite conclusion as to the date of a particular work? Considering that some Gāṇapatya sects had evolved by about the tenth century and that Gaṇapati was already a pan-Indian deity it is probable that texts relating to him existed by at least the eleventh/twelfth centuries. The *Mudgala Purāṇa,* like other Purāṇas, is a multi-layered work and the kernel of the text must be old. It must have continued to receive interpolations until the seventeenth/eighteenth centuries as the worship of Gaṇapati became more important in certain regions. Important additions pertaining to the philosophical aspect of the Gāṇapatyas must have been made when, under the Peshwas, Gaṇapati became a family deity of a royal house and the practice of making pilgrimage to the *aṣṭavināyaka* shrines was popularised because of royal patronage. Probably the tone of the Purāṇa also underwent some change during that period because of the audience for which it was being compiled. The portions dealing with the myths, for instance, are certainly older and appear to be directed at a more popular audience. Many of these myths are nothing but a modified version of older Puranic myths, with Gaṇapati in the place of Śiva, Viṣṇu or Durgā. Some of these myths must have been well known and making Gaṇapati the chief protagonist in the place of some other deity must have thrilled devotees in villages and at the same time created a more fervent clientele for a particular category of temple priests.

The edition of the *Mudgala Purāṇa* that I have consulted makes reference to the *Gaṇeśa Purāṇa.*[55] Likewise, the latter also refers to Mudgala's Purāṇa.[56] Hence both these recensions are based on two older versions of these texts. There are other reasons for supposing that some parts of these two texts belong to the twelfth century or so. Jñāneśvar praises Gaṇapati as the Supreme God, synonymous with *Brahman* in the thirteenth century. During this period there is evidence of Gaṇapati having temples devoted to him and whole portions describing his ritual and worship in some of the sacred texts such as the Āgamas. The deity was evidently popular with certain categories of society. He is invoked systematically before other deities in the inscriptions of some ruling houses such as the Śilāhāras or the Kalachuris. The *Mudgala Purāṇa* talks of an *ardhanārīśvara* (half-man half-woman) form of Gaṇapati. There is inscriptional evidence of such a form in the eleventh century. A verse in the *Halayudhastotra* inscribed in AD 1063 on the Amreśvara temple at Mandhata in the East Nimar District, Madhya Pradesh, refers to this form of Gaṇapati as well.[57] The *Sammoha Tantra* (*c.* fourteenth century) also makes reference to the literature of the Gāṇapatyas and specifically mentions two Purāṇas as being part of it. Probably there were versions of these two texts, which were lost or remained an oral tradition and were set in writing around the sixteenth century at one of the sacred sites of Gaṇapati in Maharashtra. The deity is constantly referred to with Siddhi and Buddhi. These goddesses are mentioned alongwith Gaṇapati in inscriptions from the twelfth century. Like the *Mudgala Purāṇa*, there is another text, the *Devī Rahasya*, which I discuss further on. It contains references which definitely date to the eighteenth century or so and yet, the entire text cannot be said to be of such late origin.

The *Gaṇeśa Purāṇa* has been published three times (Poona 1876, Bombay 1876, and Bombay 1892) before the edition of the Śrī Yogīndra *maṭha*. I have not been able to compare the text I have used, with these older publications. However, R.C. Hazra in his article on the *Gaṇeśa Purāṇa*[58] states that he has based his analysis on the edition published by Gopal Narayana and Co., Bombay, 1892. His various descriptions, quotations and references are found easily in the version that I have consulted and it is possible, therefore, that they are based on a common source.

Lawrence W. Preston, who has made a study of the sub-regional religious centres associated with Gaṇapati in Maharashtra, considers that the period AD 1100-1400 would appear to be the most reasonable date for the *Gaṇeśa Purāṇa* since this period agrees with the apparent age of the sacred sites mentioned by it.[59] Hazra places the *Gaṇeśa Purāṇa* between AD 1000-1400[60] and Farquhar between AD 900-1350.[61] It appears likely that the core of the text came into existence around the twelfth/thirteenth centuries for the same reasons that I have mentioned in the case of the *Mudgala Purāṇa*. This text, too, has been subject to interpolations during the succeeding ages. The *Gaṇeśa Purāṇa* was translated into Tamil in the eighteenth century[62] and the Tamil version is referred to as the *Vināyaka Purāṇa*.[63]

The Śaiva Āgamas and Upāgamas constitute another important part of the literary sources. The Āgamas are a set of sacred texts believed to have been dictated by Śiva himself. The term Āgama literally means 'tradition'. Of the texts that I have consulted, the *Mṛgendrāgama, Rauravottarāgama* and *Ajitāgama* have been critically edited and published by the FIP. The sections on Vināyaka that I consulted from the *Svayambhuvāgama* and the *Diptāgama* are in transcript form.[64] The latter has since been published. In addition, there are some texts, such as the *Vināyakavratakalpādi* which are collections of material on Gaṇapati drawn from a series of Āgamas, essentially the *Kāraṇa, Kāmika* and the *Svayambhuva.* This, again, is in the form of a transcript.[65]

According to Gopinatha Rao, the majority of the Śaiva Āgamas have to be looked upon as being later than the ninth century. They are mainly situated between the ninth and twelfth centuries AD.[66] But the descriptions of the images as contained in them may, nevertheless, be based on an older tradition. He gives the example of Varāhamihira (sixth century AD) whose description of certain images is not in any way different from those found in later Āgamas.[67] Gonda considers the oldest Āgamas to have been composed in the period between AD 400 and 800. According to him, Śaiva Āgamic literature had been widely recognized before the tenth century AD. The earliest manuscript of an Āgama—the *Kiraṇa*—is dated AD 924. However, it is difficult to ascertain the dates of individual Āgamas.[68]

The Āgamas, unlike the Purāṇas, contain little or no mythology of Gaṇapati. They provide details of the rituals and festivals associated with the deity and of the numerous possibilities for his iconogrphy. They are, therefore, later than the early Purāṇas, and contemporary to some of the later ones. It is certain that the sections on Vināyaka in the Āgamas that I have consulted are, by and large, post tenth century. They often describe sixteen or more forms of Gaṇapati and discuss the very elaborate rituals and festivals in his honour. In contrast, the *Mayamata,* a text of Tamil sculpture and architecture, which is accepted as being older than the Āgamas—the *Kāmikāgama* reproduces entire passages of it—only describes one form of the deity.[69] The *Mayamata* also provides instructions for making the image of the Buddha and the Jina.[70] It is, therefore, probably a text of the seventh or eighth century when Buddhism and Jainism were still in a flourishing condition even though Śivaism was becoming increasingly popular. It is in the Āgamas that Gaṇapati acquires a variety of forms but these are limited to south India. Most of these forms are never mentioned in the Purāṇas.

I have consulted certain ritual manuals such as the *Somaśambhupaddhati* and the *Īśānaśivagurudevapaddhati*. They draw much of their material from the Āgamas.[71] The former appears to have been written in AD 1073 or 1096. It draws mainly on the (Uttara) *Kāmikāgama.*[72] The *Īśānaśivagurudevapaddhati* has been edited by T. Gaṇapati Śāstri. Scholars are unanimous in accepting its date to be sometime in the twelfth century AD.[73] In the 'Preface' to the second volume, Gaṇapati Śāstri quotes Haraprasad Śāstri's views on the date and identity of Īśānaśiva. He considers Īśānaśiva to have belonged to Mithila or somewhere in the north and that even though manuscripts of the work were obtained from Kerala, the work itself is not a contribution of Kerala.[74] Other scholars, however, hold that there is enough evidence in the text itself to show that Īśānaśiva must have been from Kerala.[75]

Gaṇapati Śāstri states that Īśānanśiva's book embodies the teachings of a long line of Śaiva Yogis who were very influential all over India between the ninth and eleventh centuries. The *Ajita, Kiraṇa* and *Svayambhuva Āgamas* are quoted by name.[76] It also states that one of the Gaṇapati *mantras,* that of Prapañcagaṇapati, is told and explained in *Lalitāgama, Makutāgama* and *Vatulāgama.* The *Makutāgama* and *Lalitāgama* have not been published. As for the *Vatulāgama* which is the twenth-eighth Āgama, only its sub-Āgamas exist of which only one has been published.[77] The *Īśānaśivagurudevapaddhati* is, therefore, a useful text since it throws light on some texts that one is not able to consult.

Among the Tantras consulted, the *Prapañcasāra Tantra* has an important section on Gaṇapati. It is evidently older than Īśānaśiva's work since the latter quotes from it. The authorship of this text is attributed to Śaṅkarācārya,[78] although it is certain that some writings which pass under the name of Śaṅkara are not really his. This has been the case in some of the hymns edited and published by Avalon, which have been credited to Śaṅkara and then have been found in another manuscript ascribed to other works and authors.[79] It is difficult to reconcile Śaṅkara's teaching with the rituals of Tantric *pūjā* as described in this text. They present a contrast to his strict monistic teachings. The tone is also quite different to Śaṅkara's works like the *Vivekachuḍāmaṇi* or the *Bhaja Govindam.*

The *Devī Rahasya* is traditionally supposed to form part of a bigger compilation called the *Rudrayāmala Tantra.* The text is evidently composed by a writer from Kashmir because it refers to the goddesses Jvālāmukhī, Sārikā Mahārājñi, Śāradā, Bhīda and Bālā all of whom are popular and have shrines in the Kashmir Valley.[80] The reprint that I have consulted is based on an edition prepared by Pandit Ramachandra Kak and Hara Bhatta Shastri and published by the Government of Kashmir in 1941. However, the text in its present form, or at least parts of it, appear to be a late composition because of the appearance of the words *safak* and *phirangaha* which the editor feels refer to the the Mohammedans and Europeans.[81] Nonetheless, much of the section on Gaṇapati appears similar to that of other Tantric texts associated with the period between the tenth and fourteenth centuries.

Ānandagiri's *Śaṅkaravijaya* is another work which has been accorded varying dates. Farquhar situates it betweeen the thirteenth and fourteenth centuries.[82] Courtright considers it to belong to about the tenth century or so.[83] Lorenzen states that most modern authorities agree that the author of the text was not Śaṅkara's disciple Ānandagiri but an obscure author of about the fifteenth century.[84] The text refers to six sects of Gaṇapati—those of Mahāgaṇapati, Heramba Gaṇapati, Ucchiṣṭa Gaṇapati, Haridra, Navanīta, Svarṇa and Saṃtāna Gaṇapati who are condemned by the Śaiva philosopher, Śaṅkarācārya, because they do not accept his philosophy of Advaita Vedanta. Some of these forms are mentioned in the *Īśānaśivagurudevapaddhati,* or in some of the Āgamas. If this text does belong to the fifteenth century, it is surprising that it makes no reference to the *Smārta* Gāṇapatyas. The core texts of the *Smārta* Gāṇapatyas are the *Gaṇeśa* and *Mudgala Purāṇas* and the influence of this sect appears to have been far more widespread than those of the sects mentioned in the *Śaṅkaravijaya.* The *Smārta* Gāṇapatyas are, evidently, associated with the period subsequent to the *Śaṅkaravijaya.* The teachings of the Āgamas, the Yāmalas and the Tantras, in which the forms of Gaṇapati described in the *Śaṅkaravijaya* appear since long before the twelfth century, are in many ways contrary to Śaṅkara's views and teachings.[85] The Gāṇapatya sects described in the *Śaṅkaravijaya* must have come into existence by the tenth century. There are inscriptions and literary references to Gaṇapati temples in the period prior to the twelfth century. Therefore, the *Śaṅkaravijaya*, or at least the portion relating to the Gāṇapatyas, appears to belong to the period between the tenth and the eleventh century. During this period, various forms of Gaṇapati were known and these must have been the focus of worship of a number of people.

Some of the texts I have consulted are more recent. They often quote from older sources which are not available and so the information they provide is very useful. The *Tantrasāra* compiled by Kṛṣṇānanda Āgamavāgīśa with his own commentary is one such text. Pratapaditya Pal considers that the *Tantrasāra* was compiled around AD 1590, although some scholars situate the author some decades earlier and make him a contemporary of Caitanya.[86] The author cites from the *Śāradātilaka Tantra*, some Yāmalas and some Purāṇas. Among the more obscure texts cited by him is the *Gaṇeśavimarṣiṇī*.

The *Śrī Ucchiṣṭa Gaṇapati Stottra Satanāmāvalī* is a collection of prayers, rituals, myths and other details pertaining to the worship of Gaṇapati drawn from all available sources. It has been compiled and published by Śrī Sundareśa Śarmā in Tanjore in 1959. What makes it relevant is the fact that a list of the traditional literature on which this work is based is stated in the beginning of the work itself and the text is used for the contemporary worship of Gaṇapati. The *Prāṇatoṣiṇī* is also a relatively recent work. It was compiled by Rāmatoṣaṇa Vidyālankara in 1743 SE (AD 1821) at the instance of Prāṇkṛṣṇa Biswas, a landlord of Khardaha near Calcutta.[87] It has some sections which are faithful copies of earlier texts such as the rite of *Gajasampādana*. It is exactly like the one described in the *Prapañcasāra Tantra* which is a good thousand years older, if not more.

Data on the current worship of Gaṇapati is based on what I observed in about forty Gaṇapati temples in: Maharashtra (Bombay, Pen, Pune, Cincvad, Titwala and the *aṣṭavināyaka* (eight Vināyakas) temples at Moregaon, Ranjangaon, Theur, Sidhtek, Mahad, Pali, Ojhar and Lenyadri); Karnataka (Bangalore, Kurudumale in Kolar District, Gokarna, Amdalli and Idagunji in the Uttara Kannada District, Kumbhasi in the Dakshin Kannada

District; Tamil Nadu (Madras and the surrounding region); Kerala (Cochin, Ernakulam, Trichur and Guruvayoor); and Varanasi. I visited temples in small villages, in towns and in cities. Some of these are old *tīrthas* whereas others are recently built. Some are modest shrines in the city frequented only by members of a locality. Others are large well-known temples receiving important patronage. In each temple I had discussions with the *pujārī(s)* and, where the temple was served by several priests, I found it worthwhile talking, in addition, to the younger generation of the priesthood. There were always members of the laity from a cross section of society present to offer their points of view. In many places I met members of the Trust as well. In addition, I was fortunate to be able to meet several erudite persons in these various regions who shared my interest in Gaṇapati and who helped deepen my understanding of some of the current regional perceptions of the deity. Their knowledge of sacred texts was far greater than that of most temple priests. I talked at length to numerous friends, acquaintances and people from different walks of life in these regions to understand how they perceived Gaṇapati. In addition, I visited several manufacturers of Gaṇapati statues to see things from the artisans' point of view and how they catered to their varied clientele.

There are numerous Gaṇapati temples in the regions that I covered and it is not possible to visit them all. Although in Kerala there has been no evidence of Gāṇapatyas, I considered it worthwhile to include it in my intinerary in order to be able to contrast it with the other three regions because of its proximity to them and because in recent times, this is the only region, besides Maharashtra, where one of the royal families, that of the Rājās of Edapilli, worshipped Gaṇapati as their family deity. I based my selection of temples on the following considerations: those temples that are central to the Gāṇapatya tradition such as the *aṣṭavināyaka* shrines and some temples associated with the Peshwas who patronized this deity; some old *tīrthas* which are well known such as Idagunji and Gokarna but which have not been mentioned by scholars working on Gaṇapati; several small temples in cities because they cater to a large cross-section of society; temples within the same region such as Kumbhasi and Kurudumale in Karnataka, for example, where the officiants belong to different religious sects; finally, some virtually unknown and rarely frequented temples like the one in Panangad, Kerala, where Gaṇapati is the principal deity and where efforts are underway by some members of the local population to maintain a temple and prevent a tradition from disappearing because of paucity of funds.

NOTES

1. A.L. Basham, *The Wonder That Was India,* p. 321.
2. Ibid.
3. Debiprasad Chattopadhyaya, *Lokāyata,* p.248. Chapter Three of this book is devoted to a discussion on Gaṇapati ; M.C.P. Srivastava, 'Gaṇeśa and Jyeṣṭhā: A Comparative Study', *JBRS,* Vol. 58 (1-4), 1972, pp. 165-70.
4. Alice Getty, *Gaṇeśa.* See 'Introduction' by Foucher; J.R. Riviere, 'Problem of Gaṇapati in the Purāṇas', *Purāṇa* IV, 1962, pp. 96-102.
5. H. Mitra, *Gaṇapati,* p. 19.
6. T.G. Aravamuthan, 'Gaṇeśa: Clue to a Cult and a Culture', in *Journal of Oriental Research,* Madras, 1949, Vol. 18, pp. 224-43.
7. A. Coomaraswamy, 'Gaṇeśa' in *BMFA* (Boston), 1928, pp. 30-1.
8. Alice Getty, op. cit., p. 2.
9. H. Heras, *The Problem of Gaṇapati,* p. 54.
10. Robert L. Brown, ed., *Ganesh: Studies of an Asian God.*
11. A.K. Narain, 'Gaṇeśa: A Protohistory of the Idea and the Icon', in Robert L. Brown, ed., op. cit., pp. 19-48.
12. Paul B. Courtright, *Gaṇeśa : Lord of Obstacles, Lord of Beginnings.*
13. Laurence W. Preston, 'Subregional Religious Centres in the History of Maharashtra: The Sites Sacred to Gaṇeśa', in N.K. Wagle, ed., *Images of Maharashtra. A Regional Profile of India,* pp. 102-28.
14. M. Winternitz, *History of Indian Literature,* Vol. II, p. 93.
15. K.R. Norman, *Pali Literature,* pp. 84-5. (Vol. VII, of J. Gonda, ed., *A History of Indian Literature*).
16. Ibid.
17. B.C. Law, *A History of Pali Literature,* Vol. I, p. 275.
18. Uma Chakravarti, 'Women, men and beasts: The Jātaka as popular tradition', *Studies in History,* Vol. 9, No. 1, NS, Jan.-Jun. 1993, pp. 43-70.
19. Ibid., pp. 79-80.
20. E.B. Cowell, *The Jātaka,* Bk. II, No. 156, pp. 13-17.
21. Ibid., No. 163, pp. 31-4.
22. Ibid., Book III, No. 276, pp. 251-60.
23. I have quoted relevant passages of this text from Heinrich Zimmer's *Myths and Symbols in Indian Art and Civilisation.*

24. See Franklin Edgerton, *The Elephant Lore of the Hiṇdus: The Elephant Sport (Mātaṅgalīlā) of Nīlakaṇṭha.* This is the English translation of the only Sanskrit text available, edited by Gaṇapati Śāstri.
25. Ibid., see p. 1 of 'Introduction', fn. 1. Edgerton does not accept Keith's view of the *Mātaṅgalīlā* being more modern than the *Hastyāyurveda* since there is no evidence on the matter.
26. Ibid., p. vii of the 'Preface'.
27. Christopher Wilkinson, 'The Tantric Gaṇeśa: Texts Preserved in the Tibetan Canon', in Robert L. Brown, ed., op. cit., pp. 235-75.
28. Since elephants are not native to Tibet, this ritual is centered around the image of an elephant made from sacred substances. But the purpose of the ritual remains the same.
29. A.K. Warder, *Indian Buddhism,* p. 489. See also Christopher Wilkinson, op. cit., pp. 238-41.
30. Franklin Edgerton, op. cit., p. viii of 'Preface'. The *Mātaṅgalīlā* also describes the mythology of the elephant.
31. R.P. Kangle, *The Kautilya Arthaśāstra,* Part II, chaps. 31-2. The *Arthaśāstra* is a treatise on statecraft believed to be the work of Kauṭilya, the famous minister of Chandragupta Maurya (fourth century BC). However, the work as we know it is generally accepted as being a later text of the first or second century AD.
32. *Prapañcasāra Tantra,* XVII. 32-42.
33. *Prāṇatoṣiṇī,* p. 604.
34. P.V. Kane, *History of Dharmaśāstra,* Vol. I, Pt. I, pp. 14-15.
35. Arthur A. Macdonell, *A History of Sanskrit Literature,* p. 208.
36. J. Gonda, *The Ritual Sūtras,* p. 582.
37. Maurice Winternitz, op. cit., Vol. II, p. 238.
38. Ibid., p. 245; A.B. Keith, *A History of Sanskrit Literature,* p. 492.
39. P.V. Kane, op. cit., Vol. I, Pt. I, p.443.
40. Arthur A. Macdonell, op. cit., p. 365.
41. M. Winternitz, op. cit., Vol. III, p. 598.
42. J.N. Farquhar, *Outline of the Religious Literature of India,* p. 188.
43. Suvira Jaiswal, *The Origin and Development of Vaiṣṇavism* , pp. 178 and 220.
44. The *Mudgala Purāṇa* was published in October 1976. The *Gaṇeśa Purāṇa,* Upāsanā Khaṇḍa, was published in 1979, and the Krīḍā Khaṇḍa in 1985.
45. *Mudgala Purāṇa,* see 'Introduction'.
46. Phyllis Granoff, 'Gaṇeśa as Metaphor: The Mudgala Purāṇa', in Robert L. Brown, ed., op. cit., pp. 85-99.
47. R.C. Hazra, 'The Gaṇeśa Purāṇa', *JGJhRI,* Vol. 9, 1951, pp. 79-99.
48. Ibid., p. 96. See also J.N. Farquhar, op. cit., p. 270.
49. Lawrence W. Preston, op. cit., p. 104.

50. P.V. Kane, op. cit., Vol. II, Pt. II, p. 725.
51. Paul B Courtright, op. cit., p. 214.
52. There are three Upaniṣads devoted to Gaṇapati. Of these the *Śrī Gaṇapati Atharvaśīrṣa* is well known. It was probably composed during the sixteenth or seventeenth century. The other two are the *Heramba Upaniṣad* (See *Unpublished Upaniṣads*, eds., Pandits of Adyar Library, pp. 390-1) and the *Gaṇapati Upaniṣad* (See G. Srinivasa Murti, ed., *Śaiva Upaniṣads*, pp. 76-85). Although the date of these two texts are not known, they are certainly later than the fourteenth century and were probably the product of the *Smārta* Gāṇapatyas.
53. Phyllis Granoff, op. cit.
54. Paul B.Courtright, op. cit., pp. 252-4.
55. *Mudgala Purāṇa,* II.34.20; II.34.38.
56. *Gaṇeśa Purāṇa,* II.51.35 and 11.50.1.
57. Samaresh Bandyopadhyay, 'A Note on Gaṇapati', in *JOIB,* Vol. 21, 1971-2, pp. 328-30.
58. R.C. Hazra, 'The Gaṇeśa Purāṇa', op. cit., see fn. 1 on p. 79.
59. Lawrence W. Preston, op. cit., p. 103.
60. R.C. Hazra, 'The Gaṇeśa-Purāṇa', op. cit., p. 97.
61. J.N. Farquhar, *An Outline of the Religious Literature of India,* pp. 226 and 270.
62. Lawrence W. Preston, op. cit., see note no. 14 on p. 123.
63. T.S. Sundaresa Sharma, *Śrī Ucchiṣṭa Gaṇapati Stottra Satanāmāvalī* , p. 63.
64. Because of many *Āgamas* being in the Grantha script, or in private possession, or in a poor state of preservation, one of the tasks of the Sanskrit Department of the FIP, is to transcribe the texts into Devanagiri. This faithful copy of the text is catalogued as a transcript. Eventually, it is hoped, that these several transcripts will be critically edited and published. Chap. 58 of the *Svayambhuvāgama* that I have referred to is from Transcript no. 39 of the FIP. It is based on a manuscript belonging to Kilvelur, Tamil Nadu, which is in private possession. The *Diptāgama* I consulted was in transcript form (Nos. 15 and 16). It was copied from manuscripts in private possession at Kilvelur and Madurai. It has been critically edited by Dr. S.N. Bhatt and published by the FIP.
65. Transcript No. 1001 copied from Manuscript No. 43428 of the FIP.
66. T.A. Gopinatha Rao, *Elements of Hindu Iconography,* Vol. I, Pt. I, p. 56.
67. Ibid., p. 58.
68. J. Gonda, *Medieval Religious Literature in Sanskrit,* pp. 164-5.

69. Bruno Dagens, ed. and trans., *Mayamata (Traité Sanskrit d'Architecture)*, Vol. II, p. 410.
70. Ibid., Vol. II, pp. 410 and 466.
71. J. Gonda, op. cit., p. 213.
72. J. Gonda, op. cit., p. 214.
73. N.N. Bhattacharya, *History of the Tantric Religion*, p. 51. See also introductory remarks by T. Gaṇapati Śāstri, ed., *Īśānaśivagurudevapaddhati.*
74. T. Gaṇapati Śāstri, ed., *Īśānaśivagurudevapaddhati*, see p. 11 of 'Introduction'.
75. Ibid., p. 12.
76. Ibid., p. 15.
77. Ibid., Vol. II, p. 13, v. 236.
78. Arthur Avalon, ed., *Prapañcasāra Tantra*, see 'Introduction', p. 1.
79. Ibid., 'Introduction', p. 2.
80. Pandit Ramachandra Kak and Hara Bhatta Shastri, eds., *Devī Rahasya with Pariśiṣṭas*, Introduction, p. 3.
81. See pp. 307 and 317 of text as also p. 3 of 'Introduction'.
82. J.N. Farquhar, op. cit., p. 270.
83. Paul B. Courtright, op. cit., p. 218.
84. David N. Lorenzen, *The Kāpālikas and Kālāmukhas*, p. 31.
85. J. Gonda, *Medieval Religious Literature in Sanskrit*, p. 4.
86. Ibid., p. 3.
87. N. N. Bhattacharya, op. cit., p. 71.

CHAPTER 2

The Elephant

The most striking feature of Gaṇapati is his elephant head. The Brahmanical deities Śiva, Pārvatī or Viṣṇu could resurrect the dead, provide heads for the headless and perform numerous other miracles. Yet none could give Gaṇapati a human head. Clearly, the reason why he had to have an elephant head was because without it he would have lost his identity and, thereby, his *raison d'être.* The elephant head links him to some ancient cult or concept of a sacred elephant. This concept must have existed prior to the Brahmanical texts in which Gaṇapati makes his debut, for, the references in these texts throw little light on his past. Even his images appear suddenly in the early centuries of the Christian era. The motif of the elephant, however, appears from as early as the Harappan period. Enquiries into the significance of the elephant must, therefore, begin at this stage.

THE ELEPHANT IN HARAPPAN CULTURE

There are many common symbols and motifs in the civilizations of the ancient world, all with more or less the same connotations. Some of these such as the bull, the snake, the tree of life, mountain and water formulae and the wheel representing the sun are common in the Sumerian, Hittite, Assyrian, Mycenean, Cretan, Trojan, Lydian, Phoenician, Achaemenid, Scythian and Indian cultures.[1] The motif of the elephant, however, is restricted to the Indian context. It first appears in the Harappan civilization although it is not present in the earliest stages of this culture.

The Early Indus Period (late fourth and early third millennia BC) is associated with the hill valleys of Baluchistan, the Gomal Valley and the plain of Bannu in the north-west, the Potwar plateau, the Indus Valley and the Saraswati system to the east.[2] The most common painted designs from numerous sites of this period such as Kot Diji, Burzahom, Gumla, Rahman Dheri, Sarai Khola and Lewan are those representing heads wearing the horns of a buffalo,[3] female figurines of the 'Mother Goddess' type[4] and the motifs of birds, the humped bull, snake, eagle, goat, pig and ram. Fish and aquatic plants are also quite common. Some of the horned heads, like the one from Sarai Khola, have a plant growing between the horns.[5] The elephant did exist in this region because the faunal remains of a single specimen of the animal have been found at one of the pre-Harappan sites, namely, Mehrgarh in Kachi District, Baluchistan [c. 6300-5300 (calibrated) BC][6]. However, the animal does not seem to be represented in any art form during this period.

The elephant motif appears during the Mature Indus period (2550-2050 BC)[7] when it is rendered in terracotta art and represented on seals and amulets at sites such as Harappa, Mohenjo-daro and Chanhu-daro. A single seal with the elephant motif has also been found at Allahdino.[8] Elephant bones have been found at Harappa, Mohenjo-daro, Lothal, Kalibangan, Rupar and Bara.[9] The area associated with this period is much larger. It includes parts of modern Rajasthan, Gujarat, Kutch, Punjab, Haryana and western Uttar Pradesh. During this period the motifs of the unicorn, the tiger and rhinoceros also make an appearance.[10] The introduction of these motifs appears to coincide with a series of developments in this period, notably the expansion of existing settlements and the founding of new ones; growth of cities such as Mohenjo-daro; the first development of a full system of writing; manufacture of inscribed seals; an 'unprecedented extension of internal trade in all manner of raw materials and commodities and a distribution of the specialist craft and products of the cities'.[11] This is also the period when, for the first time, class stratification appears in society with evidence of a ruling elite and the ruled.

On the basis of the evidence available, the elephant motif on seals appears to be restricted to Sind and to one site in the Punjab. Elephant terracotta figurines are rare though a few have been reported from Chanhu-daro and Harappa.[12] The motif of the unicorn is by far the most widespread and the most frequently represented. It appears at nine sites both on seals and in the form of terracotta figurines.[13] The rhinoceros is represented at six sites including the four associated with the elephant. At Chanhu-daro, however, it does not figure on seals but in the form of a few terracotta figurines.[14] It is also found at Banawali (Haryana) in the form of terracotta figurines and at Shortughai (Afghanistan) where it is depicted on the only seal available from the Mature Harappan level. The tiger appears at a total of five sites of which three (Harappa, Mohenjo-daro and Chanhu-daro) are associated with the elephant motif. The other places where it was found are Kalibangan (Rajasthan) and Banawali. The motif of the bull is another popular motif but is not found at sites in Gujarat and Rajasthan. This shows that none of these animal symbols were ubiquitous and the only sites at which they all appear to have been represented were Mohenjo-daro and Harappa. At these two sites the unicorn is the most frequently represented animal followed by the short-horned bull and the elephant. The tiger, rhinoceros and *gharial* (crocodile) also appear to be among the more popular symbols.

These animals are sometimes represented by themselves, while at other times they appear as syncretic creatures. One copper tablet contains the image of a composite animal which is partly bull, partly elephant.[15] This signifies the combination of old and new symbols since the bull motif exists at the early Indus sites whereas the elephant makes an appearance only during the Mature Indus period. Another seal depicts an animal which is a composite of the bull, elephant and tiger.[16] A third seal depicts a creature with a man's face, the trunk or tusk of an elephant, horns of a bull, forepart of a ram and the hindquarters of a tiger.[17] Here, again, the ram is an old symbol which is combined with newer ones. This suggests the development of a richer and more complex set of beliefs and symbols which appear to be associated with the supernatural or with divinity. Many of these seals must have had a secular function. Others, however, are perforated and must have had a string passed through them to be worn as amulets. It is generally accepted that the motifs depicted on them were derived from religion and mythology. The division between the secular and the religious was not distinct in the ancient world. Sacred symbols represented, and possibly ensured, auspiciousness even in secular functions.

The appearance of these particular animal motifs coincides with the geographical spread of Harappan culture which implies the inclusion of new people. The development of new cities implies a new polity and a new elite. Ratnagar suggests that the seal symbols were the emblems of Harappan descent groups and were, quite possibly, old totemic symbols which distinguished various kin groups from the rest of the population.[18] In that case their appearance at this juncture would suggest the ascendance of new and powerful families or different segments of a kin group. The animal motifs on the Harappan seals can be compared to those of the early punch-marked coins of the second half of the first millennium BC. In Kośala, for example, when the Mātaṅga (elephant) dynasty comes to power, the motif of the elephant, so far absent on Kośalan coinage, makes an appearance.[19] Similarly, the symbol of the peacock on arches on one Magadhan coin originates from the totem of the peacock associated with the Mauryas (*morīya* meaning 'of the peacock').[20] Even when totemism ceases to exist the old totemic symbols can continue with a renewed significance. An example of the process of modification of ancient totems is that of the *gotras* of the *brāhmaṇas*. Many of these *gotras* which exist even in present times are, by and large, the names of animals, fish or birds which must have been the totems of the early Indo-Aryan clans or tribes. Examples include the Kāśyapa (tortoise) *gotra*, the Vatsa (calf), Śunaka (dog), Ṛkṣa (bear), Mudgala (a species of fish), Bhāradvāja (a species of birds), Gotama (cow) and the Māṇḍūka (frog).[21] There even is a *gotra* called Āne (elephant) among the Shivalli *brāhmaṇas* of Karnataka.

It is hard to imagine that an animal as powerful and majestic as the elephant would not play a significant role in the psyche of people who had adopted it as a symbol. Since the elephant was indigenous to the Indian subcontinent, its symbol in the ancient world is restricted to the Indian context. For that reason, there is no possibility of making any cross-cultural comparisons with other ancient civilizations as far as this symbol is concerned. Yet in Africa where the elephant is indigenous and where the social structure is in many cases a tribal one, myths associated with the animal do exist. In the myths of some contemporary African tribes, the elephant is closely associated with the origin of the tribe. The Nandi and the Maasai believe that three things existed on earth prior to all other creation—thunder, a mythical ancestor and the elephant. Another tribe, the Yao, believes that the first human being emerged from the primeval wilderness bearing an elephant on his shoulders. This first human being was, of course, a hunter and it is the elephant that taught him to hunt and survive. This first man also found his wife in the land of elephants.[22] This myth implies that the tribe is descended from both elephant and man, or that the elephant and man were originally one and the same. In southern Africa, it is widely believed that elephants can transform themselves into human beings and vice versa.[23] These myths portray the psyche of a hunting people. Because of its might and size, the elephant inspires awe, fear and reverence. The wild elephant is potentially the most destructive animal and the African tribesmen identified themselves with it and made it their equal, their companion and ancestor, thereby legitimizing within themselves the very same characteristics so essential for survival among the jungles of Africa. There are, besides, other similarities between the elephant and man such as similar life-expectancy and social habits.

In the Indian context, too, similar myths associated with the elephant exist and at least one such myth dates to the second half of the first millenium BC. King Prasenajit of Kośala, a contemporary of the Buddha, is described in Buddhist literature as *mātaṅga cyuti upapannam* (born of elephant semen).[24] He belonged to the Mātaṅga dynasty and in this case descent is claimed from a male elephant. This myth evidently harks back to a period of totemism. According to the *Mātaṅgalīlā,* the founding of scientific elephantology is attributed to a mythical sage, Pālakāpya (keeper of elephants) who was born to an elephant cow after she had drunk the seed of a man called Sāmagāyana.[25] Here, as in the case of one of the African myths, descent is from a human male and an elephant cow. I am not suggesting that these very myths existed in the Harappan period. However, if the elephant did represent a descent group then it is possible that it was associated with some such origin myths and that these myths were gradually adapted during the Mature Indus period to fit into the religious system of an urban civilisation.

The possibility that some of the animals depicted on Harappan seals did indeed represent certain groups is all the more plausible since there is evidence in the early historical period (post 600 BC) of people and dynasties named after these very animals. Those named after the elephant were associated with a fairly widespread area in the early historical period. The *Vāyu Purāṇa* gives a detailed description of Ketumala which corresponds to the region of old Bactria.[26] It mentions the Gajabhūmikā (land of the elephant) among the many places and people associated with the region.[27] The Mahiṣa (buffalo) is also included as a people[28] inhabiting the region. Further evidence of a people named after the elephant comes from Gandhāra with its two capitals of Taxila and Puṣkalāvatī. Greek historians, while describing Alexander's campaign from Kapīśa to the Indus through Gandhāra, mention the Astakinoi[29] as one of three important warlike people. Pāṇiṇi refers to them as the Hastināyana (descended from *hastin* which signifies 'elephant') who had their capital at Puṣkalāvatī.[30] Much of the area in the north-west such as Kapīśa (modern Begram which lies about 80 km. north of Kabul) and Gandhāra, where there is evidence of people named after the elephant, lies within the zone of the Harappan civilization. The Late Harappan and Post Harappan phases witnessed a push eastwards towards the Ganga basin and southwards towards the Deccan. In the Ganga Basin there is reference to the Mātaṅga dynasty of Kośala during the lifetime of the Buddha. The Khaḍgas (rhinoceroses) too, appear as a dynasty of kings in east Bengal in the seventh century A.D.[31] Tempting though these parallels are, I would be untrue to historical processes if I were to suggest that they represent a continuous tradition from Harappan times. What is more likely is that during the course of the several centuries that separate the Harappan culture from the early historical period, different groups of people named themselves after these animals but the exact nature of the symbolism of these animals varied according to the material milieu in which the people lived.

One of the most quoted seals in the context of Harappan religion is the one of the horned deity seated in what has commonly been described as a 'yogic pose'[32] and surrounded by four animals; an elephant and tiger on its right, a rhinoceros and buffalo on its left.[33] I am not aware of any similar pose in yoga although it has variously been referred to as *padmāsana*,[34] *kūrmāsana*,[35] *siddhāsana* or *baddhakonāsana*.[36] The central figure wears what some scholars consider to be the mask of a wild water buffalo with a head-dress of buffalo horns.[37] while others consider it to be the mask of a horned tiger.[38] The figure is also described as being ithyphallic. Marshall's explanation of this image being the proto-type of Śiva-Paśupati has been contested by those who prefer to associate it with a prototype of Mahiṣa, the buffalo-demon (who in Puranic myths is slain by Durgā in her form as Mahiṣāsuramardinī), the later pan-Indian deity, Yama (God of Death whose *vāhana* is the buffalo), as also of certain regional figures such as the south Indian Pōtu Rāju ('Buffalo King') and the Maharashtrian Mhasobā/ Mhaskobā (Marathi for Mahiṣa).[39] Some like Atre have considered this figure to be the Great Goddess of animals and vegetation,[40] the animals around her being symbolic of her divine strength. Volchok considers the surrounding animals to be representative of the four cardinal points.[41] This is the only seal of its kind. Although the central figure is depicted on some other seals and 'sealing amulets' it is not depicted with the four animals. The seal, may therefore, be commemorative of a particular event or a ritual performed on rare occasions associated with what may have been the principal kin groups that constituted the ruling elite of Mohenjo-daro.

The central figure is seated in what looks like a dance pose. It is significant that none of the Brahmanical, Buddhist or Jaina deities in the later Indian pantheons are ever depicted in this position. The head-dress of the central figure simulating the tiger/buffalo head, the bangles on his arms, his pose and the animals around him may well be suggestive of some shamanistic ritual. Shamanism, to put it very simply, is 'a technique of ecstasy' or, as Nevill Drury defines it, 'an ancient practice of utilising altered states of consciousness to contact the gods and spirits of the natural world'.[42] The shaman acts as an intermediary between the dead, demons, gods and nature spirits and the more familiar realm of everyday domestic affairs. He has the ability of entering a trance state during which his soul is believed to leave his body and ascend to the sky or descend to the underworld. By communicating with the world beyond, he is able to find the cure for diseases, avert evil influences and misfortune, and ensure the well being of his community. Shamanism has existed in several primitive societies and continues to be practised today in many parts of the world. Indologists have not engaged with this concept in any major way. However, the studies of ethnologists on existing shamanistic beliefs and practices have created a greater awareness of the details of this practice and it is possible to discern certain elements in the Harappan motifs which are suggestive of shamanism.

In the seal referred to above, the elephant, the buffalo and the rhinoceros appear in a static pose which is in contrast to the tiger which has its front paws raised as though it is about to spring on the seated figure. The seal thus appears to suggest the presence of opposing forces—the one dynamic, the other static. Further, if one compares the four animals, it is evident that the elephant, the rhinoceros and the buffalo are similar in that they all symbolise masculine strength and virility. They are also herbivorous. The tiger, in contrast, is carnivorous. It is a natural enemy of the other three animals. Several other seals depict the tiger in what appears to be an aggressive posture. There are seals which depict the so-called 'contest' motif where a man is seen attacking a tiger, or those with the 'Gilgamesh' motif showing a figure standing between two rampant tigers.[43] An elephant is depicted in the lower register of one such seal.[44] It is as if the elephant represents a counterbalance to the tiger(s). At other times the tiger is depicted with a manger on both sides which makes it appear to be more pacific. This would suggest that the wild animal signifying dissent or discord could be conquered or subdued (by the shaman?). It must be borne in mind that the Indus populace most probably consisted of several ethnic groups.[45] This presupposes the existence of tensions and rivalries. Probably the four animals on the seal in question represent, at one level, the benign and malignant spirits which constitute the world of the supernatural and which have a parallel in the material world. They also represent the ancestors or spirits of certain powerful groups of people who could be communicated with through the shaman. The disguise of the creature to be propitiated is a prominent feature of shamanism in many cultures.[46] If the mask of the 'shaman' on the seal in question is indeed a tiger mask, probably the tiger represented the evil spirit that had to be propitiated before the shaman could have access to the other three animals. Here the tiger's pose suggests that it needs to be controlled. It possibly represents a dissenting group, evil forces and obstacles. Only after propitiating it can the shaman gain access to divine and ancestral wisdom so necessary for rulers, from the animals representing their mythological ancestors.

In the contemporary context of Indian shamanism, the benign spirits are those of *pitṛs* or ancestors. The malignant ones are those of beings who died an unnatural death or who were mad, dissolute or violent-tempered and who are not allowed into the world of ancestral spirits and, therefore, cause harm to the living.[47] If the elephant in the Harappan context was the symbol of a kin group it is likely that it also represented the spirit of the mythical ancestor of the group and was an object of veneration for that particular group, a form of ancestor worship.

The elephant's association with some other animals throws further light on its possible symbolism in the Harappan context. The bull is more or less unanimously accepted as being an object of worship or a symbol of the sacred in Harappan culture,[48] largely because of the fact that it is the most frequently represented animal and because it was worshipped or considered sacred in several other ancient civilizations. Since some Harappan seals depict a composite creature which is a combination of the elephant and the bull, we can assume that the elephant was also gradually given a divine status or, at least, associated with the divine. There are three seals and one pottery plaque depicting a representation which combines two bulls, an elephant and a feline animal with a central figure of a crocodile with open jaw.[49] Another seal depicts an animal having the fore-quarters of a tiger and the hind-quarters of a bull or similar animal.[50] What is striking is that the composite creatures are always made up of a few specific animals such as the bull, the elephant, the rhinoceros, the tiger, crocodile, antelope or unicorn and appear to have some special significance. Animals like the monkey, pig, dog or turtle do not appear on seals and do not constitute the composite creatures. Often the composite creatures are half beast half human. Although there are human forms with bovine horns, legs and tail,[51] or with the hindquarters and middle of a tiger, no motif depicting a creature that is half human and half elephant has been found.

Of all these animals, the unicorn is the only one which is a mythical creature. Atre considers that the composition of the unicorn is dominated by the symbolism of male virility because of the emphasis on its male member and the single horn. She associates the creation of this animal by the Harappans with the transitional phase towards agriculture.[52] If the unicorn represents male virility, then it has a somewhat similar symbolism to that of the bull. There is a seal from Chanhu-daro which shows a bull bison with erect penis, standing over and fecundating a supine human figure from whose head emerges a sprouting plant.[53] This image is suggestive of ritual intercourse. It could very well be symbolic of the Earth Goddess being fecundated by her consort in his bull form. Related to the concept of the Earth Mother is that of the male principle responsible for her fecundation. This role would appear to have been played by the bull and possibly also by the unicorn, elephant and rhinoceros. There is a seal from Mohenjo-daro where the rhinoceros is depicted with the 'sacred brazier' which is mainly associated with the unicorn.[54] This 'sacred brazier' is, in rare cases, also depicted with the short-horned bull, the antelope[55] and in one case with the elephant (at Allahdino).[56] Perhaps this shows an attempt to give the elephant the status of the unicorn, but it may have remained a restricted belief, at least in the earlier stages.

The single horn of the unicorn has its parallel in the single horn of the rhinoceros and the long trunk of the elephant. The single horn of various animals has a special significance in the later Indian religions and how and why this idea came about is not clear. The *Arhants*, the Śravaks and other enlightened persons within the framework of Buddhism are referred to as *khaḍgaviṣaṇa* (having the horn of a rhinoceros).[57] Gaṇapati has only a single tusk and no Puranic myth adequately explains why that had to be so. Nandi, Śiva's bull, is referred to as 'the bull who has a single illuminated horn'.[58] Sometimes Śiva himself is invoked as 'the long-horned, single-horned, humped bull.'[59] The *matsya* incarnation of Viṣṇu is described as 'a golden fish with one horn'.[60] Similarly, the boar form of Viṣṇu is described as having one tusk.[61] The bull, the boar and the elephant are all animals that naturally have two horns or tusks. The fish has no horns. The single horn evidently distinguished these particular animals from the ordinary animal and symbolised divinity or superhuman strength and qualities.

According to Eliade, the single horn has traditionally been associated with the moon and fertility. The two horns of oxen, which are used to characterize the great divinities of fecundity, are an emblem of the divine *Magna Mater.*[62] Wherever they are found in Neolithic cultures, either in iconography or as part of idols in the form of oxen, they denote the presence of the Great Goddess of Fertility. The two horns are the symbol of two crescents, the full moon, the womb, the whole. The single horn, in contrast, is symbolic of the new moon. It is, likewise, also symbolic of the plough, of the male organ, the fertiliser, the initiator. In Indian mythology, the *makara* (crocodile) is also sometimes represented with horns. It symbolizes not just the waters but the fertilizing aspect of water, the principle of life. Matsya, the fish-incarnation of Viṣṇu, by saving the life of Manu and others was, in fact, the giver of new life. The bull and boar, likewise, are also representative of male fertility. The Varāha incarnation of Viṣṇu is associated with the myth of rescuing the Earth Goddess from the primal waters. He is depicted iconographically as a boar or a boar-headed human bearing the Goddess on his shoulder. In Greek mythology, contact with the bull's horn enabled the sacred king to fertilize the land in the name of the Moon Goddess by making rain.[63] The Greek God Dionysus holds a cornucopia, torn from a bull, and because of this is called Plutodotes or 'wealth-giver'. Heracles offers to Oeneus the horn snapped off from the bull-headed Achelous as a bridal gift.[64] The horn's association with fertility is implicit in this gesture. These comparisons with Greek mythology are not out of place because in several ancient civilizations there are common symbols. This does not necessarily imply borrowing or influencing by one or the other but signifies the common ideas and expressions of people in different regions. It is such comparisons which have led scholars to believe that the bull does, in all probability, represent the sacred or that it may have been an object of worship in the Harrapan context. In the same manner, the horn is associated with the creation of life and with prosperity in both the Greek and Brahmanical contexts. It is quite likely that it represented something similar in the Harappan context.

It would appear that the elephant, like the unicorn, bull and rhinoceros symbolised not just virility but, in a broader sense, prosperity and well-being. The unicorn, by reason of its distinction as a mythical creature and by its importance, was possibly some sort of cultic figure. However, the other animals, if they were originally totems which had become symbols of descent groups, and if they were associated with origin myths of these groups, probably came to be considered as the symbols of mythical ancestors and were attributed with special powers. As animal spirits they probably complimented what appear to be tree spirits represented on seals by a human figure standing in a tree.[65] In the context of the development of a more complex mythology and ritual, these animal symbols were gradually associated with the broad spectrum of fertility symbolism.

The seals depicting the so-called 'yogic figure' do not appear at any site other than Mohenjo-daro where the greatest variety of seal symbols have been found. Probably the shamanistic rites suggested by one of these seals were restricted to this centre and more specifically with its elite. There are various reasons why I consider that the elephant was associated with the elite. The numerous small terracotta masks which have been found do not represent this animal. Of the numerous terracotta figurines that have been found, those of the elephant are rare. Only few have been found at Chanhu-daro and Harappa. Most of these figurines are believed to have served as votive offerings rather than as cult images. At Mohenjo-daro they have been found, smashed, in large numbers mainly from the habitational areas of the settlement. None were found in an area which could be considered as a shrine or temple.[66] This would suggest that by and large the elephant was not associated with the masses. The elephant motif only emerges in the Mature Harappan period and it probably represents one group of people who rose to a position of power during that period.

The image of the elephant has also been found in sites which are recognised as being Late Harappan or Post Harappan. One such site, Daimabad in the Ahmednagar District of Maharashtra, has yielded some copper images which include those of a rhinoceros, a buffalo, an elephant and that of a chariot driven by two bulls with a male figure at the rein.[67] According to Allchin, these copper images date to between *c.* 1500 and 1050 BC.[68] Other scholars date them to *c.* 1800-1600 BC.[69] Some, like Ratnagar, warn that Daimabad has no stratigraphic context and, for that reason, it is difficult to assess the date of these images. Dhavalikar has suggested that these statues may have been imported into the Deccan from Harappa.[70] The statues are fairly large. That of the elephant stands 25 cm. high on a platform that is 27 centimetres long. The images of the rhinoceros and the buffalo are on wheels. The elephant statue is on a platform which has four brackets beneath, pierced to take axles.[71] This suggests that the images may have been used for processions. They are too heavy to have been toys. The elephant statue weighs over 60 kg. According to Dhavalikar, copper was extremely scarce in the Deccan and these bronzes may have been created on the order of the 'ruling chief/ priest' of Daimabad.[72] The images mounted on wheels, suggestive of ritual processions, have a long history in the Harappan context. The earliest evidence of bull figurines designed to be mounted on wheels comes from Mehrgarh Period VII (first half of the third millennium BC) just before the Indus Civilization makes its appearance.[73] Ratnagar has discussed how processions constituted an important public activity revealed by the architectural provisions in the Harappan and Kalibangan Citadels.[74] She suggests that the hole or hollow on the back of some animal figurines from Mature Harappan sites may indicate that animal emblems could have been fixed to walls with the use of nails or else attached to the tops of poles to be carried in processions. The elephant does not figure as one of these emblems. Possibly the animals on wheels, such as the elephant, were associated with fewer and the more important occasions and, consequently, were made bigger and supplied with wheels.

THE ELEPHANT FROM *c.* 600 BC–AD 200

Between the Post Harappan period and about the sixth century BC, there is a blank in the availability of data relating to the elephant. In the post 600 BC period there is evidence of people and places named after the animal. The motif appears on coins and sculpture. It is striking that, once again, the appearance of the elephant motif coincides with the rise of new urban centres and the formation of States in and around the Gangetic plain. The elephant symbol is adopted by certain kings and there is reference in literature to rituals associated with the animal. It is also associated with early Buddhist, Brahmanical and Jaina mythology. All this is very valuable evidence. When carefully collected and organized, it provides an interesting picture of the regions where the elephant was associated with royalty and divinity, of people who claimed descent from it and the nature of its symbolism.

PEOPLE AND PLACES NAMED AFTER THE ELEPHANT

There are two broad zones associated with the elephant. One includes areas that lie in modern India such as the Doab and part of the Ganga basin, as also some areas in modern Orissa and Gujarat. The second zone includes the north-west of the sub-continent and covers areas which today form part of Afghanistan and Pakistan.

Hastināpura (*hasti* signifies elephant) is an example of a place named after the elephant. It is situated on the river Ganga in the present Meerut district of Uttar Pradesh. According to the *Mahābhārata,* the city was named after its founder, King Hastin of the Paurava dynasty.[75] However, this same text refers to the town more frequently as Gajapura,[76] Gajasāhvaya,[77] Gajahvaya[78] and Nāgahvaya[79] than as Hastināpura.[80] Even according to the *Mahāmāyūrī,* the town was known as Hastināpura, Gajasāhvaya, Hastisāhvaya and Nāgasāhvaya.[81] The words *gaja, hasti* and *nāga* are synonyms for 'elephant'. These various names with the same meaning suggest that the town was associated with the elephant rather than with one king of the family of Kuru, long before the compilation of the *Mahābhārata.* Since places are often named after their inhabitants, Hastināpura was probably associated at some time with a people named after the elephant. King Hastin himself was probably named after the elephant for what it symbolised at that time. He may have been responsible only for having made the city famous or for having enlarged it. Excavations at Hastināpur have revealed a large number of elephant terracotta images and the motif appears to have been the favourite animal theme in the context of the Northern Black Polished Ware culture dated at this site between the early part of the sixth and the end of the third centuries BC.[82] This presents a contrast to the earlier and subsequent periods when bulls were more popular.[83]

In Magadha, in the early medieval period, the names of places such as Hastipada and Hastigrāma occur several times in the records of the period between AD 475-1030.[84] On the basis of these records it is not possible to know when or why these places acquired their names. It is quite likely that these places had been associated with people who were named after the elephant or for whom the elephant had a special significance. Magadha was associated with the Mātaṅga (elephant) dynasty of Kośala when Biṃbisāra, king of Magadha, married a princess of that royal house. The Buddhist text, *Lalitavistara Sūtra,* describes a debate amongst the gods when a family has to be chosen for the Buddha to take birth in. The ruling family of Kośala is considered unsuitable since it is descended from the Mātaṅgas and, therefore, neither the father's nor the mother's line is considered pure. The text describes the family as 'ignoble' and states that it patronized base people.[85] Biṃbisāra married the sister of Prasenajit of Kośala, a contemporary of the Buddha. His son, Ajātaśatru, subsequently absorbed Kośala in the Magadhan empire. Although there is no reference to the Mātaṅgas worshipping the elephant, the fact that they are named after it would show that they attached some significance to the symbol.

The term Mātaṅga is synonymous with Caṇḍāla and Kirāta. The Caṇḍālas are a particularly despised caste in early Brahmanical and Buddhist literature. They appear to have been a large and widely dispersed caste. Jha considers them to be aboriginal tribes who, as a caste, had probably evolved long before the close of the Vedic period.[86] The Kirātas were a moutain tribe who lived by hunting. Since Prasenajit of Kośala was a contemporary of the Buddha, it is evident that the Mātaṅga lineage was older than Buddhism. It was looked down upon by the *brāhmaṇas* and Buddhists because the beliefs and practices of its members did not conform to Vedic and Buddhist norms. Ultimately, however, Buddhist and Brahmanical literature developed a new perspective towards these people or, at least, a category of them. Prasenajit of Kośala was converted to Buddhism and this probably led to a gradual change in Buddhist attitude towards the Mātaṅgas. The *Mātaṅga Jātaka* refers to a Caṇḍāla by the name of Mātaṅga, the Elephant, who attained wisdom and became an enlightened soul. This Caṇḍāla was associated with Kāśī, outside which he is said to have been born. The *Lalitavistara Sūtra* refers to a *pratyekabuddha* named Mātaṅga who lived on the mountain Gotangulaparivartana in Rājagṛha. A *pratyekabuddha* literally means 'isolated *buddha*' or 'private *buddha*' meaning one who has attained enlightenment on his own in the forest, without being taught by a *buddha*, and who also does not venture to teach anyone else after his enlightenment.[87] This portion of the *Lalitavistara Sūtra* is evidently later than the portion which refers to the ruling family of Kośala in a derogatory manner. Even the Brahmanical texts eventually speak of a certain noble Mātaṅga. The *Mahābhārata* refers to him as 'the law-abiding royal seer Mātaṅga, having become a hunter, at a time of disaster'.[88] I am tempted to believe that this refers to a conversion to the Buddhist and Brahmanical faiths by some eminent members of the Mātaṅga lineage along with their followers. Since royal patronage was equally important to both the Buddhists and the *brāhmaṇas*, the new patrons were often given fabricated geneologies and fitted within the framework of the growing mythologies of the two religions. The reference in the *Mahābhārata* to Mātaṅga having become a hunter at a time of disaster appears to be an attempt to justify and explain the existence of such a past.

Aśoka (third century BC) made use of various animal symbols and it is pertinent to enquire why the elephant symbol appears where it does. The figure of an elephant is drawn on the north face of a rock bearing edicts at Kālsī (Uttar Pradesh). Below the drawing is the Brāhmī label *gajatame*, 'the best of elephants'.[89] A pillar at Sankisā (Uttar Pradesh) is said to have originally had a single elephant capital.[90] Although the capital is lost, it has been described by Fa-Hien in the fourth century AD. Below the XIII Girnār rock-edict (Kathiawar, Gujarat) is engraved, 'the entirely white elephant bringing indeed happiness to the whole world'.[91] This probably served as the label of the figure of an elephant that Aśoka caused to be carved and that has now disappeared. Finally, the Dhauli rock edicts (Bhubaneshwar, Orissa) are surmounted by the fore-part of an elephant, four feet high, hewn out of solid rock. At the end of the sixth Dhauli rock-edict is engraved the word *seto*, 'the white one', evidently referring to the figure of the elephant.[92]

The reference to the elephant as 'the white one' has led many scholars to believe that it represents the *Buddha*.[93] According to Buddhist mythology, Māyā Devī, the *Buddha's* mother, dreamed of a white elephant entering inside her when the *Buddha* was conceived. Yet, none of the places where the motif appears is particularly sacred to the Buddhists. It is also uncertain whether the elephant had been adopted as the symbol of the *Buddha*'s conception in Aśoka's lifetime.

In early Buddhist art (fourth-third centuries BC), the symbols representing the four principal episodes in the *Buddha*'s life were: the Bodhi tree, symbol of his enlightenment; the wheel representing the Wheel of Law; the lotus, symbol of his divine birth and the *stūpa* representing his *parinirvāṇa*.[94] Other episodes of the *Buddha*'s life such as the departure from home is represented by a riderless horse and his presence by that of an empty throne. In the Jātakas, the white elephant sometimes represents the Bodhisattva in a previous life and at other times it is distinct from him. In all cases it is associated with auspiciousness and well-being. Those stories where the white elephant is distinct to the Bodhisattva probably belong to the earlier layer of the Jātakas. According to them, the white elephant is sometimes a noble animal who bears the precious relics of the *Buddha* to the *stūpa* where they are finally deposited;[95] or, as described in the *Alīnacitta Jātaka*, it is an auspicious animal acquired by the king of Kāśī, thanks to which his posthumous son (the Bodhisattva) is able to ward off the attack of the king of Kośala and live in prosperity.[96] In the *Dummedha*, *Śīlavanāga* and *Chaddanta Jātakas* the Bodhisattva himself is born as an elephant. These Jātakas give the impression that there did exist some tradition of a white elephant which was gradually associated with Buddhist mythology. Whether this had already happened in the lifetime of Aśoka is doubtful.

While on his deathbed, the *Buddha* is believed to have prescribed four places as being sacred: Kapilavastu, where he was born; Bodh-Gaya, where he received enlightenment; Sārnāth where for the first time he preached his doctrine; and Kuśinagara where he entered *parinirvāṇa*.[97] Aśoka erected a pillar at Lumbinī (Kapilavastu) stating that this was the birth place of the Blessed One.[98] Surely, this would have been an appropriate place to establish the figure of the elephant, if indeed during this period it was the symbol of his conception. Yet, nowhere near the region of his birth is there any evidence of the elephant in sculpture or inscription.

The Sārnāth pillar of Aśoka is surmounted by four lions bearing a great wheel over which are represented an elephant, a bull, a horse and a lion.[99] All these animals were eventually associated with the *Buddha*; the lion became his epithet as Śākya-Siṃha (lion among the Śākyas); the horse, representative of his departure from home; the bull, the symbol of the constellation of his birth and the elephant, the symbol of his conception. Yet, the Aśokan lions have come down to us without any association with Buddhism. Probably these were symbols which were important before Aśoka's time and even before the birth of Buddhism. Those of the elephant and bull obviously signified something even in Harappan times. They were probably adopted by different religious groups and kings down the ages and modified for their own purposes.

I have suggested earlier that the elephant appears to have been associated with divinity and with royalty, before the birth of Buddhism. Possibly, the Aśokan elephant was meant to symbolise

Aśoka himself. If the motif was used in only a few specific areas, it was probably because those were the very regions where such a tradition existed. Aśoka availed of existing local symbols of divinity and kingship to proclaim his suzerainty over a vast empire.

Kālsī and Sankisā, like Hastināpura, lie in the Doab region. From that area, and from places around it, coins dating from the third to the first centuries BC from various *janapadas* (Republics) bear the elephant motif quite consistently. Those of the Ārjunāyanas (approximately 100 BC, provenance from the triangle of Delhi-Jaipur-Agra),[100] for example, have one variety which depicts, on the obverse, an elephant with uplifted trunk before a tree in railing. The reverse has a bull before a *liṅga.* The coins of the Audumbaras (about 100 BC, provenance from the Kangra District, north of the Doab) have one variety which depicts, on the obverse, a tree in enclosure with the forepart of an elephant to the right.[101] Some Kada coins (approximately latter half of third century or early second century BC, provenance from the Punjab) have, on one side, an elephant and on the other a snake, taurine symbol and legend.[102] There are some coins from around Varanasi (approximately third/second centuries BC) having an elephant/taurine with the svastika symbol on the obverse.[103] Among the coins of the Yaudheyas, there is a variety having on the reverse an elephant with a *nandipada* above it. The obverse has a bull before a sacrificial post or what appears to be one.[104] The tree, *liṅga* and bull had, and continue to have, a religious significance. If they are represented with the elephant on these early coins it is certain that the latter was also associated with the sacred.

There is evidence of the elephant being associated with rain and fertility in ancient Kaliṅga where the Dhauli rock edicts are situated. The *Kurudhamma Jātaka*[105] refers to a belief in Kaliṅga according to which the presence of a certain auspicious elephant warded off drought. According to this Jātaka the Boddhisattva was born as the son of the King of Indapatta (Indraprastha) city in the Kuru kingdom. During this time there was drought in the city of Dantapura in Kaliṅga. The people converged on the king of Kaliṅga and told him about the state elephant in the city of Indraprastha called Añjana-vasabho whose mere presence guaranteed rain. The elephant was acquired from the King of Indraprastha; still it did not rain in Kaliṅga. Finally, only when the king practiced the five virtues of the Kurus did it rain. Of course, the purpose of the Jātaka is to show the futility of existing superstitions and beliefs and the necessity of following the teachings of the *Buddha* in order to avert calamity. The Jātaka, however, confirms the existence of such a belief both in Kaliṅga and Indraprastha. The latter lies in the Doab area, not far from Hastināpura.

The name Dantapura suggests some association with the elephant. *Danta* signifies 'tooth' and *Dantin* means 'elephant'. Dantapura is the ancient name of Puri (Orissa) and according to legend it is believed to have been named after the shrine for the *Buddha*'s left canine tooth.[106] The Buddhist legends of preserving the tooth of the *Buddha* appear to be derived from some older tradition. It is striking that the tooth relics of the *Buddha*, in all cases, appear to be associated with the elephant and with places where the elephant motif appears or where there are stories of the elephant in some supernatural role. There is a legend according to which a Kashmiri monk acquires a tooth relic of the *Buddha* from a herd of elephants.[107] Hsuan Tsang refers to a milk tooth of the *Buddha* in Kapīśa.[108] Another tooth relic is associated with Gandhāra and a third with Kaliṅga while a fourth is traditionally believed to be honoured by the *nāgas* (serpents) in their abode.[109] The term *nāga* signifies both elephant and serpent and its exact meaning in literature is often ambiguous. The measurements of these relics indicates that they are not those of human teeth. The one from Kaliṅga which is preserved in Kandy (Sri Lanka) is described as being five centimeters long and two and a half centimeters wide.[110] In another case the tooth of a *pratyekabuddha* is described as being twelve and a half cm. long and ten cm. wide. Obviously, it is not of human origin.[111] Possibly, the tradition of preserving tooth relics was earlier associated either with serpents or elephants, or both.[112]

There does not appear to be any evidence of an elephant cult in the region of Junagarh. This is understandable considering that much of the available evidence comes from Buddhist sources and that this area was relatively far away from the middle Ganga basin where Buddhism was born and where it initially developed. It is also far away from the north-west where Buddhism spread and gained an early foothold. However, if the elephant is referred to alongside an edict in Junagarh it is likely that it enjoyed some local significance in the region in Aśokan times.

There is reference to an elephant deity in some Buddhist texts. In the Niddesa commentary of the *Suttanipāta* there is mention of *Hātthivatika* (worshippers of the elephant), besides the *Assavatika, Govatika, Supannavatika* (worshippers of the horse, the cow and bird), *Punnabhaddavatika, Maṇibhaddavatika,* (worshippers of Pūrṇabhadra and Maṇibhadra), etc.[113] This text, in all probability, refers to cults in and around the middle Ganga plain where Buddhism flourished from the earliest times. The reference to Maṇibhadra and Pūrṇabhadra confirms this, since these two *yakṣas* were particularly associated with Rājagṛha and Gwalior.[114]

There is literary and numismatic evidence which points to the existence of an elephant deity in the north-west of the subcontinent as well (modern Afghanistan and Pakistan). The motif of the elephant appears on one coin of Antimachus Theos who belongs to the early group of Greek kings of Bactria.[115] Demetrius II (180-165 BC) who probably succeeded him, wears the elephant scalp as his helmet.[116] The elephant was not native to Greece nor does it figure in Greek mythology. It was evidently appropriated by the Greeks because of its relevance in the region where they settled and where it was, perhaps, a symbol of royalty and divinity. I have mentioned earlier how the *Vāyu Purāṇa* refers to the Gajabhūmikā (land of the elephant) as one of the many people associated with the region of Ketumāla which corresponds to old Bactria. Gajabhūmikā may refer to a people or to a sub-region.

Kapīśa also appears to have been associated with some cult of the elephant. *Kapi* itself signifies 'elephant' and the word *Kapīśa* signifies 'Elephant Lord'.[117] There are some coins, attributed to Eucratides, which bear on the reverse the image of a female deity and the superscription *Kaviśiye nagaradevatā* (the city-deity of Kapīśi). It is accompanied by two symbols, a mountain and the head of an elephant.[118] The deity bears a palm-branch in her hand.[119] Kapīśa's city goddess was associated with a mountain and with the elephant. J.N. Banerjea considers that this elephant represents Indra. Other scholars associate it with Buddhism.[120] In all likelihood, it is connected with neither. At no point is Indrāṇī more important than Indra. Therefore, the representation of the elephant along with the goddess of Kapīśa can hardly be symbolic of Indra. Besides, Indra is never represented by the elephant. The latter remained his mount and was never synonymous with him as the bull sometimes was with Śiva. As regards Buddhism, from Hsuan Tsang's description of the elephant deity of Kapīśa, it is clear that it was distinct from the *Buddha.* This Chinese Buddhist pilgrim who visited India in the seventh century speaks of a mountain which lay to the south-west of Kapīśa. The deity of this mountain had the form of an elephant. Hsuan Tsang goes on to state that the *Buddha* was once invited by this god to the mountain. Aśoka, subsequently, built a *stūpa* on this mountain over the *Buddha's* relics. In this manner, Buddhism was associated with older places of pilgrimage. The mountain in Kapīśa is referred to by Hsuan Tsang as Pi-lo-sho-lo. The Chinese translation of this term is 'elephant solid'. Julien refers to it as Pīlusāra.[121] In fact *pīlu* signifies 'elephant' and *sāra* means 'the best', 'the highest'. The term also signifies 'strength' and 'vigour'.[122] The name Pīlusāra appears to be related to 'Piḷḷaiyar' which is the Dravidian name for Gaṇapati. 'Piḷḷaiyar' is derived from the Dravidian words *paḷḷu* or *peḷḷa* both signifying 'tooth', i.e. 'tusk of elephant'. In the present form of the word, however, there is no meaning of tusk. Piḷḷaiyar means 'noble child'. However, since the Pali word *piḷḷaka* has the significance of 'a young elephant' it is possible that *piḷḷe* originally meant the young of the elephant.[123] Kapīśa's elephant deity was evidently older than Buddhism and Brahmanism.

According to Philostratus, it was a custom in Taxila in the first century AD to keep a sacred elephant in the Sun Temple.[124] He describes how an elephant that had once belonged to Porus was dedicated in the same temple by Alexander and named Aias. People used to anoint it with myrrh and adorn it with fillets.[125] Further reference to rituals of a religious nature associated with the elephant comes from the *Susīma Jātaka*[126] which specifically mentions the elephant festivals of Taxila. It describes how the Bodhisattva in a previous life, as the son of the priest of the King of Kāśī, goes to Taxila to learn from a reputed teacher the ceremonies associated with the elephant festival. These references from two independent sources confirm that such a practice did exist in Taxila. The Jātaka also confirms that this ritual was known in Kāśī.

The elephant appears on the coins of Agathocles (180-165 BC), the first Indo-Greek king who had some hold over Taxila. His coins bear the elephant with a plant before it on the obverse and a star above the horse on the reverse.[127] Sometimes the elephant and bull are depicted together as on a coin of Heliocles II (120-115 BC).[128] This combination appears again in the money of Maues, Axes and Axilises. On one of the coins of Maues (who probably occupied Taxila about 85 BC) the bust of the king is depicted on the obverse and the elephant on the reverse. Menander also occupied Gandhāra with its two capitals.[129] Some of his coins have a standing elephant on the obverse, with a goad on the reverse.[130]

The elephant scalp appears again on a coin of Lysias (120-110 BC) where the latter wears it as a headgear. The reverse depicts the naked Heracles crowning himself.[131] The king is closely associated with the elephant. On another coin the obverse has the bust of Heracles and the reverses depicts an elephant.[132] Narain describes a silver drachma of Hermaeus which he believes depicts, on the reverse, a male deity with elephant's head, trunk to his left, tusks invisible, holding a sceptre palm in left hand.[133] He considers this to be an incipient Gaṇapati and the first evidence of a deity having a human form and an elephant-head. This suggestion has been refuted by Cribb and Bopearachchi who consider that what Narain takes for the trunk of the elephant is, in fact, 'a badly copied Zeus-Mithra nose, beard and a fold in the gown'. Besides, as Bopearachchi points out, the coin in question was not issued by Hermaeus but is an imitation issued by nomads who occupied the Kabul Valley after the death of the Greek king.[134]

The elephant is not the most frequently depicted symbol on Taxila coins.[135] By the close of the first millenium BC, other religious forces had come to exert a considerable influence in the region. Therefore, newer religious beliefs and rituals may have begun to undermine the influence and importance of the elephant deity. Moreover, the animal had, by this time, begun to acquire a new significance within the fold of the Brahmanical and Buddhist religions.

RITUALS ASSOCIATED WITH THE ELEPHANT

Earlier, I referred to a tradition of keeping a sacred elephant at the Sun Temple at Taxila and to elephant festivals at Taxila and Kāśī mentioned in the *Susīma Jātaka*. These references come without any description of what the elephant festival was actually about and what it involved. Fortunately, the *Hastyāyurveda* provides such a description and one can surmise that all elephant festivals involved certain similar rites. These festivals are not associated in any way with the elephant-headed Gaṇapati and appear to be an ancient practice, linked to the concept of the elephant as a symbol of the sacred from very early times. According to the *Hastyāyurveda* the elephant festival was an annual event where the elephant was worshipped. This ritual was performed for rainfall and the associated fertility of crops, fecundity of cattle and man, and the general prosperity of the kingdom. An elephant painted white with sandal paste was led in solemn procession through the capital. The ritual involved the wearing of women's attire by the male attendants and the utterance of licentious remarks aimed at stimulating the dormant sexual energy of the living power. Finally, the elephant was worshipped by the high officials of the realm, both civil and military.[136]

According to the *Hastāyurveda*, the white elephant, if worshipped as a divinity, bestowed on man all those earthy blessings which the goddess, Śrī-Lakṣmī, Fortune and Prosperity, the Mother Earth, fertile and abundant with water and riches, has in store.[137] The elephant was the fertilising agent and because of it, the Earth Goddess brought forth crops, animals and human beings. In fact, Gajalakṣmī represents this very concept: the fertilizing of a female being, representing the earth or the fields, by rain-clouds. It is significant that the term *kumbhin* means 'elephant' and the feminine form of the word, *kumbhini* means the 'earth'.

The elephant festival, as described in the *Hastyāyurveda*, has certain common elements with another famous ritual, that of the *aśvamedha* (horse sacrifice) associated with later Vedic culture. The latter, too, was performed by kings and high officials of the realm for the prosperity of the lands, fertility of the soil and material well being of the king and his kingdom. Women played an important role in this ritual and, in fact, all the women of the realm participated in it. The central ritual of the *aśvamedha* was the union of the queen with the dead horse while obscene language was exchanged between the priest (*hotṛ*) and the crowned queen.[138] The *Ṛg Veda* knows nothing of this ritual horse sacrifice.[139] It was probably borrowed from the existing rituals of the non-Vedic people in the Later Vedic period. It is quite possible that the elephant festival has its origin in some ritual that was older than the *aśvamedha* since the elephant appears as a sacred symbol from an earlier period than the horse. Some of the ceremonies may have been adapted to the horse in the Vedic context. Quite possibly, the elephant festival had the sacrifice of the elephant as the central ritual at some stage.

According to the *Mātaṅgalīlā*, 'the creation of elephants was holy and for the profit of sacrifice to the gods and especially for the welfare of kings'.[140] There is evidence in later literature that elephant sacrifice did exist at some point in time. There are Tantric texts which describe *homas* which must be performed with elephant's stool and elephant's meat.[141] *Yantras* (mystical diagrams) are made with a mixture consisting of secretions from an elephant's temples, blood and semen.[142] Other rituals include the drawing of an image on the meatless shoulder blade of an elephant.[143] Although Tantric texts belong to the post-Christian era, many of the rites described by them appear to be much older. Even when the elephant evolves into the Brahmanical Gaṇapati, the latter's beheading retains the idea of sacrifice. According to some texts of the early medieval period, human sacrifice is associated with the rituals of the Buddhist Tantric Gaṇapati where the *bali* offered is said to be a human leg.[144] It is not possible to say when exactly such a practice began and when it was given up. Some of the Tantric practices may well have originated in ancient shamanistic rituals. Divination through shamanism was often carried out through animal bones and reference to the meatless shoulder blade of the elephant suggests some such practice.

The sacrifice of elephants was probably given up eventually, not only because of the difficulties related to the procurement of the animal but also because it is less easily bred in captivity. Elephants have not been domesticated in the same sense as the buffalo. They were most probably captured from the wild and then trained. As they came to be used increasingly in battle and for heavy physical work it was simpler and more economical to sacrifice some of the other domesticated animals.

According to the *Hasti Ratna Dhanaṃyeti Upadeśa* (Instructions for Acquiring Wealth through the Precious Elephant), a text which forms part of the Tibetan Buddhist canon, a ritual is performed before the image of an Indian elephant for the purpose of achieving earthly prosperity of all kinds.[145] This text, which belongs to about the eighth century AD, evidently refers to a practice that is later than that described in the *Hastyāyurveda*. The text makes no reference to Gaṇapati nor to any elephant deity. It is just the elephant which has the power to fulfil all desires. The worship of its image is sufficient and there is no reference to a procession or a festival. It is likely that since elephants were not native to Tibet, a real elephant could not be associated with this ritual. However, the idea itself appears to stem from the tradition described in the *Hastyāyurveda.* In the Tibetan Buddhist canon, this text is grouped together with the largest body of texts on Gaṇapati,[146] because anything relating to elephants in the sacred context came to be associated with him. Even prayers to Gaṇapati in the Buddhist Tantric context retain a reference to his association with rainfall. There is a text in which Gaṇapati is invoked to send down hail. He has to be meditated upon as riding a dragon (the equivalent of the *nāga* of the Indian tradition). Similarly, there are rituals for stopping hail.[147]

From the *Hastyāyurveda* it is evident that the worship of the elephant was associated with that of the Goddess. Possibly, the latter was also sometimes represented in the form of an elephant. The *Matsya Purāṇa* lists about two hundred goddesses including Vaināyakī and Mātaṅgī.[148] Whereas Vaināyakī evidently refers to the *śakti* of Gaṇapati-Vināyaka when the latter had become an important god, Mātaṅgī harks back to an older period since Mātaṅg signifies 'elephant' and Mātaṅgī suggests the existence of an elephant goddess. In the contemporary context, Mātaṅgī is a woman of the Mādiga community (one of the untouchable communities in Andhra Pradesh) who is associated with buffalo sacrifice at the village goddess festivals. She is an unmarried woman who is initiated as a special representative or manifestation of the goddess, an office which she holds for life.[149] She is symbolically married to a tree and thereafter her life knows no moral restrictions. Perhaps that is why Mātaṅgī is also a name for a class of prostitutes.[150] Since the term *mātaṅga* signifies 'elephant' it is surprising that the term Mātaṅgī should be associated with the goddess and with buffalo sacrifice (the slaying of the buffalo itself is done by the chief Mādiga). It is quite likely that her prototype originally played a similar role in the context of elephant sacrifice and when that ritual ceased to be practiced she was associated with the buffalo sacrifice since her role and symbolism in that context remained unchanged.

The wearing of women's attire by the male attendants in

the performance of the elephant festival is a practice that continues to be followed in many village or popular rituals associated with other deities who constitute the non-Sanskritic tradition. In Maharashtra and Karnataka, an officient from one of the untouchable communities such as the Māṅg, Mahar or Holeya, is responsible for killing a sheep or goat prior to or after the sacrifice of the buffalo in the goddess festivals. Known as Potrāj (the term literally means 'buffalo king'), he is often dressed as a woman.[151] In Andhra Pradesh and Tamil Nadu, Pōtu Rāju is the name of the divine attendant of the Goddess. Whitehead mentions that an Andhra image of Pōtu Rāju carries 'nine glass bangles belonging to his sister Ellamma'. This practice aims at a symbolic unification or identification with the Goddess.[152] Even among the Mālas (Andhra Pradesh and Karnataka), who act as bards and priests in the worship of Aṅgalamma, the poet-priest, dressed as a woman, accompanies the sacrificial animals being taken to the shrine of the goddess.[153] Similar rites are also associated with *nāga* worship. Vogel describes a sacred ceremony called Nāga-*maṇḍala* practiced by people in the Dakshin Kannad District of Karnataka, either to get rid of an affliction due to the wrath of a serpent for having killed a snake in a former life, or to get progeny. The figure of a serpent is made and then worshipped. The ritual is performed to the accompaniment of music provided by a group of male musicians dressed in women's attire and bedecked with jewels.[154] The parallels between the buffalo sacrifice and *nāga* worship in the contemporary context and rituals centred around the elephant described in ancient texts are striking.

THE ELEPHANT IN THE MYTHOLOGY AND ART OF EARLY BRAHMANISM, BUDDHISM AND JAINISM

BRAHMANISM

The Vedic Indra does not ride an elephant. It is only in the epics that he acquires the animal as his *vāhana* (vehicle). The explanation generally given for this is that by the mid-first millennium BC the elephant had become the symbol of royalty and so it came to be considered the most appropriate mount for Indra, king of Gods. Yet, an understanding of who Airāvata is, provides another possible explanation.

According to the *Atharva Veda,*[155] Airāvata is the son of Irāvan who is the chief Nāga. He is also known as Dhṛtarāṣṭra. In some other texts he is described as a sage of the Sarpa ethnic unit, who acted as a priest. In this case, his name is mentioned as Dhṛtarāṣṭra of the Airāvata lineage.[156] In the *Ṛg Veda,* a hymn is devoted to the worship of *sarpas* (serpents). Evidently snake worship required a special category of priests. In the *Ṛg Veda,* the Sarpas and Nāgas are mentioned as two different people.[157] Over time the distinction seems to have become blurred since in later texts Airāvata is sometimes a Nāga and at other times a Sarpa. The question arises as to why he became the *vāhana* of Indra. If Indra had to be given an elephant *vāhana,* why did it have to be named Airāvata?

A *vāhana* is generally associated with the personality and role of the deity it bears. The goat, a sacrificial offering, is the *vāhana* of Agni (Fire) who carries all oblations to the gods. The antelope, a swift animal, bears Vāyu (Wind). The goddess Gaṅgā is borne by the alligator, one of the bigger and more powerful riverine creatures. Indra and Airavata also have some common associations. One of Indra's epithets is *Vṛtrahā* Indra (destroyer of Vṛtra). Originally, the term *vṛtra* expressed the general idea of 'resistance'.[158] As Indra came to be considered the hero who destroyed the foes of the Vedic Aryans, *vṛtra* came to denote those very human foes.[159] When Indra was made into a deified hero, Vṛtra became the mythical dragon that he destroys.[160] Since Indra was also regarded as the rain-god, Vṛtra was also looked upon as the cloud-demon. Indra destroys the cloud-demon and releases the rain. The mythological dragon and the *nāga* are closely related. However, the term *nāga* had come to signify 'elephant' in addition to 'serpent'. Both the elephant and serpent were associated with clouds and rain but since the elephant was considered the mount of kings, it was considered more appropraite as a *vāhana* than the serpent. So Indra acquired the elephant as a mount and the latter was named after one of the oldest lineage of Nāga priests possibly signifying the superiority of Indra over the *nāga* deities.

In the Purāṇas, Airāvata is sometimes described as a snake and at other times as an elephant. He is named as one of the eight *diggajas* (elephants of the quarters) along with Kumuda, Padma, Puṣpadanta, Vāmana, Supratīka, Añjana and Nīla.[161] In the *Vāyu Purāṇa,* Airāvata is described as being born from the ocean.[162] He is the white elephant churned from the ocean along with Lakṣmī, the white horse, Ucchaiśravas, and others. The association of the elephant with water and with the Goddess is constant. Here, Lakṣmī is associated with Airāvata, even as she is associated with Gaṇapati at a later stage. This has its parallel with the goddess of Kapīśa and the elephant deity of the mountain. In Buddhist texts Airāvata is described as one of the four great *nāga* kings. Among the Bharhut reliefs is one which shows the Lord *Buddha* being worshipped by the Nāgarāja Airāvata or Elāpattra. An inscription confirms the identity of the *nāgarāja* who, in Buddhist art, is depicted either as a five-headed serpent or as a human being with a five-fold serpent crest.[163]

The elephant first makes its appearance in the Brahmanical pantheon as Airāvata, the mount of Indra. In the last couple of centuries before the Christian era, Indra was still an important God. Airāvata, therefore, was given an equally important role. He was made the ruler of all the elephants[164] and was invoked in the propitiatory rites to destroy the diseases of elephants along with Viṣṇu and Śrī on the fifth lunar day (*nāga pañcami*).[165] In the early centuries of the Christian era, however, Indra's importance began to decline. Viṣṇu and Śiva ascended to take his place. Many of Indra's functions and attributes were taken over by these gods who represented the aspirations of a changing society. Along with Indra, Airāvata also lost his importance. As Puranic myths describe the humiliation of Indra in order to glorify one or the other of the newer Gods, so also is Airāvata humiliated. In one instance, he is described as being struck on the head by the mace of an *asura* (demon) and, consequently, falling in a swoon. He is then abandoned by Indra who mounts a chariot.[166] On more than one occasion, he is forced to retreat during combat because of severe head wounds.[167]

In Puranic mythology the elephant, along with serpents, is often used as a metaphor for clouds. This suggests common functions and symbolism for the two creatures. According to the *Vāyu Purāṇa* elephants, mountains and clouds along with serpents belong to one and the same family since water is known as the source of their origin.[168] 'Clouds arising from the waters of ocean ... assume the shapes of buffaloes, boars and elephants in their rut. They are called *jīmūtas* since they are the source of living beings'[169] by virtue of the fact that they provide the earth with fecundating rain. It is this association with the clouds that probably gave rise to the myths of flying elephants. According to the *Mātaṅgalīlā*, elephants could originally fly in the sky until they were cursed by the sage Dīrghatapas. Only the elephants of the quarters escaped the curse.[170] This idea is present even in the Buddhist texts like the *Chaddanta Jātaka* which refers to eight thousand royal elephants who, by exercise of supernatural powers, were able to move through the air.[171] Similarly, the *Dummeda Jātaka* describes an elephant who flies from Rājagṛha to Kāśī.[172] There is a close parallel between the *diggajas* and the *dignāgas* (serpents of the quarters).

In the Vedas the elephant is referred to as *hastin, gaja, mṛgha* or *vāraṇa*.[173] It is not clear when exactly the term *nāga* came to be considered as a synonym of *hastin*.[174] The grammarian Pāṇini (*c.* fifth century BC) provides the earliest evidence of the term having this dual significance.[175] *Nāga* also means 'mountain' and snakes and elephants appear to be associated with mountains as well. Sometimes specific mountains are mentioned as the abode of certain *nāgas*.[176] The sacred elephant of Kapīśa was associated with the mountain referred to by Hsuan Tsang as Pi-lo-sho-lo. There are parallels between the function of rain-bearing clouds which fertilize the earth, the fertility symbolism of the sacred elephant/serpent, and the role of mountains as the abode of clouds and the source of rivers. This perhaps explains why the term *nāga* signifies these different things. Even the term *mātaṅga* signifies both 'elephant' and 'cloud'.[177]

At times the *nāgas* also appear to be synonymous with *yakṣas*. Maṇibhadra is sometimes referred to as Maṇināga[178] and at other times as Maṇibhadra *yakṣa*.[179] Both *nāgas* and *yakṣas* share common functions. They are intimately connected with the waters and associated with vegetation. The great tutelary *yakṣas* control the rains essential to prosperity.[180] Since some *nāga* deities were *yakṣas* too, it is possible that the elephant deity was also a *yakṣa*. This idea is clearly present in the context of early Buddhist art which is discussed further on. The association of the elephant with water and mountains finds an echo in the worship of the later Gaṇapati. In the Āgamas, a *dhyāna* of Gaṇapati describes him as seated on a jewelled mountain located in a sea filled with sugar-cane juice. Inside the sea are crocodiles, *śankhas* (conches) and fish.[181]

BUDDHISM

In the three or four centuries following the death of the *Buddha*, a substantial mythology began to be woven around this historical figure. Buddhist art acquired newer forms in order to embellish the great *stūpas*. The conventional symbols representing the *Buddha* without showing him in his human form did not provide much scope for such a display of art as was required. So animal stories, which became the Jātaka stories, began to be sculpted along with the newly fabricated myths.

According to one such myth, Māyā Devī, mother of the future *Buddha*, dreamed of a young, white elephant entering her side. This was symbolic of the conception of the *Buddha* and the scene has been sculpted at the *stūpa* at Bharhut (second century BC).[182] It is significant that even in the context of Buddhism the elephant retains his role as a fertilising agent.

The elephant motif is one of several motifs sculpted on the walls of the early Buddhist *stūpas*. In some cases it recalls the elephant motif on the early punch-marked coins. That of the elephant with uplifted trunk, before a tree in railing, on the coins of the Ārjunāyanas, or the tree in enclosure with the forepart of an elephant to the right in the coins of the Audumbaras referred to earlier, has another variation on a stone railing at the *stūpa* of Bharhut. Three elephants offer worship to a tree with altar. The scene appears to be a mountain. Two elephants are approaching the stone seat, the bigger one bears a bundle of lotus fibres in its trunk; the smaller sprays itself with water from the brook.[183] Another bas relief of the Bharhut *stūpa* shows a big banyan tree with a seat in front it of it, decorated with an ornamental band and strewn with flowers. On either side, three elephants, one of which is a very young animal, are bowing or offering garlands. On the right are figures of two men. One stands with his hands joined in devotion. On the altar is engraved: 1. Bahuhathiko nigodho, 2. Nadode; the banyan tree *Bahuhathika* (of many elephants) on (Mount) Nadoda.[184] Although the sacred tree in the Buddhist context evidently refers to the Bodhi tree under which the *Buddha* achieved enlightenment, the motif itself is clearly older than Buddhism. The artisans employed to sculpt and decorate the Buddhist *stūpas* made use of skills and traditional motifs handed down since before the birth of Buddhism. Occasionally, this motif is combined with a pair of worshippers bearing rooted plants or saplings.[185]

In early Buddhist art, the serpent and the elephant sometimes perform the same functions. In Bharhut, Sanchi and Bodh Gaya, as also at Mathura, the new born *Buddha* is bathed by two elephants standing on a lotus.[186] A couple of centuries later, in the Gupta period, a sculpture from Sārnāth shows the infant *Buddha* being bathed by two serpents who float in the air above him and hold round, inverted water-jars which the elephants of the earlier *stūpas* held with their trunks.[187] At other times, the elephants and serpents appear closely associated although they remain distinct. For example, a piece of sculpture (from its style it may be assigned to the Kuṣāṇa period—first-second century AD) which was excavated at Sārnāth and is now preserved in the local museum, shows a *stūpa* being worshipped by a wild elephant with an offering of lotus-flowers and at the same time protected by some triple-headed serpents which form a garland round its dome.[188] The parallels between the serpents and elephants has already been pointed out earlier within the framework of Brahminism. Its existence in the Buddhist context points to it being a well-established notion which was recognized by both religions.

In Buddhist art, the elephant symbolising the immaculate conception of the *Buddha* is depicted with six tusks.[189] It is distinct from the elephant-headed *yakṣa*, the earliest representation of which exists at Amarāvatī in the lower Krishna Valley (second century AD)[190] and at the Kantaka Celinga *stūpa* in Sri Lanka (second century AD).[191] Even some *nāgas* acquire human forms retaining their *nāga* identity because of the capello over their heads. This elephant-headed *yakṣa* and the humanised *nāgas* are distinct from the purely decorative motif of the elephant and the snake.

The earliest *yakṣa* statues date to the Mauryan period. Those found at Parkham and Noh (in the Bharatpur region of Rajasthan) are colossal statues.[192] These tall and well built super-human figures became the models of the Bodhisattva and Viṣṇu images of later times. As the *Buddha* and Viṣṇu took the place of these local divinities the latter had to be shown in an inferior position and without the perfection of the newer deities. The problem was solved by making them smaller in size, often in the form of dwarfs with pot-bellies. In early Buddhist art the *nāga*, the elephant and other animal deities were differentiated from ordinary animals by being given a therianthrophic form. The functions of many of these old deities such as those of protection, bestowing of wealth and well-being got transferred to the greater ones. However, the role of guardian so essential to these older deities was transformed. They now became the guardians or attendants of the principal deities and were placed at the entrance to or around the main shrines of the newer gods.

JAINISM

In Jaina iconography, the elephant is sometimes associated with Pārśvanātha, the twenty-third Jina. The latter is normally depicted seated in *padmāsana* (lotus pose) with a hooded cobra over his head. In fact, the cobra is the *lāñchana* (characteristic mark) of Pārśva and is represented by five or seven snake-hoods over his head.[193] However, in some sculptures the elephant appears to substitute for the snake-hooded attendants or worshippers. A statue found at Tumain, district Guna (Madhya Pradesh, seventh century AD) depicts Pārśvanātha with the canopy of seven snake-hoods but attended on each side by an elephant carrying in its raised trunk a lotus-bud with a long stalk. The upper parts of the sculpture are badly mutilated; however, the figure of an elephant is visible on the upper left end. Perhaps there was an elephant on the other side and both the elephants were performing an *abhiṣeka* (ritual bathing) on the Jina. Another sculpture of Pārśvanātha preserved in an old Jaina temple at Rājgir shows him sitting in *padmāsana*. Part of the pedestal is mutilated but there is an elephant just to the left of the place where the *dharmacakra* (wheel of *dharma*) was but is now mutilated.[194] In the Department of Archaeology, Hyderabad (Andhra Pradesh), there is a stone statue of Pārśvanātha standing under a canopy of seven snake-hoods. Two small figures of *cāmaradharas* (chowry bearers) stand on elephants by the side of Pārśva's shoulders. The sculpture is dated to about the twelfth century AD.[195] There is even a legend according to which Pārśvanātha was once worshipped by an elephant when he visited the Kadambari forest near a mountain named Kali with a *kuṇḍa* (tank) nearby. King Karakaṇḍu of Campa knowing this, visited the spot but arrived when Pārśvanātha had already left the place. The king was dejected, but on digging near the spot found a beautiful jewel-image of the Jina which was then installed in a shrine.[196] It is worth mentioning that Pārśva who, according to Jaina tradition, lived in the eighth century BC, was from Kāśī and is reported to have travelled widely in eastern India and Kaliṅga.[197] The area of Banaras, Magadha and Kaliṅga, as we have seen earlier, were regions where the elephant appears to have been worshipped as a deity. The close association between elephant and snake is present in some icons of Pārśvanātha. Since his *lāñchana* is the snake and since *nāga* signifies both 'snake' and 'elephant' the latter was sometimes associated with him. However, these elephant motifs are the exceptions rather than the rule in the depiction of Pārśvanātha who is usually flanked either by a male or female worshipper, or standing *cāmaradharas* on each side, sometimes with snake hood, sometimes in half-snake, half-human form. At other times he is flanked by his *yakṣa* and *yakṣi* both of whom have a snake-hood above the crown.

Ajitanātha, the second Jina, has the elephant as his *lāñchana* and the twenty-fourth Tīrthaṅkara, Mahāvīra, has Mātaṅga as his *yakṣa* and Siddhyāyikā as his *yakṣiṇī*. Mahāvīra is the the most important Tīrthaṅkara for the majority of Jainas. If he is associated with Mātaṅga, the latter must have been one of the more important minor deities from the Jaina point of view. Although Mātaṅga is not represented as an elephant the name itself signifies 'elephant'. Siddhyāyikā's name is somewhat similar to Siddhi, one of the consorts of Gaṇapati. The fact that she accompanies Mātaṅga as the *yakṣiṇī* of Mahāvīra further confirms the impression that Mātaṅga represents one of the aspects of the prototype of Gaṇapati. Just as the snake, which was worshipped from the earliest of times, was absorbed in one form or another in the art and mythology of Vedic religion, Brahminism, Buddhism and Jainism, so also was the worship of the elephant very old and the animal found a place in the pantheons of the these newer religions.

It is from the Gupta period onwards that the *yakṣa* and *yakṣiṇī* figures began to be regularly appended to the sculptures of the Tīrthaṅkaras.[198] Many statues depicting Mahāvīra with his *yakṣa* and *yakṣiṇī* are post tenth century when Gaṇapati had been accepted into the Jaina pantheon. Therefore, even if Mātaṅga and Siddyāyikā are latecomers in the Jaina pantheon and even if parallels exist between them and Gaṇapati and Siddhi, they remain distinct to them. Besides, their appearance in art does not rule out the possibility of their being associated with Mahāvīra from an earlier period. The name Mātaṅga evokes a deity older than Gaṇapati. Like so much else in Indian tradition, the old continued to coexist with the evolving new.

By the turn of the Christian era the elephant had found a place in the mythology and art of Brahminism and Buddhism. At a later stage the animal was associated, directly or indirectly, with some of the Jaina Tīrthaṅkaras. However, this elephant was distinct to Gaṇapati. It is not ever referred to by any of the epithets associated with Gaṇapati. Although by the second century AD the elephant-headed *yakṣa* form exists, it cannot be presumed to represent Gaṇapati-Vināyaka. There is no evidence of a deity by this name having an elephant or elephant-headed form at this early stage. Gaṇapati-Vināyaka had yet to make his debut.

NOTES

1. Ananda K. Coomaraswamy, *History of Indian and Indonesian Art*, p. 11.
2. B.P. Sahu, *From Hunters to Breeders*, p. 112.
3. Bridget and Raymond Allchin, *The Rise of Civilization in India and Pakistan*, p. 163.
4. B.P. Sahu, op. cit., pp. 116-17.
5. Ibid., p. 163.
6. Richard Meadow, 'Animal Domestication in the Middle East', in Gregory Possehl, ed., *Harappan Civilization*, p. 298.
7. The dates for this period are cited from Bridget and Raymond Allchin, op. cit., p. 214.
8. Shubhangana Atre, *The Archetypal Mother*, p. 142.
9. B.P. Sahu, op. cit., pp. 166-7.
10. Ibid.
11. F.R. Allchin, 'The Legacy of the Indus Civilization' in Gregory L. Possehl, ed., Ibid, p. 386.
12. Shubhangana Atre, op. cit., p. 140.
13. These sites are Harappa, Mohenjo-daro, Chanhu-daro, Allahdino, Balakot, Kot Diji, Amri, Desalpur, Surkotda, Lothal, Rangpur, Rojdi (Srinathgarh), Kalibangan, Banawali, Alamgirpur, Hulas, Rupar, Manda, Shortugai, Sutkagen-dor and Sotka-Koh. See Shubhangana Atre, op. cit.
14. Ibid.
15. Bridget and Raymond Allchin, op. cit., p. 215.

16. Ibid., p. 211.
17. E.J.H. Mackay, *Further Excavations at Mohenjo-daro,* p. 333.
18. Shereen Ratnagar, *Enquiries into the Political Organization of Harappan Society,* p. 146.
19. D.D. Kosambi, *An Introduction to the Study of Indian History*, p. 157.
20. Ibid., p. 176.
21. Debiprasad Chattopadhyaya, *Lokāyata: A Study in Ancient Indian Materialism,* p. 206.
22. Mircea Eliade, *The Encyclopaedia of Religion,* Vol. 5, pp. 81-2.
23. Ibid.
24. Debiprasad Chattopadhyaya, op. cit., p. 142.
25. Franklin Edgerton, trans., *The Elephant Lore,* pp. 45-6, vv. 15-19.
26. *Vāyu Purāṇa,* Vol. I, p. 283, fn. 2.
27. Ibid., I. 44.9-15.
28. Ibid.
29. V.S. Agrawala, *India as Known to Pāṇini,* p. 456.
30. Ibid.
31. D.C. Sircar, *Studies in the Geography of Ancient and Medieval India,* p. 149.
32. The term 'yoga' appears anachronistic for the Bronze Age since it appears to have developed much later and is associated in its early stages with Patañjali in the second century BC.
33. T.M.P. Mahadevan, 'Śaivism and the Indus Civilisation', *JGJhRI,* Vol. IV, Nov. 1946, pp. 1-10.
34. Elizabeth C.L. During Caspers, 'Some Thoughts on the Indus Script', in Ellen M. Raven and Karel T. Van Kooij, eds., *Indian Art and Archaeology,* pp. 54-67.
35. Alf Hiltebietel, 'The Indus Valley 'Proto-Siva', Reexamined through Reflections on the Goddess, the Buffalo and the Symbolism of *vāhanas*', *Anthropos,* Vol. 73, 1978, pp. 767-97. See, in particular, p. 768.
36. Personal communication from Shereen Ratnagar.
37. Alf Hiltebeitel, op. cit., pp. 771-2.
38. E.C.L. During Caspers, 'Magic Hunting Practices in Harappan Times', in K. Friefelt and S. Sprensen, eds., *The Indus Civilization,* SAA, 1985, pp. 227-36.
39. Ibid., pp. 775-6.
40. Shubhangana Atre, op. cit., p. 191.
41. Alf Hiltebeitel, op. cit., see p. 776 where the author discusses this view put forth by Volchok, a member of the Russian team that has studied the Indus Valley script since the mid-1960s.
42. Nevill Drury, *Shamanism,* p. 1.
43. Shubhangana Atre, op. cit., pp. 99-199.

44. Ibid., p. 41.
45. E.C.L. During Caspers, 'Magic Hunting Practices in Harappan Times' in K. Friefelt and S. Sprensen, eds., op. cit.
46. Elizabeth C.L. During Caspers, 'Some Thoughts on the Indus Script' in Ellen M. Raven and Karel T. Van Kooij, eds., op. cit.
47. Sudhir Kakar, *Shamans, Mystics and Doctors*, pp. 56-7.
48. Shereen Ratnagar, op. cit., p. 182; Shubhangana Atre, op. cit., p. 195.
49. Shubhangana Atre, op. cit.., p. 203.
50. Ibid., p. 89.
51. Ibid., p. 80.
52. Ibid., p. 196.
53. Bridget and Raymond Allchin, op. cit., p. 215.
54. Shubhangana Atre; op. cit., p. 182.
55. Shereen Ratnagar, op. cit., p. 152.
56. Shubhangana Atre, op. cit., p. 142.
57. H.W. Bailey, ed., *Corpus Inscriptionum Iranicarum,* Part II (Inscriptions of the Seleucid and Parthian Period and of Eastern Iran and Central Asia), Vol. V, (Śaka), p. 68. This reference occurs in the context of an eulogy of the *Buddha.*
58. *Liṅga Purāṇa,* I.21.25.
59. *Vāyu Purāṇa,* I.24.110.
60. *Bhāgavata Purāṇa,* I.ii.7.1.
61. Ibid.
62. Mircea Eliade, *Patterns in Comparative Religion*, p. 164.
63. Robert Graves, *Greek Myths*, p. 484, see fn. no. 1.
64. Ibid., p. 553.
65. Shubhangana Atre, op. cit., p. 102.
66. Alexandra Ardeleanu-Jansen, 'The Terracotta Figurines from Mohenjo-Daro: Considerations on Tradition Craft and Ideology in the Harappa Culture (CA. 2400-1800 BC)', *Lahore Museum Bulletin,* Vol. I, No. 2, July-Dec. 1988, pp. 9-28.
67. Ibid., p. 211.
68. Bridget and Raymond Allchin, op. cit., pp. 273, 278-9.
69. Cited in M.K. Dhavalikar, 'Daimabad Bronzes', in Gregory L. Possehl, ed., *Harappan Civilization*, pp. 421-6.
70. M.K. Dhavalikar, op. cit.
71. Ibid., p. 424.
72. Ibid.
73. Alexandra Ardeleanu-Jansen, op. cit.
74. Shereen Ratnagar, op. cit., p. 147.
75. B.B. Lal, 'Excavation at Hastināpura and Other Explorations in the Upper Ganga and Sutlej Basins, 1950-52', in *Ancient India,*

Nos. 10 and 11 (1954 and 1955), p. 148.

76. S. Sorensen, *An Index to the Names in the Mahābhārata,* p. 287 (*Mhb.* XIII,7711).
77. Ibid., p. 287 (*Mhb.*I,1700, 3000, 4360, 4441, 4460, 4468, 5034, 5149; II,1676, 2647; III,9, 1348; V,6092, 7106; XIV,1476, 1479).
78. Ibid., (*Mhb.* II,2600, 2640; III,279; V,6071; XII,2121; XIV,370; XV,439; XVIII,181).
79. Ibid., p. 494 (*Mhb.* I,3,793, 796, 815, 823; III, 82, 5055; V,97, 3980, etc.).
80. Ibid., p. 320 (*Mhb.* I,2,512,514; I,3,672; I,102, 4125, etc.).
81. D.C. Sircar, '*Mahāmāyūrī*: List of *Yakṣas*', *Journal of Ancient Indian History,* Vol. V, Parts 1-2, p. 33.
82. Vidula Jayaswal and Kalyan Krishna, *An Ethono-Archaeological View of Indian Terracottas,* p. 115.
83. Ibid., pp. 115-16.
84. *EI,* Vol. XIV, No. 23, pp. 327-8. See lines 48-49; *IHQ,* Vol. XX, p. 328; *IO,* Vol. IV, p. 100.
85. *The Lalitavistara Sūtra,* trans. into English from the French by Gwendolyn Bays, Vol. I, pp. 37-38.
86. V.N. Jha, 'Varṇasaṃkara in the Dharma Sūtras: Theory and Practice', *JESHO,* Vol. 13, nos. 1-3, 1970, pp. 273-88.
87. A.K. Warder, *Indian Buddhism,* p. 203.
88. J.A.B. Van Buitenen, *Mahābhārata,* Vol. I, p. 162. .
89. Ramaprasad Chanda, 'The Beginnings of Art in Eastern India with Special Reference to Sculptures in the Indian Museum', *Memoirs of ASI,* No. 30, 1927, p. 33.
90. Ibid., p. 32.
91. Ibid.
92. Ibid.
93. Ibid.
94. A. Foucher, *The Beginnings of Buddhist Art,* p. 25.
95. Thomas Watters, *On Yuan Chwang's Travels in India (AD 629-645),* p. 236.
96. *Alīnacitta Jātaka* in E.B. Cowell, op. cit., Bk. II, No. 156, pp. 13-17.
97. A. Foucher, *Etudes Sur l'Art Bouddhique de l'Inde,* p. 11.
98. Ibid.
99. Ibid., p. 33.
100. John Allan, *Catalogue of the Coins of Ancient India,* see 'Introduction', pp. lxxxi and lxxxiii.
101. Ibid., pp. lxxxiii-lxxxiv.
102. Ibid., pp. xcii-xciii.
103. Ibid., p. xcv.
104. Ibid., pp. cxlvii and cxlix.

105. E.B. Cowell, op. cit., Bk. III, No. 276, pp. 251-60.
106. *Nārada Purāṇa,* Vol. IV, p. 1350, fn. 4. Presently Puri is a Vaiṣṇava sacred site and the location of the famous Jagannātha temple.
107. Ibid., p. 144.
108. Thomas Watters, op. cit., p. 128.
109. H. Kern, *Histoire du Bouddhisme dans l'Inde,* p. 141.
110. Ibid., p. 142.
111. Ibid., p. 147.
112. See *EI,* Vol. IX, No. 19, pp. 160-1, where reference is made to Dantewara, a village or small town not far from Jagdalpur in the Bastar area. Numerous images of *nāgas* have been found in the villages around. Dantewara contained the shrine of Danteśvarī, the tutelary goddess of the former ruling family of the state. She was a form of Mahiśāsuramardinī. This temple was associated with human sacrifice. The only explanation one can offer for the association of a Mother Goddess with such a name, especially in an area which was never associated with the tooth relic of the *Buddha,* is that since Danti signifies 'elephant' (and it may have also signified a snake) this practice of preserving teeth was associated with a goddess whose worship may originally have been associated with the elephant and with serpents. See Chapter III for further discussion on Danti.
113. V.S. Agrawala, *Ancient Indian Folk Cults,* p. 10.
114. Ibid.
115. A.K. Narain, *The Indo-Greeks,* p. 52.
116. Ibid.
117. There are scholars such as Basham and Sircar who write the name as Kāpiśa (A.L Basham, *The Wonder that was India,* see map on first page; D.C. Sircar, *Studies in the Geography of Ancient and Medieval India,* pp. 51n and 293). Both *Kapiśaṃ* and *Kāpiśaṃ* signify 'spirituous liquor' (V.S. Apte, op. cit., pp. 334 and 348). It is possible that this name was given to the place as it came to be associated with Bacchanalian festivals as a result of Greek influence. The cultivation and drinking of wine is believed to have been introduced in the region by Greek settlers during the time of Cyrus the Great, king of Persia (George Woodstock, *The Greeks in India,* pp. 17, 21-2). *Kapiśa* signifies 'reddish-brown', or 'reddish' which may refer to the colour of wine (V.S. Apte, op. cit., p. 334). However, the name Kapīśa may well have been an older name, especially since the elephant is definitely associated with this place. There are other scholars such as Narain and Dhavalikar who refer to the city as Kapiśa and Kapiśā respectively (A.K. Narain, 'Gaṇeśa: The Idea and the Icon' in Robert L. Brown, ed., *Ganesh: Studies of*

an Asian God, pp. 19-48. See, in particular, p. 35; M.K. Dhavalikar, 'Gaṇeśa: Myth and Reality' in Robert L. Brown, ed., op. cit., pp. 49-68, see p. 53), Probably Kapīśa (Kapi + īśa= Kapīśa) in this case is shortened to Kapiśa. Kapiśā appears to refer to the feminine form of Kapiśa. This may have been the name of the tutelary goddess of the city.

118. A.K. Narain, op. cit., pp. 62-3.
119. A.N. Lahiri, *Corpus of Indo-Greek coins,* p. 126-7.
120. A.K. Narain, op. cit., p. 63.
121. Thomas Watters, op. cit., p. 129.
122. V.M. Apte, op. cit., pp. 621 and 982.
123. Alice Getty, *Gaṇeśa,* p. 1.
124. Frederick E. Zeuner, *A History of Domesticated Animals,* p. 286.
125. W.W. Tarn, *The Greeks in Bactria and India,* p. 164.
126. E.B. Cowell, op. cit., Bk. II, No. 163, pp. 31-4.
127. A.K. Narain, op. cit., p. 53.
128. Ibid., p. 65.
129. Ibid., p. 79.
130. A.N. Lahiri, op. cit., p. 158.
131. Ibid., pp. 145-6.
132. Ibid., pp. 147-8.
133. A.K. Narain, 'On the Earliest Gaṇeśa' in J.E. Van Lohuizen De Leeuw *et al.*, eds., *Studies in South Asian Culture,* Vol. VII, (Senarat Paranavitana Commemoration Volume), pp. 142-4.
134. Osmund Bopearachchi, 'On the So-Called Earliest Representation of Gaṇeśa', in Marie-Francoise Boussac and Jean Francois Salles, eds., *Athens, Aden, Arikamedu,* pp. 45-73.
135. Ibid., p. 30. The elephant is found on no more than three of Allan's nine classes of local Taxila money and only on forty-seven of the one hundred and seventy one specimens described.
136. Heinrich Zimmer, *Myths and Symbols in Indian Art and Civilization,* p. 108.
137. Ibid.
138. N.N. Bhattacharya, *Ancient Indian Rituals and their Social Content,* pp. 3-5.
139. Ibid., p. 5.
140. Franklin Edgerton, trans. into English, *The Elephant Lore of the Hindus. The Elephant Sport (Mātaṅgalīlā) of Nīlakaṇṭha,* p. 47.
141. *Devī Rahasya,*, XXVI.54; *Guhyasamāja Tantra* , VI.23.
142. Christopher Wilkinson, 'The Tantric Gaṇeśa: Texts Preserved in the Tibetan Canon', in Robert L. Brown, ed., *Ganesh: Studies of an Asian God,* p. 263.
143. Ibid.

144. Ibid., p. 258. (*Śrī Ājnā Vinivarta Gaṇapati Sādhanaṃ.*)
145. Ibid., pp. 270-4.
146. Ibid., p. 270.
147. *Mahāgaṇapatitantra,* see Christopher Wilkinson, op. cit., p. 250.
148. V.S. Agrawala, *Ancient Indian Folk Cults,* pp. 21-3.
149. Richard L. Brubaker, 'Barbers, Washermen and Other Priests: Servants of the South Indian Village and its Goddess', *History of Religions,* Vol. 19, No. 2, Nov. 1979, pp. 128-52. See in particular pp. 136-7.
150. Alf Hiltebeitel, 'Rāma and Gilgamesh: The Sacrifices of the Water Buffalo and the Bull of Heaven', *History of Religions,* Vol. 19, No.3, Feb. 1980, pp. 187-223. See p. 197.
151. Ibid., p. 190.
152. Alf Hiltebeitel, 'The Indus-Valley Proto-Śiva', op. cit., p. 791.
153. Pupul Jayakar, *The Earth Mother,* p. 83.
154. J. Ph. Vogel, *Indian Serpent Lore,* p. 275.
155. Ralph T.H. Griffith, *Hymns of the Atharva Veda,* Book VIII, Hymn X, pp. 350-3.
156. Ibid.
157. G.S. Ghurye, *Vedic India,* p. 414.
158. R.N. Dandekar, *Vedic Mythological Tracts,* p. 173.
159. Ibid., p. 174.
160. Ibid., pp. 190-1.
161. *Agni Purāṇa,* III.269.14-23.
162. *Vāyu Purāṇa,* I.1.124.
163. J.Ph.Vogel, op. cit., p. 39.
164. *Agni Purāṇa,* I.19.27.
165. Ibid., III.291.1.
166. *Bhāgavata Purāṇa,* III.viii.11.14-16.
167. Ibid., II.vi.11.10-11; *Padma Purāṇa,* I.67.42-4.
168. *Vāyu Purāṇa,* I.51.44.
169. Ibid., I.51.29-31.
170. Franklin Edgerton, op. cit., I.11-12 (pp. 43-4).
171. E.B. Cowell, op. cit., Vol. III, Bk. XVI, No. 514, pp. 20-31.
172. Ibid., Vol. I, Book I, No. 122, pp. 269-71.
173. *Ṛg Veda,* X.40.4.
174. In the *Bṛhadāraṇyaka Upaniṣad* (I.3.22) the term *nāga* is translated as 'elephant' and in the context it makes sense (S. Radhakrishnan, *The Principal Upaniṣads,* p. 161). Similarly, there is reference to *nāga* side by side with *gaja, hasti* and *kuñjara* in the old ballad of the six-tusked elephant known indisputably to be prior to the bas-reliefs of Bharhut. Cited by A. Foucher in 'On the Iconography of *Buddha*'s Nativity', *Memoirs of ASI,* No. 46, p. 4.

175. V.S. Agrawala, *India as known to Pāṇini,* p. 218.
176. J. Ph. Vogel, op. cit., p. 33.
177. V.S. Apte, op. cit., p. 734.
178. *Mahābhārata,* Ādi Parva, 31.6.
179. D.C. Sircar, 'Two Brāhmī Inscriptions' in *JBRS,* Vol. XXXIX, Pts. 1-2, pp. 41-8; V.S. Agrawala, *Ancient Indian Folk Cults,* p. 183.
180. Ananda K. Coomaraswamy, *Yakṣas,* Part II, p. 13.
181. *Īśānaśivagurudevapadhati,* Vol. 2, 15.20-1.
182. B.M. Barua, *Barhut,* Bk. III, p. 50.
183. H. Luders, ed., *CII,* Vol. II, Part II, p. 165.
184. Ibid., p. 168.
185. Bridget and Raymond Allchin, op. cit., p. 214.
186. A. Foucher, 'On the Iconography of the *Buddha*'s Nativity', *Memoirs of ASI,* No. 46, 1934, p. 11.
187. Ibid., p. 16.
188. J. Ph. Vogel, op. cit., p. 130.
189. A. Foucher, *The Beginnings of Buddhist Art,* p. 188.
190. Ananda K. Coomaraswamy, op. cit., Pt. I, plate 23.
191. H. Heras, *The Problem of Gaṇapati,* p. 28.
192. R.C. Agrawala, '*Yakṣa* Torso from Bharatpur Region', in *JOIB,* Vol. 17, Nos.1-4, 1967-8, pp. 64-5.
193. Umakant P. Shah, *Jaina-Rūpa-Maṇḍana (Jaina Iconography)*, Vol. I, p. 181.
194. Ibid., p. 183.
195. Ibid., p. 186.
196. Ibid., p. 187.
197. Ibid., p. 172.
198. R.P. Hingorani, *Jaina Iconography in Rūpmanḍana,* p. 29.

AREAS ASSOCIATED WITH THE ELEPHANT
(Pre-Harappan Period up to Circa A.D. 200)

BACTRIA
• Gajabhūmikā
AFGHANISTAN
Kapīsī
KAPISA ✛ ⊤⊤⊤ Hastinapuras
GANDHARA ✛ Puṣkalāvatī
▨ Taxila
River Indus

0 100 200 300 400 500
Kilometers

PAKISTAN

Rupar
Mehrgarh Harappa ○ Bara ■ Kalsi
Kadas ○
Mohenjo-daro Kalibangan ■ Hastinapur
Chanhu-daro ○ Ārjunāyanas ○
Sankisa ○
Allahdino ○ Yaudheyas ○ Kāśī ▨
Lothal ■
Girnar ▲ Daimabad 🐘
River Narmada
River Godavari
River Krishna
Amaravati
River Kaveri

Audumbaras ▲
River Brahmaputra
KOSALA ▨ ⊤⊤⊤ Māṭaṅgas ⊤⊤
River Ganga
MAGADHA
Hastigrāma ⊼ Hastipada
KALINGA ⊞ Dhauli ▲

Mihintale

Arabian Sea

Bay of Bengal

INDIAN OCEAN

◓	Evidence of faunal remains of a single specimen of the elephant at a pre-Harappan site.
○	Elephant motif in terracotta art and on seals/amulets in the Mature Indus period.
■	Elephant bones discovered at sites of the Mature Indus period.
🐘	Image of elephant discovered at the Post-Harappan site of Daimabad.
⊼	Places named after the elephant in *circa* post 6th century BC.
⊤	Tribes named after the elephant in *circa* post 6th century BC.
▲	Asokan pillar/inscriptions with image or reference to the elephant.
◓	Tribal coins with elephant motif (3rd - 1st century BC).
●	Coins of Indo-Greek kings with elephant motif (2nd - 1st century BC).
▨	Places associated with the elephant in Buddhist mythology.
✛	Tooth relics of the Buddha associated with the elephant.
∿	Buddhist stupas where earliest representation of the elephant-headed yakṣa exists (circa 2nd century AD).

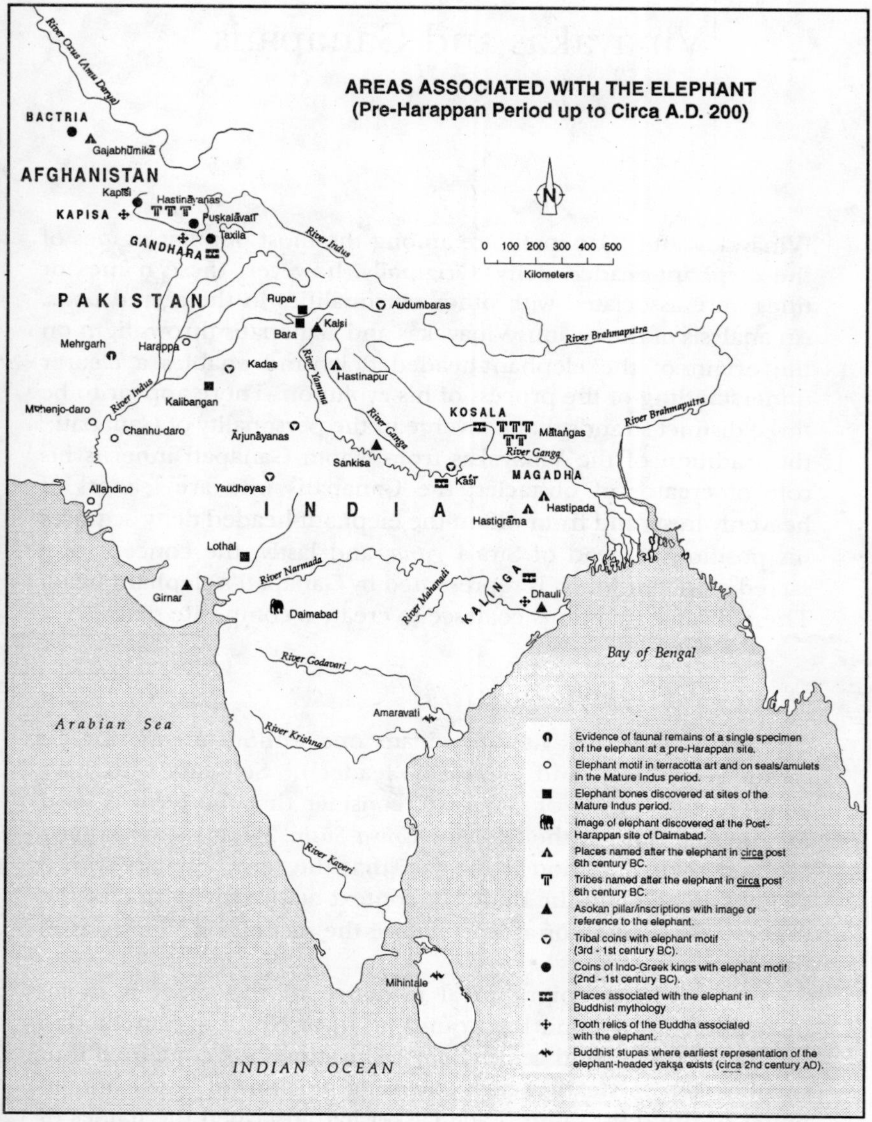

Map 1. Sites mentioned in Chapter II.

CHAPTER 3

Vināyakas and Gaṇapatis

'Vināyaka' and 'Gaṇapati' are among the most popular names of the elephant-headed deity. Originally, however, these names or titles were associated with other personalities in the sacred texts. An analysis of the various Vināyakas and Gaṇapatis throws light on the origin of the elephant-headed deity and enables a clearer understanding of the process of his evolution. There appear to be three distinct strands that converge in the personality of Gaṇapati:[1] the tradition of the Vināyakas from whom Gaṇapati inherits his role of creator of obstacles; the Gaṇapatis who are leaders of heavenly hosts and from whom the elephant-headed deity acquires his position as head of Śiva's *gaṇa*; and lastly, the concept of a sacred elephant which is represented by Gaṇapati's elephant head. These diverse traditions coalesce to create a composite deity.

VINĀYAKAS

The word 'Vināyaka' literally means one without a superior (*vi* signifies 'without' and *nāyaka* a 'leader').[2] Scholars who have analysed the origins of Gaṇapati, consider that the term is used for the first time in the *Mānava Gṛhya Sūtra*. What seems to have escaped their attention is the fact that the term appears with a distinct meaning in the Buddhist context before the period of the *Mānava Gṛyha Sūtra* or at least before the section on Vināyakas in that text.

The first epigraphical evidence of this term is in an inscription on a stone box found at *stūpa* No. 2 at Sanchi (last quarter of the second century BC).[3] The stone box contained four small caskets of steatite, each enclosing portions of burnt human bones of Buddhist saints. Each casket had inscribed the names of the saints whose mortal remains were contained within it. The stone box itself had the following inscription:

1. *Savina vināyakāna aram Kāśapa-*
2. *gotam updaya aram cas vachi-*
3. *Suvijayitam vināyaka*

The translation of this, according to Marshall is: '(Relics) of all the teachers, including ara Kāśapogota (Arhat Kāśyapa-gotra) and ara Vachi (Arhat Vatsi) Suvijayita the teacher (or teachers)'. Whether or not the term 'vināyaka' actually means teacher is not explicit. What is significant is the fact that it is associated with exalted personalities. Marshall goes on to point out that these 'teachers' belonged to different generations. The name Kāśapagota,[4] is found also in inscriptions from the *stūpas* of Sonari and Andher in the neighbourhood of Sanchi. He was a contemporary of Aśoka. All these 'teachers' belonged to different generations of the same Haimavata school. Therefore, 'vināyaka' probably signified a Buddhist spiritual teacher or a saint, at least, as early as the third century BC and, possibly, even earlier. It is certain that the term did not have any derogatory connotation at this time otherwise it would not have been associated with the saints. The term continued to have the same meaning in the Buddhist context even several centuries later. According to the *Amarakośa* (*c.* AD 500) 'Vināyaka' signifies one of the names of the Buddha, a Buddhist deified teacher and a spiritual preceptor. It also signifies Gaṇeśa, Garuḍa and Viṣṇu.[5] So, by the fifth century AD, the term was used for some Brahmanical deities as well, other than the elephant-headed deity.

In the Brahmanical context, the term is used for the first time in the *Mānava Gṛhya Sūtra*, a text of the *Kṛṣṇa Yajur Veda*, where it denotes a group of four demons.[6] A chapter in this text describes the wide range of calamities caused by these demons, which affect virtually every category and age-group of society. The possessed people develop the following symptoms:

A person possessed, pounds clods, tears grass, writes on his limbs and has various inauspicious dreams in which he sees waters, men with shaved heads, men with matted hair, persons wearing red clothes, camels, pigs, asses, Caṇḍālas and so on. He feels that he is moving through the air; and when walking along the road, he thinks that somebody is pursuing him from behind. When possessed by these Vināyakas, princes do not get their kingdoms, although they are otherwise qualified; girls cannot secure husbands although eager to do so and possess auspicious signs. Women do not get any issue although anxious for and capable of bearing them; children of virtuous women die; a learned teacher fails to attain the position of an *ācārya*; students face great interruptions in the course of their study, merchants' trade fails and agriculture of husbandsmen yields poor crops.[7]

The *Mānava Gṛhya Sūtra* then describes the rituals that must be performed for the propitiation of these Vināyakas. These include a wide range of offerings that are to be made at the crossroads of a village, a town or a market place. They include husked grains, unhusked grains, uncooked and cooked meat, fish, flourcakes, pounded, fragrant substances, a fragrant beverage, a white wreath, red, yellow, white, black, blue, green and multi-coloured garments, beans, fragrant rice, roots and fruits. All these must be offered with a new winnowing basket.[8] Also included in the ritual is the worship of a host of other associated beings. The names of the four Vināyakas are Śālakaṭaṇkaṭa, Kuṣmāṇḍarājaputra, Usmita and Devyajana. No physical description of them is given, the term Gaṇeśa or Gaṇapati is not used and there is no reference to their association with the elephant.

It is surprising that no attempt has been made to understand who these four Vināyakas were. The fact that they have names, shows that they were identities in their own right. What did they have in common and why were they four in number? If each had a name, why were they collectively referred to as the Vināyakas? We also need to ask whether and why the term acquired a derogatory connotation only within the Brahmanical context. A fuller understanding of the four personalities does provide some answers.

ŚĀLAKAṬAṆKAṬA

According to the *Rāmāyaṇa*,[9] Śālakaṭaṇkaṭa is a *vaṃśa* (lineage) of *rākṣasas* (demons) like that of the Pulastyas. Rāvaṇa's mother came from this family. Possibly, Śālakaṭaṇkaṭa was the tutelary deity of this family which was named after him. The name is also associated with Skanda. A stanza of the Dhūrta Kalpa hymn from the *Pariśiṣta* of the *Atharva Veda*, invokes Skanda as follows: 'Hail to Dhūrta, Skanda, Viśākha, Pinakasena, ...Śālakaṭaṇkaṭa.'[10] In the first case it is clear that Śālakaṭaṇkaṭa referred to a category of people looked upon as *rākṣasas* by the author(s) of the *Mānava Gṛhya Sūtra*. In the second case, since he is associated with Skanda, Śālakaṭaṇkaṭa had probably come to be looked upon as a *graha* (grasper)like so many other non-Vedic deities. One of Śiva's epithets in the *Vāyu Purāṇa* is Kaṭaṇkaṭa,[11] and in the *Mahābhārata,* Kālakaṭaṇkaṭa.[12] If Śiva, as Kālakaṭaṇkaṭa, was Lord of Time, so also Śālakaṭaṇkaṭa was perhaps the deity of the *śāla* (*Shorea Robusta*) tree. This tree is also associated with the third Jaina Tīrthaṅkara, Sambhavanātha, who is believed to have obtained *kevalajñāna* (highest knowledge) under a *śāla* tree.[13] Similarly, even the Buddha died under a group of *śāla* trees at Kuśinagara.[14] Neither in the *Rāmāyaṇa* nor in the Dhūrta Kalpa, is Śālakaṭaṇkaṭa refered to as Vināyaka.

KUṢMĀṆḌARĀJAPUTRA

The name literally means the son of the king of *kuṣmāṇḍas.* The term *kuṣmāṇḍa* has two meanings. It signifies a kind of pumpkin gourd and it is also the name of a category of demi-gods in early Buddhist literature and sculpture. These demi-gods are referred to as the *kuṣmāṇḍas* or *kumbhāṇḍas.* In some of the early Buddhist texts such as the *Dīgha Nikāya,* Virūḍhaka is mentioned as the Lord of Kumbhāṇḍas and guardian of the southern quarter.[15] At Bharhut (mid second century BC) Virūḍhaka is sculpted as a guardian *yakṣa* on the corner pillar of the South Gate. An inscription beside the sculpture confirms the identity of the *yakṣa.*[16] The *kuṣmāṇḍas* and Virūḍhaka are also depicted on the Sanchi gateways. Although the former are depicted as bandy legged, pot-bellied, huge headed and short armed little dwarfs, their leader, Virūḍhaka, is shown with no such deformity.[17]

In the literature of a later period, references to the *kuṣmāṇḍas* make it quite clear that they were a tribe or clan. In one of the Jātakas, the name of one of the *kuṣmāṇḍa* chiefs is Kumbhīra. He is otherwise called a *yakṣa* who lived on the Vepulla mountain outside the city of Rājagṛha.[18] This is the region where Buddhism initially developed, which accounts for the early association of the *kuṣmāṇḍa* people and their deity with Buddhism. There are other references in Buddhist literature to the chiefs of *kumbhāṇḍas, kuśmāṇḍas* or *kuṣmāṇḍas* (*kumbhāṇḍa-gaṇendras*), invariably in the plural and in a mythologised form.[19] Further information on the *kuṣmāṇḍas* can be gleaned from the Purāṇas. Although the Purāṇas belong to a later period than the *Mānava*

Gṛhya Sūtra they do throw some important light on this category of beings. According to the *Vāyu Purāṇa*, the *kuṣmāṇḍas* are one of sixteen pairs of *piśāca* twins, each pair comprising of a boy and a girl.[20] Possibly, this implies that the *kuṣmāṇḍas* were one of sixteen *piśāca* clans or tribes. Each pair of twins probably represented the progenitors of a different clan or tribe. This evokes the sibling marriage symbolism associated with origin myths of many *kṣatriya* lineages that were the founders of the *janapadas* (Republics) in the mid-first millenium BC, such as the Licchavis or the Śākyas.[21] Many of these *kṣatriya* families were associated with the Buddha, Mahāvīra and other heterodox teachers. Such myths of marriages between twins enabled the clans to claim purity of lineage since each was descended of parents of identical blood. Since the *kuṣmāṇḍas* are referred to as *piśācas* which have the same connotation as *asuras* or *rākṣasas* in Brahmanical literature, they were probably people who did not abide by Brahmanical norms. They also appear to have been associated with the *nāgas* because the name *kuṣmāṇḍa* appears as one of the numerous *nāga* names in the epics.[22]

On the basis of both sculptural and literary evidence, it is clear that some *kuṣmāṇḍa* chiefs had adopted Buddhism in the centuries preceding the Christian era. Their deities found a place in the growing Buddhist pantheon. Virūḍhaka, probably a tutelary *yakṣa* of the *kuṣmāṇḍas*, had become one of the four Buddhist *lokapālas*. During this period when Buddhist mythology was developing and had acquired Kubera, Dhṛtarāṣtra, Virūpākṣa and Virūḍhaka as the *lokapālas*,[23] the Brahmanical guardian deities of the quarters were still eight Vedic divinities. They were Indra, Vāyu, Yama, the Pitaraḥ, Varuṇa, Mahārāja or Kubera, Soma, Mahendra, with Vāsuki in the nadir and Brahmā in the zenith.[24] The *Manu Smṛti* mentions them as Indra, Vāyu, Yama, the Sun, Agni, Varuṇa, Soma and Kubera.[25] Even in the Purāṇas, the Brahmanical guardians of the quarters were never the same as those of the Buddhists, with the exception of Kubera who was common to both traditions. They are generally described as Indra, Yama, Varuṇa and Kubera.[26] At other times there are references to the *diggajas* (elephants of the quarters) or the *dignāgas* (serpents of the quarters).

The *kuṣmāṇḍas, yakṣas, piśācas* and *nāgas* appear to have been closely associated with each other. Virūḍhaka, a *kuṣmāṇḍa*, is depicted in later Buddhist art with the helmet made of the skin of an elephant's head.[27] Hsuan Tsang, when describing the Four Lords who divide Jambudvīpa when no one has the fate to be universal sovereign over that island, refers to the Lord of the South (Virūḍhaka) as the Elephant-Lord.[28] While describing the different pairs of *piśāca* twins, the *Vāyu Purāṇa* refers to one pair as *vakra* and *vakramukhī*.[29] The term *vakra* does not mean just twisted but rather turned or twisted backwards as only the trunk of an elephant can be. A later epithet of Gaṇapati is *Vakratuṇḍa* which conveys the same idea.

The word *kuṣmāṇḍa* appears in the *Taittirīya Āraṇyaka* where a special *kuṣmāṇḍa homa* (oblation to the gods) is prescribed for a man who regards himself as impure.[30] In this case the term signifies a kind of pumpkin gourd. By offering a sacrifice with *kuṣmāṇḍas*, accompanied by the appropriate *mantras* (incantations), a man is able to purify himself. It is prescribed that a person performing such a *homa* must shave his head as well as his upper lip. He must also abstain from eating flesh. What could have been the origin of this rite? Was there any link between this rite and the people called *kuṣmāṇḍas*? The *Vāyu Purāṇa* states that 'the Piśācas called Kuṣmāṇḍikas are devoid of hair on their heads or bodies. Skins and hides constitute their garments. They always eat gingelly seeds and flesh.'[31] Is it coincidence that performers of the *kuṣmāṇḍa* homa had to shave their heads and abstain from eating flesh? I wonder whether the origin of the *kuṣmāṇḍa* homa in the *Taittirīya Āraṇyaka* was in any way related to contact of a category of Vedic priests of the *Kṛṣṇa Yajur Veda* with this very clan or tribe whose name is associated with a particular plant. Possibly, the *kuṣmāṇḍa*, or pumpkin gourd, was an ancient totem of the *kuśmāṇḍa* clan or tribe who derived their name from it. Perhaps it was to ward off the contaminating effect of contact with these and other similar people that this rite was elaborated by the Vedic priests. In that case, was such a ritual appropriated from the people referred to as the *kuṣmāṇḍas* and converted into a Vedic ritual? There is a similar process described in the Purāṇas where it is said that by visiting a certain *piśācatīrtha* the devotee avoids the possibility of becoming a *piśāca*.[32] It is more likely that the *tīrtha* (place of pilgrimage) was originally associated with the *piśācas* and then included in the Brahmanical list of *tīrthas*. The association remained but in an inverse sense. The reference to the *kuṣmāṇḍas* appears only in texts of the *Kṛṣṇa Yajur Veda*. Even the *Padma Purāṇa* states that priests of the *Yajur Veda* should recite a hymn addressed to the demons called *kuṣmāṇḍas*.[33]

In the modern context the *piśācas* are believed to be the ghosts of those men who were either mad, dissolute or violent-tempered.[34] As malignant spirits, they are believed to possess individuals and have to be placated in order to rid the individual of them. An impending spirit attack usually announces itelf through certain omens in dreams. Symptoms of dizziness and nightmares are also widespread among victims of spirit attack.[35] In case of possession, sometimes the spirit demands a full ritual worship or an annual sacrifice.[36] This sounds very similar to Vināyaka possession and shows how certain concepts persist and how the term *piśāca* has continued to have a maleficient connotation even in present times.

USMITA

There does not appear to be any reference to this name in the sources that I have consulted. It may have signified a local deity popular in the region where the *Mānava Gṛhya Sūtra* was compiled.

DEVAYAJANA

The word literally means the worship of or sacrifice to the *deva*. The term *deva* signifies both 'god' and 'spiritual guide'. The term *Devayajana* signifies the worship of certain non-Vedic divinities or spiritual guides. The worship or sacrifice to these deities or spiritual guides must have been performed by some *brāhmaṇas* for material gain and they must have, consequently, been looked down upon. There is epigraphical reference to a grant being made to a *brāhmaṇa* of the Taittirīya *śākha* of the *Kṛṣṇa Yajur Veda* by the Vākaṭāka Pravarasena II. The *brāhmaṇa* is referred to as *gaṇa-yājin* (one who performs sacrifices on behalf of various categories and groups other than the ones prescribed in the Vedic texts) and the grant was possibly made to him on the occasion of a *gaṇa-yajña* at which he officiated as priest. Pravarasena is stated to be a devotee of Maheśvara.[37] Numerous cults were associated with Śiva which did not form part of Vedic tradition. The *Manu Smṛti* refers to the performers of *yajña* for the *gaṇas* and excludes such persons from the funeral feast.[38]

The four Vināyakas, therefore, represented certain people and practices in the region of the middle Ganga basin, that were viewed with hostility by adherents to the Vedic tradition in that same region. These beliefs and practices must have been widespread to eventually find expression in the *Mānava Gṛhya Sūtra*. In the description of the dreams which result as a consequence of possession by the Vināyakas, the reference to the sight of men with shaven heads, matted hair and those clad in red garments is significant. The shaven heads suggest the *kuśmāṇḍas* or the Buddhists, the red robes indicate the Buddhist monks, and the matted hair points to the ascetics of the Yoga and Sāṃkhya schools or to the early Pāśupata Śaivas. Equally significant is the fact that the Vināyakas first find mention in a domestic manual, and one which is associated with the region where Buddhism, Jainism and several other new faiths originated and developed. The *brāhmaṇas* of the Maitrāyaṇīya School, to which the *Mānava Gṛhya Sūtra* adheres, were associated mainly with the region between modern Gujarat and Banaras.[39]

The *Mānava Gṛhya Sūtra* is closely related to the *Varāha Gṛhya Sūtra*, which, although also belonging to the Maitrāyaṇīya School, does not mention the Vināyakas. Similarly, the *Kāthaka Gṛhya Sūtra*, the manual of another school of the *Kṛṣṇa Yajur Veda*, that of the Kāthakas, does not mention the Vināyakas. Yet, these three domestic manuals are otherwise very closely related.[40] It is probably the difference in the region of their compilation which is responsible for such minor variation. The *Kāthaka Gṛhya Sūtra* was mainly followed by the *brāhmaṇas* of Kashmir.[41] The demonic beings described as the Vināyakas by the *Mānava Gṛhya Sūtra* are associated with the region of the middle Ganga plain. This region witnessed the development of numerous non-Vedic sects and philosophies in the mid-first millenium BC. During the Mauryan period, Jainism and then Buddhism received royal patronage and became the greatest rivals of the declining Vedic religion.

To the individual, domestic rites were more important than the elaborate Vedic rituals which only a very limited section of society could afford and perform. The only way in which the *brāhmaṇa* priests could find a large and satisfied clientele was by acknowledging certain existing beliefs and practices among the common people or by creating new rites to satisfy their needs. All aspired to prosperity, progeny, beauty and health. Popular superstition about evil spirits being the obstacles to the realisation of these desires necessitated such rites. They were, therefore, prescribed by the *Mānava Gṛhya Sūtra.* Rival deities and cults were held responsible for all calamities and made into demons. The rites associated with them were absorbed into the framework of Brahmanism.

The Vināyakas are associated with a host of demonic beings: Vimukha, Syena, Baka, Yakṣa, Kalaha, Bhīru, Vināyaka, Kuṣmāṇḍarājaputra, Yagñavikśepi, Kulāṅgapamāra, Yupakeśi, Suparakrodi, Haimavata, Jambhaka, Virūpākṣa, Lohitākṣa, Vaiśravaṇa, Mahāsena, Mahādeva and Mahārāja.[42] An analysis of these beings will throw more light on the identity of the Vināyakas.

Syena (hawk) and Vimukha (ugly face or one without a face) could well refer to some *piśāca* deities.[43] The *piśācas* are described in the Purāṇas as having all kinds of strange faces. Those called Arkamarkas have the forms of monkeys while those called Pāṇipātras have stout heads like those of elephants and camels.[44] Baka is described as a man-eating *rākṣasa* in the *Mahābhārata.*[45] The *Vāyu Purāṇa* describes Baka and Yakṣa as the brothers of Pūrṇabhadra and Maṇimān. Their father, Maṇivara, is stated to be the brother of Maṇibhadra[46] the famous *yakṣa* associated with the region of Rājagṛha. The Jambhakas appear to be a category of *bhūtas* in the *Sāmavidhāna Brāhmaṇa* of the *Śukla Yajur Veda* which lays down special rites for bringing them under control.[47] Clearly, these were local gods or deified ancestors or leaders who, from the Brahmanical perspective, were demons.

Kuṣmāṇḍarājaputra (Virūḍhaka), Mahārāja, Vaiśravaṇa and Virūpākṣa are names of the Buddhist *lokapālas* as described earlier. Whereas for the Buddhists, Virūpākṣa is the Lord of Nāgas, Brahmanical literature refers to him as a *dānava*[48] or a *rākṣasa.*[49] The name Haimavata is also associated with Buddhism. It is in the masculine gender and there is no deity by this name in either the Buddhist or the Brahmanical pantheons. Yet, as indicated earlier, the teachers mentioned in the casket inscription of the *stūpa* at Sanchi, all belonged to the Haimavata school. This may then be an oblique reference to the tradition, which that group of teachers represents. What is interesting is the reference to a single Vināyaka as one of a host of demonic beings associated with the four Vināyakas. Who he represents is not clear. Possibly it refers to the concept of the Buddhist spiritual leader if not to the Buddha himself.

The inclusion of Mahāsena and Mahādeva indicates that the Vināyakas were associated not only with Buddhism but also with the non-Brahmanical Śiva and his entourage. Although Rudra is acknowledged as a deity in later Vedic religion, the Śiva of the non-Vedic tradition is associated with numerous other beings that are not mentioned in the Vedic texts. Some form of sectarian worship of Śiva appears to have been in existence from as early as the fourth century BC,[50] although at this stage, Śivaism, as a definite religious group with its own tenets and theology, had not come into being. The earliest Śaivas were the non-Vedic Pāśupatas and the deity they worshipped was probably closely associated with Yoga. The yogis and ascetics, like the Buddhists, did not differentiate between castes. *Śūdras* and outcastes could join their orders as readily as they could the Buddhist *saṃgha.* There were parallels between the *pramāthas* of Śiva and the army of the Buddhist *māras,* between the worship of the *liṅga* and that of the Buddhist votive *stūpa.*

If the *kuṣmāṇḍas,*Virūpākṣa and other *yakṣas* form part of the Buddhist mythology at an early stage, they were later associated with the Brahmanical Śiva as well. In the Purāṇas, Kuṣmāṇḍa becomes a *gaṇa* of Śiva, all *kuṣmāṇḍas* being represented by the one. Iconographically he is depicted as a stout, dwarf-like dancing figure[51] like the *kuṣmāṇḍas* of the *stūpa* at Sanchi. Virūpākṣa becomes an aspect of Śiva and is described as one of the Rudras.[52] Kubera is closely associated with Śiva and, with him, a host of other *yakṣas* and *rākṣasas,* including Śālakaṭaṇkaṭa, are also indirectly associated with him. The Puranic deity Gaṇapati-Vināyaka remains distinct from Kuṣmāṇḍa, Virūpākṣa, Śālakaṭankaṭa and others.

This brings us to the question as to why Śālakaṭaṇkaṭa, Kuṣmāṇḍarājaputra, Usmita and Devayajana were identified as Vināyakas by the authors of the *Mānava Gṛhya Sūtra.* If, in the Buddhist context, the term signified one without an equal in spiritual achievement, in the Brahmanical context it signified one without an equal in evil. Had the term originally had a negative connotation it is unlikely that it would have been used by the Buddhists to denote their saints. The term is used specifically by the *brāhmaṇa* authors of the *Mānava Gṛhya Sūtra* in a derogatory context to express their antagonism against rival religious sects, especially the Buddhists. Such antagonism between rival faiths is manifest in several texts and icons during the succeeding centuries. Some such examples, even if they belong to a later period, permit a clearer understanding of the phenomenon taking place in the creation of the Vināyakas.

The Purāṇas are sometimes explicit in their denunciation of rival sects. The *Brahmāṇḍa Purāṇa* states: 'Formerly, in the battle between the *devas* and the *asuras*, the *asuras* were defeated. They created the heretics like Vṛddhaśrāvakas, Nirgranthas (nude Jainas), Śākyas (Buddhists), Jivaskas and Kārpatas.'[53] Here the Buddhists and others are clearly equated with *asuras* and this idea appears to be inherent in the concept of Vināyakas in the earlier *Mānava Gṛhya Sūtra*. There is a constant lament in the Purāṇas for 'the danger and fear to people owing to wrong performance of sacrifices, neglect of (Vedic) studies ... misleading religious scriptures and faults in the performance of holy rites of *brāhmaṇas*'.[54] Regret is also expressed about the fact that 'people do not accept the authority of the *Smṛtis*'.[55]

A similar antagonistic attitude exists in certain Buddhist texts where Śiva, Viṣṇu, Brahmā and Indra are described as *duṣṭa-raudra-devatās* (mischievous, terrible deities) and designated as *catur-māras*, or 'the four evil ones'.[56] If the Buddha and his *lokapālas* are Vināyakas (demons) from the Brahmanical point of view, the four principal Brahmanical deities become *māras* from the Buddhist point of view. According to the *Bhaktiśataka* by Rāmacandra, 'Brahmā is overpowered by *avidyā*, Viṣṇu is embraced by great illusion by which it is difficult to discriminate, Saṅkara holds Pārvatī in his own person, owing to excessive attachment, but in this world the great *muṇi*, the Lord, is without *avidyā*, without illusion, and without attachment'.[57] There are several early medieval representations of Brahmanical deities being trampled under the feet of Buddhist Gods. The Buddhist remover of obstacles, Vighnāntaka, trampling upon the Brahmanical Gaṇapati is only one such example.[58] In another example the Buddhist goddess Mañjūśrī holds Gaṇapati prostrate under one foot.[59]

A further comparison with present day belief in spirits would not be out of place here. In the course of his research on traditional Indian methods of healing 'psychic distress', psychoanalyst, Sudhir Kakar, describes how many patients claimed to be possessed by a Muslim spirit. In his words, 'the Muslim seems to be the symbolic representation of the alien in the Hindu unconscious. Possession by a Muslim *bhūta* reflects the patients' desperate efforts to convince himself and others that his hungers for forbidden foods, tumultuous sexuality and uncontrollable rage belong to the Muslim destroyer of taboos and are farthest away from his 'good' Hindu self.'[60] Similarly, from the perspective of the Vedic priest, the Buddhists, Pāśupatas and others of the heterodox tradition all represented everything that was alien to him and they were collectively blamed for the ills in society.

The Vināyakas are, therefore, not original deities, but an epithet given to a concept: that of the *vighnakartas* (creators of obstacles). This concept had existed since the earliest times. The *vighnakartas* are personified in the *Mānava Gṛhya Sūtra* as the more important rival deities which existed in the region where this text was composed and which had been absorbed into the Buddhist fold. Each deity keeps his original name but they are collectively named after the greatest of rivals, the Buddhist spiritual guide if not the Buddha himself. The fact that a term associated with the highest of Buddhists is selected to nominate what are described as demonic beings by the author(s) of the *Mānava Gṛhya Sūtra*, is significant. Eventually, this term loses its negative connotation, not because the elephant-headed Gaṇapati evolves from a maleficient to a beneficient being, but because the term did not have a negative meaning in the first place, except in a limited number of Brahmanical texts.

The four personalities which the *Mānava Gṛhya Sūtra* names as the Vināyakas are probably meant to evoke the idea of the four directions. Brahmanism saw itself threatened from all sides by rival faiths. That is why every category of society—men, women, children, kings, students and others—is described by the *Mānava Gṛhya Sūtra* as being prone to Vināyaka possession which resulted in the worst conceivable tragedies and disasters. The concept of the four Vināyakas representing the four directions finds expression, several centuries later, at the pillar at Ghatiyala established by King Kakkuka of the Pratīhāra dynasty in *samvat* 919 (AD 861). This pillar is surmounted by four images of Gaṇapati facing the four quarters.[61]

The Vināyakas evolve into one being with four names in the *Yājñavalkya Smṛti* (second/third century AD). This Vināyaka is stated to have been created by Brahmā and Rudra for the purpose of creating obstacles.[62] Whereas in the *Mānava Gṛhya Sūtra* seven goddesses personifying Beauty, Prosperity and other such qualities are invoked after the worship of the Vināyakas and their demoniacal entourage,[63] in the *Yājñavalkya Smṛti* Ambikā alone is invoked. She is worshipped along with Vināyaka for granting the very qualities personified by the seven goddesses in the *Mānava Gṛhya Sūtra*. The worship of Ambikā is followed by that of the *grahas* and finally that of Āditya (Sun). The concluding line of the chapter states that he who applies *tilaka* to Swāmī (Kārttikeya) and Mahāgaṇapati obtains all success.[64]

Vināyaka was absorbed into the Brahmanical pantheon and his worship was associated with that of Ambikā, Śiva and Skanda. Mahāgaṇapati, no doubt, refers to Śiva in this context. Vināyaka acquires that title not before the end of the sixth or the seventh century AD. In the early centuries of the Christian era, the epithet remains an appellation for Śiva. The *Yājñavalkya Smṛti* is a text of the *Śukla Yajur Veda* and in the *Yajur Veda* the epithet Gaṇapati is applied to Rudra.[65] Most of the demoniacal beings that are worshipped along with the Vināyakas in the *Mānava Gṛhya Sūtra* are associated with Mahādeva. If these beings now no longer find mention, it is because they are all personified by Mahāgaṇapati (Śiva), even as all the mothers are personified by Ambikā and the four Vināyakas by the one Vināyaka. Mahāsena was already associated with Śiva in the *Mānava Gṛhya Sūtra* and had grown in importance since. He is, therefore, mentioned separately. It is unlikely that the worship of Vināyaka could include that of Ambikā, the *grahas*, Āditya and Skanda and ignore that of Śiva. Therefore, I consider that Mahāgaṇapati refers to Śiva. If, however, the term does signify Vināyaka, then this last line is a very late interpolation (post seventh century).

There is a Vināyaka Kalpa in the *Nārada Purāṇa*[66] which is similar to that of the *Yājñavalkya Smṛti*.[67] These sections of the *Yājñavalkya Smṛti* and the *Nārada Purāṇa* represent a second stage in the development of the personality of Vināyaka. He has become a well established concept. He is associated with Rudra, Ambikā, Skanda and the *grahas*. The association with the *grahas* comes about quite naturally because of the evils that he causes. Yet, being derivative of different local deities, there is no indication of his having any particular image. No physical description of him is given. The epithet Gaṇapati is not associated with him nor is there any indication of a link with the elephant.

Some of the references in the Purāṇas, to the many Vināyakas, probably belong to the earliest layers of these texts, perhaps between the third and fifth centuries of the Christian era. They are mentioned along with *bhūtarākṣasas, bhramarākṣasas, guhyakas, gandharvas, apsaras, siddhas, devas, dākinīs* and *kṣetrapālas* as forming the entourage of Śiva.[68] Elsewhere, there is reference to 'the cruel ones belonging to Skanda, Vināyaka, Pramatha and Guhyaka which are greatly inimical and terrible'.[69] Even the single Vināyaka in some Purāṇas appears as a minor and maleficient being and he does not seem to be associated with the elephant. It would be misleading to identify every reference to 'Vināyaka' in the Purāṇas with the elephant-headed deity. It is not obvious in all cases. In one version of Śiva's fight with Andhakāsura in the *Kūrma Purāṇa,* Andhaka is said to create thousands of *daityas* called Andhakas. Eight of these Andhakas are said to be prominent and they include Meghanāda and Vināyaka. Śiva cannot defeat Andhaka and finally seeks refuge in Viṣṇu. Finally, by the grace of Viṣṇu, Andhaka is defeated by Śiva, praises him and gains the chieftancy of the *gaṇas.* Meghanāda is the son of Rāvaṇa in the *Rāmāyaṇa* (therefore related to Śālakaṭaṇkaṭa). If Vināyaka is associated with him he is, quite evidently, equated with the *rākṣasas.* There is no indication of his being the son or a *gaṇa* of Śiva. Skanda is not mentioned along with him. At this stage the epithet 'Gaṇeśa' does not appear to be associated with Vināyaka.

GAṆAPATI/GAṆEŚVARA/GAṆEŚA

The term 'Gaṇapati' is used in early Vedic literature as an appellation for several deities. In the *Ṛg Veda* it is used for Bṛhaspati[70] as well as for Indra.[71] In the literature of the *Yajur Veda,*[72] however, it denotes Rudra. The epithet Gaṇapati has no negative connotation. The term '*gaṇa*' signifies a 'multitude' in the Vedic context. It also signifies the followers of a deity or cult associated with specific regions or categories of society. According to the *Milindapañha,* followers of different cults under the guidance of a spiritual head were referred to as *gaṇas.*[73] Evidently, there were numerous *gaṇas.* Some of the heads of the better known sects had a specific title. Makkhali Gośāla of the Ājīvikas is referred to as Gaṇanāyaka and Nigaṇṭha Nātaputta (Mahāvīra) of the Jainas, as Gaṇāchārya.[74] The *Lalitavistara* refers to the Gaṇapatis (in plural) along with a long list of deities which include Brahmā, Indra, Rudra, Viṣṇu, Devī, Kumāra, Mātṛ, Āditya, Vaiśravaṇa, the *nāgas, yakṣas, gandharvas, kumbhāṇḍas, piśācas,* etc.[75] Kṛṣṇa in the *Mahābhārata* is referred to as Suragaṇeśvara.[76] Similarly, Śiva is referred to as Gaṇādhīpa.[77] The terms Gaṇeśa, Gaṇeśvara, Gaṇādhīpa and Gaṇapati are synonymous since they all mean 'lord of the *gaṇa*'. In that respect, some of the four Vināyakas were also Gaṇeśas since they were deities of a category of people.

The epithet 'Gaṇeśa' is frequently used for the various *gaṇas* of Śiva who act as doorkeepers. Satī, on her way to Dakṣa's sacrifice, is accompanied by 'eight hundred groups of the thousand strong-armed Gaṇeśas equal in brilliance to Lord Śiva'.[78] The attendants at the portals of Śiva's abode are referred to as Gaṇeśas.[79] According to one Purāṇa, all those who eulogise and worship Mahādeva at Varanasi are forgiven all sins. They then become Gaṇeśvaras.[80] 'Gaṇeśvara' is also an epithet of Śiva[81] and so are 'Vighneśvara' (Lord of Obstacles)[82] and Vighnakāraka (Creator of obstacles).[83] In fact, Śiva is worshipped by many names which include those of his *gaṇas* - Nandin, Nandīśvara, Kumāra, Skanda and Gaṇeśvara. What is striking is that he is not referred to as Vināyaka.[84]

The first time that the Vināyakas are acknowledged as Gaṇeśvaras is in the *Mahābhārata,* where the Gaṇeśvara-Vināyakas are described as the Lords of all the worlds (*Īśvarāḥ sarva-lokānāṃ gaṇeśvaravināyakāḥ*).[85] Although it is not specifically stated that there are four Vināyakas, since the term is used in the plural, we can presume it does, indeed, imply four. They are mentioned along with several other deities including Nandīśvara, the Rudragaṇa, *bhūtagaṇa, yogagaṇa, nakṣatra,* the rivers, seas, Himālayas, Skanda and Ambikā. They are no longer demons, but one category of numerous deities that Bhīṣma advises Yudhiṣṭhira to worship. This worship ensures the destruction of all sins. These Gaṇeśvara-Vināyakas appear in the same role as the Buddhist *lokapālas,* the *diggajas* and the *dignāgas.* With the rise of Śiva and Viṣṇu several local cults, each represented by its Gaṇapati or Gaṇésvara, are recognized by the Brahmanical religion. As these numerous Gaṇésvaras find acceptance, so do the Vināyakas. The adding of the title Gaṇeśvaras (which has no negative connotation) to the epithet Vināyakas, confirms this acceptance.

Elsewhere in the *Mahābhārata* the Vināyakas, again in the

plural, are referred to as evil beings associated with *piśācas, bhūtas* and *rākṣasas*[86] all of whom are believed to be responsible for creating obstacles. This description belongs to the earliest portions of the *Mahābhārata,* and would be more or less contemporary with the chapter on Vināyakas in the *Mānava Gṛhya Sūtra,* or perhaps a little later but certainly before the Christian era. The Anuśāsana Parva is believed to contain some of the latest additions to the epic[87] and this would perhaps explain how the evil Vināyakas of the Śānti Parva become the Gaṇeśvara-Vināyakas worthy of worship in the Anuśāsana Parva. This portion of the *Mahābhārata* probably belongs to the second century AD, and is a little earlier than the section in the *Yājñavalkya Smṛti* where the four Vināyakas have merged into one.

If the Vināyakas are viewed as demons around the second century BC, by about the end of the second century AD they are identified with the Gaṇeśvaras and begin to find acceptance as deities in their own right. However, they continue to form part of the entourage of Śiva. By the end of the third century they have evolved into a single being who does not appear to have an iconographical form at this stage. How was he to be represented since he was a syncretism of several cults? Perhaps an iconographical form was not even necessary since he formed part of special domestic rites and did not require daily worship. Besides, did Jambha, Syena and so many other *gaṇas* have an iconographical form?

At this stage Vināyaka is still distinct from the elephant deity. There is no evidence that the early images of an elephant-headed figure are indeed those of the syncretic Vinayaka-Gaṇapati. Brahmanical literature, prior to the Christian era, makes no reference to such a deity and existing references are generally accepted as being later interpollations.[88] How and when does the merger between Gaṇapati-Vināyaka and the elephant deity take place?

VINĀYAKA-GAṆAPATI-ELEPHANT DEITY

The earliest references to an elephant deity in Brahmanical literature are in the *Mahābhārata.* In the Sabhā Parva, one of the personalities present in Kubera's abode is Danti. He is mentioned along with Saṅkukarṇa, Kutīmukha and Kāṣṭha who form part of

Śiva's retinue.[89] Skanda is not mentioned. When Skanda and Gaṇapati-Vināyaka become sons of Śiva and, therefore, brothers, they are usually mentioned together in descriptions of Śiva's entourage. In this case Danti is just one of Śiva's retinue. There is no indication of him being a son or a *gaṇa* of any particular importance. In addition, there is reference to a *yakṣa* by the name of Gajakarṇa (elephant ears) in the retinue of Kubera.[90] This would suggest that just as there were several *nāga* deities, similarly, there was more than one elephant deity. The *Mahābhārata*, elsewhere, has a long list of deities to be worshipped for the removal of sins. These include Śiva, Skanda, Ambikā, the Gaṇesvara-Vināyakas, various *gaṇas* and a deity called Mahākāya (one with a huge body).[91] Since Śiva is already mentioned, this is possibly a reference to the elephant deity. It is true that Mahākāya is an epithet of Śiva,[92] but it is essentially used for him in the *Śiva Sahasranāma* (thousand names of Śiva). The term is also an epithet for Gaṇapati[93] and one of the *śaktis* associated with him is referred to as Mahākāyā.[94] Among the most popular *ślokas* for Gaṇapati, is the one where he is invoked as:

> *Vakratuṇḍa Mahākāya sūrya koti sama prabha*
> *Nirvighnaṃ kurū me deva sarvakāryeṣu sarvadā.*
>
> O Lord with the twisted trunk, the huge body and
> the brilliance of a million suns,
> May you always rid me of all obstacles, in all I do.

In fact, many of the epithets of Śiva are those of minor deities associated with him and with each other. Nandīśvara is an epithet of Śiva but it is also the name of a *gaṇa*. Nandin is the name of Śiva's bull but also another name for the *gaṇa* Nandīśvara.[95] Similarly, Mahākāya does not appear to represent any particular aspect of Rudra-Śiva as depicted in Vedic, epic or early Puranic literature. There are Puranic myths about the giant *liṅga* of fire, but the term Mahākāya is descriptive of some being having an enormous body. It is possible that it refers to an elephant deity. The epithet 'Mahodara' (having a large stomach) is frequently associated with Gaṇapati especially in the Gāṇapatya *Purāṇas*. Yet the latter is obviously an allusion to his human form with pot-belly. Mahākāya is a more appropriate description for the earlier elephant form.

These references throw light on an important phase in the evolution of Gaṇapati. They point to the existence of an elephant deity along with the Gaṇeśvara-Vināyakas in Śiva's entourage. The elephant deity appears to have been accepted into the Brahmanical Śiva's pantheon, as a minor deity, at a relatively early date. In this new situation, neither Danti nor the Gaṇeśvara-Vināyakas seem to have any negative connotation.

Danti is mentioned in two other texts of the *Kṛṣṇa Yajur Veda*, the *Maitrāyaṇī Saṃhitā* and the *Taittirīya Āranyaka*. Both texts contain a *gāyatrī* to an elephant-god where he is invoked as Vakratuṇḍa, Danti and Hastimukha. None of these *gāyatrīs* mentions Vināyaka or Gaṇeśvara. Danti remains an epithet rarely used for Gaṇapati-Vināyaka. The epithet Hastimukha (elephant face) suggests that the deity has a human body but the face of an elephant. These *gāyātris* are generally considered to have been interpolated at a period when Gaṇapati had become an important god. However, since the form of the elephant-headed *yakṣa* exists from about the second century of the Christian era and since, as I have already discussed, this form is not the syncretic deity Gaṇapati-Vināyaka but simply the elephant deity, it is possible that this interpolation was made as early as the second or third centuries AD.

In the first two or three centuries of the Christian era, the Vināyakas are mentioned only in the *Mahābhārata* and in the literature of the *Kṛṣṇa Yajur Veda*. Similarly, Danti also finds mention both in the *Mahābhārata* and in the texts of the *Kṛṣṇa Yajur Veda*. The region associated with the *Kṛṣṇa Yajur Veda* texts included what had been the stronghold of Buddhism since the time of the Buddha himself. The cult of the elephant was also associated with this area. This was precisely the region where the threat to the Brahmanical religion from rival cults was the strongest, thereby giving rise to the concept of Vināyakas. Even references to the Vināyakas and Danti in the *Mahābhārata* are limited to certain editions which shows that the tradition was restricted to specific regions and was only reflected in texts associated with those regions. Like the Vināyakas, the elephant deity was not widely acknowledged or accepted by Brahmanism at this stage. It was restricted to a particular area and to a certain category of *brāhmaṇas*.

At a first stage, the propitiation of the Vināyakas became an established practice. At a second stage, they evolved into a single being. Finally, they came to require an iconographical form in a milieu where iconography was developing and where rituals of worship necessitated the use of images. No form existed since the Vināyakas were derivative deities. Yet, two of the Vināyakas had a link with the elephant. Virūpākṣa, one of the deities who forms part of the entourage of the four Vināyakas, is described as the Lord of *nāgas* but depicted as an elephant when, along with Airāvata, he stands as one of the eight *diggajas*.[96] Kuṣmāṇḍa-rājaputra, one of the four Vināyakas, as described earlier, is also associated with the elephant. The Gaṇeśvara-Vināyakas in the *Mahābhārata* play the same role as the *diggajas* and *dignāgas*. They are, therefore, equated with the elephants and serpents of the quarters. The *nāgas*, *kuṣmāṇḍas*, *piśācas* and *yakṣas* were all closely related and form part of the antecedents of the Vināyakas. Some of them are also associated with the elephant. Since the elephant was the deity of a particular group of people, he must have had his own *gaṇa*. He was, therefore, a Gaṇeśa or Gaṇapati in his own right. The rituals for the four deities, collectively referred to as the Vināyakas, and for Danti must have been similar, outside the Brahmanical fold.

Worship of some of the more famous *nāgas* was gradually adopted into the Brahmanical tradition. In the early centuries of the Christian era, the *brāhmaṇa* priests of the Maitrāyaṇīya school were especially associated with the worship of Maṇibhadra or Maṇināga.[97] Maṇibhadra is both a *yakṣa* and a *nāga* and was famous in the region of Rājagṛha. Two of the demonic beings that are to be placated along with the Vināyakas, Baka and Yakṣa, were associated with Maṇibhadra. It was within this same school of the Maitrāyaṇīyas that the concept of Vināyakas had emerged and it is within a text of this school, the *Maitrāyaṇī Saṃhitā*, that Danti finds early mention. The rituals for Vināyaka propitiation, borrowed from outside the Brahmanical tradition, must have been similar to the rituals associated with the *nāga* deities, including those of the elephant deity. Vināyaka had become one deity by the time of the *Yājñavalkya Smṛti*. He had lost his evil connotation. Since both the Vināyakas and Danti find mention essentially in the works of the Maitrāyaṇīya School in a particular region, and since there are parallels between them, it is likely that the two are gradually identified with each other by the Maitrāyaṇīya *brāhmaṇas* in the region of the middle Ganga basin around the fourth century AD or so. However, it is only in the Śaiva *Purāṇas* that Gaṇapati-

Vināyaka acquires the myths and personality that we know today. Probably, the manufacture and worship of Gaṇapati icons was also popularised by the Śaivas.

The iconographical form of the elephant-headed *yakṣa* already existed (Amarāvatī, second century AD).[98] It was distinct to the form of Airāvata (elephant figure with four tusks) and the symbol of the Buddha's conception (an elephant with six tusks) and was accepted as the form for the syncretistic deity Gaṇapati-Vināyaka-sacred elephant. Some Śaiva myths attempt to explain why the elephant-headed figure has the name Vināyaka. After all, there are numerous heads of *gaṇas* so why is only one referred to as Vināyaka. In the *Skanda Purāṇa,* Śiva tells Pārvatī that the head is normally considered to be the leader (*nāyaka*) of the body. Since Gaṇapati's head is so large, it represents a greater leader than the normal head. Therefore, he is named Mahāvināyaka.[99]

The elephant-headed *yakṣa* from Amarāvatī and the one from Mihintale in Sri Lanka have often been quoted in discussions relating to Gaṇapati's origins. Distinction, however, must be made between Gaṇapati and the elephant headed *yakṣa.* The latter represents only one aspect of Gaṇapati's origin whereas Gaṇapati represents the syncretistic deity Vināyaka-Gaṇapati-elephant. Therefore, I prefer to refer to these representations as those of the elephant-headed *yakṣa* or as incipient Gaṇapatis. Five elephant-headed figures also appear on the lowest band of a fragmentary relief of the Kuṣāṇa period found at Mathura.[100] These are also considered by some scholars to represent the five Vināyakas. However, the bas-relief is badly damaged making it difficult to determine whether the elephant figures are similar to the elephant-headed *yakṣa* of the Amarāvatī sculpture. In the case of the figure in the centre, the proboscis is turned to the proper left, a common feature of the Gaṇapati statues of the Gupta period from Mathura and elsewhere.[101] Yet, the band of the frieze on which these images are sculpted is only partly preserved. There is no knowing if it was not a motif which covered an extended portion of the frieze. Secondly, even if the number is actually five, it does not necessarily associate this image with the concept of four or five Vināyakas. Five is an important number in both Mahāyāna Buddhism as also in Śivaism and was probably used for a variety of representations since it was considered auspicious. In fact, on the second band, just above the five elephant figures, are sculpted the busts of five worshippers while the top-most band has the design of a railing. The relief dates to around the same time as the Amarāvatī elephant-headed *yakṣa*. It may well have been a purely decorative motif, forming part of a Buddhist or Jaina *stūpa* since most of the products of the Mathura School of Art under the Kuṣāṇas were Buddhist or Jaina images. One of the common themes in the decoration on the railings of Buddhist and Jaina *stūpas* is that of worshipping figures paying homage to the *stūpa* representing either the Buddha or the Jina. Therefore, it is very likely that these five elephant *yakṣas* are not Gaṇapati-Vināyaka even though the theme of five elephants in a group gave rise to similar sculptures associated with Gaṇapati in a later period.[102]

According to Coomaraswamy, the full-fledged image of Gaṇapati, and which I take to be that of Gaṇapati-Vināyaka-elephant deity, begins to occur quite commonly in Gupta art, from about AD 400.[103] Some of the earliest statues of Gaṇapati have been found in and around the region of *madhyadeśa*: at Sankisa mound[104] and the Mathura region[105] (Uttar Pradesh), Bhūmāra[106] and the Udayagiri caves[107] (Madhya Pradesh) and Rājgir (Bihar).[108] All are dated to approximately between the end of the fourth and sixth centuries of the Christian era and this would correspond to the period when Gaṇapati begins to find mention in the *Purāṇas*. Some scholars, on the basis of reference to Gaṇeśa's trunk in the Gāthāsaptaśatī,[109] consider that this deity, in its present form, was already in existence around the first century AD. However, this work, traditionally attributed to Hāla Sātavāhana, is believed to have been regularly added to almost up to the eighth century.[110] Hence, I do not consider this reference to be suggestive of such an early date for Gaṇapati.

Dhavalikar argues against the generally accepted theory that Gaṇapati images appear only from about the fourth/fifth centuries AD.[111] He refers to three images, presently in the Mathura museum, all carved in the round and similar to each other and which he ascribes to the Kuṣāṇa period. They depict the deity with two hands. The left holds a bowl of sweets into which the trunk dips. Dhavalikar considers that, since carving figures in the round was the speciality of the Kuṣāṇa artists of Mathura, these statues have to be assigned to *c.* first to third century AD. Similarly, the image from Sankisa mound which Getty dates not before the fifth century is assigned by Dhavalikar to the late second or early third century AD. Literary evidence at the close of the first millenium BC points to the existence of the cult of the elephant but there is no evidence to show that the animal was worshipped in an therianthropic form. This elephant-headed *yakṣa* gradually became popular through Buddhism and was accepted as the basis for the iconography of the syncretistic Brahmanical deity Gaṇapati. Therefore, I prefer to consider the Kuṣāṇa images as incipient Gaṇapatis which represent the elephant deity who, because of the influence of Buddhist iconography, had acquired a newer form but whose worship was old. What appears quite clear is that the few early images of the elephant-headed figure attributed to the third century or so were not common. After *c.* 400 AD, the number of images increases greatly and this corresponds to the period when Gaṇapati begins to be mentioned in Puranic literature.

Finally, all the three distinct strands in Gaṇapati's personality are apparent in later literature—*Purāṇas, Tantras* and *Āgamas*—on which the present-day Gaṇapati worship is based. As a relic of his elephant past, he is invoked in special *homas* for calming elephants and for granting them *śānti* and prosperity.[112] He himself is to be meditated upon as an elephant.[113] His *nāga* past is reflected in the special rites performed in his honour for the purpose of driving away both serpents and elephants.[114] The various myths in the Purāṇas about his head associate him with some older and important elephant. In some cases it is the head of Airāvata that is transferred on to the trunk of Gaṇapati.[115] At other times it is the king of elephants[116] or an ordinary elephant that lends its head to him. As a remnant of his evil side deriving from the Vināyaka tradition, there are *homas* in his honour prescribed to rectify *graha doṣa* (evil effects of graspers) and diseases. Like the Vināyakas he is associated with the *piśācas.* He is sometimes referred to as Hastipiśācīśa[117] and his consort as Hastipiśācī.[118] At other times, he is referred to as the god of *kuṣmāṇḍas.*[119] He has special propitiation rites which require the offering of *bali* at the crossroads.[120] It is also the Vināyaka strand which is responsible for making Gaṇapati the creator and remover of obstacles. Originally, that was the role of the *vighnakartas* personified as the Vināyakas by the Maitrāiyaṇīya *brāhmaṇas.* The theme of four Vināyakas is echoed in the four headed form of the deity.[121] As Gaṇapati, he remains the head of a *gaṇa* and has numerous Vināyakas as his followers.[122] These three distinct strands are responsible for his numerous powers and attributes and are responsible for raising him, eventually, to the status of a major god. They are equally responsible for the many dichotomies that exist in his character.

NOTES

1. The first scholar to suggest these strands in the personality of Gaṇapati is V. Ramasubramaniam in his article 'The Gaṇapati-Vināyaka-Gajānana Worship: Analysis of an Integrated Cult', in *Bulletin of the Institute of Traditional Cultures*, Madras, 1971, pp. 110-46. A.K. Narain also bases his analysis of Gaṇapati on these three different aspects in his article 'Gaṇeśa: A Protohistory of the Idea and the Icon' in Robert L. Brown, ed., *Ganesha: Studies of an Asian God,* pp. 19-48. However, the analysis and conclusions of these scholars are quite distinct to those put forward by me.
2. For discussion on the various possible meanings of the term 'Vināyaka' see A.K. Narain, op. cit.
3. J. Marshall and A. Foucher, *Monuments of Sanchi,* p. 289.
4. Ibid., p. 294.
5. A.A. Ramanathan, *Amarakośa: With Unpublished South Indian Commentaries,* p. 302.
6. *Mānava Gṛhya Sūtra,* II.14.
7. Trans. from R.C. Hazra, 'Gaṇapati-worship and the Upapurāṇas dealing with it', *JGJhRI,* Vol. 5, Pt. 4, 1948, pp. 263-76.
8. *Mānava Gṛhya Sūtra,* II.14.28.
9. *Rāmāyaṇa,* 8.23.
10. P.K. Agrawala, *Ancient Indian Folk Cults,* p. 69.
11. *Vāyu Purāṇa,* I.30.203.
12. *Mahābhārata,* cri. edn., Anuśāsana Parva, 17.56.
13. Umakant P. Shah, *Jaina Rūpa Maṇḍana (Jaina Iconography)*, p. 132.
14. A. Foucher, *Etudes Sur l'Art Boudhique de l'Inde,* p. 9.
15. Cited by H. Luders, ed., *Bharhut Inscriptions,* in *CII,* Vol. II, Pt. II, p. 76.
16. Ibid., pp. 73 and 76.
17. P.K. Agrawala, 'The Kumbhāṇḍa Figures in Sanchi Sculpture', *EW,* Vol. 37, 1987, pp. 179-89. See in particular, p. 184.
18. P.K. Agrawala, 'The Kumbhāṇḍa Overlord Virūḍhaka', in Devendra Handa and Ashvini Agrawal, eds., *Ratna-Chandrika: Panorama of Oriental Studies* (Shri R. C. Agrawala Festschrift), pp. 67-74.
19. Ibid.
20. *Vāyu Purāṇa,* II.8.198-9 and II.8.251-2.

21. Romila Thapar, 'Origin Myths and Historical Tradition', *Ancient Indian Social History*, pp. 294 -325. See in particular, pp. 311-12.
22. J. Ph. Vogel, *Indian Serpent Lore*, p. 191.
23. Ibid. See also, P.K. Agrawala, 'The Kumbhāṇḍa Overlord Virūḍhaka', in Devendra Handa and Ashwini Agrawal, eds. op. cit., p. 68.
24. J. Gonda, *Viṣṇuism and Śivaism*, p. 36.
25. J.L. Shastri, ed., *Manusmṛti with the Sanskrit Commentary Manvarthamuktāvali of Kulluka Bhaṭṭa*, V.93.
26. *Padma Purāṇa*, II.1.41.17b-18a; *Varāha Purāṇa*, II.158.18-19.
27. P.K. Agrawala, 'The Kumbhāṇḍa Figures in Sanchi Sculpture', *EW*, op. cit., p. 180. See also J.Ph. Vogel, op. cit., p. 213.
28. Thomas Watters, *On Yuan Chwang's Travels in India*, p. 35.
29. *Vāyu Purāṇa*, II.8.198-9 and 210.
30. *Taittirīya Āraṇyaka (With Commentary of Sāyaṇa)*, II.7-8.
31. *Vāyu Purāṇa*, II.8.262.
32. *Nārada Purāṇa*, V.71.24.
33. *Padma Purāṇa*, I.27.32b-35a.
34. Sudhir Kakar, *Shamans, Mystics and Doctors*, p. 56.
35. Ibid., p. 110.
36. Ibid., p. 99.
37. V.V. Mirashi, ed., *CII*, Vol. V, No.3, p. 10.
38. F. Max Muller, ed., *Manu Smṛti (The Laws of Manu)*, III.164.
39. J. Gonda, *The Ritual Sūtras*, p. 600.
40. Ibid.
41. Ibid., p. 598.
42. *Mānava Gṛhya Sūtra*, II.14.30.
43. The Piśācas are believed to have been a tribe of people who originated in the north-west, in the region of Kafiristan. They gradually spread southwards and eastwards to the Ganga basin and the region near the Vindhyas. (See A.N. Upadhye, 'Paiśāci Language and Literature', *ABORI*, Vol. 21, 1940, pp. 1-37). The *Bṛhatkathā* of Guṇādhya is believed to have been written in the Paiśāci language around the third century AD in the region of Ujjain or Kausambi (see Maurice Winternitz, *History of Indian Literature*, Vol. III, p. 346).
44. *Brahmāṇḍa Purāṇa*, II.3.7.390 and II.3.7.394.
45. *Mahābhārata*, cri. edn., Ādi Parva, 151.26-7.
46. *Vāyu Purāṇa*, II.8.153-7.
47. *Sāmavidhāna Brāhmaṇa (with Vedarthaprakāśa of Sāyaṇa and Padarthamātṛvivṛti of Bharatsvāmin)*, III.7.10.
48. J.A.B. Van Buitenen, Trans., *The Mahābhārata*, Vol. I, p. 149.
49. *Vāyu Purāṇa*, II.8.168.

50. Sudhakar Chattopadhyaya, *Evolution of Hindu Sects,* p. 110.
51. *Agni Purāṇa,* I.50.40.
52. T.A. Gopinatha Rao, *Elements of Hindu Iconography,* Vol. II, Pt. II, p. 387.
53. *Brahmāṇḍa Purāṇa,* II.3.14.38b-42.
54. *Vāyu Purāṇa,* I.58.36.
55. Ibid., I.58.34.
56. H. Mitra, *Gaṇapati,* p. 43.
57. Cited by S. Radhakrishnan in *Indian Philosophy,* Vol. I, p. 462.
58. Pratapaditya Pal, *Bronzes of Kashmir,* pp. 166-7.
59. Alice Getty, *Gaṇeśa,* pp. 44-5.
60. Sudhir Kakar, op. cit., p. 87.
61. *EI,* Vol. IX, No. 38, p. 279.
62. *Yājñavalkya Smṛti (With the Commentary of Vijñāneśvara called the Mitaksara),* Vol. I, pp. 174-5.
63. *Mānava Gṛhya Sūtra,* II.14.30.
64. *Yājñavalkya Smṛti,* p. 178.
65. Cited by R.C. Hazra, op. cit., p. 268.
66. *Nārada Purāṇa,* II.51.58-79.
67. There is a chapter in the *Garuḍa Purāṇa* entitled 'Teachings of Yājñavalkya' which also describes the symptoms of Vināyaka possession and treatment. It is an abbreviated and somewhat modified version of that described in the *Yājñavalkya Smṛti.*
68. *Nārada Purāṇa,* III.77.64-77.
69. Ibid.
70. *Ṛg Veda,* II.23.1.
71. Ibid., X.112.9.
72. *Taittirīya Saṃhitā,* IV.1.2.2 and *Vajasaneyi Saṃhitā,* II.15 and 22.30. Quoted by R.C. Hazra, op. cit., p. 268.
73. *Milindapañhapali,* I.1.5 (p. 3 for original text and p. 6 for Hindi translation).
74. Ibid.
75. Gwendolyn Bays, Trans., *The Lalitavistara-Sūtra,* Vol. II, p. 381.
76. *Mahābhārata,* cri. edn., Droṇaparva, 124.9.
77. Ibid., Anuśāsana Parva, 17.116.
78. *Śiva Purāṇa,* Vāyavīyasaṃhitā I, IV.18.33-4.
79. Ibid., IV.27.2.
80. *Kūrma Purāṇa,* I.31.53b-56a.
81. *Liṅga Purāṇa,* II.98.40.
82. Ibid., I.1.2-4.
83. Ibid., II.98.712.
84. Ibid., II.98.40, 477, 618, 804 and 805. For a current version of the *Śiva Sahasranāmastotram and Nāmāvalī* see the publication by the Central Chinmaya Mission Trust, Bombay.

85. *Mahābhārata*, cri. edn., Appendix 18.54. In Geeta Press edn., Anuśāsana Parva, 150.25-8.
86. Ibid., In Geeta Press edn., Śānti Parva, 284.197.
87. Suvira Jaiswal, *The Origin and Development of Vaiṣṇavism*, p. 13.
88. R.C. Hazra, in his article 'Gaṇapati Worship and the Upapurāṇas Dealing with It', discusses the reference to a deity called Hastimukha along with Vināyaka, Vighna, Lambodara and others in the *Baudhāyana Gṛhyaśeṣasūtra and the Baudhāyana Dharmasūtra.* He considers this portion of these works as being of doubtful authenticity. Since there is no evidence of the syncretistic deity Gaṇapati-Vināyaka with the elephant head before the Christian era, these portions were evidently interpolated much later. It is worth pointing out, however, that both these texts also belong to the Kṛṣṇa *Yajur Veda.*
89. *Mahābhārata*, Geeta Press edn., Sabhā Parva, X.35.
90. Ibid., Sabhā Parva, 10.16.
91. *Mahābhārata*, cri. edn. Appendix 18.53 and 54. In Geeta Press edn., Anuśāsana Parva, 150.25-8.
92. *Liṅga Purāṇa*, II.98.527.
93. *Agni Purāṇa*, IV.312.16-22.
94. *Liṅga Purāṇa*, II.27.142-7.
95. Ibid., II. 9. 4-10a.
96. *Agni Purāṇa*, III. 291.2-5a.
97. D.N. Das, 'Serpent Worship in Ancient Kalinga', *PIHC*, 1965, pp. 43-4.
98. Ananda K. Coomaraswamy, *Yakṣas*, Pt. I, plate 23. A similar elephant-headed *yakṣa* belonging to the same period is also present on a frieze from a *stūpa* near Mihintale, Sri Lanka. See Alice Getty, op. cit., p. 25.
99. *Skanda Purāṇa*, Venkateshwar Steam Press edn., Śrī Prabhāsa Khaṇḍa, 3.32.15-17.
100. P.K. Agrawala, *Goddess Vināyakī*, p. 4.
101. Ibid.
102. See P.K. Agrawala, 'A Pañca-Gaṇeśa Panel from Varanasi', *JOIB*, Vol. 25, pp. 71-3. The article describes three sculpted panels of Gaṇeśas dating to between AD 800 and 1200 found in Rajasthan and Varanasi. Two of these panels depict four elephant headed figures in a row with the fifth figure being that of an elephant. The third shows five elephant headed figures in a row. These are obviously Gaṇapati because in two of the three cases the rat is also depicted. These examples show how older iconographical forms influence the art of the succeeding centuries. However, this does not justify the consideration of the five Kuṣāṇa *gajānana yakṣas* as Gaṇapati-Vināyaka.

103. Ananda Coomaraswamy, op. cit., Pt. I, p. 7.
104. D.C. Sircar, *Studies in the Religious Life of Ancient and Medieval India,* p. 114.
105. V.S. Agrawala, 'Miscellaneous Architectural Sculptures: Buddhist', *Journal of the Uttar Pradesh Historical Society*, Vol. XXIV-XXV, 1951-52, pp. 77-118. See in particular, p. 96.
106. D. C. Sircar, op. cit., p. 114.
107. R.C. Agrawala, 'Ūrdhavaretas Gaṇeśa from Afghanistan', *EW,* Vol. 18 (NS), 1968, pp. 166-8.
108. Shiela L. Weiner, *From Gupta to Pāla Sculpture,* p. 173.
109. *Gāthāsaptaśatī,* IV.72 and V.3.
110. V.V. Mirashi, ed., *CII,* Vol. V, see 'Introduction', pp. lvi-lix and pp. 76-9.
111. M.K. Dhavalikar, 'Gaṇeśa: Myth and Reality' in Robert L. Brown, ed., *Ganesh: Studies of an Asian God,* pp. 49-68.
112. *Īśānaśivagurudevapadhhati,* II.16.121.
113. Ibid., II.16.21.
114. Ibid., II.15.118.
115. *Bṛhaddharma Purāṇa,* 2.60.50-2; *Mudgala Purāṇa,* IV.47.47.
116. *Brahmavaivarta Purāṇa,* 3.12.9-22.
117. *Gaṇeśa Purāṇa,* I.46.4.
118. T.S. Sundaresa Sharma, *Śrī Ucchiṣṭa Gaṇapati Stotra Satanāmāvalī,* p. 58.
119. *Kūrma Purāṇa,* I.22.47.
120. *Svayambhuvāgama,* 58.52.
121. *Ajitāgama,* Vol. III, 55.7.
122. *Varāha Purāṇa,* I.23.20-5.

CHAPTER 4

A Brahmanical Deity

In the early centuries of the Christian era, as Śiva and Viṣṇu grow in importance, a new body of literature known as the *Purāṇas* comes into being. These texts reflect a changing material and social milieu. As Brahmanical culture spreads from the *madhyadeśa* region into the peripheral areas and tries to cope with the challenge of Buddhism and Jainism, it comes in contact with a variety of new ethnic groups and undergoes a process of syncretism. As a result, newer gods take precedence over the Vedic divinities. A variety of new myths or new versions of old myths are created with the purpose of glorifying Śiva and Viṣṇu and, later, the Goddess. The rise in stature of these new gods results in the inclusion of several non-Vedic deities as part of their expanding pantheons. The temple is closely associated with the worship of these sectarian gods. Consequently, new beliefs and rituals are incorporated into the Purāṇas, festivals develop and holy sites are associated with each deity. The practice of making pilgrimages becomes popular. Several religious traditions such as the Vedic, Tantric, Pāśupata and Pañcarātra are reflected in the Purāṇas. It is within this context, between approximately AD 400 and AD 1400, that Gaṇapati gradually acquires the personality and role that we associate him with today. From a simple *gaṇa* of Śiva, he rises to become the principal *gaṇa* and the son of Śiva and Pārvatī. Initially, the younger brother of Skanda-Kārttikeya, he is eventually considered the elder. He is associated with other Brahmanical deities besides Śiva and develops a cult of his own.

GAṆAPATI AND THE ŚAIVA PANTHEON

The first definite reference to an elephant-headed deity exists in the context of Śivaism as it is described in the Purāṇas. References in the *Mahābhārata* are limited to the Gaṇeśvara-Vināyakas or to

Danti. Whereas the Vināyakas are not described as having any form, Danti clearly designates an elephant. The two do not appear to be synonymous. The elephant-headed human deity is described only in the Purāṇas. It is essential, therefore, to understand the nature of Śivaism in the early centuries of the Christian era because it influences, to a large extent, the character and role of Gaṇapati.

Pāśupata Śivaism appears to be the oldest form of Śivaism. In its earliest stages it prevailed in north-western and western India in the two or three centuries before the Christian era. The early Pāśupatas were looked down upon by the followers of the Brahmanical tradition because they did not accept the authority of the Vedas and because they did not follow the *dharma* of the *varṇa* (caste) and *āśrama* (four stages of life).

In the early centuries of the Christian era, the Lakulīśa sub-sect of the Śaivas emerged. This form of Śivaism is described in the *Pāśupata Sūtra* (*c.* AD 100-200) which is supposed to have been taught by Lakuli to his pupil Kuśika.[1] Lakuli is believed to have lived in the country of Lāṭa in the Kathiawad region which lies in modern Gujarat.[2] This sub-sect represented a limited rapprochement with the Brahmanical tradition. However, like the heterodox Pāśupatas, Lakulīśa-Pāśupatism emphasised *yoga* (meditation) and *bhakti* (devotion).[3] Lakulīśa had four disciples who, in their turn, became the chiefs of four distinct lines of teachers concerned with the propagation of the Pāśupata religion.[4] In early medieval times, Lakulīśa was deified and subsequently worshipped as a cult-person. He came to be looked upon as the twenty-eighth incarnation of Śiva. His icons have been found dating from the sixth century in Karnataka and in temples of the Cālukyas of Bādāmi dating to the seventh-eighth centuries.[5] He also appears at the Kailāśa temple at Ellora. Temples to Lakulīśa have also been found in Gujarat and Rajasthan.

Pāśupata Śivaism in the earlier portions of the Purāṇas is, in fact, a mixture of Vedic, Sāṃkhya and Yoga practices. In the *Vāyu Purāṇa*, Śiva states:

> Having established the *Vedas* with their six ancillaries together with the Sāṃkhya and Yoga and performing penances inaccessible to *devas* (gods) and *dānavas* (demons), the Pāśupata rite has been evolved by me. This rite is accompanied by objects of worship. It is evolved in secret and is unintelligible to the unintelligent. In some respects it agrees with the functions of different castes and stages of life. In some respects it is

contrary to them. It is determined by the meanings of the Vedic passages ... it can be followed by a person in any stage of life.[6]

These three different streams of thought and practice—Sāṃkhya, Yoga and Veda—are largely responsible for the many dichotomies in the character of Śiva and, by extension, in the character of his *gaṇas* (a group of demi-gods considered as Śiva's attendants).

The school of Yoga with its strict physical and mental discipline is responsible for the ascetic aspect of Śiva. With Sāṃkhya comes the importance of the *śakti*, since according to Sāṃkhya philosophy, *puruṣa* (the soul—conceived as the male principle) alone is inactive and inert without *prakṛti* (primeval matter—conceived as the female principle). This idea is best represented in the *ardhnārīśvara* aspect of Śiva where the latter combines in himself both the male and female principles. The left side is feminine and the right, masculine. The earliest such statues date to the Kuṣāṇa period. The role of *śakti* was later reinforced with the influence of Tantrism. From the Vedic tradition and, more specifically, from the character of Indra, Śiva acquires the aspect of the demon-killer and destroyer of the cities of his enemies aided by a host of *gaṇas*.

Conflict with and destruction of *asuras* (demons)is an intrinsic aspect of Śaiva mythology in the Purāṇas. These *asuras* are overcome by Śiva's numerous *gaṇas*. Their battles represent, among other things, a reflection of the conflict with other developing religious sects, local cults and also with the Vedic tradition. Perhaps some of these myths are also part of the oral traditions of war-like tribes and other ethnic groups that were associated in one way or another with Brahmanical society and culture.

Śiva has two aspects to his character, one the *śiva* (calm and pleasing) and the other *ghora* or terrible. Each of these aspects is said to be manifold.[7] These various aspects are often manifested in his *gaṇas* who are essentially of two types. They are either repositories of profound spiritual knowledge or they are fierce demonic creatures that inspire terror. To the first category belong Nandin, Nandīśvara and Upamanyu. Nandin is the name of Śiva's bull who is always positioned outside the sanctum sanctorum of Śiva's shrine or temple. It is also the name of a *gaṇa* described as an incarnation of Śiva, born to the *brāhmaṇa* Śilāda, as a boon for his unswerving devotion to Śiva.[8] This second Nandin is also known as Nandīśvara.[9] There is, however, another Nandīśvara who is described as a sage who performed severe penance in order to propitiate Śiva. In return he was granted a form and splendour like that of Śiva himself and the lordship of the *gaṇas*. Śiva tells him 'O *brāhmaṇa*, you will be the foremost among my attendants and will be known as Nandīśvara'.[10] Similarly, Upamanyu is also a *brāhmaṇa*. As a young boy he invoked Śiva when, due to poverty, he could not get milk to drink. As a reward for his severe penance, Śiva told him: 'You have been adopted as my son now.... Immortality is bestowed upon you. So also the perpetual chieftaincy of the *gaṇas*'.[11]

There is a second category of *gaṇas*, those created specifically as fierce beings for the purpose of destroying Śiva's foes or the foes of his devotees. To this category belong Caṇḍa or Vīrabhadra. The latter is created, according to one version, from the mouth of Rudra and is described as being 'a goblin that resembled the fury of fire', with a thousand heads, a thousand feet and eyes. Vīrabhadra's appearance inspires fear and awe. Like most demonic forms he has 'curved fangs'[12] and is said to be 'the terrible form' of Śiva.[13] It is Vīrabhadra who assumes the form of the Śarabha incarnation of Śiva (Śarabha is a mythological creature that is half animal and half bird, with eight legs and stronger than a lion) to kill Narasiṃha, the half-man half-lion incarnation of Viṣṇu.[14] Likewise, it is he who destroys the sacrifice of Dakṣa.[15]

What is common to both categories of *gaṇas* is that they are created by Śiva alone. None are connected with the Goddess except for the fact that when Śiva makes some of his *gaṇas* his sons, Ūmā/Pārvatī accepts them as her sons as well. In the myths associated with the birth or exploits of these different *gaṇas*, Skanda and Gaṇapati are not mentioned. Nandin, the bull, appears to be the earliest associate of the Puranic Śiva.

The various deities that were gradually associated with the Puranic Śiva are described as his *gaṇa*. In this way the elephant deity also becomes a *gaṇa* of Śiva. However, there appear to be two aspects to the evolution of the elephant deity in the Puranic pantheon. On the one hand, as some myths suggest, Śiva was already associated with the elephant outside the Puranic framework in the early centuries of the Christian era and these myths seek to justify this association. On the other hand, there is the creation of an elephant-headed human figure who becomes a *gaṇa* of the Puranic Śiva and is, subsequently, elevated to the position of son of Śiva and Pārvatī. The first aspect is suggested by the myth of Gajāsura (elephant demon). Gajāsura is described as the lord of *dānavas*. As a result of a penance performed by meditating on Brahmā he acquired the boon of being invincible to humans, gods, the guardians of the worlds and others. The *asura* then conquered all the quarters, the three worlds, the gods, demons and human beings. Finally, when he reached Kāśī, the abode of Śiva, he was defeated by the latter. As his body was pierced by Śiva's trident he begged for a boon: that his hide would be worn by Śiva. The latter accepted and, moreover, declared that on his death, the *asura's* body would become the *liṅga* known as *Kṛttivāseśvara* (he who is clad in hide).[16] In another version of this myth Śiva appears out of a *liṅga* and kills the demon with his trident[17] and then wears his hide.

Earlier literature refers to Śiva clothed in animal skin[18] or in dripping animal hide but does not specify whether it is the hide of an elephant.[19] In the Purāṇas, he is specifically associated with the elephant hide. Not only does he wear the hide but, according to one myth, he also creates a *liṅga* from the body of Gajāsura which becomes one of the more famous *Śivaliṅgas* in Kāśī. By these actions the elephant becomes a part of Śiva in Kāśī. The significance of the myth of Gajāsura is better understood when compared to that of Mahiṣāsura (buffalo-demon). The latter is slain by Durgā. Yet he is different to other *asuras* in that he is a devotee of Śiva and a leader of his *gaṇas*.[20] As a result of a curse of sages whom he had insulted, he had been transformed into a buffalo. When the goddess beheads him, not knowing that he is a devotee of Śiva, a *liṅga* emerges from within his head and it is then worshipped by the goddess.[21] Hence both Mahiṣāsura and Gajāsura are associated with the *liṅga*. In one case the *liṅga* is a part of the *asura's* body and, in the second case, the *asura's* body is converted into a *liṅga*. This makes these two *asuras* distinct from others slain by Śiva or the goddess.

In one version of the Puranic myth of Mahiṣa, the latter asks the goddess to marry him. [22] In fact, there are folk traditions where Mahiṣāsura is looked upon as Śiva himself. He is worshipped as an *avatāra* (incarnation) of Śiva in some parts of Rajasthan and Orissa where *śākta* conceptions are at their strongest.[23] At Kothrūḍ,

Vākaḍ and Vīr in Maharashtra, Mahiṣāsura, under the name Mhātobā, Mhasobā or Maskobā, is worshipped as the husband of Jogubaī who is none other than Durgā. This identification of Śiva with a deity of the non-Sanskritic tradition is something which occurred time and again throughout the centuries. Nandin, the bull deity, was ultimately identified with Śiva as the latter became a more popular deity. Similarly, the elephant deity was also identified with Śiva, at least in a few regions. By the time the Purāṇas came into being the association between Śiva and Nandin must have been well established. However, that between the sacred elephant and Śiva was not so old and found reflection in a myth which sought to justify the deity's association with the elephant.

In the Purānas, Gajāsura is said to be the son of Mahiṣāsura.[24] If, in folk tradition, Mahiṣāsura is Śiva, then Gajāsura is also the son of Śiva. Since the son represents an aspect of his father, Gajāsura is but an aspect of Śiva. Mahiṣāsura in his fight against Durgā transforms himself, turn by turn, into a lion, an elephant and a man and each time he is beheaded by Durgā.[25] In temple art the *mahiṣa* demon is depicted variously as a buffalo, as a man,[26] as a man emerging from the buffalo body[27] or as a man with horns.[28] Śiva is sometimes described as wearing horns.[29] Besides, since he wears the elephant hide, has his *liṅga* symbol made of the elephant demon's dead body and since one of the forms of Mahiṣāsura is also the elephant, it would appear that Gajāsura is another form of Śiva. In the Purāṇas the term *asura* is often equated with the ignorant and the non-believer. The *asura* ceases to be an *asura* when he accepts the superiority of Śiva and becomes his devotee. He is then converted into a *gaṇa.* Gajāsura becomes more than that. He becomes a permanent part of Śiva. The Bhairava form of Śiva is specifically associated with the elephant hide. Bhairava's complexion is described as being dark as the rain cloud, he has a flabby belly and side-tusks all which make him similar in concept to Gaṇapati.[30] Among the sixty-four Bhairavas described in the *Rudrayāmala Tantra* three are referred to as *Modaka-priya* (he who is fond of the sweatmeat, *modaka*), *vighna-santuṣṭa* (he who grants peace from obstacles) and *Mahākāya* (he who has a huge body).[31] These names suggest a close affinity with Gaṇapati since they are also his epithets.

The Heramba form of Gaṇapati also appears to have some association with *Mahiṣa.* The term *heramba* is synonymous with *mahiṣa* and signifies 'buffalo'. Why would Gaṇapati, who has no association with the buffalo, be named after the animal? This form of Gaṇapati has five heads and rides on a lion instead of the mouse (photo 11). The five heads recall the five heads of some forms of Śiva. The lion mount is borrowed from Durgā. There appears to be some kind of Śiva and Durgā melding in the Heramba Gaṇapati form.

In the one or two centuries before the Christian era Śiva already had a following outside the Brahmanical fold. Since the Pāśupatas appear to have been the earliest sect of the Śaivas it is possible that in certain regions local deities were associated with Pāśupata Śiva even as the various village goddesses were eventually associated with Pārvatī. The Mahiṣāsura and the Gajāsura of the Purāṇās probably represent the cults of the buffalo and the elephant which were identified, in some regions, with Pāśupata Śiva as he grew in importance and popularity and as the various goddesses came to be considered as forms of his consort. This association is grudgingly acknowledged in the Purāṇas by making the elephant into an *asura* that is defeated and then identified with Śiva. In other regions, however, the elephant's association with Śiva was recognized but he remained a distinct deity. In this case he became the *gaṇa* of Śiva. Possibly, it was because the elephant was popular over a wide region that an attempt was made to reconcile these two differing traditions. The elephant deity, therefore, eventually acquired an independent status in the Puranic framework in the form of an elephant-headed son of Śiva.

The myth of Gajāsura appears to be associated with the earlier stages of Śiva's mythology in the Purāṇas since there are some early images depicting this myth. There is a sixth century image of Bhairava Śiva from Pandrenthan (Kashmir) dated to the second half of the sixth century. It depicts the deity holding aloft the elephant hide attached to the elephant head.[32] The image is presently in the Sri Pratap Singh Museum, Srinagar. Its representation in Cave No. XVI at Ellora is another early example.[33] Elsewhere, the Gajāsura motif appears more frequently from the eighth/ninth century AD. The motif also appears in the Coḷa temples. However, this does not necessarily imply that the myth did not exist earlier than the sixth century when it first appears in sculpture. Many of the Jātaka stories that were sculpted on the walls of the early Buddhist *stūpas* had already existed before being incorporated in Buddhist art. Similarly, in the Brahmanical context, as temple building became more complex and elaborate, a greater number of myths were required to embellish the temple walls. It was perhaps at this point that the myth of Gajāsura came to be represented in sculpture. Just as in the Jātakas the Buddha is said to have been a noble elephant in a previous life so also is Śiva associated with the elephant. The elephant in the early centuries of the Christian era was associated with the non-Brahmanical Śiva as it was with the Buddha and that is why it came to be regarded as an *asura* from the Brahmanical point of view. Even when Gaṇapati-Vināyaka is made Śiva's son, the older myth of Gajāsura continues unchanged until, finally, Gaṇapati himself is made the slayer of Gajāsura. According to a south Indian version of this myth there was a giant-demon with the face of an elephant who was unconquerable either by god or by man. Gaṇapati, being only a demi-god, was able to fight him. At the first encounter, the giant-demon, Gajamukhāsura, broke off Gaṇapati's right tusk. But Gaṇapati caught his broken tusk and hurled it at the giant-demon who instantly turned into a rat, whereupon Gaṇapati took him into his service as his *vāhana.*[34] Here the demon is not an elephant but only elephant-faced which makes him even closer in concept to Gaṇapati. Similarly, the demon becomes a part of Gaṇapati since it becomes his *vāhana* even as the elephant skin is worn by Śiva.

The Puranic Śiva is also sometimes clad in tiger skin. According to one myth, it was at Kāśī that a certain *daitya* assumed the form of a tiger. Śiva killed him, wore his skin and was thus known as *Vyāghreśvara* (Tiger Lord).[35] At the place where the tiger was killed Śiva established a *liṅga* called Vyāghreśvara.[36] Just as there is a *liṅga* associated with the elephant demon so also is there a famous *liṅga* associated with the tiger demon.

Śiva wears the elephant hide and also has an elephant-headed *gaṇa.* Similarly he also wears the tiger skin and has a tiger *gaṇa.* Both *gaṇas* are associated with the Goddess. According to one myth, when Kālī retires to a lonely grove to do penance in order to attain a fair complexion, a tiger waits upon her with great devotion and piety. The Goddess comes to regard him as her son. Upon her request, Śiva converts him into a Gaṇeśa (Lord of the *gaṇas*) called Somanandin[37] and he assumes guard of the entrance to her appartment. Similarly, Pārvatī creates the elephant-headed

Gaṇapati to guard her door. This association between the goddess, the tiger, the elephant and the buffalo suggests that these animals represented the consorts of various village goddesses who eventually were identified as different forms of Pārvatī. The animals associated with them sometimes became a form of Śiva and at other times the *gaṇas* of Śiva. Several ancient cults coalesced in the personality of the non-Brahmanical Śiva as he grew in popularity. They helped shape the personality of the Puranic Śiva and provided scope for his growing mythology. Śiva was already known to have animal forms. In the form of a bull, the Greeks knew him as the god of Gandhāra.[38] It was during the Kuṣāṇa period that the bull came to be regarded as his mount and his human form became predominant. In fact the earliest icons of Brahmanical deities were made at Mathura during the Kuṣāṇa period. They include the *liṅgas* with one or four faces of Śiva, Durgā as Mahiṣāsuramardinī, Varāha and Ardhanārī.[39] The Mahiṣāsuramardinī image also appears in Gupta Art in Udayagiri caves (Madhya Pradesh),[40] and seems to be closely associated with early Śivaism and with *liṅga* worship.

Śiva's association with the tiger, the elephant and the *liṅga* has a parallel in some of the early statues of Gaṇapati-Vināyaka which strongly suggest an identification of the two deities in some specific regions. Some of the early images of the elephant-headed deity depict him in an *ūrdhavamedhra* (ithyphallic) form wearing the *vyāghracarma* (tiger-skin) Two such statues were found at Gardez and Sakar Dhar, both near Kabul, Afghanistan,[41] in the region of ancient Kapīśa. These statues are dated between the fourth and seventh centuries. Another statue from Mathura depicts Gaṇapati wearing a *vyāghrajina* (tiger-skin) and his face has both tusks intact.[42] An image carved on the facade of cave no. 6, Udayagiri, Madhya Pradesh, also depicts Gaṇapati in the *ūrdhvamedhra* form.[43] In all these images the mouse is absent. There are several reasons for thinking that these statues represent a syncretic form of Śiva and the elephant deity. Firstly, the statues from Afghanistan are in the region of Kapīśa where evidence of the elephant cult has been discussed in the previous chapter. Early Śivaism is also associated with this region. Similarly no other deity, other than Śiva and these few examples of Gaṇapati, is shown in the ithyphallic state. The earliest depiction of *ūrdhvamedhra* Śiva appears to be on a gold coin of the Kuṣāṇa king, Huviṣka. In fact the *ūrdhvaliṅga* is common in sculptural representations of Śiva from the late Kuṣāṇa period onwards.[44] The tiger skin also appears for the first time on one of the coins of Vāsudeva where it adorns a three-headed Śiva. There is a stela with Śiva from Uttar Pradesh, now in the Los Angeles County Museum of Art, where Śiva is depicted with the *ūrdhvaliṅga* and what appears to be an ascetic's staff.[45] Even Lakulīśa, believed to be an incarnation of Śiva, is represented naked in an ithyphallic state. A sculpture from Mukhalingam, Andhra Pradesh, shows Lakulīśa as a four-armed ithyphallic god seated on a double-petalled lotus.[46] Therefore, the erect phallus and tiger skin became part of Śiva's early iconology and only later were they associated with the early statues of Gaṇapati. They did not, however, become a regular feature of Gaṇapati's iconology.

The earliest literary evidence of Śiva being ithyphallic comes from the *Mahābhārata* where he is described as draped in dripping animal hide, having a serpent-form, being of short stature, ithyphallic, four-faced and carrying skulls.[47] The suggestion that some of these early statues of Gaṇapati represent a syncretic form of Śiva-elephant deity is more plausible when compared to some of the representations of Nandin. The latter, originally Śiva himself in theriomorphic form and, later, his mount, is carved exactly like Śiva in late mediaeval and modern reliefs of southern India. The only distinction lies in the fact that his 'front' hands are in the *namaskāra* pose (the 'back' hands, like those of Śiva, carry the *paraśu* (axe) and *mṛgha* (deer)) while Śiva's front hands are shown in the *abhaya* (freedom from fear) and *varadā* (boon granting) poses.[48] There is even a description of Nandin wearing a tiger-skin garment.[49] In some Purāṇas there are indications that Gaṇapati resembles Śiva. According to the *Skanda Purāṇa*, Gaṇeśavara has the same form as that of Śiva.[50]

This syncretism between Gaṇapati and Śiva is also seen in some statues in southeast Asia which evidently had their prototypes in some early Indian images. In the eighth century Cambodian Gaṇeśa from Triton, the two armed figure holds a *kalaśa* (water jar) in one hand and a rosary in the other.[51] These attributes highlight his ascetic nature and recall the Pāśupata form of Śiva. Another statue from Mī-so'n in Vietnam depicts Gaṇapati with the tiger's skin worn around his hips, the only known instance of this in southeast Asian art.[52] I have referred earlier to statues of Lakulīśa also being depicted in an ithyphallic state. It is possible that one reason why Gaṇapati becomes so important in Cambodia at an early stage (by the sixth century he had temples devoted to him) is because he was considered an aspect of Śiva. To make an analogy, Varāha whose images became popular in the early Gupta period was worshipped as a deity in his own right even though he was considered an incarnation of Viṣṇu. It is true that religious literature is not explicit on this point. However, Gaṇapati's iconological and mythological developments do not always proceed in a parallel manner. As we shall see further, there is much in his images which remains unexplained by literature. It should be borne in mind that Brahmanical literature, by and large, reflects only the accepted practices and beliefs of a limited few. The images, however, suggest other possibilities.

All the early images of the elephant-headed figure cannot be referred to as Gaṇapati. There is a terracotta bas-relief from Akra (Bannu district, North West Frontier Province, Pakistan) which some scholars date to about the fifth century,[53] and others to the second century.[54] It depicts the figure in a dancing pose holding a round object. The latter is, according to Brahmanical texts, the *modaka* (a sweetmeat). However, most Brahmanical statues depict Gaṇapati holding a bowl of *modakas* rather than the single *modaka.* Besides, in many Puranic myths of Gaṇapati's birth there is no reference to the *modakas.* There is, moreover, no satisfactory explanation provided for Gaṇapati's penchant for these sweetmeats or how he came to be associated with them. In the Buddhist context, the round object is stated to be the *cintāmaṇi* (wish fulfilling jewel). However, the earliest Buddhist texts that deal with Gaṇapati date from about the seventh century or so. It would, therefore, appear that the elephant deity of the north-west region was associated with this round object which may have been a fruit and it eventually took on a specific connotation in the Brahmanical and Buddhist contexts.

In most of the surviving Gupta temples, Śiva in the form of the *liṅga* was the principal cult image. The elephant deity also appears to have been associated with a form of *liṅga* worship in that it was associated with jutting out rocks and promontories. In the previous chapter, I have referred to the elephant deity at Kapīśa who was associated with the mountain. In the myth of Gajāsura, the demon's body is converted into a *liṅga.* In Kashmir three famous pilgrimage sites are associated with Gaṇapati. One is a rock lying at the foot of the Hariparbat hill near Srinagar which is worshipped as Gaṇapati under the name of Bhīmasvāmin. Another *svayambhū mūrti* (self-existent image) of Gaṇapati lies near the village of Gaṇes-bal in the Lidar river near its right bank. The third pilgrimage site is called Gaṇeśa Ghati or Gaṇeśagiri.[55] It is located in the Upper Kiśangaṅgā valley and is close to the shrine of Śāradā. The *Rājataraṅgiṇī* refers to a castle called *Śiraḥśilā* which Stein identified with this site.[56] *Śiraḥśilā* literally means the rock with the shape of a head. This rock was identified with Gaṇapati.

Ganapati is ithyphallic, is associated with the *liṅga* and wears a tiger-skin. Yet there are no myths that explain how he got a tiger skin or that even mention his wearing one. Similarly, the Purāṇas stress that Gaṇapati has only one tusk. Yet the statue of Gaṇapati from Mathura has his two tusks intact. It is true that in some of the Buddhist Tantras Gaṇapati is described as having both tusks intact and possibly that is why Agrawala classifies this statue as a Buddhist one. However, some of Śiva's *gaṇas,* as also some manifestations of Śiva such as Vīrabhadra, are described as having two curved fangs which would correspond to Gaṇapati's two tusks. In that case, this statue is probably a syncretic Śiva-elephant deity in a fierce form like that of Vīrabhadra. Another possible interpretation is that this is an early statue when Gaṇapati-Vināyaka's elephant head is represented in a realistic fashion before the myths about his single tusk evolved. Śiva's association with Gaṇapati in the Purāṇas is subsequent to his association with the elephant deity outside the newly emerging Puranic fold. The *Kṛtyakalpataru* quoting from the *Narasiṃha Purāṇa* describes Gaṇapati as having one, two or four tusks.[57] This in itself is suggestive of the different sources of Gaṇapati's origin: Airāvata with his four tusks, an ordinary elephant with its two tusks and the Brahmanical version of the single tusked elephant.

The second aspect of Gaṇapati's development in the Purāṇas is centred around the process of beheading, acquiring an elephant head and the name Vināyaka. This process of death and rebirth with a different form and name is common to several of Śiva's *gaṇas*. Andhakāsura is transformed by Śiva into his *gaṇa* chief called *Bhṛngi*. Dakṣa is killed, resurrected with the head of a sacrificial animal and granted the chieftancy of the *gaṇas*.[58] Brahmā is beheaded by Śiva (only his fifth head) and then brought back to life by the yogic power of Śiva, who he then accepts as the greatest god.[59] Gaṇapati is also beheaded and acquires a new form and a new name. The elephant thus becomes a human deity retaining the elephant head for identity. Death represents the transition to *gaṇahood* and to the entourage of the Puranic Śiva. Some of the *gaṇas* are, in fact, incarnations of Śiva, such as Lakuliśa. Others, like Mahākāla or Virūpākṣa, were originally deities in their own right and were later identified with Śiva. Gaṇapati, like Nandin, represented the cult of the elephant even as Nandin represented the sacred bull. Both were identified with Śiva, initially, outside the Brahmanical framework. Later, both became distinct from, but closely related to, the Puranic Śiva.

In the myths regarding the birth of Skanda and Gaṇapati, their association with the Goddess is evident which again points to a pre-Puranic tradition. Neither is born from the sexual union of Śiva and Pārvatī. Skanda is born from the semen of Śiva,[60] but is also fathered by Agni and mothered by Gaṅgā, the Kṛttikās and then, finally, accepted by Pārvatī. The concept of his having several mothers, and several heads with which to feed from, is an echo of his older association with the *mātṛkās* (mothers) who possessed children. Gaṇapati, on the other hand, is generally associated with one mother. He is frequently referred to as 'the son of the daughter of the king of mountains'[61] as 'son of Ambikā'[62] or as the 'son of Pārvatī'.[63] This is an echo of his earliest personality, the elephant deity who, as a fertility deity, was intrinsically associated with the worship of the Earth Goddess. Images of Gaṇapati in the company of the *mātrkās* begin to appear from as early as the sixth century AD. No myths, however, explain his association with them. The earliest representations of this kind are found at: Deogarh (along the Betwa River ghats on the border of Uttar Pradesh and Madhya Pradesh);[64] at Śāmalājī, a village in Gujarat and close to the Rajasthan border;[65] at Mandor (near Jodhpur, Rajasthan);[66] in the Cālukyan temples at Aihoḷe, Bādāmi (Karnataka), and at Elephanta and Ellora (Maharashtra).[67] These *mātṛkā* images formed part of Śaiva shrines and their cult was already established in these regions, prior to Gaṇapati's association with them.

There are basically three kinds of myths relating to the origin of Gaṇapati: where he is formed by Pārvatī; where he is created by both Śiva and Parv̌atī; where he is created by Śiva alone. Yet, even in the last case, the creation of Gaṇapati is indirectly associated with the Goddess. In the *Śiva*,[68] *Skanda*,[69] and

Matsya Purāṇas,[70] Gaṇapati is formed by the scuff that Pārvatī rubs off her body during her bath. In the *Bhaviṣya*[71] and *Vāmana*[72] *Purāṇas,* Gaṇapati is a creation of both Śiva and Pārvatī but not through sexual union. According to the *Bṛhaddharma*[73] and *Varāha*[74] *Purāṇas,* Śiva alone creates Gaṇapati. Yet the association with the goddess remains because in the former case, he is created out of a piece of Pārvatī's garment and, in the latter, it is because Pārvatī is enamoured by Śiva's creation, Gaṇapati, that he is cursed by a jealous Śiva to assume his ugly form. The Purāṇas themselves justify these numerous and often contradictory versions about Gaṇapati's creation by stating that the several myths are related to different *kalpas* (ages).

Gaṇapati is different to the other *gaṇas* in that he acquires a childhood. He is described as a happy dancing child whose dance amuses Śiva who crowns his son as lord of *gaṇas.* He is described as playing pranks even as Kṛṣṇa did with Yaśodā. He hides the moon in the matted locks of his father's hair. He is depicted as dancing and singing in order to amuse his mother. At the same time, he is described as having independent power.[75] Just as Kṛṣṇa acquires a childhood in the *Bhāgavata Purāṇa* which he does not have in the *Mahābhārata,* similarly, Gaṇapati also acquires many dimensions to his personality, which make him more lovable to the public and lend the austere Śiva a more human side. If he cannot be approached, his son acts as an intermediary.

The child god is a new phenomenon in the early medieval period. During this period temple ritual corresponded closely to palace ritual. The temple was the Lord's palace and the deity was awakened, bathed, fed, entertained and put to bed in the same manner as the king. Similarly, he acquired a family at par with the royal family. Perhaps that is why even Viṣṇu's incarnations have families since that made it possible for devotees to identify the cosmic world with the human world. Just as Kṛṣṇa became the subject of so much folklore, being more popular than the Viṣṇu of the Sanskritic tradition, so also Gaṇapati provided the same possibilities in the Śaiva context. Śiva and Viṣṇu, as they rose to the position of major gods, gradually grew more distant. Their sons or incarnations provided them with the dimensions necessary to make them the objects of veneration for all levels of society. Epigraphical evidence, remains of temples and statues show that

Viṣṇu and Śiva were the deities that enjoyed royal patronage. Gaṇapati or Kṛṣṇa were more popular with the other categories of society. There is another parallel between the secular and religious world in the early medieval period. Just as kings of lesser dynasties often observed the formality of claiming *kṣatriya* status, or at least of participating in a common *kṣatriya* past as embodied in the *itihāsa-purāṇa* tradition, so also were non-Brahmanical divinities converted into family members or incarnations of the Puranic gods.

At first, Gaṇapati appears as a malevolent deity. He is described as being surrounded by Vināyakas, all elephant-faced like him, who are dark-coloured and who hold various weapons. 'They have fierce eyes, flowing ichor and massive bodies'. They represent beings that invoke fear and terror.[76] Yet, the instances when Gaṇapati is depicted in the role of a warrior are few indeed. In the *Śiva Purāṇa* he is described as bravely and single-handedly resisting Śiva and his *gaṇas* at Pāravatī's door until Śiva has to use cunning to behead him.[77] In the same *Purāṇa*, he is depicted as bravely fighting against the *asura* Śumbha.[78] However, in most of the battles fought by Śiva it is Skanda and the other *gaṇas* that are actually engaged in battle and Gaṇapati's role remains somewhat ambiguous. Kārttikeya is the perfect general, created specifically to destroy the Tripuras (three cities), a task that Indra and the other gods are unable to accomplish. Perhaps it is Gaṇapati's role as a *gaṇa* which led him, in a few cases, to be identified with rituals pertaining to war. There is an inscription which records the installation of an image of Vināyaka by a prince of the Viṣṇukuṇḍin family at the command of Viṣṇukuṇḍin Mahendravarman (*c.* AD 556-616). According to the inscription, the prince set up a military drum, brought an image of the elephant-faced Vināyaka and installed it after having worshipped it with great care.[79] Traditionally, prayers to the war-drum were offered by the king on the occasion of *raṇa dīkṣā* or the preparation of war. This association of Gaṇapati with the war-drum perhaps came about because of his role as Śiva's *gaṇa* and also because of his elephant-head. Elephants formed an important arm of the army and their role was crucial to success in battle. The king himself often participated in the battle on elephant-back.

Initially, Skanda was the older brother of the two. He was accepted as part of the Brahmanical Śiva's pantheon at an earlier date than Gaṇapati. In the *Brahma,*[80] *Liṅga*[81] and *Matsya*[82] *Purāṇas,* Skanda is stated to be the the older brother. In the *Śiva Purāṇa,* the chapters dealing with the birth of Gaṇapati follow upon those dealing with the birth of Kārttikeya making Gaṇapati the younger brother.[83] In the *Brahmavaivarta*[84] and *Nārada*[85] *Purāṇas* he is referred to as *Guhāgraja* (elder than Guha, another name for Skanda). In the *Varāha Purāṇa* the chapter describing the birth of Gaṇapati precedes that of the birth of Skanda, so we may presume that he is the elder.[86] However, it is not certain whether these different texts represent a chronological development or merely a regional difference in the importance given to each of these two deities. Possibly, in some regions and among some categories of people, as Gaṇapati became more important Skanda received less attention and was relegated to the status of a younger brother. A clearer idea can be had if one examines some of the inscriptions of the early medieval period. By the eighth century, in some regions at least, Gaṇapati was considered the older or, at least, the more important of the two. An inscription from Baijnath in Kangra, dated to about AD 750 begins with an invocation to Śiva, followed by one to Gajāsya (elephant face), Skanda, Nandi and Vīrabhadra.[87] However, in Bengal, in the Barrackpur grant of Vijayasena's thirty-second year (eleventh/twelfth centuries during the reign of the Sena dynasty), Śiva is invoked first and, thereafter, Kārttikeya and Gaṇapati.[88]

Some myths depict how Gaṇapati is the cleverer of the two and, therefore, more important. The *Śiva Purāṇa* narrates the myth of Śiva and Pārvatī holding a competition—a race round the earth—for their two sons. While Kārttikeya sets off on his peacock, Gaṇapati merely circumambulates his parents seven times since he believes that his parents represent his whole world. He is declared the winner and is married to the daughters of Prajāpati, Siddhi and Buddhi. From Siddhi he has a son, Kṣema, and from Buddhi, another son, Lābha. Kārttikeya on his return is furious to learn what has taken place and departs to the Krauñca mountain where he remains an eternal bachelor.[89]

Gaṇapati wins the race because of his intelligence and devotion. By this he adds yet another dimension to his personality -that of a householder. He was a *gaṇa,* a child, and now, by his marriage to Siddhi and Buddhi, he becomes a husband and a father. This would also reflect a changing society where, what

Kārttikeya represented was not valid any longer. Just as Indra, the warrior god, cedes his place to Śiva and Viṣṇu, so also Kārttikeya, as protector of children and then as warrior, cedes his important position to Gaṇapati. The latter acquires greater and wider powers since he removes obstacles of every kind. He can be manipulated to suit a larger number of needs for many more categories of society. Perhaps, in the early centuries of the Christian era, continuous invasions made war a constant feature of life. Skanda, therefore, was very popular as a warrior God. However, over time, especially in north India, his importance within the Puranic pantheon and, more specifically, within the Śaiva pantheon, declined. After being declared the winner of the race, Gaṇapati is told by Śiva: 'He who has intelligence possesses strength as well. How can he who is devoid of intellect have strength'.[90] Gaṇapati represents intelligence which is considered more important than martial might. He is also the perfect *bhakta* and, against a background of a growing *bhakti* movement, he acquires greater significance.

Within the Śaiva pantheon, Gaṇapati and Kārttikeya, as indeed all the other *gaṇas*, remain essentially an extension of Śiva. If Śiva acquires many of the characteristics of Vedic Indra, so do his sons. Kārttikeya, as *Senāpati*, is shown riding on the elephant Airāvata,[91] the mount of Indra. In fact, he is created to destroy the Tripuras, a task that Indra is unable to accomplish. Similarly, in one myth, Gaṇapati also acquires the head of Airāvata. The *gaṇas* have great yogic powers and yet they are warriors. Kārttikeya is the commander of the army and yet he is 'conversant with the reality of the teaching in the *Vedas* and *Sāstras*'.[92] The *gaṇas* are described as being celibate, perfect yogins, and yet, at other times, they are said to be married. Nandin is married to Suyāsa, the daughter of the Maruts.[93] However, he is also described as being 'stationed in the harem of the lord',[94] a role normally associated with a eunuch. Kārttikeya is a bachelor and yet he is described as being attended to by two *śaktis.*[95] At other times he is described as having a wife called Devasenā.[96] Similarly, Gaṇapati is married to Siddhi and Buddhi. At other times, he is said to be married to Puṣṭi, the daughter of Dakṣa.[97]

At another level, Kārttikeya and Gaṇapati represent the two contradictory aspects of Śiva. The former is tall and handsome, the eternal youth, whereas the latter is short and potbellied. Śiva is always iconographically depicted as tall and slim, yet in his *Bhairava* form he resembles the short stout form of Gaṇapati.[98] Kārttikeya is born on the sixth day of the bright half of the lunar month of *mārgaśirsa.* (November/December).[99] He is associated with the sun, the fire, with brilliance and purity. Gaṇapati, on the other hand, is born on the dark half of the month of *bhādrapada* (August/September) at the auspicious hour of moonrise.[100] He is associated with the moon, with death and regeneration, hence with fertility and prosperity. Śiva's *tapas* (asceticism) and austerity is brilliant and pure as the sun. Yet he wears the moon in his locks. In Śaiva philosophy, Śiva is the embodiment of the five elements which together make up every form of life. Skanda represents both fire and water, the *liṅga* represents air, the Goddess the earth, and Gaṇapati the sky or ether.[101] Both Gaṇapati and Kārttikeya thus appear to be extensions of Śiva himself, the only deity who is both erotic and ascetic at the same time, who has a family with two sons, but who is also the eternal *yogi* living on the peak of Mount Kailāśa. The conflict between Gaṇapati and Kārttikeya, as represented by the myth of Gaṇapati's marriage, can be seen as a parallel to the constant conflict in the personality of Śiva because of his dual personality.

Within the framework of Pāśupata Śivaism as described in the *Purāṇas,* all the *gaṇa* chieftains are extensions of Śiva, but they are not Śiva himself. This is because the Pāśupata School is dualistic. The supreme and individual souls are distinct entities. In its delivered condition the individual soul shakes off its ignorance and acquires the supreme and ultimate knowledge and purity. It attains perfect resemblance to Śiva without, however, the power of creation.[102] In describing such a delivered soul it is said: 'if he is unattached, Sadaśivā, Lord of Gods, teaches him the purport of the great *mantra,* crowns him as the chief of the *gaṇas,* and gives him a body similar to him'.[103] Śiva is lauded as 'the one having the face of a great elephant',[104] or as the one assuming the form of an elephant.[105] He is 'One who has the form of a boy, or one assuming the form of a boy.'[106] 'You are the animals, beasts and birds.'[107] Śiva was also worshipped in eight forms which were considered to represent his diverse manifestions—the five elements together with the sun, the moon and the sacrificer. Gaṇapati, similarly, also acquires eight forms and is invoked with eight names—Gaṇeśa, Ekadanta, Heramba, Vighnanāyaka, Lambodara, Surpakarṇa, Gajavaktra and Guhāgraja.[108]

At an initial stage, before Gaṇapati acquired the right to be worshipped first, various leaders of *gaṇas* enjoyed this honour. Caṇḍa, Nandin, Bhṛṅgin, Skanda, Ādityas, the Maruts and the goddess are all, at some point or the other, stated to have the privilege of being worshipped first. So also are Vīrabhadra, the *bhūtas*, the *pretas* and the *kuṣmāṇḍas.*[109] In the case of Kīrtimukha, it is stated that 'this *gaṇa* shall be specially worshipped in the course of the adoration of Śiva. Those who do not worship him at the outset will find their worship in vain'.[110] At other times, it is recommended that Nandin be worshipped at the outset and only then, Mahākāla, Gaṅgā, Yamunā, *gaṇas* and others. There is no specific mention of Skanda and Gaṇapati.[111] There are some descriptions of Śiva worship in which the ritual begins with the adoration of the eight cosmic bodies of Śiva. This is followed by worship of his retinue consisting of Īśāna, Nandi, Caṇḍa, Mahākāla, Bhṛṅgin, Skanda, Kapādīśa, Soma and Śukra. Vīrabhadra is placed in front of Śiva and Kīrtimukha at the back. Gaṇapati is not mentioned.[112] Being a latecomer into the Brahmanical fold, he was, initially, not included in the worship of the Puranic Śiva. Sometimes his name appears as a superimposition on an already established ritual. In the *Liṅga Purāṇa,* for example, there is a chapter on the worship of Śiva in the form of a *liṅga.*[113] In the entire chapter, which describes the procedure in detail, there is no mention of Gaṇapati. Only at the end of the chapter is it stated that for the achievement of all desired objects, Gaṇeśa, the lord of the universe, shall be worshipped at the outset, and in the end, by *brāhmaṇas* and *devas.* This instruction appears to have been inserted at a later stage and shows that the worship of Gaṇapati was not, initially, an intrinsic part of this rite.

Gaṇapati, in the context of Śivaism, is either a *gaṇa* which makes him a warder deity, or he is the son of Śiva. As 'Vināyaka' he is usually depicted in the role of attendant along with other *gaṇa* chiefs. In the *Agni Purāṇa*, for example, in the context of the intial consecration of an image, the warder-gods Nandi and Mahākāla, Bhṛṅgi and Vināyaka, Vṛṣabha and Skanda, Goddess and Caṇḍa, are all worshipped first.[114] As 'Gaṇeśa', too, the elephant-headed deity usually appears as a warder-deity. In the *Matsya Purāṇa,* for instance, in the context of the installation of an image of Śiva and its worship, Gaṇeśa's worship is part of the worship of Śiva's attendants, along with that of Nandi, Bhṛṅgi or Kārttikeya.[115] These are probably references to the earlier stages in the development of Gaṇapati-Vināyaka in the Śaiva pantheon. However, his worship as 'Gaṇapati' is distinct from that of the warder deities and, in this case, he appears as an independent deity who is worshipped as the Lord of Obstacles. According to the *Maheśa Mantra-Kathanam* described in the *Nārada Purāṇa*, meditation on Maheśa is followed by the worship of the nine *śaktis*. This is followed by the worship of the Lord of Obstacles. Only then are the eight attending deities, including Gaṇeśa, worshipped.[116] A definite evolution is perceptible. He is both an attendant deity and yet he has acquired the right to worship at an independent level but, of course, within the framework of Śivaism. At other times, instead of being worshipped as an attendant of Śiva, he is worshipped as his son along with his parents and brother. In this case, the worship begins with Nandin, as an aspect of Śiva, and only then, inside the sanctum sanctorum, is Śiva worshipped along with the Goddess and their two sons.[117]

Gradually, Gaṇapati comes to be worshipped for a variety of purposes: for warding off impediments, for the fulfilment of all desires, for emancipation and enjoyment,[118] for the sake of victory, for prosperity and for the power to subdue.[119] He is worshipped for progeny, for the achievement of holy rites, to bestow equality on those men and women who worship him on all occasions and for achieving oneness with Śiva.[120] The *Padma Purāṇa* adds that, among other things, worship of Gaṇapati ensures control of the entire universe. Evil spirits become calm. Such a devotee is not troubled by disease. Being free from all sins, he eternally obtains heaven.[121] According to the *Bhaviṣya Purāṇa*, by worshipping Gaṇapati, kings become powerful, kingdoms prosper, a beautiful virgin can be acquired as a bride and victory in battle is ensured.[122]

Gaṇapati in the Śaiva pantheon has a counterpart in Lakṣmaṇa of the Vaiṣṇava pantheon. It is said that if a man desires success in the worship of Rāma he must first worship Lakṣmaṇa.[123] The *mantra* of Lakṣmaṇa must be repeated before that of Rāma if the devotee wishes to achieve *siddhi* (success).[124] By worshipping Lakṣmaṇa, a devotee regains lost kingdoms, overcomes premature death, achieves victory in battles and never suffers from illness and poverty.[125]

At other times, Gaṇapati has his perfect counterpart in Hanumān. The latter is sometimes an attendant of Rāma and, at other times, he is entitled to independent worship. Rāma considers Hanumān as his child.[126] Like Gaṇapati, he is described as 'the young *brahmacārin*, who confers all auspiciousness'.[127] By the worship of Hanumān 'the various harassing calamities from goblins, poison, evil planets, and diseases as well as adverse planets and demons perish at the same instant'.[128] These are the very dangers with which the evil Vināyakas of the *Mānava Gṛhya Sūtra* were associated. By the worship of Hanumān the devotee 'obtains wealth, grain, son, grandson, good fortune, unequalled renown, intellect, learning, lustre, kingdom, victory in arguments, activities facilitating the control of people and victory in battle'.[129] Human problems, fears and aspirations are common to all categories of society and to all regions. To that extent, Hanumān and Gaṇapati both represent the same thing within different contexts. The image of Hanumān is stated to face the south[130] as is often the case with images of Gaṇapati in the Śaiva temples. Both have faces that are red with the application of *sindūra* (red lead) and Tuesday is the special day for their worhip.

GAṆAPATI AND THE OTHER PURANIC DEITIES

In the sectarian Purāṇas there are two distinct themes. On the one hand, there is animosity and rivalry between different religious sects and on the other, there is an emphasis on the essential unity of the different deities. The efforts at syncretism between various Brahmanical sects were embodied in distinct iconic types such as the *Hari-Hara* (Viṣṇu and Śiva),[131] the *Ardhanārīśvara* (Śiva in his form as half man and half woman)[132] or the *Sarvatobhadra* images. The latter depict Śiva, Viṣṇu, Sūrya and Durgā on four sides of a pillar. These forms evolved during the Gupta period.[133] The efforts at syncretism resulted in Vaiṣṇava deities being associated with Śiva and vice-versa. Kubera and his entourage begin to find mention in the context of Viṣṇuism.[134] In the same manner, Hanumān is described as doing obeisance to Śiva.[135] It is said that he can be worshipped in the pedestal of images of either Śiva or Viṣṇu.[136] Gaṇapati, the son of Śiva, is accepted into the Vaiṣṇava pantheon and described as 'one who served Kṛṣṇa as well as Śiva, who made the *gopīs* (cowherd maids) laugh, who is single-minded by being devoted to the Lord of the *gopīs*'.[137] Some *Purāṇas* go a step further and bestow upon Kṛṣṇa the role of having given Gaṇapati his elephant head.[138] In fact even his birth is described as being the result of Kṛṣṇa's propitiation by Pārvatī.[139] Eventually Gaṇapati becomes an *aṃṣavatāra* (partial incarnation) of Kṛṣṇa.[140] His worship ensures the attainment of *Viṣṇuloka* (world of Viṣṇu).[141] The *caturthī* (fourth) day, normally associated with the worship of Gaṇapati, is said to be the special day for some Vaiṣṇava deities as well. The *caturthī* in the month of *vaiśākha* (April/May) is associated with the worship of Śaṅkarṣaṇa (brother of Kṛṣṇa) and that in the month of *jyeṣṭha* (May/June) is associated with Gaṇapati in the form of Pradyumna (the son of Kṛṣṇa and Rukmiṇī).[142] So completely is Gaṇapati absorbed within the fold of Puranic Viṣṇuism that, according to some Purāṇas, even the *caturthī* day in the bright half of the month of *bhādrapada*, normally associated with Gaṇapati alone, is celebrated as the holy day for the *bahuladhēnuka vrata* (a vow observed for the acquisition of many cows) . On this day the cow is to be worshipped and the devotee attains *goloka*, the realm of Kṛṣṇa.

In the context of certain Vaiṣṇava *tīrthas* (pilgrimage sites) such as that of the Viśrānti *tīrtha* at Mathura, Hanumān is worshipped first followed by Gaṇapati. Only then, are Viṣṇu and the Goddesses evoked.[143] This would suggest that Gaṇapati is accepted in his own right into the fold of Vaiṣṇava worship, but not in the highest rung of secondary deities. Subsequently, the worship of Gaṇapati at the beginning of any rite and ritual was accepted. According to the *Narasiṃha Purāṇa*, for example, Gaṇapati is first honoured at the beginning of any sacrifice or worship.[144] King Ikṣavāku is described as first worshipping Lord Vināyaka before settling down to practice penance.[145] In Uttar Pradesh, the Mathura *praśasti* (eulogy) of the reign of Vijaypalla (AD 1149-50) refers to a temple of Viṣṇu but it begins with an invocation and then *maṅgala* (invocation for auspiciousness) to Gaṇapati[146] which shows that by the twelfth century this was an accepted practice in some regions.

Some Purāṇas recommend that the Sun or the *pitṛs* (ancestors) be worshipped at the beginning of any prayer or ritual. According to the *Brahma Purāṇa*, 'The devotee should not worship Viṣṇu, Śiva or the Lord of *devas* unless the water-offering has been made to the Sun-god in the manner prescribed in the *Śāstras*'.[147] At other times, the worship of the *pitṛs* is considered imperative before the worship of any other deity. According to the *Vāyu Purāṇa*, 'One should especially worship *pitṛs* before *devas*'.[148] Both the sun and the *pitṛs* are closely associated in their roles. The sun is the source of all life on earth even as the *pitṛs* are the source of existing generations. The *pitṛs* are sometimes conceived of as dwelling in the sun's orb or the moon's rays.[149] In fact, there are many parallels between the *pitṛs*, the sun, the moon and Gaṇapati.

The *pitṛs* are said to have their abode in the sky (or in the ether) and their quarter is the south.[150] The *nāgas* too, are associated with the south and with the sky. The myth, quoted earlier, whereby Rudra does not have a form in the sky and therefore creates Gaṇapati, suggests the latter's association with the sky. As a warder god of Śiva, Vināyaka is positioned in the south along with Bhṛngi.[151] *Pañcāyatana-Gaṇeśa* is always placed either in the south-east or in the south-west.[152] Only when worshipped as the principal deity is he placed in the centre. Gaṇapati temples often face the south.[153] The south is also the abode of Yama, of death and, thereby, of regeneration. In the *Mahābhārata*, the southern region is described as being the abode of the deceased ancestors and also the location of the town named Bhogāvati, ruled by Vāsuki, the Nāga Takṣaka and by Airāvata.[154] In Buddhist literature, the southern region is presided over by Virūḍhaka, the Lord of *kumbhāṇḍas*. As discussed in the preceding chapter, the *kumbhāṇḍas* and the nāgas form one aspect of Gaṇapati's origins.

The worship of some *nāgas* and *pisācas* appears to be little other than *pitṛ-pūjā* (ancestor worship) and this would account for the close association between them and the *pitṛs*. The *nāgas* and the *piśācas* were, originally, a people before becoming mythological figures. The *Nīlamata Purāṇa*, recommends the worship of Nikumbha who is said to have been the attendant of Nīla, the most famous of the *nāga* kings to have ruled over Kashmir at the dawn of civilization in the valley. According to this text, the earliest inhabitants of the Kashmir Valley were the *nāgas* and then the *piśācas*. Nikumbha is described as a *piśāca* chief and it is prescribed that oblations for him and the *piśācas* should be placed, among other places, in cemetries, rivers and on the tops of mountains.[155] Nikumbha appears to be a deified leader or chief of some of the early inhabitants of Kashmir. Similarly, several *nāgas* such as Takṣaka were also probably deified rulers or ancestors. Since

Gaṇapati is partly derived from the *nāgas/piśācas/kumbhāṇḍas*, it is hardly surprising that he shares a common symbolism with them on the one hand and with the *pitṛs* on the other.

Pitṛs, when worshipped, confer many good things. '*Pitṛs* in the form of grandfathers grant nourishment, progeny and heavenly pleasure to him who desires nourishment or who desires progeny'.[156] 'A man devoted to *pitṛs* immediately attains all the jewels, vehicles and women on the earth'.[157] A king regains his kingdom; a poor man becomes wealthy; a man about to die, attains longevity. In fact, a man devoted to *pitṛs* has all his wishes fulfilled by them. In a nutshell, worship of *pitṛs* ensures a better material life and it is precisely this that Gaṇapati comes to represent as he grows in importance.

Gaya is the most famous place for the performance of *pitṛ-pūjā*.[158] Because of its age-old sanctity, it eventually became associated with the important deities and sages. The *padas* (footprints) of different deities here are said to include those of Viṣṇu, Śiva, Indra, Ravi, Kārttikeya, Krauñca and Mātaṅga. The other holy places for the performance of *śrāddha* (rites for the dead) are the mountain Amarakaṇṭaka (in Bilaspur District, Madhya Pradesh), and other places situated in present day Kurnool District (Andhra Pradesh), and Kośala (part of modern Uttar Pradesh). These very regions were associated in one form or the other with the sacred elephant. The earliest evidence of an elephant-headed *yakṣa* was found at Amarāvatī in Andhra Pradesh; Kośala was associated with the Mātaṅga dynasty. Gaya has a special association with elephants, for it is stated that 'by granting elephants in Gaya, one can be free from all worries about *śrāddhas*'.[159]

The *pitṛs*, the moon, the sun, *nāgas* and the Goddess are all symbols of fertility and the theme of fertility is woven around the waters, vegetation, women and the mythological ancestor. All five are associated with periodic regeneration—the sun that rises and sets each day as does the moon, the ancestors who die but are reborn in their descendants, and the Goddess who, as the personification of the earth, gives and sustains life and takes back the dead into her fold. This theme of regeneration is evoked by the *nāga* and other lunar animals, by the opposition of light and darkness (night and day), the sky and the underworld. In fact 'To Śakti, the Sun and Vighneśvara red cloth is offered'.[160] Red is the sign of virility and fertility.

The association of Gaṇapati with the *pitṛs*, the moon, the sun, *nāgas* and the Goddess is never explicit in the Purāṇas. Yet, the parallels are striking. Sometimes, the images of the deity are eloquent testimony of this association. An early image of the elephant-headed deity (*c.* fifth century) from Rājgir depicts him seated and entwined by cobras. This image was one of several figures forming the base of a structure of an old temple of Maṇiyar Maṭha. The other images on the base of this statue are: a nude six-armed dancing Śiva, a *liṅga* garlanded with glowers, a *nāginī* and five *nāgas*.[161] Even today, there are many places, particularly in south India, where Gaṇapati is worshipped with *nāgas*. In Madurai, for example, he is worshipped in the presence of *nāgas* at the Gaṇeśa Natarāja temple where there is a belief that childless couples who bathe the image and circumambulate it in the early morning for forty-eight days will have their wishes for progeny fulfilled.[162] There are no myths in the Purāṇas, however, which throw any light on this aspect of the deity. It is evident that in the Purāṇas Gaṇapati's personality is being remodelled to fit into the Brahmanical framework. However, older associations which were popular and well-established continued and were gradually incorporated into Brahmanical practices even if the texts did not prescribe or describe them. From the iconological point of view, Gaṇapati retains his link with the *nāgas* because of the serpent that he usually wears in the form of a sacred thread or as a waist band.

Gaṇapati figures on the lintels of Sun temples in Gujarat belonging to the Maitraka (AD 470-788) and the post-Maitraka (eighth/ninth centuries) period. In the Sun Temple at Sutrapada (District Junagadh, Gujarat), each doorway has an image of Gaṇapati on the dedicatory block.[163] Similarly, in the Sūrya temple at Kalasar (District Bhavanagar), Gaṇapati is carved on the lintel of the door. This association between Sūrya and Gaṇapati is never explained in the *Purāṇas*. Yet the association was old. In Chapter II, I have referred to the description by Philostratus of the practice of keeping a sacred elephant in the Sun Temple of Taxila in the first century of the Christian era. This is yet another example of how pre-Puranic associations of the sacred elephant are reflected in a Brahmanical context without any explanation or justification in religious texts.

What also remains unexplained in the Purāṇas is

Gaṇapati's association with the *navagrahas* (nine planets). Images of the deity with the *navagrahas,* dating to about the seventh century, have been found essentially in Orissa, Bengal and Gujarat.[164] Gaṇapati is always placed at the extreme right of the *navagrahas,* next to Ravi, the sun. A carved *navagraha* slab was found near the ancient ruins of Kankandighi (District of 24 Parganas, West Bengal), where the images of the Nine Planets are represented standing in a row with Gaṇapati. Although two *navagraha* slabs have been found in Bengal with the image of Gaṇapati accompanying them, it is not known where these slabs originally came from since there is no ancient temple in Bengal still standing.[165] In Orissa, often, only eight planets were depicted and they were found in Śaiva temples. They belong to the late sixth or early seventh century. In the famous Paraśurāmeśvara temple (AD 650), which is the best known of the earliest Orissan temples, images of the *mātṛs,* the *navagrahas,* Lakulīśa, Gaṇapati and Kārttikeya are present. Although the *Purāṇas* do not provide any explanation, the origin of this association can be sought in the Vināyaka propitiation rites described in the *Mānava Gṛhya Sūtra* where the planets are invoked after the Vināyakas.

AS AN INDEPENDENT DEITY IN THE PURĀṆAS

There are some Purāṇas, like the *Agni Purāṇa,*[166] where chapters are devoted to the worship of Gaṇapati as a deity in his own right. He is depicted as a personality quite distinct to the Gaṇeśa who is Śiva's *gaṇa.* The nature of the *pūjā* itself shows how the Purāṇas have absorbed a non-Brahmanical ritual wholesale into their fold. It does not include the worship of any other deity and the influence of Tantrism is evident. There is emphasis on the importance of the preceptor, the *yantra* (mystical diagram) the *mudrā* (gesture) and the *mantra* (incantation)[167] As in the case of the Tantras the *sādhanā* (worship) consists of two parts, *pūjā* (ritual worship) and *yoga* (meditation).[168] However, unlike Tantric texts which recommend the use of the *pañcamakāras* (five essentials, i.e. wine, meat, fish, gesture and sexual intercourse), the offerings to Gaṇapati in Puranic religion are purely vegetarian, and do not include any intoxicants either. Clearly, non-Brahmanical practices related to Gaṇapati cannot be ignored once the deity has been Brahmanized. The process of evolution is a continuous one. On the one hand, the deity is used to perpetuate Brahmanical norms of caste and *dharma*. On the other hand, he is associated with all categories of society and with rituals that are borrowed from non-Brahmanical sources, thereby, making him a Brahmanical deity, accessible to all.

Like in other aspects of Gaṇapati's personality and worship, there is ambiguity in his association with the *caturthī* at an initial stage. According to the *Rudrasaṃhitā* of the *Śiva Purāṇa*, Gaṇapati was born on the fourth day of the waning moon in the *bhādrapada* month at the auspicious hour of moonrise, and so this is the most auspicious day for his worship.[169] According to the *Vidyeśvarasaṃhitā* of the same *Purāṇa*, the days of special worship of Gaṇapati are Fridays, the fourth days of the waxing moon in the months of *śrāvaṇa* (July/August) and *bhādrapada*.[170] At other times the *caturthī* in the month of *āṣādha* (June/July) is considered specially auspicious for the worship of Gaṇeśa.[171] According to the *Varāha Purāṇa*, the *vighnahara* rite, for the purpose of warding off obstacles should be performed on the *caturthī* in the month of *phālguna* (February/March).[172] Yet, at other times the *caturthī* in the month of *pauṣa* (December/January) is considered specially auspicious.[173] If sometimes Fridays are considered particularly auspicious for the worship of Gaṇapati, at other times it is stated that if the *caturthī* coincides with Sunday or Tuesday in any of the twelve months, it yields special benefits. Further, all the *caturthīs*, whether of the dark half or of the bright half of the month, are considered auspicious for the worship of Vighneśa, the Lord of Obstacles. Eventually, the month of *bhādrapada* becomes the most popular one for the celebration of the Gaṇeśa *caturthī*.[174]

Gaṇapati, like the other Gods who figure in the *pañcāyatana pūjā*, is to be worshipped in his image. Clay idols are particularly recommended. However, an idol made of metal, coral or white *arka (Calotropis gigantea)* flowers can also be installed.[175] Among the articles that are specially associated with Gaṇapati worship are vermillion, the *ketaka (Pandanus odoratissimus*, the Screw Palm or the modern *keora*) flower, the *arka* flower and root.[176]

The *gāyatrīs* to the the elephant deity mentioned in the *Maitrāyaṇī Saṃhitā* and the *Taittirīya Āraṇyaka* are modified and there is specific reference to Mahāgaṇapati. The *Bhaviṣya Purāṇa* describes the *mantra* as *Mahāgaṇapataye vidmahe, vakratuṇḍāya dhīmahī, tanno Dantiḥ pracodāyāt.*[177] The *Agni Purāṇa* describes it as

Lambodarāya vidmahe mahodarāya dhīmahī tanno Dantiḥ pracōdayāt. In both cases, the appellation *dantiḥ* is retained which associates these *gāyatrīs* with the earlier ones in the *Maitrāyaṇī Saṃhitā* and the *Taittirīya Āraṇyaka.* However, the epithets Mahāgaṇapati and Lambodara are those that are clearly associated with the Puranic elephant-headed deity.

Gaṇapati-Vināyaka is created by the *brāhmaṇas.* He is then imposed upon the community at large and Brahmanical rites and practices are superimposed on his non-Brahmanical associations. According to the *Padma Purāṇa,* a *brāhmaṇa* should first worship Gaṇeśa before performing any sacrifice. This ensures great religious merit.[178] In the *Liṅga Purāṇa,* Śiva tells Gaṇapati, 'my son, you are born for the destruction of *daityas* and for rendering help unto *devas* and *brāhmaṇas,* the expounders of the *Vedas*'.[179] If Gaṇapati is created to destroy *asuras,* it is because at the origin, he was looked upon as an *asura* himself. It is typical of the Purāṇas that the most powerful and popular non-Brahmanical element in the cultural tradition of a region is isolated and then transformed and used for the promotion and transmission of Brahmanical norms. The worship of Gaṇapati is thrust upon all other rituals by the menace of ill-luck if this injunction is not adhered to. Śiva is made to say 'O son, even when the *brāhmaṇas* worship me as Nārāyaṇa or Brahmā or when they perform sacrificial rites you will be worshipped at the outset. If any one performs auspicious rites laid down in the *Sruti* or *Smṛti* or any wordly ceremony without worshipping you at the outset, it will be turned inauspicious.'[180]

Once Gaṇapati is made into a Brahmanical god, he is used to ensure the maintenance of the caste structure. One prayer implores the deity to 'remove the vital breaths of men and women fallen off from their castes'.[181] Patronage of the *brāhmaṇas* is ensured by prayers to Gaṇapati to create impediments in the rituals performed without the offering of monetary gifts to *brāhmaṇas.*[182] In a myth of the *Skanda Purāṇa,*[183] Gaṇapati is depicted as looking after the welfare of the *brāhmaṇas.* The text describes how before the *Kali yuga,* women, barbarians, *śūdras* and other sinners entered heaven by visiting the shrine of Somanātha. Asceticism, gifts to *brāhmaṇas* and other obligatory rites ceased to be performed and heaven became crowded with men. Sacrifice was destroyed and the earth emptied; heaven became so overcrowded that people had to stand holding their arms straight up. Then Indra and the gods became distressed at being overrun by men, and sought refuge with Śiva blaming him for the overpopulation of heaven. But Śiva could do nothing. So Pārvatī created Gaṇapati to impose obstacles before men so that they would be deluded and defeated by desire and go to hell instead of coming to Somanātha. Gaṇapati is obviously associated with the *śūdras* but used by the *brāhmaṇas* to defend themselves against this very category.

NOTES

1. Sudhakar Chattopadhyaya, *Evolution of Hindu Sects*, p. 113.
2. Ibid., p. 123.
3. Ibid.
4. R.N. Nandi, *Social Roots of Religion in Ancient India*, p. 102.
5. Ibid.
6. *Vāyu Purāṇa*, I.30.291-3.
7. *Liṅga Purāṇa*, II.96.106.
8. Ibid., I.42.1-15.
9. Ibid., I.42.32.
10. *Varāha Purāṇa*, I.213.30-70.
11. *Liṅga Purāṇa*, II.107.55-8.
12. *Vāyu Purāṇa*, I.30.122-4.
13. *Liṅga Purāṇa*, II.96.4-5.
14. Ibid., II.i.96.64-75.
15. Ibid., II.i.99 and 100.
16. *Śiva Purāṇa*, II.v. 57.
17. *Kūrma Purāṇa*, I.32.16-18.
18. *Vājasaneyī Saṃhitā*, III: 61, III:58. Quoted by Sukumari Bhattacharji, *The Indian Theogany*, p. 109;
19. *Mahābhārata*, XIII:17. Quoted by Sukumari Bhattacharji, op. cit., p. 111.
20. *Skanda Purāṇa*, III.11.72b-77.
21. Ibid., III.11.44b-49.
22. Ibid., III.10.53.
23. Madeleine Biardeau, 'The Śamī Tree and the Sacrificial Buffalo', *Contributions to Indian Sociology (NS)*, Vol. 18, 1, 1984, pp. 1-23.
24. *Śiva Purāṇa*, II.V. 57.7.
25. Alf Hiltebeitel, 'The Indus Valley "Proto-Śiva", Reexamined through Reflections on the Goddess, the Buffalo and the Symbolism of *vāhanas*', *Anthropos*, Vol. 73, 1978, pp. 767-97. See in particular, p. 782.
26. K.V. Soundara Rajan, *Cave Temples of the Deccan*, p. 82.

27. Ibid., p. 191.
28. Carol Radcliffe Bolon, 'Two Chalukya Queens and their Commemorative Temples', in Vidya Dehejia, ed., *Royal Patrons and Great Temple Art*, p. 71.
29. In the *Mahābhārata* Śiva is referred to as *śṛṅgī* (having horns—Anuśāsana Parva, 17.147), *śṛṅgapriya* (fond of horns—ibid.), *vṛṣaśṛṅga* (having horns like those of a bull—Droṇa Parva, 173.30) and *viṣāṇi* (wearing horns—Anuśāsana Parva, 17.69). He is also referred to as *vṛṣaṇa* Saṅkara (horned Saṅkara—ibid., 17.80).
30. T.A. Gopinatha Rao, *Elements of Hindu Iconography*, Vol. II, Part II, p. 177.
31. Ibid., p. 180.
32. V.N. Drabu, *Śaivāgamas, A Study in the Socio-Economic Ideas and Institutions of Kashmir (200 BC -AD 700)*, p. 221
33. K.V. Soundara Rajan, op. cit., pp. 192-3.
34. Alice Getty, *Gaṇeśa*, p. 15.
35. *Nārada Purāṇa*, V.50.55-6.
36. *Liṅga Purāṇa*, I.92.79-80 and 84.
37. *Śiva Purāṇa*, IV.i.27.
38. J.N. Banerjea, *The Development of Hindu Iconography*, p. 129.
39. J.C. Harle, *The Art and Architecture of the Indian Subcontinent*, pp. 64-5.
40. Ibid., p. 95.
41. R.C. Agrawala, 'Ūrdhavaretas Gaṇeśa from Afghanistan', *EW*, Vol. 18 (NS), 1968, pp. 166-8. The author discusses the dates ascribed to these two statues by various scholars. Tucci considers the statue from Gardez to belong to the end of the fifth or beginning of the sixth century. D.C. Sircar prefers to ascribe it to the sixth or seventh centuries. As for the one found at Sakar Dhar, T.N. Ramachandran in his unpublished report of the Indian Archaeological Delegation in Afghanistan in 1956 suggests the fourth century as the probable date of this Gaṇapati.
42. Photo No. 509 in the Mathura Museum. See V.S. Agrawala, 'Miscellaneous Architectural Sculptures: Buddhist', *JUPHS*, Vol. XXIX-XXV, 1951-2, pp. 77-118. See in particular p. 96.
43. R.C. Agrawala, 'Ūrdhvaretas Gaṇeśa from Afghanistan', *EW*, op. cit.
44. J.N. Banerjea, op. cit., p. 123.
45. J.C. Harle, 'Towards Understanding Gupta Sculpture', in Karl Khandalavala, ed., *The Golden Age*, p. 8.
46. Ibid., 104.
47. *Mahābhārata*, XIII:17. Quoted by Sukumari Bhattacharji, op. cit., p. 111.
48. J.N. Banerjea, op. cit., p. 536.

49. Ibid., p. 534.
50. *Skanda Purāṇa*, I.10.28.
51. Robert L. Brown, 'Gaṇeśa in Southeast Asian Art', in Robert L. Brown, ed., *Ganesh*, pp. 171-99.
52. Ibid.
53. D.C. Sircar, op. cit., p. 114.
54. M.K. Dhavalikar, 'Gaṇeśa: Myth and Reality,' in Robert L. Brown, ed., op. cit., pp. 49-67.
55. Alice Getty, op. cit., p. 22.
56. M.A. Stein, *Kalhaṇa's Rājataraṅgiṇī*, Vol. II, p. 282.
57. *Narasiṃha Purāṇa*, 26.6,8,13, cited in P.V. Kane, *History of Dharmaśāstra*, Vol. V, Pt. I, p. 149.
58. *Liṅga Purāṇa*, II.100.41-51.
59. *Kūrma Purāṇa*, II.31.31.
60. Sukumari Bhattacharji, *The Indian Theogony*, p. 181.
61. *Liṅga Purāṇa*, I.72.114-21.
62. *Brahma Purāṇa*, IV.44.8. (Gautami Māhātmya)
63. *Viṣṇudharmottara Purāṇa*, I.225.3.
64. Sara L. Schastok, *The Śāmalājī Sculptures and Sixth Century Art in Western India*, p. 70.
65. Ibid., p. 1.
66. G. S. Ghurye, *Gods and Men*, p. 77.
67. Alice Getty, op. cit., pp. 27-8. See also Aschwin de Lippe, *Indian Medieval Sculpture*, p. 138.
68. *Śiva Purāṇa*, II.iv.13.20.
69. *Skanda Purāṇa*, Venkateshwara Press edn., Śrī Brahmkhaṇḍa, II.12.23.
70. *Matsya Purāṇa*, I.154.502-4.
71. *Bhaviṣya Purāṇa*, 2.4.31-3.
72. *Vāmana Purāṇa* , 28.64-6 and 28.57-9 (Saromāhātmya)
73. *Bṛhaddharma Purāṇa*, 2.60.35-50.
74. *Varāha Purāṇa*, I.23.9-18.
75. *Brahma Purāṇa*, IV.44.10-12 (Gautamī Māhātmya).
76. *Varāha Purāṇa*, I.23.20-9.
77. *Śiva Purāṇa*, II.iv.16.
78. Ibid., II.v.21.13-18.
79. *EI*, Vol. XXXVII, pp. 125-30
80. *Brahma Purāṇa*, IV.44.11.
81. *Liṅga Purāṇa*, I.82.92-5.
82. *Matsya Purāṇa*, II.158.24-42.
83. *Śiva Purāṇa*, II.iv.2. for birth of Kārttikeya and II.iv.13 for Gaṇeśa.
84. *Brahmavaivarta Purāṇa*, III.44.85.
85. *Nārada Purāṇa*, IV.i.113.31-7.
86. *Varāha Purāṇa*, I.23 and I.25.

87. G.S. Ghurye, op. cit., p. 70.
88. *EI*, Vol. XV, No. 15, pp. 278-86.
89. *Śiva Purāṇa*, II.iv.19 and 20.
90. Ibid., II.iv.19.52.
91. *Liṅga Purāṇa*, I.82.92-5.
92. Ibid.
93. Ibid., I.44.38-9.
94. Ibid., I.82.26-9.
95. *Śiva Purāṇa*, IV.11.17-21.
96. *Brahmavaivarta Purāṇa*, III.17.14-19
97. Ibid., III.17.23.
98. In the *Viṣṇudharmottara Purāṇa*, Śiva, in his aspect of Bhairava, is described as having 'a flabby belly (other texts give pot-belly) and round yellow (or red) eyes, side tusks and wide nostrils'. See Alice Getty, op. cit., p. 13. There is an image dated to late fifth century AD, from Mansar, Maharashtra, presently at the National Museum, Delhi, which depicts Śiva as a corpulent dwarf. Sivaramamurti has drawn attention to the *Śatarudriya*, a celebrated Vedic text, in which allusions are made to the dwarf form of Śiva, and this unique image may be related to some such concept.
99. *Śiva Purāṇa*, II.iv.2.68.
100. Ibid., II.iv.18.35-7.
101. *Varāha Purāṇa*, I.23.10-15.
102. R.G. Bhandarkar, *Vaiṣṇavism, Śaivism and Minor Religious Systems*, p. 127.
103. *Śiva Purāṇa*, IV.ii.21.21-2.
104. *Liṅga Purāṇa*, I.21.59.
105. *Skanda Purāṇa*, VII.i.325.2.
106. *Vāyu Purāṇa*, I.30.214.
107. Ibid., I.30.238.
108. *Brahmavaivarta Purāṇa*, III.44.85.
109. *Liṅga Purāṇa*, I.82.25-110.
110. *Śiva Purāṇa*, II.v.19.51.
111. *Agni Purāṇa*, I.21.9-14.
112. Ibid., I.2.22.
113. Ibid., II.25.
114. Ibid., I.96.
115. *Matsya Purāṇa*, II.266.42-9.
116. *Nārada Purāṇa*, III.i.91.1-30.
117. *Liṅga Purāṇa*, I.27.1-23.
118. *Agni Purāṇa*, II.i.179.1-5.
119. Ibid., III.i.301.1-7.
120. *Liṅga Purāṇa*, II.i.104.3-6.
121. *Padma Purāṇa*, II.i.63.29-31.

122. *Bhaviṣya Purāṇa*, I.30.19-21.
123. *Nārada Purāṇa*, III.73.146-7.
124. Ibid., III.i.73.148-51.
125. Ibid., III.i.73.152-63.
126. Ibid.,III.i.78.20-3.
127. *Varāha Purāṇa*, II.i.160.10.
128. *Nārada Purāṇa*, III.74.19.
129. Ibid., III.74.199-202.
130. Ibid., III.75.79; III.75.42-4.
131. *Skanda Purāṇa*, Venkateshwara Press edn., V.i.3.34; VII.ii.17.115.
132. *Matsya Purāṇa*, II.260.1-21.
133. Pratapaditya Pal, *The Ideal Image*, p. 30.
134. There is a myth in the *Bhāgavata Purāṇa* about a pair of Arjuna trees who in their former birth were two *guhyakas* and sons of Kubera (IV.x.9.22-3 and IV.x.10). They were known as Nala Kubera and Maṇigrīva. Due to a curse by Nārada they were transformed into trees. Eventually they are uprooted and redeemed by the child Kṛṣṇa, whose fervent devotees they then become.
135. *Nārada Purāṇa*, III.79.131-5.
136. Ibid., III.75.49.
137. *Brahmāṇḍa Purāṇa*, II.iii.43.6.
138. *Brahmavaivarta Purāṇa*, III.12.14-22.
139. Ibid., III.6.92.
140. *Brahmavaivarta Purāṇa*, II.34.62 and IV.9.10-12.
141. Ibid., III.13.60.
142. *Nārada Purāṇa*, IV.113.2-5.
143. *Varāha Purāṇa*, II.i.160.11-14.
144. *Narasiṃha Purāṇa*, I.25.24.
145. Ibid., I.25.1-4.
146. *EI*, Vol. I, No. 33, pp. 287-93.
147. *Brahma Purāṇa*, I.26.40.
148. *Vāyu Purāṇa*, II.14.2.
149. *Mārkaṇḍeya Purāṇa*, 96.31.
150. *Vāyu Purāṇa*, II.14.34. and *Nārada Purāṇa*, I.14.89.
151. *Agni Purāṇa*, I.96.3.
152. *Nārada Purāṇa*, III.i.65—see footnote on page 936 of this text.
153. H. Cousens, *The Chalukyan Architecture of the Kanarese Districts*, pp. 21-2. This is usually the case when the Gaṇapati temple is not the principal one in a complex. The *aṣṭavināyaka* and some of the other important Gaṇapati temples generally face east or, in some cases, north, like many Śiva temples.
154. J. Ph. Vogel, op. cit., p. 201.
155. Ved Kumari, *The Nīlamata Purāṇa*, Vol. I. p. 162.
156. *Vāyu Purāṇa*, II.21.84.

157. Ibid., II.18.58 and 62.
158. *Mārkaṇḍeya Purāṇa*, 33.8 and *Matsya Purāṇa*, II.204.7-8., and many other references.
159. Ibid., II.21.84.
160. *Nārada Purāṇa*, III.i.67.56.
161. Shiela L. Weiner, *From Gupta to Pāla Sculpture*, p. 173.
162. Lawrence Cohen, 'The Wives of Gaṇeśa', in Robert L. Brown, ed., op. cit., pp. 115-40.
163. Kantilal F. Sompura, *The Structural Temples of Gujarat*, p. 81.
164. In the *Mānava Gṛhya Sūtra* the rites for Vināyaka propitiation are followed by the worship of the seven goddesses and then of the Sun. In the *Yājñavalkya Smṛti* Vināyaka propitiation precedes the rites for the *grahas*. These different themes gradually manifest themselves in the cult of Gaṇapati.
165. Alice Getty, op. cit., p. 30.
166. *Agni Purāṇa*, I.71.
167. *Śiva Purāṇa*, II.iv.18.
168. Sanjukta Gupta, Dirk Jan Hoens and Teun Goudriaan, *Hindu Tantrism*, p. 121.
169. *Śiva Purāṇa*, II.iv.18.35-7.
170. Ibid., I.ii.16.21-2.
171. *Nārada Purāṇa*, IV.113.6.
172. *Varāha Purāṇa*, I.59.
173. *Nārada Purāṇa*, IV.i.113.70b-71.
174. In the contemporary worship of Gaṇapati in Maharashtra, both the fourth day of the bright half of the lunar month as also the fourth day of the dark half are considered important. The fourth day of the dark half of the month is called *Saṅkaṣṭa caturthī* (dangerous fourth) and is considered inauspicious to begin any new undertaking. *Pūjā* performed on this day is done with the aim of averting ill luck and obstacles. However, the fourth day of the bright half of the month is called *Vināyaka caturthī* (Gaṇapati's fourth) and this is the day believed to represent Gaṇapati's positive side and considered auspicious for new undertakings. This day is also celebrated as his birthday.
175. *Śiva Purāṇa*, II.iv.18.42-3.
176. *Bhaviṣya Purāṇa*, I.20.3.
177. Ibid., I.30.15.
178. *Padma Purāṇa*, II.i.63.20-1.
179. *Liṅga Purāṇa*, II.i.105.15.
180. Ibid., II.i.105.22.
181. Ibid., II.i.105.15.
182. *Liṅga Purāṇa*, II.i.105.15-23.
183. *Skanda Purāṇa*, Venkateshwara Press edn., VII.1.38.

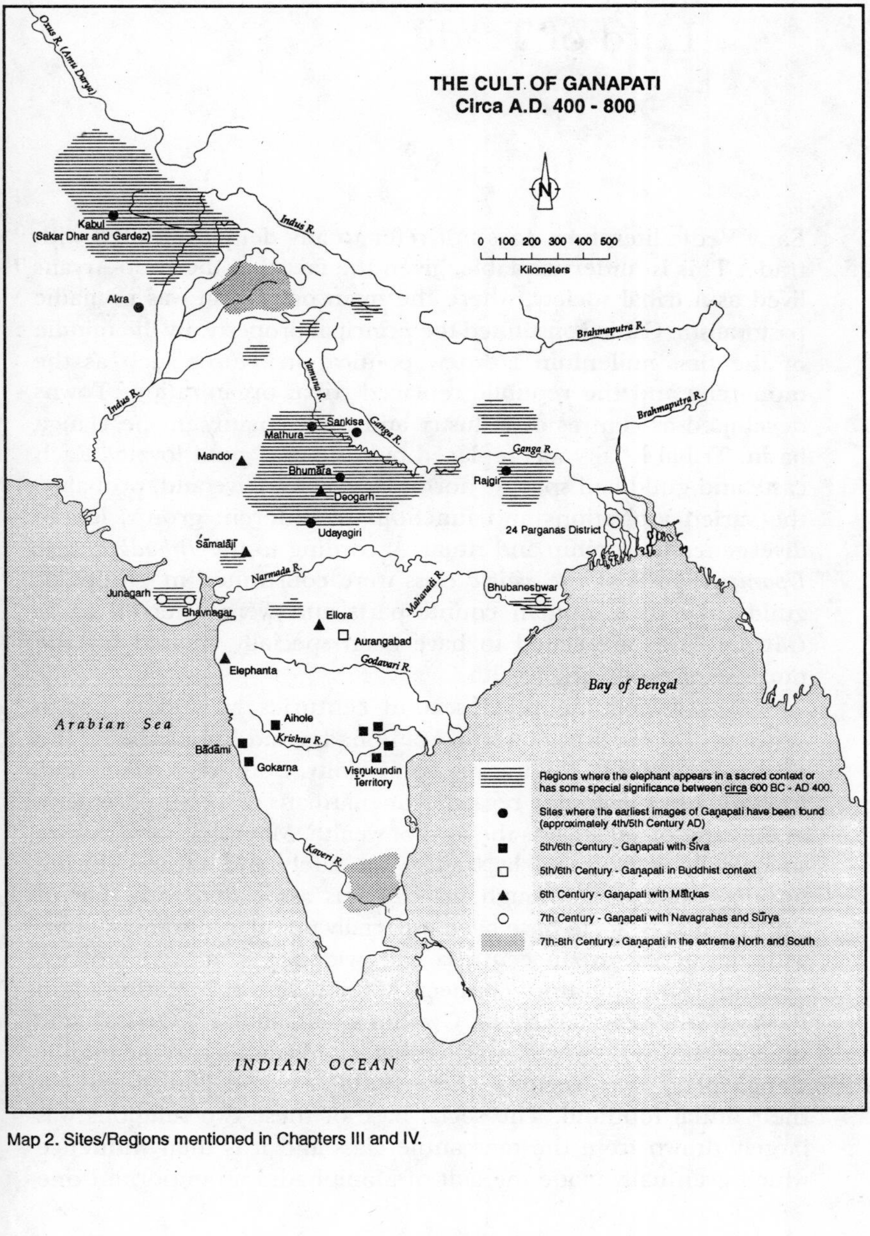
THE CULT OF GANAPATI
Circa A.D. 400 - 800
N
0 100 200 300 400 500
Kilometers
Oxus R. (Amu Darya)
Indus R.
Kabul
(Sakar Dhar and Gardez)
Akra
Brahmaputra R.
Yamuna R.
Indus R.
Brahmaputra R.
Sankisa
Mathura
Ganga R.
Ganga R.
Mandor
Bhumāra
Rajgir
Deogarh
Udayagiri
24 Parganas District
Śāmalāji
Narmada R.
Mahanadi R.
Junagarh
Bhavnagar
Bhubaneshwar
Ellora
Aurangabad
Godavari R.
Elephanta
Bay of Bengal
Arabian Sea
Aihole
Krishna R.
Bādāmi
Gokarṇa
Viṣṇukundin
Territory
Kaveri R.
INDIAN OCEAN
Regions where the elephant appears in a sacred context or has some special significance between circa 600 BC - AD 400.
Sites where the earliest images of Gaṇapati have been found (approximately 4th/5th Century AD)
5th/6th Century - Gaṇapati with Śiva
5th/6th Century - Gaṇapati in Buddhist context
6th Century - Gaṇapati with Mātṛkas
7th Century - Gaṇapati with Navagrahas and Sūrya
7th-8th Century - Gaṇapati in the extreme North and South

Map 2. Sites/Regions mentioned in Chapters III and IV.

CHAPTER 5

Lord of Trade

Early Vedic literature does not refer to any deity associated with trade. This is understandable, given the fact that the Indo-Aryans lived as a tribal society, where the main ocupation was nomadic pastoralism. Cattle constituted the principal property. By the middle of the first millenium BC, new political structures such as the monarchy and the republic replaced tribal organization. Towns developed as centres of industry and trade mainly in the Ganga basin. Tribal loyalty was replaced by caste and guild loyalty. Each caste and guild had specific norms by which to live and, probably, the varied aspirations and functions of different groups led to divergence in worship and ritual. According to the *Bṛhadāraṇyaka Upaniṣad,* gods of the *vaiśya* class were constituted in groups or guilds like their human counterparts and were referred to as *Gaṇaśa.* They are stated to have been specially created for the purpose of producing wealth.[1]

Between the third/second centuries BC and the sixth century AD there is evidence of Maṇibhadra and Kubera being the principal deities of the trading community. Both were *yakṣas* and, traditionally, *yakṣas* were regarded as guardians of treasure. Kubera, as the king of *yakṣas,* was the lord of wealth. Maṇibhadra was more specifically worshipped by traders for safety and success during business voyages. Although his cult was associated with that of Kubera, it appears to have been especially popular in some regions with important urban centres. The evidence from archaeology, epigraphy and literature connects Maṇibhadra with Mathura and Pawaya (old Padmāvatī in Gwalior),[2] Magadha,[3] Orissa[4] and Brahmavatī (in the region of Gandhāra).[5] Magadha and the middle Ganga plain were regions where Buddhism and Jainism gained their initial foothold. The social base of these two religions was largely drawn from the mercantile class and it is their influence which eventually made the cult of Maṇibhadra an important one within the Buddhist and Jaina contexts. The deity is often mentioned in the Pāli works of the Buddhists and the Prākrit canons of the Śvetāmbara Jainas.

Until the first two centuries of the Christian era, Maṇibhadra was associated with categories of people who were not particularly high in the caste hierarchy. The *Milindapañha*[6] refers to Maṇibhaddas or followers of the Maṇibhadra cult together with tumblers, jugglers and actors. His gradual acceptance by Buddhism and Jainism and his growing popularity with a category of people who were affluent, eventually led to his worship being adopted even by some *brāhmaṇas* because of the wealthy patronage that ensured. A story in the *Mahābhārata* describes how a *brāhmaṇa* who, in his desire to perform *yajñas,* is constantly in need of wealth. He finally turns to Maṇibhadra to provide him with what he needs. The *yakṣarāja* Maṇibhadra, who is referred to as *Dhanadātā Deva,* fulfills his demands but only with the permission of the Brahmanical gods.[7]

There is evidence of images of Maṇibhadra being worshipped from as early as the first century BC. The Parkham image of the *yakṣarāja* Maṇibhadra[8] dates to this period and appears to be the earliest of its kind. A second image was found at Pawaya and is dated to the first or second century of the Christian era.[9] The dedicatory inscription declares that the members of the *goṣṭha* (corporation) for whom the image was set up called themselves Maṇibhadra *bhaktas* (devotees).[10] The left hand of the image grasps a money bag. This *goṣṭha* was obviously one of merchants or traders. An inscription discovered in the vicinity of Kosam, the ancient Kausambi,[11] records the erection of a stone railing (*vedikā*) by a certain Gotiputa who was a caravan-merchant and a votary of Maṇibhadra. The inscription begins with a salutation to a certain Bhagavat whose name, unfortunately, is not given and ends with the wish that the deity may be pleased. The deity probably refers to Maṇibhadra given the fact that Gotiputa was his devotee.

The title *Mahārāja-Sirī-Gaṇaśa* appears in the first line of a poorly preserved inscription of about the third century AD.[12] D.C. Sircar interprets this as reference to a ruler called Śrī-Gaṇa during whose reign the grant recorded in the inscription was made. However, the existence of such a ruler is not confirmed by any other source. It is, therefore, not improbable that Sirī-*Gaṇaśa* refers not to a ruler, but to a deity. Since one of the meanings of the term *gaṇa* is a 'corporation of traders and artisans',[13] *Gaṇaśa* (Lord of the *Gaṇa*) could also signify the lord of a guild of traders or artisans. The inscription records the installation of three idols by a certain Mūlajapa. This may have implied the setting up of a shrine dedicated to *Gaṇaśa* and other deities associated with him. Mahārāja may be an honorific title for the deity just as it sometimes is for Kubera or the Buddhist *lokapālas.* The inscription has been found in Orissa. While it cannot be definitely said that Sirī-*Gaṇaśa* signifies Maṇibhadra, it is likely that he was a deity associated with traders. Mūlajapa must have been a wealthy man if he could set up three idols and gift land for their maintenance. Since he does not claim to be a king or a member of a royal family, and does not associate himself with any particular geneology, it is possible that he was a merchant of some means. The inscription suggests that traders had their own deities and it was not uncommon for them to set up their images for worship. Some of the earliest inscriptions of the Christian era are those of traders.

The Jātakas provide numerous examples of rituals performed by traders before setting out on their perilous travels. They made animal sacrifices to some deity and vowed to make more if the journeys were profitable. Such deities were usually associated with a tree outside the village, in a grove or in the dense jungle. Sacrifices were also made at the cross-roads with fish, flesh and wine in bowls or sherds for the purpose of averting evil influences and obstacles.[14] The erection of a stone railing referred to in the Kosam inscription, mentioned earlier, may have been in commemoration of a safe return. Maṇibhadra probably had shrines in the town as well as special sacred trees in the forest or on the periphery of the town. There is reference to a temple of Maṇibhadra in the city which served as a place for determining whether husbands and wives had been unfaithful.[15] Such a practice must have been particularly relevant in the case of travelling merchants who had to absent themselves for long periods.

The Āraṇyaka Parva describes the plight of a group of merchants attacked by wild elephants in a jungle. Many are killed and much merchandise is ruined. The survivors ask themselves why it happened. They come to the conclusion that it was because the *Mahāyakṣa* Maṇibhadra and Kubera were not worshipped.[16] They further state that they did not perform *pūjā* of the *vighnakartas* (creators of obstacles) at the outset. These *vighnakartas* represented the various evils and obstacles that could beset those setting out on long, perilous journeys. That is why the worship of the guardians of the quarters was considered important. The twenty-fourth chapter of the *Lalitavistara* and the *Mahāvastu* describe the meeting of the Buddha with two merchants. The chapter concludes with a benedictory hymn, in which the protection of the four quarters is invoked for itinerant merchants.[17] According to these two texts, each quarter is represented by a group of seven *nakṣatras,* one of the Buddhist *lokapālas* and one Brahmanical *lokapāla.* If Kubera was the guardian of the northern quarter for the Buddhists, the latter considered Maṇibhadra to be his Brahmanical equivalent.[18] The Vināyakas of the *Mānava Gṛhya Sūtra* were similar in concept to the *vighnakartas* in that they represented the numerous ills that threatened every category and age-group of society. They were eventually identified with the *vighnakartas.*

Initially, Maṇibhadra was an insignificant deity in the Brahmanical context. This was probably due to the fact that traders and their activities were looked down upon. According to the *Vāyu Purāṇa* a merchant is among the persons who cannot be invited to a *śrāddha* (ceremony performed in honour of the dead). It is said that, 'what is given to a trader is not beneficial here or hereafter.... That which is given to a merchant or an artisan devoid of virtue becomes lost; a merchant despises (underrates) the commodities while purchasing and praises (the same) while selling. Hence a merchant, the abode of untruth, does not deserve (invitation to) a *śrāddha.*'[19] Again, according to the *Vāyu Purāṇa,* 'In this *yuga,* people will have trading propensity. By false measures, the buyers will be deceived of their due share in the commodities'.[20] One reason for this attitude was because many of the wealthy traders and merchants were Buddhists or Jainas. Since they did not patronize the *brāhmaṇas,* the latter felt cheated of the privileges and wealth they had received from this community in the past.

Maṇibhadra's association with the trading class is suggested in some of the *vaiśya* professions and caste names which carry the epithet 'maṇi' (jewel). The *Smṛtis* and *Dharma Śāstras* refer to a caste, the Maṇikara, who were believed to be the offspring of a clandestine union between a *kṣatriya* male and a *vaiśya* female. Members of this caste gained their livelihood by working on beads, by perforating pearls and dealing in coral and conches. According to the *Sūtasaṃhitā*, however, they were the clandestine offspring of a *vaiśya* male from a *vaiśya* female.[21]

Eventually, Maṇibhadra came to be associated directly with wealth rather than with protection from dangers during business travels. He is invoked as Dhaneśvara in the *Nīlamata Purāṇa* which states that one becomes rich by the mere sight of him.[22] Since the *Nīlamata* reflects beliefs and practices in Kashmir between approximately the seventh and ninth centuries AD it is clear that Maṇibhadra appears to have taken on the role of Kubera who perhaps did not have a regular cult. In the *Karpūracarita Bhāṇa* of Vatsarāja (twelfth/thirteenth centuries AD),[23] Maṇibhadra is described as the giver of victory in gambling, which confirms his position as the bestower of wealth.[24]

Like Maṇibhadra, Kubera, too, was often depicted holding a money bag. Several Gupta images of Kubera have been found in Rajasthan where he is depicted as a pot-bellied deity holding a money bag in one hand and a cup in the other.[25] Sometimes the cup is replaced by a round object as is the case of a Jaina sculpture discovered at Bansi and dated to about the seventh/eighth century AD. At Bhinmal there is a sculpture of a four armed Kubera in the famous temple of Varāha-Ghanaśyāma. It depicts the deity holding a purse like object in the upper two hands.[26] An elephant stands to his left. The concept of prosperity and plenty is determined largely by the ecology of a place. In Rajasthan, where water is scarce, the image of Kubera is often found near step-wells. One such sculpture was found on a brick platform in front of the step-well inside the Caṇḍināth temple at Bhinmal (*c.* seventh/eighth centuries AD).[27]

Unlike Maṇibhadra who is usually invoked alone, Kubera appears to have been closely associated with Lakṣmī, the goddess of wealth and prosperity. The *Mahābhārata* describes Lakṣmī as being present in the abode of Kubera.[28] Several sculptures of the Kuṣāṇa period provide evidence of the worship of Lakṣmī together with that of Kubera.[29] This is not surprising. Originally, Lakṣmī was a non-Vedic goddess connected with vegetation and fertility. She was popular with agriculturists and herdsmen. As trade became an important activity and prosperity took on different connotations, even traders came to worship her. The Buddhist sources reflect this association between Śrī or Lakṣmī and the merchant community. Their names often contain the prefix Śrī and these names are very common in the Buddhist votive inscriptions of the second/first century BC.[30]

The affiliation between Lakṣmī and traders is further borne out by some ancient coins, such as the *negama* series of the inscribed coins of Taxila. *Negama* corresponds to the 'traders' or 'market merchant guild quarter of a city'. In any case, it indicates mercantile money tokens issued by traders (second century BC).[31] On the obverse of some of these coins a female figure is depicted with a lotus in the right hand. Her pose is similar to that of the Lakṣmī on the coins of Mathura and elsewhere, although she does not stand on a lotus. Among the coins of Mathura, dated between 200-50 BC and included as tribal coins, the standing figure of a goddess holding a lotus in her uplifted right hand appears on the obverse. She is quite clearly meant to represent Lakṣmī. On the reverse are depicted three elephants with riders holding goads.[32] These, evidently, represent merchants.[33] The traditional symbol of the merchant class was the elephant goad. It probably signified the travels of merchants and the transport of large-scale merchandise which often must have taken place on elephant back.

Śrī was first accepted into the Vedic pantheon and associated with Indra. Like her, the latter, too, was the bestower of rain, fertility and abundance. Just as Pārvatī came to represent the various Mother Goddesses, so also Lakṣmī absorbed within her the cult of the several goddesses of fertility and prosperity. She was associated with Indra, then with Kubera. On rare occasions she was associated with Maṇibhadra but in the company of Kubera. In the seventh hymn of the *Śrī-Sūkta* the worshipper implores the goddess to come to him with Devaśakha (Kubera), Kīrti and Maṇi.[34]

Gaṇapati's association with Kubera and Lakṣmī begins from around the late fifth/early sixth centuries. There are numerous examples of images from Mathura where Gajalakṣmī is shown flanked by the pot-bellied figures of Gaṇapati and Kubera.[35] Mathura was one of the main centres of trade with the western countries. Jaina merchants had concentrated in this region since Sātavāhana times, generously subsidising the erection of Jaina monasteries and temples.[36] In Rajasthan, a sculpture from Ābānerī (now preserved at the archaeological museum at Amber) presents Gaṇapati, Gajalakṣmī and Kubera seated in a row. Kubera holds what appears to be a cup of wine in his right hand and a female figure holding a flask in her hands can be seen by his side. This relief is dated to the eighth century.[37] It is possible that these early statues of Gaṇapati with Lakṣmī and Kubera are Jaina ones. Probably, at this stage, Gaṇapati is not directly associated with wealth but only appears as the remover of obstacles for the acquisition of riches. This is confirmed by the Sakrai Stone Inscription, (AD 642-3)[38] found in the region of Jaipur, Rajasthan. It records the construction of a pavilion (*maṇḍapa*) in front of the goddess Śaṅkarā by an association or a committee of eleven bankers. The initial portion of this inscription invokes the blessings of three deities: Gaṇapati, Caṇḍikā and Dhanada. The invocation to Gaṇapati does not in any way associate him with trade or wealth as such. He is merely invoked to bestow blessings. It is Caṇḍikā who is invoked to shower prosperity and Dhanada to confer affluence.

It is significant that the earliest inscription where Gaṇapati is invoked before any other deity is by the merchant community. As mentioned earlier, the placation of the *vighnakartas* at the outset of a journey was an old practice performed by merchants and caravan leaders. Gaṇapati-Vināyaka gradually came to represent all forms of *vighnakartas* and was, therefore, readily worshipped before any other deity by the mercantile community. He is not generally referred to in inscriptions before the eighth century. On the rare occasions when he is, it is either to mark the setting up of his image along with that of Śiva or he is invoked after Śiva before the main text of the inscription. The eighth century Bhairavakonda Inscription of Vikramāditya (Andhra Pradesh), refers to the setting up of images of Daṇḍīśvara, Gaṇapati and Nandīśvara.[39] Another inscription from Baijnath in Kangra invokes Śiva, Gajāsya, Skanda, Nandi and Vīrabhadra. Even after the ninth century there is no epigraphical evidence of Gaṇapati being systematically invoked before other deities. More often than not, Śiva or Viṣṇu are invoked first.[40] Most inscriptions are in the name of kings and members of the nobility and Śiva and Viṣṇu were the two most popular deities with these categories. This makes the seventh century Sakrai Stone Inscription all the more significant. In at least one region, that of modern Rajasthan, Gaṇapati was invoked before other deities by a group of bankers. Neither Śiva nor Viṣṇu are mentioned. The three deities in question, Gaṇapati, Caṇḍikā and Kubera were evidently more popular with this community.

From the little evidence available, it would appear that Gaṇapati acquired this important position, initially, with specific families of bankers who were possibly, Jainas. In the case of the Sakrai Stone Inscription, it is worth noting that the bankers belong to two families—Dhūsara and Dharkkaṭa. The surname Dhūsara is still well-known in Rajasthan, but persons bearing this surname call themselves Bhārgava *brāhmaṇas,* though they are generally believed to have been originally *banias* (traders/shopkeepers). In this inscription, Maṇḍana Dhūsara, one of the members of the temple supervision committee is called a *śreṣṭhi* which clearly makes him a *vaiśya.* The name Dharkkaṭa has survived in the slightly altered form Dhākaḍ, a sub-division of the Osvāls.[41] The object of the inscription is to record the construction of a *maṇḍapa* in front of the goddess Śaṅkarā. The wordings of the inscription suggest that the pavilion was intended to receive images of various secondary deities by the side of the principal divinity that was Śaṅkarādevī. Possibly, what was dedicated by the *śreṣṭhins* was not a bare pavilion but a pavilion with images of various gods, including those of the three invoked in the inscription, each properly installed in its respective niche.[42] It is also likely that the wealthy and more resourceful merchants and bankers installed deities which were dear to them in various existing temples. At Osian there are two eleventh century images of Gaṇapati carved along with Kubera on the doorsills of small Jaina shrines that stand in the foreground of the Mahāvīra temple.[43] At the main shrine of the temple of Pippalada Mātā at Osian (Jodhpur District, Rajasthan), huge sculptures of Gaṇapati and Kubera are placed close to that of Mahiṣamardinī.[44] Here Mahiṣamardinī replaces Caṇḍikā of the Sakrai Stone Inscription.

By the ninth century in Rajasthan, Gaṇapati is specifically associated with trade and prosperity. The Ghatiyala Inscription of Pratīhāra Kakkuka[45] (AD 861) records the establishment of a *haṭṭa* (market) and *mahājanas* (traders) at Rohiṁsaka (identified with Ghatiyala) and Maḍḍodara (identified with Mandor). According to the insription, the Ghatiyala region had been deserted because of its being unsafe on account of the Abhīras. Kakkuka conquered the area and established markets in the villages of Rohiṁsaka and Maḍḍodara. *Brāhmaṇas, kṣatriyas* and *vaiśyas* were settled there by him. The inscription is engraved on a column, not far from an old ruined Jaina structure, now called Mātā-kī-sāl, about 35 km. from

Jodhpur. It begins with an obeisance to Vināyaka. No other deity is mentioned. The column itself is surmounted by a quadruple image of Gaṇapati facing the cardinal directions. This is the first time that four images of Gaṇapati are represented back to back. He evidently represents protection of the four quarters. It is significant that in this context only Vināyaka is invoked. Clearly, the deity was associated with material prosperity. It is also likely that he was a popular deity with the trading class, otherwise his image would not be installed in such a prominent position in a newly founded market centre. Possibly, it is because Kakkuka relied on the wealth generated by merchants and trade, that he accepted the establishment of the image of this deity, normally not associated with royal houses and the upper two castes. Elsewhere, images of Gaṇapati during this period appear essentially in shrines or for purposes of worship. Here the deity appears to have greater protective powers as the guardian *yakṣas* of old.

The Ghatiyala Pillar Inscription was written by a Maga *brāhmaṇa*. The Maga were originally foreigners who were associated with sun worship. They had been regarded in the early centuries of the Christian era with some suspicion from the point of view of ritual status. It is evident that by the time of this inscription they had established their bona fides even as the rulers they served had. The Pratīhāras of Mandor, who rose to prominence sometime in the eighth century, claimed descent from the *kṣatriya* wife of a *brāhmaṇa* implying *brahma-kṣatra* status. They claimed links with Lakṣmaṇa who acted as the *pratīhāra* (doorkeeper) of Rāma.[46] In fact, they were descended from Gurjara (shepherd) stock. It is possible that in the course of their rise to political prominence, this family may have been served by the Maga, themselves ritually low in Brahmanical hierarchy. As the family came into power the ritual status of the Maga serving them also improved.

Maga is another name for the Sākadvīpīya *brāhmaṇas*. These *brāhmaṇas* are known as *sevaks* in the region of Jodhpur and most of them are religious dependants of the Osvāl Śrāvakas. Some of the merchants settled in Maḍḍodara and Rohiṁsaka by Kakkuka may well have been Jainas. Perhaps one reason for the deity's early importance in this region is because this area was a stronghold of Jainism and the Jainas were a prosperous trading community. In a region where there was economic prosperity and where the merchant class was powerful, their influence must have been considerable. The period between approximately the fourth/fifth century and the tenth century is generally looked upon as one when trade and urban centres declined, when coins became scarce and when self-sufficient economies developed in most regions of the subcontinent. The Ghatiyala Pillar inscription provides an example to the contrary. Mandor and Rohiṁsaka were among the few places which actually witnessed a more advanced economy as a result of Pratīhāra Kakkuka's conquest. Vināyaka was the deity chosen to preside over this newly founded prosperity.

Another inscription dated AD 960 from the region of Alwar, Rajasthan, records the grant of the village Vyāghrapāṭaka for the purpose of defraying the expenses of performing rituals and maintenance of a Śiva temple established by a certain Mathanadeva, who claims to belong to the Gujarapratīhāra lineage.[47] This name does not appear in any other inscription or source and, possibly, Mathanadeva was a feudatory or subordinate of Vijayapāladeva who he refers to and who was king of Kanauj. The inscription records that certain additional taxes or tolls gathered from the various sources of revenue would be used for the temple as also for the shrine or image of Vināyaka which was set up close by. This inscription is addressed to the inhabitants of the village which include merchants (*vaṇik*). Further, there is reference to markets (*haṭṭa*) in the village. What is significant is that the Vināyaka shrine is given sufficient importance in this region. It is true the deity is part of a Śaiva temple but special provisions for his shrine may have been the consequence of the importance he already enjoyed with the trading community which had the inclination and the means of paying the various taxes or tolls for its maintenance.

A comparison between the origins of Maṇibhadra, Kubera and Gaṇapati would enable a better understanding of why Gaṇapati is closely linked to them and eventually takes on their role. All three were *yakṣas* and the elephant deity was originally also a *nāga* deity. The *yakṣas*, like the *nāgas*, are the traditional guardians of treasure. The term *maṇi* signifies jewel and, according to traditional belief, only the snake and the elephant carry a jewel within them.[48] The sacred elephant represented fertility and prosperity. Its cult was linked to that of the goddess. When Lakṣmī became the archetype of all goddesses of plenty, the sacred elephant, in its evolved form of Gaṇapati-Vināyaka, also came to be associated with her. If Lakṣmī has her *abhiṣeka* performed by elephants,

Gaṇapati too, in Tantric texts, has his *abhiṣeka* performed by the eight *diggajas*. Instead of water, they pour jewels and wealth upon him.[49] Ganapati's *nāga* origin associates him with water and, indeed, many of his statues, like those of Kubera, have been found near step wells or along rivers.[50] Lakṣmī's origin, in traditional literature, is also from the waters. Maṇibhadra is represented as one of the principal *yakṣas* in the Jaina context. In Jaina cosmography he occupies the position of a chief and is thus called Indra, along with Pūrṇabhadra.[51] Kubera has been conceived by the Śvetāmbara Jainas, as a deity, who rides a man, bears gems and a club. He is considered to be the treasurer of Indra.[52] Kubera is also the attendant *yakṣa* of the nineteenth Jina, Malli. The ensign of this *yakṣa* is the pot.[53] Similarly, it is as Mātaṅga, the *yakṣa* of Mahāvīra, that the prototype of Gaṇapati-Vināyaka is present in the Jaina pantheon.[54] There is also a *yakṣa* called *Mahāyakṣa* who is the *yakṣa* of the second Tīrthaṅkara Ajita.[55] Sometimes the epithet *Mahāyakṣa* is applied to Gaṇapati himself as in the case of the Gaṇapati-mantrasādhanā in the Digāmbara text *Vidyānuśāsana*.[56]

Maṇibhadra continued to be popular in Rajasthan and Gujarat during the early medieval period. He was particularly venerated by the Tapa *gaccha* of the Śvetāmbara Jainas, formed in Mewar in the thirteenth century. The followers of this *gaccha* installed images of Maṇibhadra Vīra in Jaina shrines erected by them.[57] Vastupāla, the chief minister at the Cālukya court, was favourably inclined towards this *gaccha*. Such patronage would have helped Maṇibhadra's worship gain importance.

There are two late sculptures, one from Prabhāsa Patan and the other from Diva in Saurashtra which depict Maṇibhadra as riding an elephant with three trunks. Maṇibhadra himself has the face of an elephant and he bears the mace, the goad, the snake, and holds one hand in *varada-mudrā*.[58] Almost all the images of this deity are crude or spoiled by application of oil and red lead-oxide. These sculptures are all recent and appear to have little or no historical basis. They, nevertheless, highlight some popular conceptions of the deity. The elephant head links him to Gaṇapati and to the Jaina *yakṣa* Pārśva who is also elephant-headed and who attends upon the twenty-third Jina, Pārśvanātha, in the Śvetāmbara tradition.[59] Sometimes Pārśva's elephant head has only one tusk, making him similar to Gaṇapati.[60] The association between Pārśvanātha and Maṇibhadra is suggested even by the

Rāmāyaṇa. According to this epic, Maṇibhadra's name was Pārśvamauli. He acquired this epithet because his crown had slipped to one side on being struck by the mace of Rāvaṇa when he fought the latter.[61] Maṇibhadra's elephant *vāhana* associates him with Kubera, Lakṣmī and Gaṇapati. Kubera is often shown with an elephant mount and Lakṣmī's association with the elephants is explicit in her form as Gajalakṣmī. An image from Osian depicts Gaṇapati riding an elephant.[62] This appears to be the only representation of its kind (although there is a reference to Gaṇapati riding on the elephant in one of the Purāṇas).[63] There is another Jaina image of Gaṇapati from Nāḍlāi, Rajasthan (twelfth century) where he rides a ram. This vehicle is sometimes associated with Kubera. Maṇibhadra, Pārśva, Gaṇapati and Kubera share some common characteristics in the region of modern Gujarat and Rajasthan, which suggests that all four were associated with similar functions. Pārśva, himself, could never develop an independent cult because he was an attendant deity and the Tīrthaṅkaras remained the principal figures of worship in the Jaina context. However, Maṇibhadra appears to have been as popular as Gaṇapati among certain sections of Jaina traders and merchants. Kubera is the one who eventually appears to have receded into the background. Although his image appears in temple sculpture, he does not seem to have enjoyed the same popularity as the other two deities after the tenth century.

Maṇibhadra is invoked both by the Śvetāmbara and the Digāmbara sects. He is mentioned in the Digambara *Vidyānuśāsana* also.[64] In the present day context, Maṇibhadra is the tutelary deity of the Osvāl Jainas who originated from Osian.[65] Gaṇapati is worshipped by most Jainas and he appears to have taken over certain functions of Kubera. Several images of Kubera dating to the seventh and eighth centuries AD have been found near step-wells. From the sixteenth century, inscriptions in step-wells invoke Gaṇapati. One such inscription, dated AD 1547, was found on a stone in a step-well called Gaṇeśa-*bāvaḍī* at Toda-Raising in the Jaipur District of Rajasthan.[66] The inscription invokes the grace of the god Gaṇeśa. Next follows a verse containing an adoration to the god Vighnavināśana (destroyer of obstacles) praised as the Supreme Being. The object of the inscription is to record the construction of the step-well. A series of names are given. They, evidently, do not belong to royalty otherwise it would have been stated. It is likely that they represent wealthy land-owners or merchants. There are two other inscriptions engraved on a pillar in the corner of a step-well and on a stone slab built into the wall of the same well in Rampura village, Mandasor district, Madhya Pradesh. The date corresponds to AD 1607. They record the construction of the step-well by someone who is stated to be from the *śreṣṭhi gotra* and the *vaiśya* caste. Further, the grandfather of the author of the inscription is said to be a Jaina. The second inscription begins with a passage invoking Gaṇeśa and Bhāratī.[67] Over the centuries, Gaṇapati had become the deity representing prosperity specifically associated with the *vaiśya* caste.

Images of Gaṇapati in Jaina temples of Rajasthan and Gujarat speak of the importance of this deity within the Jaina community. It is likely that since the Jainas were a powerful trading community, any deity popular with the community would eventually find a place in the Jaina pantheon. An image of Gaṇapati was found in the *pīṭha* of the Neminātha temple at Kumbharia (AD 1126), and another in the Mahāvīra temple at Kanthkot (AD 1280). They are both small images. In the Neminātha temple, Gaṇapati is present in one of a series of niches, which also contain images of Saraswatī, Lakṣmī, *vidyādevīs* and *yakṣis*.[68] Images of Gaṇapati are, likewise, found in the Jaina temples at Idar, Patan, Varakhana, Somanatha-Patan and other places. A temple at Kumbharia, North Gujarat, also contains an image of Gaṇapati carved on its rear wall.[69] He is invoked along with Saraswatī in one of the Jaina inscriptions at the Temple of Neminātha. No other deity figures in the invocation.[70] The Osvāls and the Dharkatas are mentioned in the inscription as two of the local communities that could perform the festival celebrated on the anniversary of the consecration of the temple.[71] There appears to be a constant association between the Osvāls, the Dharkatas and the deity Gaṇapati. Even today, Gaṇapati is an important deity for the Śvetāmbara community of western India and is propitiated at different auspicious occasions.

The flourishing Jaina community in Gujarat and Rajasthan also built temples to Gaṇapati. The Gaṇeśar Inscription of VS 1291 (AD 1235) refers to the construction of new temples and the repair of old ones by the chief minister of the Cālukyas, Vastupāla and his brother Tejaḥpāla. One such temple was made for the God Gaṇeśvara in the Ganauli village (near Dholka, Ahmedabad

District).[72] Diskalkar who discusses this inscription feels that 'Gaṇeśvara' probably refers to Śiva. However, in view of the fact that Gaṇapati was an established deity among the Jainas and had his own temples during this period, it is likely that this temple was, indeed, built for him.

Tibetan Buddhist texts also contain references to Gaṇapati as the lord of wealth. These texts are translations of Indian originals which have been lost and which were written and translated into Tibetan between approximately the eighth and eleventh centuries AD. Gaṇapati is often referred to as 'Great God of Wealth'.[73] There are prayers offered to him for the purpose of finding wealth without effort, without the necessity of making a profit and for obtaining power over the wealth of the world.[74] He is invoked as the 'King of Jewels'.[75] The image of Mahāgaṇapati made from 'gold' is said to ensure wealth in the house where it rests. A rain of jewels is believed to fall on the land where a golden Gaṇapati resides. Even the lord of wealth, Vaiśravaṇa, is said to serve and honour the owner of a golden Gaṇapati.[76] Although the Buddhist Tantric texts do not provide evidence of Gaṇapati being specifically the lord of trade, they confirm that he had come to be looked upon as the deity that conferred material wealth.

Eventually, Gaṇapati's association with the trading community finds reflection in the Purāṇas. According to the *Brahma Purāṇa,* Gaṇapati says that those who worship him will never experience poverty.[77] According to the *Brahmāṇḍa Purāṇa,* success in all tasks is certain for those who worship Gajānana before undertaking a *yātrā* (journey) and conducting *vāṇijya* (business trade).[78] Even the goad which Gaṇapati carries in his hand, is a symbol of the *vaiśya* class. Gaṇapati's various functions are evident in the names of his consorts and his sons. His two consorts are described variously as Siddhi and Buddhi, Ṛddhi and Buddhi, or Ṛddhi and Siddhi. Ṛddhi, however, is often referred to as the wife of Kubera.[79] Their names represent the benefits accrued by his worship. *Buddhi* means intelligence, *siddhi* signifies success and *ṛddhi,* prosperity. The two sons are Lābha (profit) and Kṣema (prosperity).

Gaṇapati's association with traders in the Brahmanical context first takes place in the far South from about the tenth century onwards. During this period, under Coḷa rule, merchants played a major role in the economic, social and religious life of the region. By the close of the ninth century AD, temple centres and the surrounding *brahmadeyas* (land granted to *brāhmanas*) had emerged as nuclei of urban growth. The tenth century onwards is a period characterized by the emergence of market centres (*nagaram*) in response to the marketing needs of the *naḍus*. Large-scale commercial activity led to the establishment of a network of market centres.[80] The Coḷas, with their expansionist ambitions patronized traders and commercial enterprises. It is against this background that a variety of forms of Gaṇapati appear and each is associated with a specific category of town or village.

In the *Āgamas*, there is a definite association between Gaṇapati and traders. It is specifically stated that his images may be placed in shops, amongst other places.[81] The *Ajitāgama* refers to a form of Gaṇapati known as Lakṣmī Gaṇapati.[83] It is described as being white, ten-handed and seated with two *devīs* (goddesses). Among the attributes he holds are a bowl of jewels, the *kalpalatā* (wish-fulfilling creeper) and a *kalaśa* (jar) overflowing with nectar. He holds one hand in the *varada mudrā* (boon granting gesture). This image recalls that of Gajalakṣmī. The latter is flanked on either side by an elephant even as Gaṇapati is by two *devīs*. The overflowing *kalaśa* recalls the water poured by the elephants for the *abhiṣekha* of Lakṣmī. Even the white colour is suggestive of Lakṣmī. This is the first time we come across such a close and direct association between Gaṇapati and the Goddess of Fortune. This form is recommended for towns which have shops and different classes of people. In other texts the description of Lakṣmī Gaṇapati is somewhat different. According to Aghoraśivācārya in his *Kriyākramadyoti*, the image should have eight hands and is to be depicted with a single goddess. The *kalaśa* and the *kalpalatā* remain the same. However, it is stated that water should be shown to be flowing from the proboscis.[83] According to the *Mantra-mahōdadhi*, the image is said to have four hands, one of which holds the *cakra* (disc) a distinct Vaiṣṇava attribute. The goddess Lakṣmī is described as embracing Gaṇapati with one arm and holding a lotus in the other.[84] The name of the goddess itself and the emphasis on the flowing proboscis and *kalaśa*, leave no doubt that it is intended to be the same Lakṣmī who had come to be regarded as the consort of Viṣṇu and who was looked upon as the bestower of wealth and prosperity. It is likely that the form of Lakṣmī Gaṇapati described in the *Ajitāgama* is the older one which later became modified, because the existing images of this variety, depict Gaṇapati with just one goddess. Such is the case with the stone image of Lakṣmī Gaṇapati in the Viśvanāthasvāmī Temple at Tenkasi which is known to have been built by a Pandya king, Arikesari Parakrama Pāṇḍyadeva, in AD 1446.[85] Another explanation could be that different versions of the same concept existed. The *Mayamata*, a treatise on architecture dated to about the seventh or eighth century AD, describes only one form of Gaṇapati.[86] The form of Lakṣmī Gaṇapati, therefore, evolved after the ninth century and it appears to have been restricted essentially to the region of modern Tamil Nadu.

According to the *Svayambhuvāgama*, Gaṇapati with two *śaktis* may be installed in a *nagara.*[87] A *nagara* is described in the *Mayamata* as a town situated in forested country with houses for all classes of people and with shops as well.[88] According to the *Diptāgama*, which is probably later than the *Mayamata*, a *nagara*, is peopled by various castes and craftsmen and has shops.[89] The *Svayambhuvāgama* does not mention any name for this particular form of Gaṇapati. According to the *Ajitāgama,* however, the only form of Gaṇapati with two *śaktis* or *devīs* is that of Lakṣmī Gaṇapati. In the case of Haridra Gaṇapati the two *devīs* are categorically stated to be his wives (*dārāḥ*).[90] Therefore, we may presume that the *Svayambhuvāgama* does indeed imply the form of Lakṣmī Gaṇapati. Since it was considered appropriate for this kind of habitation, it shows that not only was trade important, but that Gaṇapati and Lakṣmī were the presiding deities of this activity.

The *Svayambhuvāgama* further states that Lakṣmī Gaṇapati and Vijaya Gaṇapati may be installed in a *pura.*[91] According to *Mayamata*, a *pura* is the same as a *nagara*. The *Diptāgama* describes the *pura* as being inhabited by all classes of people, but weavers appear to be the main and specialised craftsmen.[92] I have not come across the description of Vijaya Gaṇapati in the sources that I have consulted. It was perhaps a localised form. The *Svayambhuvāgama* recommends the installation of Ucchiṣṭa Ganapati and Rakta Ganapati in a *paṭṭana*. The *Mayamata* describes a *paṭṭana* as a town where products from other countries are to be found. It is inhabited by people of all classes. There are shops and an abundance of merchandise such as precious stones, grains, fine cloth and perfumes. It is situated by the sea and extends along the coast.[93] According to the *Ādipurāṇa* written by a

Digambara monk of Mānyakheṭa (Malkhed, Gulbarga District, Karnataka), a *paṭṭana* is a place where people use sea-faring boats for transport.[94] Evidently, the *paṭṭana* must have been the residence of various religious communities and of foreign traders as well. The *Ajitāgama* describes both Ucchiṣṭa Gaṇapati and Rakta Gaṇapati without *śaktis.*[95] In the first case he holds a bunch of paddy and a pomegranate which would make him appear as a deity associated with agricultural wealth. In the second case he holds a mango in one of his four hands. The mango fruit has sexual overtones and, coupled with the epithet *rakta* (red), is suggestive of a fertility deity.

It is quite likely that these forms of Gaṇapati had popular appeal and were particularly important for the non-Brahmanical castes and communities that contributed in a significant manner to the generation of wealth under the Coḷas. In some other texts, however, the description of Ucchiṣṭa Gaṇapati and Rakta Gaṇapati is different. Whereas the *Kriyākramadyoti's* description of Ucchiṣṭa Gaṇapati tallies with that of the *Ajitāgama*, that of the *Mantramahārṇava* describes it as accompanied by a *devī* in a pose suggestive of attempted coition.[96] According to the *Uttara Kāmikāgama*, the nude *devī* is seated on his lap and one of his hands is touching her private parts.[97] Since most images of Ucchiṣṭa Gaṇapati depict him with a goddess on his lap, it is likely that the description in the *Ajitāgama* belongs to an earlier period when the influence of Tantric practices was not so widespread. The Ucchiṣṭa Gaṇapati of the *Ajitāgama* appears without any Tantric attributes and I wonder whether the epithet Ucchiṣṭa in this case was the result of his being worshipped by communities looked down upon by the authors of the *Āgamas*, such as the Jainas, for example. Even though Śivaism became the religion of the kings after the conversion from Jainism of the Pallava Mahendravarman, Jaina merchants and traders must have continued to function in the market centres. Since, at least, some Jaina traders of western India had adopted the worship of Gaṇapati in western India from as early as the seventh century, the practice may have found its way to the south.

This brings us to the question as to when the cult of Gaṇapati appeared in the south. From the evidence available, it would appear that it became popular in the Tamil region, in the post seventh century period, in the context of Śivaism. There is no mention of Vināyaka in the literature of the pre-Pallava period nor any evidence of his images. The earliest references to Gaṇapati appear to be in the hymns of the seventh century Śaiva Saints, Appar and Sambandar.[98] However, the deity does not appear to be well known at this period, because he is not systematically evoked in the hymns of the other saints. Nor is he mentioned in all the hymns of Appar and Sambandar. In the *Tēvāram* hymns, Śiva's *gaṇas* remain vague and undifferentiated. The goddess represents the gentle, feminine side of the lord permanently united with him in his form as Ardhanārīśvara. Śiva in the *Tēvāram* is rarely portrayed as the householder of the Purāṇas. The god's wife and his two children are no more than shadowy figures in his personal history.[99] There is only one mention of Gaṇapati in the *Tēvāram*, where Siruttondar refers to the pot-bellied Gaṇapati as one of the two sons of Śiva.[100] Siruttondar is believed to have lived at the end of the seventh and the beginning of the eighth centuries. There is also a traditional belief that the worship of Gaṇapati was brought to the Tamil country from Vātāpi (Bādāmi), capital of the Cālukyas, by Siruttondar. According to the *Periya Purāṇa*, Siruttondar, before becoming a Śiva *bhakta*, had been a commander under the Pallavas when they invaded Vātāpi. Tradition has it that the image of Vātāpi Gaṇapati presently at Thirucchengattankudi, was brought to the Tamil region by him.[101]

The earliest epigraphical reference to Gaṇapati and his sculptural representations in south India date to the eighth century.[102] In fact, the form of Gaṇapati is not found among the numerous icons of the time of the Pallava kings Mahendravarman I (AD 600-30) and Narasiṃhavarman I Mamalla (AD 630-68). The *Somaskanda* (Śiva with Ūmā and Skanda) images represent the essential part of Pallava Śivaism around AD 700. If Vināyaka had been considered a part of Śiva's family, it is unlikely that he would not have been represented along with Śiva, Ūmā and Skanda who constitute this image.

Mahendravarman I (AD 590-630), after his conversion from Jainism to Śivaism, undertook the construction of Brahmanical temples. Images of Gaṇapati have been found in temples built by Mahendravarman, such as the Cave Temples at Vallam (Viluppuram, Ramasamy District), the temple which is famous as the Ucchi-Piḷḷaiyar temple today (Tiruchchirappalli District) and at the Sikhari-Pallaveśvaram cave-temple at Melacheri (South Arcot

District). However, these images are generally accepted as being later additions, most probably during the later part of the Pallava period when the cult was better known.[103] The Ucchi-Piḷḷaiyar temple which is a famous Gaṇapati temple today, had, according to inscriptions, originally been a shrine of Śiva and Pārvatī.[104] Prior to that it had been a Jaina shrine. Similarly, the rock-cut monument known as the Gaṇeśa temple at Mamallapuram, was excavated on the orders of Parameśvara I (AD 670-700) and it was originally a Śiva temple.[105]

Perhaps one reason why Gaṇapati does not appear in early Śivaism in the south is because when Puranic Śivaism spread in the region he could not be identified with any of the earlier indigenous gods unlike Śiva, Durgā and Skanda who were identified with Ālamar Selvam, Koṛṛavai and Muruga respectively.[106] The Śiva of the Nayanars is different from the Puranic Śiva. He is closely associated with the Tamil region, language and culture and acquires a distinct Tamil identity. It is only in the Āgamas that Gaṇapati figures as a member of the Śaiva pantheon where he has sections devoted to his worship and ritual. These portions of the Āgamas appear to have been compiled during the Coḷa period. The Coḷa kings invited many Śaiva *brāhmaṇas* from the north to settle in their kingdom. Possibly, the importance given to Gaṇapati in the *Āgamas* is a result of their influence. There are also several epigraphical references to him and his shrines. In the Bṛhadīśvara temple at Thanjavur (AD 1000), a record mentions that 150 plantain fruits were offered daily to the god.[107] The earliest and perhaps the most famous of the Vināyaka temples of south India is the one at Tiruvalamjuli on the Kaveri about 10 kilometers away from Kumbhakonam in Thanjavur district (Tamil Nadu). It dates to before the eleventh century. The Vināyaka of this place is called 'Śveta Vināyaka' (white Vināyaka).[108]

It is hard to imagine that Gaṇapati was completely unknown in the south until his first icons appear or when the Nayanars first refer to him. The Viṣṇukuṇḍins and the Cālukyas who were the northern neighbours of the Pallavas had adopted his worship by the sixth century. He had become a part of Mahāyāna Buddhism from at least the end of the fifth/early sixth century. Jaina traders in western India invoke him from as early as the seventh century. Jainism and Mahāyāna Buddhism flourished in south India prior to the conversion of Mahendravarman. Even after that, it is unlikely that the two communities disappeared altogether. The relative decline of trade and communication networks between the fourth/fifth centuries and the ninth/tenth centuries does not presuppose the total disappearance of inter-regional movement of commodities, ideas and people. The motif of the early prototype of Gaṇapati, the elephant headed *yakṣa* or *gaṇa*, appears in the Rāmānuja-maṇḍapa, a Śaiva shrine, at Mahabalipuram.[109] This temple belongs to the period of Parameśvaravarman I (AD 670-700). In the depiction of a *bhūtagaṇa* frieze, there is an elephant headed *gaṇa* occupying the central place, perhaps indicating that he is the head of the *gaṇa*.[110] This theme of a group of *gaṇa*, including an elephant-headed one, carrying a garland, is an old one. It is present at Amarāvatī and at the Kantaka Celinga Stūpa at Sri Lanka in the second century AD. It was an old Buddhist motif, and its appearance here in the south is not surprising. From Hsuan Tsang, who visited the Pallava country during the time of Narasiṃhavarman (AD 630-8), we know that Mahāyana Buddhism was in a flourishing condition in this region. Buddhist art traditions were obviously borrowed for decorating Brahmanical shrines.

Appar and Sambandar describe a version of the Puranic Gajāsura myth according to which Śiva created Gaṇapati for the purpose of destroying Gajāsura.[111] Nagaswamy suggests that since Appar refers to this myth it was already well known.[112] This appears possible in view of what I have said earlier. Gaṇapati was known but did not become popular. He could not be identified with a local deity. Puranic Śivaism was rejected by adherents to the *bhakti* ideal as it was synonymous with Brahmanical beliefs and practices. The *bhakti* ideal developed in a situation of conflict, presumably as a protest against the ritual exclusiveness of the *brāhmaṇas* and as a challenge to Jaina and Buddhist dominance. It sought to redefine Śivaism or Viṣṇuism in more popular, but increasingly sectarian, terms. *Bhakti* hymns were popularized by the Coḷas through temple rituals and grants for such rituals and the construction of temples in the centres associated with the *bhakti* hymns.[113] The cult of the Śiva *liṅga* became the primary cult in these temples. However, the Coḷas settled many northern *brāhmaṇas* in their kingdom and associated them with the temple rituals. It was probably partly as a result of their influence that the cult of Gaṇapati developed in a big way.

It is also possible that various forms of Gaṇapati existed at a local level among some communities and these were subsequently adopted by the *Āgamas.* Religious literature does not reflect all existing beliefs and practices. In certain standard texts of Āgamic ritual such as the *Somaśambhupaddhati* which belongs to the eleventh century, none of the numerous forms of Gaṇapati are mentioned. As 'Vināyaka' he figures as one of eight *dvārapālas*[114] (guardians of the threshold) of Śiva. As 'Gaṇapati'[115] or 'Vighnanāyaka'[116] or 'Lambodara'[117] he is a deity in his own right, to be worshipped before the *guru,* as part of Śiva's pantheon. The fact that the different forms exist in only a few texts would show that they were popular with only certain sections of society. Why would the Āgamas include such forms or create new ones? Probably, they represent an effort at syncretism to ensure that Śivaism remained the primary religion. Just as the Purāṇas adopted a variety of deities and rituals associated with regional and ethnic groups making them part of the entourages of Śiva or Viṣṇu, and using them to propagate the Brahmanical world-view, the Āgamas, too, appear to have synthesized the beliefs and rituals of cross-sections of society in the region. One such category was that of the traders and merchants. As they became more affluent and powerful, their support for the state became indispensable. Royal patronage was reflected through religious recognition of their deities by texts of the local 'high tradition'. Within this framework, deities representing the aspirations of various categories of society were accommodated. In this manner, conflicting and divergent groups were united under the common umbrella of Śivaism.

The process by which new iconographical forms are created can be clearly illustrated by the example of the *Brahmādhirāyar.* It is a special icon which was created under Coḷa rule. It represents the *brāhmaṇas* who served as commanders of the imperial army, especially under Rajaraja I, Rajendra I and his successors, distinguishing themselves in every war. They were given the title Brahmādhirāja, i.e. king among *brāhmaṇas.* Several of these images were set up in the temples as devotees of the lord.[118] These icons of the *Brahmādhirāyar* have a shape and stature similar to that of Gaṇapati. They are sparsely dressed, with little jewellery and are depicted with short, plump bodies and pronounced bellies. One wonders why, as military commanders, they were depicted with such a form. Since the concept of these generals was new, an iconographical type had to be found. Gaṇapati, perhaps, represented, at a spiritual level, what these generals symbolised at the material level. Both were Gaṇapatis. One served Śiva and the other served the King. Both are examples of supreme valour and devotion but lower in hierarchy to Śiva and the King. It is tempting to see such an idea behind the choice of an iconographical form for the *Brahmādhirāyar*. Similarly, if Gaṇapati acquires numerous forms it is because he represents a variety of things to the various categories of society. As some of these categories became more influential and since they patronized temples and provided funds for their maintenance, their deities also found a place in the temples and in the religious literature on which temple-ritual was based. All over the south, the king was equated with Viṣṇu and Śiva. The Śiva of the *Āgamas* had his human counterpart in the Coḷa king. By extension, the secondary deities in his pantheon were associated with the lower orders of society. There is a second parallel between Gaṇapati and officers of the Coḷa king. The deity has been popularly known as Piḷḷaiyār (son or noble child) in Tamil Nadu. This term was also the title of princes of the Coḷa family. After about AD 1150 it became an honorific title for officers occupying a senior position in the Coḷa administration.[119]

Coḷa conquests of northern territories in the present day regions of south Karnataka and Andhra Pradesh led to the developments of *nagarams* and the growth of urban activities in these regions from about the tenth-eleventh centuries.[120] Guild activities spread to the Andhra and Karnataka region in the wake of the Coḷa conquests. After the twelfth century, Gaṇapati appears in inscriptions of the merchant community in Karnataka. A stone inscription set up near the Mulesingeśvara temple (Nagamangala taluk, Belur district), Karnataka, and dated AD 1296, constitutes a charter of agreement entered into between the *mahājanas* of several villages. The only deity invoked is 'Gaṇādhipati'.[121] Another inscription on a stone set up near the sluice on the bund of a large tank at Byadarahalli (Hassan taluk, Hassan district), dated AD 1341, states that a lady purchased a site from the *mahājanas* of Bēḍarahaḷḷi and got a tank excavated. The *mahājanas* made a grant of land towards the upkeep of the tank.[122] Here, again, only 'Gaṇādhipati' is invoked.[123] An inscription on the wall near the southern entrance of the Hoysaleśvara temple, dated AD 1287, records an endowment made by a messenger of the deity Iṇḍeya

Benaka (Vināyaka) from his salary. A part of the salary was to be lent for interest and the latter was to be paid on the occasion of the festival of *Bhādrapada śuddha chauthī* for covering the expenses of the celebration.[124] What is significant is that monetary transactions are associated with this deity. There are other references in the inscriptions of this region to Gaṇapati being 'the cause of continual wealth'[125] (fourteenth century), 'the cause of unobstructed prosperity'[126] (fourteenth century) and 'abundant prosperity'[127] (fifteenth century), and as the one who gives 'eternal prosperity'[128] (fifteenth century). An inscription on a lamp-post opposite the ruined Āñjaneya temple at Gumballi (Yalanduru, Mysore district) records the setting up of a lamp-pillar by a sculptor. Obeisance is made to Gaṇādhipati alone.[129] Another inscription from Ratnapura (Hunasur, Mysore district), records a charter laying down the punishments to be awarded for crimes committed and fines levied upon the tenants in the village, including those that may settle down in the future. There is no reference to any ruler and the only deity invoked is Gaṇādhipati. The inscripion is dated AD 1417. A sixteenth century inscription from Alakere (Yalanduru, Mysore district), records a grant of lands to a number of *mahājanas* of Alakere and Benskere, free from several taxes for the merit of his master by the chief minister of the Vijayanagar ruler, Kṛṣṇārāya (AD 1519).[130] Only Gaṇapati is invoked. Normally grants in the name of Kṛṣṇārāya and other kings of Vijayanagar invoke Sambhu, Varāha and Gaṇapati.[131] It is also quite clear that in royal inscriptions it is insufficient to invoke Gaṇapati alone, even though he may be invoked first. In matters that concern other people, mainly traders, invocation to this deity alone is considered appropriate.

In the ninth century, Pratīhāra Kakkuka established a town and a quadruple image of Gaṇapati was installed to ensure prosperity. Several centuries later, a similar phenomenon occurs in the region of modern Andhra Pradesh and Karnataka. An incription dated AD 1289 records the gifting of a village called Marpaḍiga by the minister of the Kākatiya king, Rudradeva, to a *brāhmaṇa* scholar named Viddānācārya. The latter renamed the village Vināyakapura.[132] In Karnataka, a stone inscription from Sankalapura (Bellary district) records the grant of Sankalapura village to a temple of Gaṇapati. The village was renamed Koṭa-Vināyakapura (Vināyaka in the Fort), after its presiding deity, and converted into a town with a newly constructed tank. There is reference to worship, repairs, offerings, all entertainment and car festivals being fully provided for. This inscription is dated AD 1513 and the slab which bears the inscription has the figure of Gaṇapati engraved on it with the sun to his right and a crescent to his left.[133] This confirms Gaṇapati's association with material well-being for why else would a place be named after him if it was not to ensure prosperity. In all these cases, no other deity is mentioned in the inscriptions.

One of the more recent forms of Gaṇapati is that of Ṛṇamocaka Gaṇapati (he who removes debts) which is mentioned in the *Śrītattvanidhi,* a text compiled by Kṛṣṇarāja Wodeyar IV, king of Mysore, towards the end of the nineteenth century.[134] This form is also represented on the *prākāra* wall of the Nañjundeśvara temple near Mysore which dates to about AD 1850. In this case it is referred to as Ṛṇavimocana Gaṇapati. This form appears to be limited to the region of Mysore and is eloquent testimony to Gaṇapati's association with any kind of money transaction.

Even in the *Gaṇeśa Purāṇa,* there is an indirect reference to Gaṇapati being associated with traders. King Somakanta, who is suffering from leprosy, is told by the sage Bhṛgu that the cause of his illness can be found in his previous life. He had been a *vaiśya* and was reckless and given to killing *brāhmaṇas.* In his old age, however, he had become penitent and attempted to give away his ill-gotten wealth to *brāhmaṇas* but they refused to accept it. So, instead, he spent his fortune refurbishing an abandoned Gaṇapati temple and then died soon after.[135] Whatever else be the implications of this story, the association of rich merchants with Gaṇapati temples is evident.

By the fourteenth century, there is inscriptional evidence of Gaṇapati being the principal deity of the merchant community in other parts of south India as well. According to the Kottayam plate of Vīra Rāghava,[136] the title 'Maṇigrāmam' was conferred on a certain merchant. It implied specific honours and rights. The inscription then enumerates the sources of income available to the grantee as lord of the city (of Kodungular, near Cochin). The inscription begins with an invocation for prosperity and with an adoration of Mahāgaṇapati. No other deity is mentioned. The invocation of Gaṇapati was considered adequate, and appears to have been a form for all such organisations. Maṇigrāmams were trading corporations and seem to have existed since the early centuries of the Christian era.[137] We know from inscriptional evidence that this guild of traders was present at the port of Quilon, on the Kerala coast, as early as the ninth or early tenth centuries[138] and that its members functioned both at coastal sites and at townships in the interior.

Gaṇapati's rise in the Puranic pantheon coincides with a period considered as one of decline in trade and feudalization of Indian society and economy. Whereas from the Brahmanical point of view this deity is only one of many members of Śiva's entourage, for the trading community he appears to acquire a definite role and *raison d'être.* This development takes place in a region where economic activity continued to be important and within a community, that of the Jainas, where it was the principal occupation. The period from approximately the tenth century onwards is marked by the crystallisation of new networks of exchange, the formation of trade guilds and a resurgence of money production and circulation. South India under the Coḷas was in the forefront of this resurgence and it was during this period that Gaṇapati became associated with the traders in the region as well. Whereas in the context of the royal cult of Śiva, he remains either a *dvārapāla* of Śiva, or the Lord of Obstacles, for certain communities such as those of the traders and merchants he was the principal deity associated with their functions and transactions. It is possible that with major transformations taking place during this time, a new deity, relevant to the changed scenario, was required. Gaṇapati fitted this role and acquired numerous forms and attributes influenced by the villages and towns in which they developed. He was associated with earthy needs and, therefore, became the primary deity of those whose purpose in life was to generate wealth.

NOTES

1. *Bṛhadāraṇyaka Upaniṣad,* I.4.12 in S. Radhakrishnan's *The Principal Upaniṣads,* pp. 149-333. Refer to p. 169.
2. R.N. Misra, *Yaksha Cult and Iconography,* p. 81.
3. *Mahābhārata* , Sabhā Parva, 21.9.
4. *EI,* Vol. XXVIII, No. 51 pp. 328-31.
5. R.N. Misra, op. cit., p. 43. He cites from the *Mahāmāyūrī,* I.31.

6. Swami Dwarikadas Shastri, Trans. and ed., *Milindapañha Pali* (original text with Hindi translation), p. 191.
7. Śānti Parva, 263.15-28.
8. D.C. Sircar, *Select Inscriptions,* Vol. I, pp. 92-3.
9. M.B. Garde, 'The Site of Padmavati', *ASIAR,* 1915-16, p. 106.
10. Ananda Coomaraswamy, *Yakṣas,* Part I, p. 28.
11. *EI,* Vol. XVIII, No. 20, pp. 158-9.
12. *EI,* Vol. XXIX, No. 23, pp. 169-74.
13. J.N. Samaddar, 'Industrial and Trading Organisation in Ancient India', *JBORS,* Vol. VII, Part 4, 1921, pp. 35-54.
14. D.D. Kosambi, *Myth and Reality,* p. 103.
15. N.M. Penzer, ed., *Kathāsaritsāgar,* Vol. I, p. 162.
16. *Mahābhārata,* Appendices 10.60-2; 11.52-4; 12.14-6. In Geeta Press edn., Āraṇyaka Parva, 65.22-3.
17. J.P. Vogel, *Indian Serpent Lore,* p. 10.
18. Ibid.
19. *Vāyu Purāṇa,* II.i.21.39-42a.
20. Ibid., I.58.51.
21. P.V. Kane, *History of Dharmaśāstra,* Vol. II, Pt. I, p. 90.
22. *Nīlamata Purāṇa,* 1043-4.
23. Maurice Winternitz, *History of Indian Literature,* Vol. III, pp. 279-80.
24. R.N. Misra, op. cit., p. 82.
25. R.C. Agrawala, 'Some Interesting Sculptures of Yakṣas and Kubera from Rajasthan', *IHQ,* Sep. 1957, pp. 201-7.
26. Ibid.
27. Ibid., see p. 203.
28. Sabhā Parva, 10.19.
29. R.C. Agrawala, op. cit., pp. 102-3.
30. Suvira Jaiswal, *The Origin and Development of Vaiṣṇavism,* p. 97.
31. John Allan, *Catalogue of the Coins of Ancient India,* 'Introduction', p. cxxvi.
32. Ibid., pp. 173-6.
33. According to the description of the funeral rites in the *Gṛhya Sūtras,* the corpse is laid on a black antelope's skin. In the case of a *vaiśya,* his goad (in that of a *brāhmaṇa* his staff, and of a *kṣatriya,* his bow) is taken from his hand, broken and cast on the pyre. Quoted in A.A. Macdonell, *A History of Sanskrit Literature,* p. 256.
34. Ibid., p. 102.
35. V.S. Agrawala, 'Brahmā, Viṣṇu and Śiva, etc. in Mathura Art', *JUPHS,* Vol. XXII, 1949, pp. 150-1. The author considers these images to belong to the Gupta Art of Mathura.
36. N.R. Guseva, *Jainism,* pp. 56-7.

37. R.C. Agrawala, 'Sculptures from Abaneri', *Lalit Kala,* Nos.1-2, 1955-6, pp. 130-5.
38. *EI,* Vol. XXVII, No. 7, pp. 27-33.
39. *EI,*Vol. XXXIII, No. 13, pp. 79-81.
40. In the Koni inscription of Kalachuri Prithvideva II (K.E. 930) Gaṇapati is invoked after Śiva, Nandi and Saraswatī (See *EI,* Vol. XXVII, No. 45, pp. 276-87); An inscription from Ranod or Narod (AD 1026), about seventy five kilometers south of Narwar begins with an invocation to Śiva, followed by one to Vināyaka, Saraswatī and then to Śiva again (*EI,* Vol. I, No. XLI, pp. 351-61). The Bhera-Ghat stone inscription of Narasiṃha (Kalachuri) Year 907 begins with an invocation to Śiva then to the moon and this is followed by an eulogy of Śiva; only then is Gaṇapati invoked as the remover of obstacles (V.V Mirashi, ed., Inscriptions of the Kalachuri-Chedi Era, *CII,* Vol. IV, Pt. I, No. 60, pp. 312-21); the Ratanpur Stone Inscription of the Kalachuri king Prithvideva II (AD 1149-50) begins with an invocation to Rudra followed by one to Gaṇapati (*CII,* Vol. IV, Pt. 2, No. 93, pp. 483-8); in the Dhureti plates of Trailokyamalla of about AD 1212, Gaṇapati is invoked directly after Śiva (*CII,* Vol. IV, Pt. I, No. 72, pp. 369-74; in Bengal, the Barrackpur grant of Vijayasena's thirty-second year (eleventh/twelfth centuries AD) refers to the reign of the Sena dynasty and invokes Śiva first and makes reference to Kārttikeya and Gaṇapati (*EI,* Vol. XV, No. 15, pp. 278-86). See also Gaṇapeśvaram inscription of the time of Gaṇapati (AD 1231) in *EI,* Vol. III, No. 15, pp. 82-93.
41. *EI,* Vol. XXVII, No. 7, p. 29.
42. Ibid., p. 28.
43. Maruti Nandan Tiwari and Kamal Giri, 'Images of Gaṇeśa in Jainism' in Robert L. Brown, ed., *Ganesh: Studies of an Asian God,* pp. 101-14.
44. R.C. Agrawala, 'Some Interesting Sculptures of Yakṣas and Kubera from Rajasthan', p. 203.
45. *EI,* Vol. IX, No. 38, pp. 277-81.
46. B.D. Chattopadhyaya, 'Origin of the Rajputs: The Political, Economic and Social Processes in Early Medieval Rajasthan', *IHR,* Vol. III, No. 1, pp. 59-82.
47. *EI,* Vol. III, pp. 263-7.
48. *Garuḍa Purāṇa,* I.69.1-3.
49. *Īśānaśivagurudevapadhati,* Vol. 2, 16.55-7, p. 19.
50. V.S. Agrawala, 'Brahmā, Viṣṇu and Śiva, etc. in Mathura Art', *JUPHS,* op. cit.
51. R.N. Misra, op. cit., p. 82.

52. R.P. Hingorani, *Jaina Iconography in Rūpamanḍana*, p. 113.
53. Ibid., pp. 12-13.
54. Ibid., p. 13.
55. Ibid., p. 12.
56. U.P. Shah, 'Minor Jaina Deities', *JOIB*, Vol. 32, pp. 82-98. See particularly, p. 92.
57. Ibid., p. 97.
58. Ibid., p. 98, fn. 87. It is not stated how late these sculptures are, but they are certainly post fourteenth century. However, they reflect ideas and associations that belong to a much earlier period. Maṇibhadra is depicted in this manner even in some contemporary representations.
59. Maruti Nandan Tiwari and Kamal Giri, op. cit., p. 105.
60. Ibid.
61. R.N. Misra, op. cit., p. 80; *Rāmāyaṇa*, Uttarakāṇḍa, 15.14-15.
62. Maruti Nandan Tiwari and Kamal Giri, op. cit., p. 103.
63. *Skanda Purāṇa*, I.i.10.29-30.
64. U.P. Shah, op. cit., p. 98.
65. Ibid., p. 98.
66. *EI*, Vol. XXX, pp. 190-7.
67. *EI*, Vol. XXXVI, pp. 121-30.
68. Harihar Singh, *Jaina Temples in Western India*, p. 23.
69. U.P. Shah, op. cit., p. 92.
70. *EI*, Vol. VIII, No. 21, pp. 200-19. See, in particular, p. 208, v. 2.
71. Ibid., p. 206. See Part II of the inscriptions vv. 9-25, pp. 219-20.
72. D.B. Diskalkar, 'Some Unpublished Inscriptions of Vastupāla' in *ABORI*, Vol. 9, Pts. 1-4, 1927-8, pp. 179-81. See also footnote on p. 179.
73. Christopher Wilkinson, 'The Tantric Gaṇeśa', in Robert L. Brown, ed., op. cit., pp. 265, 261.
74. Ibid., p. 258.
75. Ibid., p. 268.
76. Ibid., p. 246.
77. *Brahma Purāṇa*, IV.44.19-25.
78. *Brahmāṇḍa Purāṇa*, II.iii.42.42-4.
79. *Padma Purāṇa*, I.17.100-18.
80. R. Champakalakshmi, 'State and Economy: South India, *c.* AD 400-1300', in Romila Thapar, ed., *Recent Perspectives of Early Indian History*, pp. 266-308.
81. *Uttara-Kāmikāgama*, 45.1-8. Cited as a footnote in the cri. edn. of the *Rauravottarāgama*, Chap. 9, p. 29, fn. 3.
82. *Ajitāgama*, Vol. III, 55.13.
83. T.A. Gopinatha Rao, *Elements of Hindu Iconography*, Vol. I, Pt. I, p. 53.

84. Ibid.
85. Ibid., p. 64.
86. Bruno Dagens, trans., *Mayamata: An Indian Treatise on Housing Architecture and Iconography,* p. 354. The form described is called Gaṇādhīpa and he has no *śakti.*
87. Quoted from the *Svayambhuvāgama* in *Ajitāgama,* Vol. III, p. 6, fn. 73.
88. Bruno Dagens, op. cit., p. 40.
89. *Diptāgama,* Transcript No. 15, Chap. 78., sloka 37. The reference in the published edition is I.I.37.
90. *Ajitāgama,* Vol. III.55.18.
91. Quoted in *Ajitāgama,* Vol. III, p. 6, fn. 73.
92. *Diptāgama,* 78.42.
93. Bruno Dagens, op. cit., p. 40.
94. R.N. Nandi, *Social Roots of Religion in India,* p. 24.
95. *Ajitāgama,* Vol. III, 55.9-10.
96. T.A. Gopinatha Rao, op. cit., p. 54.
97. Ibid.
98. R. Nagaswamy, *Śiva Bhakti,* p. 200.
99. Indira Viswanathan Peterson, *Poems to Śiva,* p. 101.
100. Ibid., p 233.
101. R. Nagaswamy, op. cit., p. 200.
102. See the Kasakkudi Plates in *SII,* Vol. II, pp. 365-6. Vināyaka is just mentioned in the invocation after six other deities. However, Gaṇapati is not systematically invoked in other inscriptions of Nandivarman II. Most often only Śiva or Viṣṇu are mentioned. See Pullur Plates of Nandivarman, (*EI,* Vol. XXXVI, No. 20, pp. 144-52), the Pattattalmangalam plates (*EI,* Vol. XVIII, p. 120), or the Udayendiram grant (*SII,* Vol. II, pp. 365-6), all dating to the eighth century.
103. K.R. Srinivasan, *Cave Temples of the Pallavas,* pp. 61, 79 and 88.
104. Ibid., pp. 79 and 88.
105. R. Gopalan, *History of the Pallavas of Kanchi,* p. 107.
106. R. Champakalakshmi, 'Ideology and the State in South India', Mamidipudi Venkatarangaiah Memorial Lecture -1, *Andhra Pradesh History Congress,* Srisailam, 1989.
107. R. Nagaswamy, *Masterpieces of Early South Indian Bronzes,* p. 136.
108. G.S. Ghurye, *Gods and Men,* p. 79.
109. This shrine was originally a Śaiva shrine. After the influence of such religious reformers as Rāmānujācārya, the Śaiva sculptures in the interiors of several Śaiva temples were destroyed and replaced by Vaiṣṇava images. Some of the decorative friezes, however, remained. In the case of the Rāmānuja-*maṇḍapa,* an old

Śaiva inscription remained intact on the floor which indicates the original nature of the shrine. See A.H. Longhurst, *Pallava Architecture,* Pt. II, pp. 5-6.

110. K.R. Srinivasan, op. cit., p. 176.
111. R. Nagaswamy, *Śiva Bhakti,* p. 200.
112. Ibid.
113. R. Champakalakshmi, 'Ideology and the State in South India', op. cit.
114. *Somaśambhupaddhati,* Pt. II, pp. 47 and 334.
115. Ibid., pp. 334, 342.
116. Ibid., p. 111.
117. Ibid.
118. R. Nagaswamy, *Masterpieces of Early South Indian Bronzes,* p. 117.
119. Y. Subbarayalu, 'The Coḷa State', *Studies in History,* Vol. IV, No. 2, 1982, pp. 265-306.
120. R. Champakalakshmi, 'State and Economy: South India, *c.* AD 400-1300', in Romila Thapar, ed., op. cit.
121. *EC,* Vol. 7, No. 82, pp. 498-9.
122. Ibid., Vol. 8, No. 206, p. 698.
123. Ibid.,Vol. 8, No. 206, p. 698-9.
124. Ibid., Vol. 9, No. 266, p. 698.
125. Ibid., Vol. 5, No. 256, p. 998; Vol. 8, No. 87, p. 493.
126. Ibid., Vol. 8, No. 115, p. 641.
127. Ibid., Vol. 6, No. 25, p. 616.
128. Ibid., Vol. 9, No. 576, p. 854.
129. Ibid., Vol. 4, No. 188, p. 779.
130. Ibid., Vol. 4, No 168, p. 772.
131. Ibid., Vol. 3, No. 113, p. 669; Vol. 5, No. 105, p. 800; Vol. 5, No. 225, p. 984; Vol. 6, No. 99, p. 480; Vol. 6, No. 26, p. 619; Vol. 7, No. 134, p. 523; Vol. 7, No. 7, p. 553. There are numerous such examples.
132. *EA,* Vol. IV, pp. 109-17.
133. *EI,* Vol. IV, pp 266-9.
134. Gudrun Buhnemann, *Forms of Gaṇeśa,* pp. 19, 45.
135. *Ganeśa Purāṇa,* Upāsanā Khaṇḍa, 7 and 8.
136. *EI,* Vol. IV, No. 41, pp. 290-7.
137. Meera Abraham, *Two Medieval Merchant Guilds of South India,* p. 29.
138. Ibid., p. 13.

CHAPTER 6

The Gāṇapatyas

Little is known of the Gāṇapatyas, a sect worshipping Gaṇapati as their special deity. Scholars who mention them[1] base their information essentially on a text of the medieval period, the *Śaṅkaravijaya* of Ānandagiri. This text is in the form of a debate between the Śaiva philosopher Śaṅkarāchārya (eighth/ninth century AD) and the heads of several religious sects, including those of the Gāṇapatyas, who oppose his philosophy of Advaita Vedānta. The text mentions six sects of Gāṇapatyas: those of Ucchiṣṭa Gaṇapati and Heramba Gaṇapati which appear to have been closely related and are clubbed together; and those of Haridra Gaṇapati, Mahāgaṇapati, Saṃtāna, Navanīta and Svarṇa Gaṇapati.[2] Each sect is described as worshipping Gaṇapati under a different name, in a somewhat different form and with a differently worded *mantra.* Moreover, members of each sect are described as having their arms and foreheads branded with the symbol of the sect.

What remains unexplained is why Gaṇapati became the focus of sectarian worship when other deities such as Kubera, Skanda or the various *nāgas* remained secondary divinities. Even Hanumān, another therianthropic deity, as closely associated with Rāma and Sītā as Gaṇapati is with Śiva and Pārvatī, did not aquire his own sect. Secondly, where and when did these sects evolve and what were the categories of society associated with them? Were the differences between the various subsects limited only to form, name and *mantra* or were they more significant?

In the introduction, while discussing the sources, I have explained why I situate the *Śaṅkaravijaya* between the tenth and eleventh centuries AD. Therefore, a preliminary discussion on the status of the worship of Gaṇapati in this period is useful. By the tenth century the deity had become important in many regions of the country. Epigraphical references confirm the existence of shrines and temples to him in the region of modern Rajasthan[3] and Gujarat.[4] While some appear next to Śiva temples suggesting that Gaṇapati was an important but secondary deity within the Śaiva context, others were temples in *pañcāyatana* complexes.[5] *Pañcāyatana pūjā* is believed to have been introduced by Śaṅkarācārya and appears to have been widely accepted by the tenth century. In this context Gaṇapati appears as a deity in his own right. The *Saraswatī Purāṇa* (Cālukyan period) refers to *tīrthas* and shrines of many deities on the Sahasraliṅga lake, including those of Vināyaka.[6]

In Uttar Pradesh, some early images of Gaṇapati have been found at Baijnath on the Sarayu river in the Kumaon region where the ruins of several old temples exist. They belong to the reign of the local Katyuri dynasty of the ninth and tenth centuries.[7] In all likelihood they were housed in their own shrines or temples. In the Purāṇas there are references to *tīrthas* associated with Gaṇapati in the region of Uttar Pradesh, such as the Avighna *tīrtha*, on the northern banks of the river Gautamī,[8] and the Vighnarāja *tīrtha* on the river Yamuna, near Mathura.[9] In central India, a stone inscription of AD 1181-2 refers to the temples of Tunta Gaṇapati and Heramba Ganapati both in the region of modern Madhya Pradesh.[10] Since there does not appear to be a form known as Tunta Gaṇapati in the sacred texts, Tunta was probably the name of the village or locality where the temple was built.

In the region of Maharashtra, Gaṇapati is invoked systematically at the beginning of nearly every inscription of the Śilāhāra dynasty between the ninth and eleventh centuries AD. Although Śiva was the tutelary deity of this royal family, it was evidently considered important to invoke Gaṇapati in his capacity as remover of obstacles at the outset of all understakings.[11] Similarly, in a grant made by a member of the Modha family, Gaṇapati is invoked first.[12] The Modhas were a local *brāhmaṇa* ruling family who probably owed allegiance to some contemporary Śilāhāra ruler. In the grants of the Śilāhāras and the Modhas there is no reference to Kārttikeya which shows that in some regions Gaṇapati was clearly the more important of Śiva's two sons. Although the inscriptions do not indicate whether Gaṇapati had any temples dedicated to him in the region of Maharashtra, it is reasonable to suppose that they did exist. Śilāhāra rule extended over parts of modern Karnataka as well, including the Konkan area, and that is where some of the oldest Gaṇapati temples exist. It is unlikely that religious traditions popular in one part of the Śilāhāra kingdom were unknown in other parts.

The Mahāgaṇapati temple at Gokarna in the Uttar Kannada district, Karnataka, is one of the most famous old Gaṇapati temples. Tradition has it that it dates from the time of the early Kadambas (fifth-sixth century AD) a major royal family whose power extended over a large part of modern Karnataka and also parts of Goa and Maharashtra. Gokarna is a Śaiva *tīrtha* and the principal temple at the site is that of Mahābaleśvara (Śiva). However, the Mahāgaṇapati temple close by, houses an image which is also very old and appears to be of early Kadamba workmanship. The deity has only two arms and is in a standing position. It is very similar to the images in some other old temples such as the Gaṇapati temple at Uppinapattan[13] and that at Idagunji in the same district. The latter is mentioned as Idakuñja and Kuñjavana and also Iḍugunjige in an inscription from the same place dated AD 1348.[14] These temples, too, are believed to exist from early Kadamba times although the structure has been renovated several times. It is not clear whether the images were part of Śaiva temples initially or whether they had their own shrines from an early period. Since Gaṇapati becomes important only after the sixth century, these temples, as also that at Gokarna, probably date to the late sixth century/seventh century at the earliest. All these images in Karnataka are extremely simple (plate 1). They are depicted with no jewellery and no crown and are in striking contrast to the more ornate forms that evolved subsequently. By the tenth century, images of Gaṇapati with two hands are rare and four hands are the most common representation. Several images in the Gaṇapati temples at Gokarna stand on a *snānadroṇī* (photo 3). This feature is found on some late seventh/early eighth century Gaṇapati statues from Vietnam and Thailand[15] and it is likely that it was borrowed from earlier Indian statues.

In Kurnool district of modern Andhra Pradesh, an eighth century inscription records the setting up of images of Danḍīśvara, Gaṇapati and Nandīśvara.[16] It is not known whether all the three were housed in the same temple or whether Gaṇapati had a shrine of his own. A tenth century inscription from the Guntur district of Andhra Pradesh refers to the *Vināyakotsava* (festival of Vināyaka) being celebrated in a village called Kākumrānu.[17] The *utsav* appears to be associated with the feast celebrating the commencement of the sowing season. In the Tamil region Gaṇapati had become an intrinsic part of the royal cult of Śiva. The Āgamas, many of which belong to this period, contain sections on his worship and associated rituals.

Thus by the tenth century there is definite evidence of Gaṇapati being worshipped in various parts of the country. He appears to have been popular with at least three royal families: the Kadambas, Śilāhāras and Coḷas. Since these families adhered to Brahmanical norms, the cult of Gaṇapati propagated by them was probably a strictly Brahmanical one. Since what royalty does is immitated by the lower orders of society, the worship of the Braḥmanical Gaṇapati became specially popular in the region of modern Karnataka, Maharashtra and Tamil Nadu by the tenth century. The deity was also associated with festivities in connection with agricultural rites and so must have been a deity of the agricultural classes as well. The latter would have had their own ritual specialists responsible for conducting these festivities. Where Gaṇapati temples existed, a category of priests must have emerged who were mainly, if not solely, associated with his worship. This, most likely, led to the gradual creation of myths associated with specific temples and to a greater number of rituals in order to attract a larger clientele. Against this background, it is worthwhile examining the textual tradition in order to understand the nature of the Gāṇapatya sects that appeared by about the ninth century.

The *Sammoha Tantra* (thirteenth/fourteenth centuries AD)[18] refers to a Gāṇapa Tantrika tradition in both the northern and southern class of *Tantras*.[19] It mentions five cults of the Gāṇapatyas and lists the extant body of Gāṇapatya literature which consists of fifty Tantras, twenty-five Upatantras, two Purāṇas and a long list of what seem to be smaller works.[20] The five cults probably signify five sects, rather than five forms of Gaṇapati because by the fourteenth century there were numerous forms of the deity. The Āgamas refer to as many as twelve[21] and sixteen forms.[22]

From the *Sammoha Tantra*, it is reasonable to conclude that by the fourteenth century the Gāṇapatyas were established in various parts of the country and that their literature was essentially Tantric. Since very few Tantric texts devoted to Gaṇapati are known it is apparent that most of this literature has either been lost or remains undiscovered. The Tibetan Buddhist canon contains about thirty Tantric texts devoted exclusively to Gaṇapati.[23] Many of these are translations of Indian originals and bear the names of their Indian authors and translators.[24] This would indicate that possibly some of the Gāṇapatya sects evolved within the Buddhist context. Others were off-shoots of the Śaivas since many Śaiva Tantras and Āgamas have sections devoted to Gaṇapati where he is worshipped independently of Śiva and his entourage. In fact, the forms of Gaṇapati worshipped by some Gāṇapatya sects, such as Ucchiṣṭa Gaṇapati or Haridra Gaṇapati, are described in detail in the Āgamas.[25] The two Purāṇas mentioned by the *Sammoha Tantra* evidently refer to the *Mudgala* and *Gaṇeśa Purāṇas* since these are the only two known Purāṇas that are devoted exclusively to Gaṇapati. They represent a third tradition outside the Buddhist and Śaiva frameworks, that of the *Smārtas.* This third category is associated with the period subsequent to the *Śaṅkaravijaya.*

I shall, therefore, begin with a discussion on the evolution of Gaṇapati in the Buddhist and Śaiva contexts; against this background, an analysis of the Gāṇapatya sects mentioned in the *Śaṅkaravijaya* becomes relevant; finally, I shall examine the *Smārta* Gāṇapatyas.

GAṆAPATI AND BUDDHISM

Gaṇapati worship appears to have been accepted into Buddhism from at least as early as the sixth century AD. At the Buddhist caves of Aurangabad, a recently discovered cave located between Caves 5 and 6 contains, as its major icon, an image of Gaṇapati. He is at the centre rear of the cave. On his right are the seven mothers with Śiva. On his left are Durgā and two Buddha images. The cave is dated to the second half of the sixth century.[26] Brown interprets this image as Gaṇapati in his capacity as remover of obstacles to further worship in the site as a whole as well as a focus for the fulfilment of specifically mundane desires. However, if the deity was looked upon as the remover of obstacles, the image of Gaṇapati should have figured in a very prominent part of the site whereby visitors would have to first pay homage to him before proceeding to the other caves. Possibly, Gaṇapati had some other significance in the Buddhist context. What is striking is his association with Śiva and Durgā but in a more important position than both of them. There is also a small Gaṇapati on the doorframe at Cave 3 at Aurangabad which dates to the second half of the fifth century.[27] It is not certain whether at this early stage Gaṇapati had the same significance in both the Brahmanical and Buddhist contexts.

There is a bas-relief of Gaṇapati in the Buddhist grotto-temple of Kung-hsien, China, dated AD 531 which depicts the deity seated cross-legged with a lotus in his uplifted right hand and what is referred to as a '*cintāmaṇi*' in his left hand which rests on his lap. An inscription in Chinese characters refers to him as the 'Spirit King of Elephants'. He is depicted in the company of nine deities : the Spirit Kings of the *Nāgas,* of the Wind, of Peals, of Fire, of Trees, of Mountains, of Fishes, of Lions and of Birds.[28] It is significant that he is not referred to as Vināyaka or by any other epithet associated with him in the Brahmanical context. As Getty points out, this image of Gaṇapati was evidently based on a model brought from India as the elephant was little known in China at that epoch. Possibly, the elephant-headed deity, in the Buddhist context, did not have the negative connotation that it had acquired in the Brahmanical religion due to his association with the obstacle causing Vināyakas. Eventually, however, he acquired some of the powers of the Brahmanical Gaṇapati, such as the ability to remove obstacles and grant success.

Textual references to Gaṇapati in the Buddhist context only appear after the eighth century or so. Unfortunately, most Buddhist texts housed in the monasteries and learning centres of Nālandā or Vikramaśīla were probably destroyed during the succeeding Afghan and Turkish invasions from the tenth century. Some of these works had, however, been translated and taken to other regions such as Tibet, Nepal and China prior to this period. It is in the Buddhist canons of these countries that many such texts are preserved. Fifteen of the thirty Gāṇapatya texts preserved in the Tibetan canon have been translated into English by Wilkinson.[29] These are vital for understanding the evolution of Gaṇapati within the Buddhist fold in the early medieval period.

Although it is difficult to date the Tibetan Gāṇapatya texts exactly, they can be situated between the eighth and eleventh centuries on the basis of the names of their authors and translators. The names include those of the most well known Indian Buddhist teachers of the period: Amoghavajra (eighth century AD); Dīpaṅkaraśrījñāna (eleventh century AD); Dombiheruka (eighth century AD), king of Magadha; Nāgārjuna of Nālandā (seventh or eighth centuries AD); Śrī Dīpaṅkarabhadra (late eighth and early ninth centuries AD); Vairocana of Kośala and Gāyadhara of Gaya (both eleventh century AD).[30] These works reflect beliefs and practices at the monasteries of Nālandā and Vikramaśīla.

In some of the Buddhist Gāṇapatya texts, certain deities are invoked before the worship of Gaṇapati. In one case homage is paid to Avalokiteśvara before Gaṇapati.[31] At other times it is to Vajradākinī[32] or Vajrapāṇi[33] or to all the Buddhas and Bodhisattvas.[34] There are other texts, however, where no other deity is mentioned and which are only concerned with the preparation of Gaṇapati's images and *maṇḍalas,*[35] the instructions about the nature of his worship, the *mantras* to be recited and the powers that are acquired thereby. A *mantra* called the Essence of Gaṇapati is described which, if recited by the devotee at the outset of any worship or activity, is considered to be equivalent to a homage to the Blessed Buddhas with flowers and incense.[36] The worship of Gaṇapati is said to lead to the fulfilment of all desires and the removal of all hindrances. Besides being invoked as the Lord of Obstacles,[37] the Buddhist Gaṇapati is also referred to as 'the noble Gaṇapati of Wisdom'[38] the 'Great God of Wealth'[39] and the 'Great Compassionate Gaṇapati'.[40] Whereas the Brahmanical Gaṇapati is also associated with wealth and wisdom, the concept of a lord of compassion is purely Buddhist.

In the Tibetan Buddhist texts Gaṇapati's zoomorphic past is evident. He is referred to as the 'chief of elephant-trunked ones'.[41] He is described as having three faces, that of a monkey, a rat and an elephant. He is also said to manifest in a monkey's body.[42] Monkey fat,[43] heart and hair are prescribed for some of the rituals in the worship of Gaṇapati along with elephant hair[44] and the meatless shoulder blade of an elephant.[45] Even his consort is said to have the face of a monkey.[46] Gaṇapati himself is said to manifest in a monkey's body to generate coarse awareness.[47] The association with the monkey links Gaṇapati to the elephant deity of Kapīśa because *kapi* signifies both 'elephant' and 'monkey' and Kapīśa, therefore, signifies both Elephant Lord and Monkey Lord. The association between the elephant and the monkey appears to have some significance in the Śaiva context as well. In a Śiva temple in Cintāmaṇi (Kolar District, Karnataka), the doorway to the temple has the figure of an elephant to the left and that of a monkey to the right.[48] The *Skanda Purāṇa* also refers to a three-headed Gaṇapati with the face of a monkey, an elephant and a lion in place of the rat of the Buddhist version.[49] I do not know what the significance of the monkey and the lion is in this case. However, even in the contemporary context, Hanumān and the Heramba form of Gaṇapati represent an association with these two animals. Hanumān nearly always has a niche in Gaṇapati temples in some regions such as Maharashtra and the Heramba form of Gaṇapati has a lion mount.

The Tibetan Buddhist texts distinguish between the Buddhist Gaṇapati and the evil Vināyaka of the Brahmanical tradition. One text called the *Vināyaka Graha Nirmocana* describes the symptoms of Vināyaka possession and prescribes the rites for ridding oneself of this demon.[50] This description is evidently derived from the *Mānava Gṛhya Sūtra* with small variations.[51] The text makes no reference to the physical form of Vināyaka who is distinct from the Buddhist Gaṇapati. The latter only removes obstacles and does not create them. He is worshipped after invoking other Buddhist deities and in one case it is stated that Gaṇapati 'the supreme king of all elemental spirits who is truly loving to practitioners' should be invoked after worshipping the *guru* and the Buddha.[52] In the Brahmanical tradition, Gaṇapati is supposed to be invoked first.

The Buddhist Tantric Gaṇapati has two aspects to his personality, the wrathful one and the peaceful one. In the former case, he is described as 'having the heart of a Buddha and the head of an animal'. The wrathful form of Gaṇapati has many characteristics and attributes of Bhairava-Śiva. He is described as wearing a garment made from the skin of a tiger holding a flaming *vajra* (a thunderbolt which is the weapon of Indra) and skull. He wears a garland of skulls which otherwise is only associated with Śiva.[53] His body is either red or blue.[54] In his peaceful aspect Gaṇapati is associated with the Bodhisattva Avalokiteśvara. He is referred to as the 'Great Compassionate One'.[55] Bodhisattvas are, by definition, markedly responsive to the needs of humans by virtue of their compassionate nature and Gaṇapati acquires this quality in the Buddhist context. He is referred to as the 'Emanation of the Most Noble Avalokiteśvara'[56] and as one who is manifested in the heart of Avalokiteśvara.[57] In one hymn Gaṇapati is described as being white and bearing in his four hands a radish, an axe, a trident and a skull. He bears the image of Amitābha on his head.[58]

This form is similar to that of Avalokiteśvara who is also often represented with the effigy of Amitābha in his crown since he is an accolyte of Amitābha.[59] Similarly, in his form as Siṃhanāda, Avalokiteśvara is often represented holding a trident or a human skull and his body is white.[60]

This syncretic Gaṇapati who acquires the attributes of both Śiva and the Bodhisattva Avalokiteśvara is also well known in Japan. According to some Japanese texts a dual form of Gaṇapati, known as Kangi-ten, is looked upon as the son of Śiva and Āryāvalokiteśvara (another name for Avalokiteśvara) in his feminine form which is identical to that of Ūmā, wife of Śiva. Gaṇapati is, therefore, believed to have two natures, masculine and feminine, symbolising the union of Brahmanism and Buddhism or, perhaps, Śivaism and Buddhism. In Japan, this Tantric form of Gaṇapati is represented by two elephant headed human figures, male and female, embracing. The female aspect is considered to be a metamorphosis assumed by Avalokiteśvara while the male part is supposed to be a metamorphosis of Mahāvairocana or of Śiva. The two figures together represent the unity between the devotee and the Buddha. This dual form of Gaṇapati was introduced into Japan from China where it was known as Kuan-shi-t'ien. According to the Chinese it symbolised the union of sky and earth.[61] This form probably came into existence in China in the eighth century and Śubhākarasiṃha, who visited China, translated into Chinese a ritual for the worship of Gaṇapati in this form.[62] It is not known whether this text was brought to China by Subhākarasiṃha from India in the eighth century or whether it had been brought to China earlier.

The idea that the dual Gaṇapati represents a union between Buddhism and Brahmanism/Śivaism is also implicit in the *Gaṇapatihṛdaya mantra* which forms part of the Tibetan texts. Here Gaṇapati plays the role of a mediator between Buddhist and non-Buddhist traditions. By using the *mantra* contained in the text, non-Buddhist ceremonies can be transformed into Buddhist ones. The presumed author of this text is the Buddha himself.[63] Perhaps, those who sought a syncretism of Buddhism and Śivaism chose to worship Gaṇapati as the symbol of this syncretism.

In several Buddhist Tantras there appears to be a syncretism between the Buddha and Śiva. There are Buddhist Tantras with titles such as *Vajrabhairava* or *Buddhakāpāla* which point to a certain Buddha-Śiva melding. At other times the syncretism is between Śiva and one of the Bodhisattvas. A brass sculpture of the early medieval period in the collection of the Ashutosh Museum, University of Calcutta, depicts the composite Śiva-Lokeśvara (Avalokiteśvara) as a two-armed ithyphallic god holding a skull and a trident. He bears the tiny seated figure of the Dhyāni-Buddha Amitābha on top of his *jaṭamukuṭa* (crest of matted hair) and has two standing male figures on either side.[64] This strange combination of Mahāyāna doctrines with the worship of Śiva has its parallel in Champa, Java, Sumatra, Nepal and Tibet during the same period. Tāranātha (sixteenth/seventeenth century AD) asserts that it was in the Vikramaśīla and Jagaddala Universities founded by the Pāla kings (between eighth and eleventh centuries AD in the region of modern Bengal and Bihar) that Tantrayāna Buddhism was fully developed and that it was from these centres that missionaries went to preach in Tibet and Nepal.[65] It would appear that Śiva was initially associated with the Buddha or with the Bodhisattva Avalokiteśvara in certain Buddhist Tantras. Later, in some regions, Gaṇapati became the symbol of this syncretism. Elsewhere he was looked upon as a purely Buddhist deity having some of the characteristics of the Buddha and none of Śiva. Getty describes three images of Gaṇapati, one Cham (eighth century), one Khmer (fourteenth century) and one Burmese (undated) where he is represented in the characteristic pose of the Buddha with some of the typical features of the Buddha such as the protruberance between the eyes (which is distinct from a third eye) and the right arm in the *bhūmisparśa mudrā* (earth-touching pose), one of the well-known attitudes of the Buddha.[66] The statues suggest that the elephant-headed deity came to represent some of the concepts associated with the Buddha without ever actually being identified with him.

It is possible that in some areas or at least in some monasteries in the regions of modern West Bengal and Bihar, Gaṇapati was worshipped in some of the esoteric forms described above. Even if some of the forms evolved in China or Japan, the idea of this syncretism probably came from India. This suggestion may be unacceptable to those scholars who insist on a clear and precise textual reference to such a phenomenon. Yet, from what I have discussed earlier, this idea sometimes appears implicit in the Tibetan Buddhist texts. Besides, actual religious practice often takes liberties with notions stated in religious texts. Take, for example, the case of Avalokiteśvara who has numerous forms. In Japan there is a tradition amongst a fairly large section of people or in certain religious congregations where this Bodhisattva is represented in some feminine forms.[67] Even in China he is sometimes conceived of in the feminine form although such a notion is non-existent in the Buddhist canons of these countries. The number of forms in which devotees may conceive of their chosen deity are infinite depending on their needs and aspirations. Many syncretic forms are the products of popular belief which, unlike the Buddhist cannon, are not fixed.

The Buddhist Gāṇapatya texts are associated with the last creative phase of Indian Buddhism under Pāla rule. This period witnessed a changing social order when the influence of *bhakti* and Tantrism led to the inclusion of popular cults and practices in both the Buddhist and Brahmanical religions. *Śūdras* and women could be initiated into these new forms of ritual and worship. Gaṇapati represented the perfect blend of a Brahmanical, Buddhist and folk deity who was equated with universally common needs and desires. He became the symbol of a new phase of religious belief which sought a rapprochement between the Sanskritic and non-Sanskritic traditions. If several texts were devoted to his worship alone it is possible that a section of persons chose to worship him to the exclusion of other deities. His powers are described as being so great that the devotee can have all his wishes granted, acquire health, wealth, learning and get compassion in time of need. Would there be any requirement then for the worship of another deity?

GAṆAPATI AND ŚIVAISM

Like the Buddhist Tantric texts, the Śaiva Tantras and Āgamas contain whole sections devoted to Gaṇapati where he figures as an independent god. These texts represent a tradition which is non-Brahmanical and, often, anti-Brahmanical. Certain Śaiva sects which drew inspiration from these traditions were looked down upon by the *brāhmaṇas* of the *Smārta* tradition.

Gaṇapati has three different roles in the Āgamas. He is, on the one hand, worshipped briefly, before any worship of Śiva begins, so that he may remove obstacles.[68] He is also one of the eight *gaṇas* who constitute the *dvārapālas* (guardians) of Śiva's shrine.[69] At the same time, in certain texts, he has sections devoted to his worship alone.[70] The former two roles are, undoubtedly, the influence of the northern *brāhmaṇas* who were settled in the South by the Coḷa kings. They represent those aspects of the Āgamas that are in line with Puranic traditions. The third aspect of Gaṇapati appears to have evolved in the far south. The sections in the Āgamas describing Gaṇapati's independent worship must have developed from about the tenth century. Śivaism had begun to enjoy royal patronage in the Tamil country from the seventh century when the Pallava king Mahendravarman I was converted from Jainism to Śivaism. The Coḷas built several famous Śiva temples. Initially, Gaṇapati's images were installed in these temples. Subsequently, he acquired his own shrines within the temples. He, therefore, came to require rituals of his own. At a later stage, he acquired independent temples. The Āgamas refer to temples of Gaṇapati where he is the principal deity with attendant deities of his own. Details regarding the location, architecture and form of deity to be installed in the different kinds of temples are also described.[71] Ultimately, this may have resulted in his being worshipped to the exclusion of other deities, by a category of people.

As an independent deity in the Āgamas, Gaṇapati acquires *utsavas* of his own.[72] He is associated with the harvest, because sowing takes place three or five days before his festival.[73] His *vāhana* is also worshipped which is not the case in the Buddhist Tantras.[74] He is worshipped with Śaiva *mantras* such as the *Mṛtyunjaya mantra.*[75] Worship of the *liṅga*[76] as also offerings of flesh[77] form part of his ritual. The radish which often figures as an attribute of the Buddhist Gaṇapati is absent in the Āgamas (as also in the Purāṇas). The Gaṇapati festival culminates with the immersion of the deity's image in water.[78] This represents a significant difference between the rituals of Śiva and those of Gaṇapati which, are very similar otherwise.

Unlike the Buddhist Tantras where Ganapati has a limited number of forms, in the Āgamas he acquires numerous forms.[79] These are not found in the Mahāpurāṇas and, therefore, appear to have evolved within the framework of Śivaism mainly in the Tamil region. They represent the various dimensions of Gaṇapati's personality. As Bāla Gaṇapati, he fulfils the role of son of Śiva and Pārvatī.[80] Bhakti Gaṇapati symbolises the important phenomenon of *bhakti.* Vijaya Gaṇapati is suggestive of the Puranic Gaṇapati who, as Śiva's chief *gaṇa,* ensures victory at all levels. Nṛtta Gaṇapati or Piṅgala Gaṇapati are close in concept to Śiva himself. Other forms such as *Śakti* Gaṇapati or Rakta Gaṇapati are evidently Tantric.[81] There is another Brahmanical form, that of Lakṣmī Gaṇapati, which is depicted with two *devīs.* It is obviously the reverse of the Gajalakṣmī concept where Lakṣmī is flanked by two elephants.[82] There is even a form called Krodha Gaṇapati which may have been borrowed from the wrathful aspect of the Buddhist Gaṇapati.[83]

Some of these forms continue to be worshipped today in independent temples of Gaṇapati in the South. At the Pañcamukha Heramba Gaṇapati temple at Mahālakṣmī layout, Bangalore, I obtained an interesting insight into a concept which must have existed centuries ago in some Gaṇapati temples. The *pujārī* (priest), Shankar Narain Shastri, considered Gaṇapati to be an '*avatāra*' of Śiva. In Chapter IV, I have said that some of the early images of Gaṇapati suggest that in a few regions, particularly in the early stages, the elephant-headed deity was looked upon as a form of Śiva. This thesis does not appear wholly unacceptable when considered in the light of some contemporary perceptions of Gaṇapati. Although no text might say so, the priest serving in the Pañcamukha Heramba Gaṇapati temple firmly believes this to be so. These beliefs must be looked at from the point of view of the laity and the priesthood to whom they are relevant. In a society where access to sacred texts is limited to very few and where the oral tradition remains important what the priest believes has greater influence on the laity than what is stated in sacred literature.

Against this background it is worth analysing the Gāṇapatya sects described in the *Śaṅkaravijaya* in order to determine whether they were really independent sects or wherther they were offshoots of the Buddhists and Śaivas.

THE GĀṆAPATYA SECTS

THE SECT OF HERAMBA GAṆAPATI

As discussed in Chapter IV, Heramba signifies 'buffalo' and this form of Gaṇapati combines in himself aspects of both Śiva and Durgā. The epithet 'Heramba' was eventually associated with the

Buddha as well. According to the *Śabdakalpadruma*,[84] Heramba is synonymous with some Tantric forms of the Buddha such as Heruka, Chakrasaṃvara, Vajrakāpāli, Vajraṭīka, Deva, Niśumbhi and Śaśiśekhara. Heruka, also signifies an attendant of Śiva.[85] In other words, Heramba is synonymous with the syncretic form of Buddha/Śiva-Kāpāla.

In the *Śaṅkaravijaya*, Heramba is visualized as embracing his *śakti* who is seated on his left thigh.[86] However, the *Devī Rahasya*, a Kashmiri text, describes Heramba Gaṇapati as a young boy, a *kumāra*.[87] Even the *Ajitāgama*[88] and the *Tantrasāra*[89] (the latter quotes from the *Śāradātilaka Tantra*, a Kashmiri text of the tenth or eleventh century AD) describe him without a *śakti*. Clearly, the Heramba Gāṇapatyas described in the *Śaṅkaravijaya* followed a tradition distinct to that described in the Kashmiri and south Indian Tantras and Āgamas. Was it Buddhist influence which led to this form acquiring a *śakti* like some of the Tantric Buddhist forms which also bear the epithet Heramba?

The iconographical form of Heramba Gaṇapati as described in the Āgamas also suggests Buddhist influence. His five heads are representative of the concept of five Dhyāni Buddhas of Mahāyāna Buddhism. His mount, the lion, is parallel to the lion-throne of the Buddha who manifests himself in the form of the five Dhyāni Buddhas. According to the *Ajitāgama*,[90] Heramba is white (like the elephant representing the Buddha's conception or like the Bodhisattva Avalokiteśvara). Five is also an important number in Brahmanism and Śiva, too, is associated with five. However, the fact that this form of Gaṇapati was initially looked down upon in the Āgamas would point to it being associated with things that were anti-Śaiva. It was recommended as being appropriate in a *kheṭa*.[91] The *Diptāgama* defines a *kheṭa* as a village inhabited by *śūdras*.[92] Possibly, some worshippers of Heramba Gaṇapati were Buddhists or Buddhists and Śaivas at the same time and were, therefore, looked down upon. It is significant that this form of Gaṇapati appears in places (Kashmir and the Tamil region) where a flourishing Buddhism was eventually replaced by a resurgent Śivaism. Consequently, there are positive indications of borrowing between the two faiths. The sect of Heramba Gaṇapati probably existed in both Kashmir and the Tamil region.

It is difficult to determine at what stage the Heramba aspect of Gaṇapati acquired its particular iconographic form. The earliest reference to a five headed form of the diety, seated on a lion and referred to as Heramba, is found in the Kashmiri text *Śāradātilaka Tantra.*[93] Since the iconographical form of Heramba Gaṇapati was already established in the tenth/eleventh centuries, and since he is described in the *Āgamas* it would appear that this form of the deity must have had a following, at least, by the end of the ninth century. I referred earlier to a twelfth century inscription recording the erection of a temple to Heramba Gaṇapati in Madhya Pradesh.[94] It is possible that it was built by adherents to the sect of Heramba Gaṇapati.

THE SECT OF UCCHIṢṬA GAṆAPATI

Ucchiṣṭa Gaṇapati, according to the *Śaṅkaravijaya,* is to be meditated upon as having four arms, three eyes, bearing the *pāśa* (rope), *aṅkuśa* (goad) and *gada* (mace). One hand is held in the *abhaya mudrā* (freedom from fear position). The tip of his trunk descends into the goddess' *yoni* (vulva).[95] According to the *Śaṅkaravijaya,* Ucchiṣṭa's cult is also known as Hairamba and I wonder whether the association between the Herambas and Ucchiṣṭas was essentially because they were associated with certain categories of society who were looked down upon by those who conformed to Brahmanical norms of worship and who did not accept these esoteric forms. When the esoteric forms were finally recognized it was with some modifications.

The *Prāṇatoṣiṇī* describes Ucchiṣṭa Gaṇanātha as the boyhood of Heramba[96] whereas the *Devī Rahasya* states the contrary.[97] Śaiva texts such as the *Īśānaśivagurudevapaddhati* describe Ucchiṣṭa Gaṇapati without a *śakti.* In some of the later Tantric texts, however, Ucchiṣṭa Caṇḍālī is described as the *śakti* of Ucchiṣṭa Gaṇapati although the *Śaṅkaravijaya* does not mention the name of the *devī.*[98] According to the *Prāṇatoṣiṇī,* Ucchiṣṭa Caṇḍālī is a form of Mātaṅgī.[99] Caṇḍālī and Mātaṅgī were goddesses of the *Caṇḍālas* and *Mātaṅgas* both originally aboriginal tribes who were eventually converted into a low caste.[100] The practices of this sect were evidently Tantric and later texts associated this form of the deity with the goddesses of the lower orders of society.

The term Ucchiṣṭa indicates a cultic practice of eating left-over food as part of the religious discipline of a deity. There are Śaiva cults with similar practices.[101] The term by itself is derogatory. The Mahāpurāṇas make no mention of this form of Gaṇapati. The members of this sect were evidently of low-caste or from rival religious sects. Since the earliest reference to Ucchiṣṭa Gaṇapati appears to be in the Āgamas, this particular sect could not have come into existence before the end of the eighth century, at the earliest. It is more likely that it evolved in the ninth century, probably around the same time as the sect of Heramba Gaṇapati, since both are said to be closely related. The *Svayambhuvāgama* recommends this form of Gaṇapati in *paṭṭans*.[102] The *Diptāgama* defines a *paṭṭan* as a town where there is international trade and where various communities reside.[103] Since the Buddhists in the region of modern Tamil Nadu resided mainly in coastal towns in the early medieval period it is possible that this deity was venerated by some Buddhists and other sects. It may have also been popular with the trading communities in a region where internal and external trade flourished.

THE SECT OF MAHĀGAṆAPATI

There is a certain uniformity of concept and form in the description of Mahāgaṇapati in the Āgamas, Tantras and in the *Śaṅkaravijaya*. The differences between this form of the deity in the Buddhist and Brahmanical contexts are minor.

The earliest texts devoted to Mahāgaṇapati such as the *Mahāgaṇapati Tantra* form part of the Tibetan Buddhist canon. Gaṇapati is described as the 'world-benefitting god of gods whose worship brings accomplishment'.[104] Whereas in the Buddhist context he is said to be white in colour with four hands,[105] the Brahmanical texts such as the *Īśānaśivagurudevapaddhati*,[106] the *Prapañcasāra Tantra*[107] and the *Śaṅkaravijaya*[108] describe him as being red with ten or twelve arms. In both cases, he is accompanied by his *śakti*. In the Buddhist text, she is not described but merely stated to be present in the *maṇḍala* of Mahāgaṇapati.[109]

The sect of Gāṇapatyas worshipping Mahāgaṇapati described in the *Śaṅkaravijaya* appear to have evolved from within the Brahmanical tradition. They claim to follow the *Śruti* and consider that Mahāgaṇapati symbolises the trinity—Brahmā, Viṣṇu and Śiva. They also appear to be adherents of the dualistic school of philosophy since they maintain that *mukti* (liberation from the cycle of birth and death) is not merging with the *Brahman* but staying forever in the same *loka* (world) as their god.[110] It is likely that they were off-shoots of the Pāśupata Śaivas or Āgamic Śaivas since both schools are dualistic.

The members of this sect appear to have been *brāhmaṇas*, for in the *Śaṅkaravijaya*, Śaṅkara is described as condemning the fact that they felt the need to brand themselves with the symbol of the sect. He goes on to state that a *brāhmaṇa* needs no symbols. He distinguishes himself from other categories of society by the fact of his birth in a *brāhmaṇa* family, by the observation of the *saṃskāras* (sacraments) stipulated in the *Vedas* and of the four *āśramas*.

In the Śaiva Āgamas Mahāgaṇapati appears as one of the sixteen forms of the deity[111] and has temples dedicated to him. This form was considered specially appropriate for installation in a *kubjaka*, but it could also be installed in all places.[112] According to the *Diptāgama*, a *kubjaka* is a village bordering a *kheṭa*. The latter, as stated earlier is a village inhabited by *śūdras*.[113] Possibly, the *brāhmaṇa* members of this sect were low castes who claimed *brāhmaṇa* status because of the ritual functions they performed in the Gaṇapati temples and who chose this deity in preference to Śiva in order to escape the secondary position they may have occupied in the hierarchy of Śiva temple priests. This sect probably came into existence around the same time as the sects of Heramba and Ucchiṣṭa Gaṇapati.

THE SECT OF HARIDRA GAṆAPATI

According to the *Śaṇkaravijaya*, the followers of Haridra Gaṇapati do not worship the *śakti*. The deity is described as being dressed in yellow with yellow *yajñopavīta* (sacred thread), having four arms and three eyes. The head of the sect recites a *mantra* from the *Kṛṣṇa Yajur Veda*.[114] This sect appears to be a purely Brahmanical one and, like the sect of Mahāgaṇapati, it probably came into existence around the tenth century.

In the *Ajitāgama*, Haridra Gaṇapati is described as a turmeric coloured elephant flanked by two wives. The word 'wives' is specifically used (*dārāyugalam*).[115] These wives are distinct to *śaktis*. This form appears closest in concept to the Gaṇapati of the *Mudgala* and *Gaṇeśa Purāṇas* where he is always flanked by his wives, Siddhi and Buddhi.[116] In these two Purāṇas they appear as an intrinsic part of Gaṇapati[117] and do not require any special rituals associated with *śakti* worship. The *Ajitāgama* recommends that this form of Gaṇapati be installed in capital cities.[118] It probably became popular with a section of the population in the cities and gradually a sect devoted to it came into existence. Yellow is the traditional colour of the *vaiśya varṇa.* Since Haridra Gaṇapati is specially recommended for capital cities it probably became popular with a growing category of wealthy clientele and gradually came to be projected as an independent deity.

THE SECTS OF NAVANĪTA, SVARṆA AND SAṂTĀNA GAṆAPATI

Navanīta, Svarṇa and Saṃtāna Gaṇapati appear to be clubbed together as one in the *Śaṅkaravijaya.*[119] They were obviously closely related. Their followers did not worship the *śakti,* wore turmeric and claimed to follow Vedic rites only. These sects, too, appear to have been limited to the far South.[120] According to the *Ajitāgama,* Svarṇa Gaṇapati is described as being white as gold and without a *śakti.*[121] Although the *Śaṅkaravijaya* states that these three forms are described in the Śaiva Āgamas,[122] the names of Navanīta and Saṃtāna Gaṇapati do not appear in the Āgamas that I have consulted nor do they appear in the traditional lists of sixteen or thirty-two Gaṇapatis available in the *Tantras* nor in the list of fifty six Vināyakas of Kāśī. However, a *mantra* of Navanīta-Gaṇapati from the Pūrvāmnāya occurs in the *Śrīvidyāratnākara.*[123]

Navanīta Gaṇapati recalls the child Kṛṣṇa and his myths about stealing butter. Saṃtāna Gaṇapati reminds one of Saṃtāna Gopāla, a form of Kṛṣṇa worshipped to obtain offspring. Possibly, both these forms were popular with the Vaiṣṇavas who also worshipped Gaṇapati and who may, in some cases, have identified him with the Vaiṣṇava deities. This suggestion becomes more plausible if one understands some aspects of the contemporary worship of Gaṇapati. There are Gaṇapati temples today where the officiants are Vaiṣṇava and where the deity is looked upon as a form of Viṣṇu although I do not know of any text where this is stated. One such temple is the Aneguḍḍe Śrī Vināyaka temple, Kumbhāsi, in the Dakshin Kannada District, Karnataka. The officiants are Vaiṣṇava *brāhmaṇas* of the Mādhava sect. The head priest (*pramukha pujārī*) who I met insisted that the Gaṇapati in this temple was considered to be a manifestation of Viṣṇu. The priest also distinguished between Gaṇapati in general who is a deity in his own right and this particular image.

Gaṇapati is the only Śaiva deity who is worshipped by the Vaiṣṇavas. He is sometimes referred to as Gaja Ālvār, the thirteenth Ālvār of the Vaiṣṇava *bhakti* tradition of the south.[124] It is not relevant whether this is mentioned in the sacred texts. Nor does it matter whether all Vaiṣṇavas accept it or not. The fact is that in some temples this is what the priests believe and what some of the laity agree with. Such beliefs are easily accepted by the Hindu mind which sees the unity behind the diversity and can readily accept seemingly disparate and contradictory concepts as different forms of the one and only.

This tendency to syncretize has been present throughout the centuries. There is a nineteenth century scroll of drawings of Gaṇapati prepared by artists attached to the Mysore Palace in the nineteenth century. One of these forms is referred to as Siṃha Gaṇapati and it is depicted as a deity with the composite head of a lion and an elephant having eight arms.[125] It is evidently a syncretism between Gaṇapati and the Narasiṃha form of Viṣṇu. This same form is also represented on the side wall of the modern Pañcamukha Heramba Gaṇapati temple at the Mahālakṣmī layout, Bangalore. Where Siṃha Ganapati is mentioned in some Tantric texts such as the *Śrītattvanidhi* he is simply described as having the face of a lion with an elephant's trunk.[126] No mention is made of the Narasiṃha form of Viṣṇu. In the modern Śrī Siddhi Buddhi Vināyaka temple at Sarojini Nagar, New Delhi, however, Siṃha Gaṇapati is merely depicted as Gaṇapati riding on a lion and is distinct from the Heramba form only in that the latter has five heads (plate 2). He forms one of a group of thirty four Gaṇapatis that decorate the sides of the hall for special *pūjās* and *utsavas* next to the main temple. There is, on the other hand, in this same temple a form called Vaiṣṇava Gaṇapati which depicts the deity as blue in colour (like Kṛṣṇa) (plate 3). In three of his hands he holds the *śankha* (conch) the *cakra* (disc) and the *gada* (mace), all typically Vaiṣṇava attributes. The fourth hand is held in *abhaya mudrā*. These descriptions illustrate that a process of syncretism has constantly been taking place and that it varies in degree between regions and temples.

Just as the various village goddesses are considered to be forms of Pārvatī, similarly, in some temples, the priests and the laity believe that Gaṇapati represents a form of the major deities Śiva or Viṣṇu. There are also forms of Gaṇapati in temple sculptures which do not appear to be described in any text. Rāma Gaṇapati is an example. It is one of thirty two forms depicted on the top parapet of the *prākāra wall* (north-west corner) of the Nañjuṇḍeśvara Temple dedicated to Śiva in Nañjungūḍ, not far from Mysore. This wall dates to about AD 1850.[127] There is another form known as Subrahmaṇya Gaṇapati described in the *Vidyārṇava Tantra.*[128] Why would these forms emerge if they did not seek to identify or at least create a link between Gaṇapati and Rāma or Gaṇapati and Subrahmaṇya? Perhaps, they emerged in those temples or villages where both deities were popular and the message they conveyed was either that both were at par, or that both represented traits and characteristics that complemented each other or, perhaps, that both were forms of each other. The Aneguḍḍa Gaṇapati temple in Karnataka has recently been renovated and has a new facade which is ornate with various Gaṇapatis in the niches. The motifs include an image of Gaṇapati with the child Kṛṇṣa on his lap. Such an image is again one that I have not come across in any text. The motifs have been made by craftsmen (*śilpis*) from Shimoga and are claimed to be based on some sacred text. Since sacred texts are numerous and since most people have no access to them, anything can be claimed to have its origin in 'sacred texts' and will be accepted by the public and most priests as well.

Strict Vaiṣṇavas and Śaivas may not accept these interpretations. Yet, in the region itself the local priesthood has created its own tradition. Often the deity acquires a name decided upon by the local priest and not because it conforms to any particular type. Major temples built by kings or rich landowners and merchants may have had images that were made in strict accordance with the *Śilpaśāstras.* However, this would not have been the case in small temples which made do with local craftsmen or with images believed to be *svayambhū.* There is a modern temple at Amdalli on the border of Karwar taluk, North Kannada District, Karnataka, called the Śrī Vīra Gaṇapati temple. Here the *mūrti* is believed to be *svayambhū.* About ten years ago a Customs Officer noticed a stone along the highway that had the shape of an elephant's head without arms and attributes. So a temple was constructed over the stone. The priest who was appointed by the local community decided that the image should be named Śrī Vīra Gaṇapati. According to the Āgamas, Vīra Gaṇapati has numerous attributes whereas this image has none. Yet that was what the priest decided and it was readily accepted by everyone concerned. Saṃtāna and Navanīta Gaṇapati must have also been named in such a way after the wishes of some priests and their laity who wished to see in Gaṇapati what they admired and loved in Kṛṣṇa. Eventually, they may have considered themselves as a separate subsect. This subsect also probably came into existence around the tenth century.

At this point, it would be relevant to ask to what extent were the Gāṇapatyas really sects in the true sense of the word. A sect generally implies a specific doctrine, a priesthood and an exclusive laity. Strictly speaking, very few Hindu sects have ever had an exclusive laity. In early medieval India a person could be both a Vaiṣṇava, a Śākta or Tantrik as well as a Yogin. A well known example is the medieval Vaiṣṇava poet, Vidyāpati (*c.* AD 1400) whose devotional songs to Rādhā and Kṛṣṇa are sung even today. Besides these devotional songs he wrote the *Śivasarvasāra, Durgābhaktitaraṅgiṇī* and a Tantrik work, so that he may be called a Vaiṣṇava, a Śaiva, a Śākta and a Tantrik.[129] In the case of the six Gāṇapatya sects described in the *Śaṅkaravijaya,* even if they had a priesthood, it is unlikely that they had an exclusive laity and they do not appear to have had any specific doctrine.

The heads of the so-called sects of Gāṇapatyas described in the *Śaṅkaravijaya* are referred to as *Mahāgaṇapatimatavādi* and *Haridragaṇapatimatavādi*[130] (propagators of the doctrine of Mahāgaṇapati or Haridra Gaṇapati) or as *upāsakas* (worshippers) of Ucchiṣṭa, Navanīta, Svarṇa and Saṃtāna Gaṇapati.[131] This implies that these so-called heads were, in fact, only devotees of this form of Gaṇapati and preached about him. They do not appear to have had any specific doctrine but based their rituals and beliefs on certain sections of the Śaiva Āgamas and the Buddhist Tantras and may have also followed some Vaiṣṇava traditions. Possibly, they were associated, in some cases, with the lower orders of society who would not have been as strict as the *brāhmaṇa* community about the distinction between different religious sects. Since the sections on Gaṇapati in the Āgamas form part of the Śaiva doctrine and cult there was nothing distinct or new about the practices of these sects. The essential difference between the Gāṇapatya sects of the *Śaṅkaravijaya* is that some, such as those of Heramba and Ucchiṣṭa Gaṇapati were Tantric and were influenced by Buddhism whereas the other four were not. The former two sects also appear to have had a following outside south India. Perhaps one reason why no *maṭha* of the Gāṇapatyas could develop was because they did not enjoy royal patronage. In the South, the Coḷa kings and the prosperous merchants extended patronage to both Vaiṣṇava and Śaiva temples. Since Gaṇapati was part of the Śaiva cult he was not considered independent of Śiva. So the small village and urban temples devoted to him remained limited local features. In the towns, particularly, the temples devoted to Gaṇapati had to share the laity with the other more important temples of Viṣṇu and Śiva.

Since in the fourteenth century the *Sammoha Tantra* speaks of five different cults of the Gāṇapatyas, they must have existed for several centuries. However, it is likely that some of these sects may have faded away gradually while others were increasingly influenced by and identified with the *Smārta* Gāṇapatyas. The reasons why they faded away were because: they do not appear to have had any influential *brāhmaṇas* or royalty amongst their followers; they had nothing new to offer; the Tantrik and esoteric rites of two of these sects were shunned by many; Buddhism was completely replaced by a resurgent Śivaism in the South during the Coḷa period and the powerful *bhakti* movement with Śiva and Viṣṇu as the principal deities must have attracted a large number of devotees from among the common folk; and finally, Gaṇapati as the son of Śiva was an intrinsic part of Śivaism and could not be accepted by the majority of people as superior to, or independent of Śiva.

GAṆAPATI AND THE SMĀRTA TRADITION

The *pañcāyatana* form of worship introduced by Śaṅkarācārya was accepted by the *Smārta* sects. The monistic philosophy preached by Śaṅkara made it possible to choose one of these as the principal deity and manifestation of the *Brahman* (all-pervading soul and spirit of the universe) and, at the same time, worship the other four deities as different forms of the same *Brahman*. Once Gaṇapati was accepted as one of the five principal deities of Brahmanism it was a matter of time before a category of *brāhmaṇas* chose to worship him as their principal deity. This is the tradition reflected in the *Mudgala* and *Gaṇeśa Purāṇas.*

One might ask why Gaṇapati was included in the *pañcāyatana* and thereby equated with the major Puranic deities. Possibly, one reason was because he was already popular with some Buddhist and Śaiva sects having been identified as an aspect of the Buddha and Śiva or the symbol of the syncretism between the two. Granting him an important position in the Brahmanical framework was one way of coping with rival sects. It was in the interest of the *brāhmaṇas* to sustain a large clientele on which their livelihood depended and, at the same time, ensure the prevalence of the traditional Brahmanical norms as spelt out in the *Smṛti.* Another reason may have been because Gaṇapati, as the creator and remover of obstacles, could be associated with all rituals and deities. Equally important was the fact that the concept of Gaṇapati was present in the Vedas (it is an epithet used for Bṛhaspati,[132] Indra[133] and Rudra.)[134] It was, therefore, easy to link the elephant-headed deity to the Vedas and, thereby, confer on him the standing of an ancient deity of the Vedic tradition. This was not the case with Kubera, Hanumān or the *nāgas.* Although they were associated with major gods, they were never identified with them. Therefore, they remained separate and secondary figures.

In content, both the *Mudgala* and the *Gaṇeśa Purāṇas* have much in common, showing a basic coherence in belief and practice. They are the products of *Smārta brāhmaṇas* and while they reflect the influences of the Tantras and the Āgamas, they strictly adhere to Brahmanical norms. They appear to have constituted the only independent sect of Gāṇapatyas in the sense that they were not offshoots of other sects. They appear to have come into existence around the eleventh or twelfth century and belong to a period later than the *Śaṅkaravijaya.*

The Gāṇapatyas lay stress on the *pañcāyatana* form of pūjā where Śiva, Viṣṇu, Durgā and Sūrya are equally important, in that they are considered different forms of Gaṇapati. However, it is Gaṇapati who is the source of all such manifestations. Most of the forms of Gaṇapati worshipped by the sects described in the *Śaṅkaravijaya* are not mentioned in these Purāṇas. The *Gaṇeśa* and the *Mudgala Purāṇas* are monistic works and are not in conflict with Śaṅkarāchārya's philosophy of Advaita Vedānta. Ānandagiri's sects had a particular symbol each, such as the elephant trunk or the elephant tusk, branded on the devotee's forehead or shoulder. These two sectarian Purāṇas make no mention of such a practice. According to the *Mudgala Purāṇa*,[135] any person of any caste can receive *dīkṣā* (initiation) to the status of a Gāṇapatya. However *dīkṣā* can only be given by *brāhmaṇas.* Once initiated, if a member leaves the sect, it is stated that he will face obstacles everywhere. In order to be initiated, a *kṣatriya* must give up the use of arms, a *vaiśya* must cease to practice trade and a *śūdra* must give up violence and other lowly activities. In addition, after initiation, the Gāṇapatya must perform his daily duties as stipulated in the Āgamas and Vedas. He has to smear sandal paste in twelve places on the body—head, forehead, both ears, neck, arms, heart, stomach, navel, both hips and back. Preferably, he should cover the whole body with red sandalpaste, taken from a statue of Gaṇapati which has been smeared with it. The Gāṇapatya must wear around the arms and neck *mālās* (rosaries) of *śamī* seeds (*śamī* is the name of a tree) or the seeds of the *mandār* tree (the coral tree).[136] If these are not available then even the *vidruma* (coral) or *akṣa* (a shrub which produces brown seeds used for making rosaries) seeds will do. It is essential for him to observe the *vrata* (a vow taken and observed for the fulfilment of specific desires) on the two main *caturthīs,* (in the months of *bhādrapada* and *māgha*), visit the *kṣetra* (sacred site) of Gaṇapati, and also recite and preach about Gaṇapati. A Gāṇapatya is also permitted to observe the *vratas* and visit the *tīrthas* of other deities. Elsewhere it is stated that Ganapati is to be worshipped only by *yogīs.* This is because he is synonymous with *Brahman* and the latter can only be achieved through *yoga* and *yogīs* alone are well established in *yoga.*[137] In this case *yoga* is synonymous with *śānti,* a tranquil state of mind. From this it would appear that a Gāṇapatya was essentially a *sanyāsi* (a renouncer) even though this is not specifically stated.

To show the importance of their deity, the *Smārta* Gāṇapatyas had to create a mythology for him distinct to that found in the Mahāpurāṇas. They had to justify his position as an equal of Viṣṇu, Śiva or the Devī, because even if the *pañcāyatana* form of *pūjā* had come into existence, these other deities were still more important. They had to elaborate a distinct theology for Gaṇapati and, at the same time, stress its antiquity. They sought to establish a special iconographical form for this deity, to distinguish it from that of the other sects. These objectives were achieved in various ways.

The *Gaṇeśa* and *Mudgala Purāṇas* appropriate whole myths from the Mahāpurāṇas with the difference that Gaṇapati is the central figure in place of Śiva, Viṣṇu or Durgā. Take, for instance, the myth of Gajāsura. In the *Mahāpurāṇas,* Śiva destroys this *asura* and then wears his skin. In the *Mudgala Purāṇa,* it is Gaṇapati who destroys Gajāsura.[138] Mahiṣāsura is killed by Gaṇapati in his form as *Śakti.*[139] Like Kṛṣṇa, Gaṇapati acquires a childhood which is vividly described. He becomes the mind-born son of Brahmā.[140] He is depicted as the five year old son of Śeṣa.[141] Some new myths are created. Daśaratha is able to obtain sons only after worshipping Gaṇapati.[142] Vyāsa is able to compile the Vedas and the Purāṇas after doing likewise.[143] Other deities are shown in an inferior position. Indra is used as a messenger of Gaṇapati,[144] or he is swallowed by Gaṇapati and inside his stomach sees the whole universe and many *brahmāṇḍas* (cosmic eggs). Then he is humbled and worships Gaṇapati.[145] Like the other gods, he acquires an abode of his own called Svānanda.[146]

Gaṇapati borrows aspects and attributes of other Puranic deities. Like Viṣṇu, he acquires eight incarnations. These are Vakraṭuṇḍa, Ekadanta, Mahodara, Gajānana, Lambodara, Vikaṭa, Vighnarāja and Dhūmravarṇa.[147] As in the case of the *avatāras* of Viṣṇu, each manifests itself for a specific purpose. Gaṇapati's incarnations destroy eight different demons (*Matsara, Mada, Moha, Lobha, Krodha, Kāma, Manmata* and *Ahaṃkāra*) who are nothing but the personification of negative tendencies. He is present in the four *yugas* in different forms. In *Kṛta Yuga* he is called Vināyaka and is the son of Kaśyap. His vehicle is the lion and he is said to be as brilliant as the sun, and has eight arms. In *Treta Yuga* he is known as Mayureśvar, he sits on a peacock, is the colour of moonlight and becomes the son of Śiva. He has six arms. In *Dvāpara Yuga* he rides a mouse, is four-armed and is called Gajānana. He is the son of Vareṇya (Sun) and is red in colour. In *Kali Yuga,* he rides a horse, is the colour of smoke and is two-armed. He is worshipped as Gaṇeśa. He gives *siddhi* in all ages.[148]

Gaṇapati acquires *mantras* of his own: one, four, five, six, eight, ten, twelve, sixteen, eighteen or twenty eight syllable *mantras.*[149] The *Gaṇeśa* and *Mudgala Purāṇas* admit that they follow what is prescribed in the Tantras, Purāṇas, Āgamas and Vedas.

But the Ṛg Vedic *mahāmantra, Gaṇānām tva Gaṇapatim havāmahe* is considered superior to all the Āgamic ones.[150] There are repeated references to the fact that the Āgamas are the sources of the Gāṇapatya *mantras, nyāsas, mudras* and much else.[151] Gaṇapati is regarded as the source of the Vedas[152] and he is identified with the Vedic sacrifice[153] and is called *yajñapati*.[154] He acquires a *Kīlakastotra*,[155] *Sahasranāmastotra*[156] enunciated by Śiva and even a *Gītā* where he expounds upon *jñāna yoga, karma yoga* and *kṣetra viveka* to King Vareṇya.[157]

The typical form of Gaṇapati in these sectarian Purāṇas is with his two consorts: Siddhi on his left and Buddhi on his right.[158] All three together are said to constitute Gaṇapati.[159] However, Gaṇapati has a female form as well. There is an episode described in the *Mudgala Purāṇa* where Gaṇapati appears before Brahmā in the form of *Śakti*. She claims to be Gaṇeśa.[160] This suggests that Ganapati is both masculine and feminine. The devotee conceives of him as he wishes. There is also an *ardhanārī* (half male half female) form described in the *Mudgala Purāṇa* and referred to as *Śakti* Vināyaka. It is stated that *Śakti* forms the left side of Gaṇeśa. Both of them together constitute *Brahman* which is synonymous with Svānanda, the abode of Gaṇapati.[161] No such icon has so far come to light. However, from inscriptional evidence we know that such a form existed in the eleventh century. A verse in the *Halāyudhastotra* inscribed in AD 1063 on the Amreśvara temple at Mandhata in the East Nimar District, Madhya Pradesh, states that, competing with the *ardhnarīśvara* form of his father Śiva, Gaṇapati assumed the same form.[162] This form of Gaṇapati represents the recognition of and the concession made to *śakti* worship in general. Such a form is also described in the *sixteenth century Silparatna* of Śrī Kumāra. A passage in this text describes *Śakti* Gaṇapati as having the head of an elephant with the lower body of a youthful female with corpulent belly, heavy breasts and beautiful hips, who is endowed with two proboscises and ten arms.[163] The *Śilparatna* describes the iconography of *Śakti* Gaṇapati under the heading *miśramūrtayaḥ* (composite images) along with several other well-known syncretistic image-types such as *Ardhanārīśvara, Lakṣmī-Nārāyaṇa* or *Hari-Hara*.[164] Is is distinct to the other composite images in that the body is completely feminine with breasts and feminine hips, and only the head remains that of Gaṇapati and, therefore, is masculine.

In the *Gaṇeśa* and *Mudgala Purāṇas*, Gaṇapati's trunk is consistently described as hanging straight down and being as firm as a rod (*śuṇḍādaṇḍa*).[165] It is as though a deliberate attempt is being made to distinguish him from the other iconographical forms where his trunk turns either to the left or to the right. This constant reference to Gaṇapati's trunk as being straight as a rod has a connotation which he does not have elsewhere. The *daṇḍa* brings to mind the club that Lakulīśa often holds. In fact Lakulīśa means the holder of the club. The *laguḍa* or club is an offensive weapon. Its association with a religious preacher was evidently aimed at holding out a threat to the followers of rival sects. In peninsular India where the chief rivals of the Saivite order were the Jainas, images of Lakulīśa show him in a militant attitude.[166] In other places where there was not such conflict as in Rajasthan and Gujarat he appears in a more pacific attitude. I am tempted to see in the straight and taut trunk of Gaṇapati the expression of a certain firmness of attitude among the *Smārta* devotees of Gaṇapati. Were they trying to depict the firm resolve and the discipline required of a Gāṇapatya or were they trying to assert the *Smārta* form of worship over narrow sectarian forms?

A new way of bowing to Gaṇapati is introduced in these texts. The *ṛsis* and gods are described as crossing arms, holding their ears and touching their heads to the feet of Gaṇapati.[167] The latter states that this method of paying obeisance to him must be followed by all people since it pleases him.[168] This is still the traditional way of bowing to Gaṇapati in Maharashtra and all over the south, except that the devotee does not actually touch his head to the feet of the deity who is at a distance in his shrine. They either cross arms to hold the ears and bow several times or turn around usually three, five or seven times. The ritual of immersing the image of Gaṇapati in water at the end of the *Vināyaka caturthī-vrata* takes on a new feature in that it is permanent,[169] unlike in the Āgamas, where the image is immersed for a prescribed period and then brought back to the temple.

The *Smārta* Gāṇapatyas appear as a sect similar to those of various Śaiva or Vaiṣṇava sects. They created a specific doctrine for themselves even if they borrowed freely from the Purāṇas, Āgamas and Tantras. They introduced new forms, myths and rituals for their deity. A distinct philosophy was also expounded in their works.[170] They were strictly Brahmanical in their rituals. There are no offerings to Gaṇapati which include flesh of any kind. Nor is the Tantric influence of the *pañcamakāras* evident. The Gānapatya Purāṇas reflect the changing material milieu of the early medieval period. The religion is opened to the lower castes but a strict hierarchy is still maintained. A *śūdra* is neither permitted to recite a *śloka* of Gaṇapati nor perform *homa*. He only has the right to recite the *nāma-mantra*.[171] There are myths of how a *śūdra* visiting Gaṇeśa's *kṣetra* acquired intelligence and knowledge and of another *śūdra* who died in this *kṣetra* and attained Svānanda.[172] Likewise, even a *Caṇḍāla* can reach Svānanda.[173] Animals, too, have the possibility of being born as Gaṇeśas if they bathe in the Gaṇeśa *kuṇḍa* (tank).[174]

The *Smārta* Gāṇapatyas appear to have been associated with Varanasi, present day Maharashtra and parts of Karnataka and Andhra Pradesh.[175] Kāśī and Mayureśpur or Moregaon appear to be specially sacred.[176] The river Narmada is considered the most sacred of rivers and the red stones found in it are believed to represent Gaṇapati.[177] The *Gaṇeśa Purāṇa* mentions Cintāmaṇipura or Kadambapura in Vidarba, as also Siddhikṣetra,[178] Gaṇeśapura, Puṣpakapura and Mayureśvara.[179] Only a few of these places can be identified. Kadambapura is identified with the village Kalamb (Yeotmal District), Maharashtra, which is referred to as Kadambgirigrāma in a copper plate grant of the fifth century AD. There is an old underground temple of Cintāmaṇi in the village but its date is uncertain.[180] Siddhikṣetra may be Siddhatek which is the site of one of the *aṣṭavināyaka* temples. The concept of eight Vināyakas and eight sacred places[181] appears to have been established by them. Indeed the *aṣṭavināyaka* shrines are among the most famous of Gaṇapati *tīrthas* today. They all lie within a radius of about a hundred kilometres from Pune at Moregaon, Siddhatek, Pali, Mahad, Theur, Lenyadri, Ojhar and Ranjangaon. In addition, the temple at Cincvad (near Pune) is also very important as it is here that the shrine associated with Morayā Gosāvī is located.

It is generally accepted that the *aṣṭavināyaka* temples rose to prominence during Peshwa times (seventeenth to nineteenth century). Although the temple structures date to Peshwa times, the sites themselves must have been considered sacred from an earlier period. The *svayambhū mūrtis* that are worshipped in each of these places do not depict Siddhi and Buddhi. Where painted images or metal icons of the latter exist they have only recently been placed and in some cases they are not even present. Yet according to the *Gaṇeśa* and *Mudgala Purāṇas* Siddhi and Buddhi are an intrinsic part of Gaṇapati. Even the temple priests in these eight spots accept that Gaṇapati is married to them and that he is not a *brahmacārin*. On the basis of textual references and epigraphs, it is certain that Gaṇapati was being worshipped with Siddhi and Buddhi, at least, by the twelfth century. Someśvaramalla (king of the Kalyāṇa branch of the Cālukya family, AD 1126-38) refers to Gaṇapati in his work *Mānasollāsa* or *Abhilāshitārthacintāmaṇi* as being accompanied by Siddhi and Buddhi and invokes him at the beginning of his work as the one who fulfils all desires and scatters away all obstacles.[182] It is possible, therefore, that the sites of the Aṣṭavināyaka temples were associated with Gaṇapati before the twelfth century. At these shrines, Gaṇapati must have initially been worshipped as a *brahmacārin* before the tradition of his wives, popularised by the *Gaṇeśa* and *Mudgala Purāṇas,* became established. Besides, none of the images of Gaṇapati at these shrines is depicted with the trunk straight. It turns either right or left. Yet the two Purāṇas refer to the straight trunk of Gaṇapati. It is only in the *ārti* to Gaṇapati composed by Rāmadās—a seventeenth century Vaiṣṇava *brāhmaṇa* saint who is believed to have been the preceptor of Śivājī, the founder of the Maratha empire—and which is sung in many Gaṇapati temples in Maharashtra is there reference to the straight trunk of Gaṇapati.[183] Possibly, he chose this form because of the firmness of resolve that it appears to symbolise.

Another reason for supposing that the *aṣṭavināyaka* sites are older than Peshwa times is because Morayā Gosāvī who is believed to be the first of a dynasty of eight incarnations of Gaṇapati at Cincvad, near Pune, was associated with some of these sites prior to the rise of the Peshwas. According to the hagiological tradition at Moregaon and Cincvad, Morayā's father and mother came on pilgrimage to Moregaon and settled there. The father, Vāmanbhaṭṭa, performed penance at this place in order to obtain a son. Because of his prolonged penance Gaṇapati finally appeared before him and agreed to incarnate as his son. This son was Morayā Gosāvī. It was at Theur that Gosāvī had his first experience of the highest state of consciouness. Later, he moved to a small shrine at Cincvad. Gosāvī underwent *jīvansamādhi* (entombment while alive) in a chamber beneath the shrine and thereby passed out of visible existence in AD 1651. Devotees believe he attained *mokṣa* from rebirth and that his presence continues to endow the shrine with sacred significance.

If Gosāvī could have been accepted as an incarnation of Gaṇapati, the cult of the deity must have already been well-established in the region. I have mentioned earlier how from the ninth century onwards Gaṇapati is almost systematically invoked first in the epigraphs of the Śilāhāras who ruled over parts of Maharashtra and the Konkan area of Karnataka. Mukundarāja, a sectarian Śaiva from Maharashtra (late twelfth century) and author of a philosophic treatise named *Vivekasindhu* also begins his work with obeisance to Śrī Gaṇeśa.[184] These examples point to a growing tradition in Maharashtra where Gaṇapati was invoked at the beginning of all undertakings by *brāhmaṇas* and kings. This phenomenon finds its culmination in the *Jñāneśvarī* (AD 1290) when the Maharashtrian poet-saint, Jñāneśvara, identifies Gaṇapati with the supreme *Brahman*. Perhaps one reason why there is no epigraphical reference to Gaṇapati temples in Mahārashtra is because after the thirteenth century Muslim rule was established in the Deccan. The region first passed under the Delhi Sultanates and then under the Bahamanis. Therefore, there was no royal patronage for Hindu temples nor the associated epigraphs which constitute an important source of information for the historian. Mughal supremacy in the Deccan ended with the death of Aurangzeb in AD 1707 when the Marathas took control under Shahu, the grandson of Śivājī. Thereafter, the Aṣṭvināyaka temples rapidly rise to prominence in the time of the Peshwas. Further south, where the Vijayanagar empire stemmed the tide of Muslim conquest for more than two hundred years, there is continuous reference to Gaṇapati in the royal and other inscriptions of the period. In AD 1565 Vijayanagar was destroyed by the combined power of the Muslim rulers of Ahmadnagar, Golkonda and Bijapur. This does not mean that the worship of the deity came to an end or that traditions ceased to exist. It is just that some of the more important temples in this region fell into neglect because of a lack of royal patronage but beliefs and traditions survived. Even today, Gaṇapati is specially popular in Karnataka.

The Peshwas were Konkanastha *brāhmaṇas* (from the Konkan area) and Gaṇapati was an important deity in this region from as early as the seventh or eighth century, borne out by the Gaṇapati temples at Gokarna and Idagunji. They were evidently *Smārtas* because they built temples to several other deities. Gaṇapati, however, was their family deity. The *Gaṇeśa* and *Mudgala Purāṇas* probably acquired substantial additions during this period. Since the lower orders of society imitate the higher orders, visiting these temples must have received an impetus. The Peshwas and some of their Maratha contemporaries further spread the cult by building new temples to Gaṇapati in different parts of their territory. Some of the well-known Gaṇapati temples in Maharashtra such as Daśabhuja Gaṇapati and the Siddhi Vināyaka temple at Puṇe were built by the Peshwas. The latter are also associated with the Śrī Siddhi Vināyaka Mahāgaṇapati temple at Titwala about seventy kilometres from Bombay and the Gaṇapati temple at Satara. In Cuttack, Orissa, there is a Varada Gaṇanātha temple which was built in the time of the Marathas. Śrī Raghuji Bhonsale, a contemporary and opponent of Peshwa Bajirao and his son, Nana Saheb, is said to have given the land for this temple, and the means for building it,[185] when his troops occupied Orissa in 1741-2.[186]

The *Smārta* Gāṇapatyas probably flourished over a fairly large region for several centuries. Their relative importance in Maharashtra is because of the tradition established by Gosāvī and also because of the subsequent patronage of the *aṣṭvināyaka* and other Gaṇapati shrines by the Peshwas. Their contribution to the religious life of the regions associated with them can only be evaluated by a study of the perceptions of Gaṇapati as also his worship in the contemporary context.

NOTES

1. Paul B. Courtright, *Gaṇeśa: Lord of Obstacles, Lord of Beginnings*, p. 218; M.K. Dhavalikar, 'Gaṇeśa: Myth and Reality' in Robert L. Brown, ed., *Ganesh: Studies of an Asian God*, p. 49; Alice Getty, *Gaṇeśa*, p. 20.
2. N. Veezhinathan, ed., *Śrī Śaṅkaravijaya of Ānandagiri*, pp. 81-91.
3. *EI*, Vol. III, No. 36, pp. 263-7.
4. *EI*, Vol. XXVI, No. 27 D, pp. 212-7.
5. B.N. Sharma, 'Abhiṣekha in Indian Art', *JOIB*, Vol. 21 (1971-2), p. 10.
6. Kantilal F. Sompura, *The Structural Temples of Gujarat*, p. 90.

7. Aschwin de Lippe, *Indian Medieval Sculpture,* p. 15.
8. *Brahma Purāṇa,* IV.44.1-2.
9. *Varāha Purāṇa,* II.154.29-30.
10. V.V. Mirashi, ed., *Inscriptions of the Kalachuri-Chedi Era,* 'Kharod Stone Inscription of Ratnadeva III: Chedi Year 933', *CII,* Vol. IV, Pt. 2, No. 100, pp. 533-43.
11. *EI,* Vol. III, No. 37, pp. 267-76; *CII,* Vol. VI, 1977, pp. 36-44 and pp. 44-54; *EI,* Vol. XXXII, pp. 63-8; *EI,* Vol. XII, No. 31, pp. 265-7; *EI,* Vol. XXIII, No. 45,pp 269-81.
12. *EI,* Vol. XXXII, No. 5, pp. 71-6.
13. *Gazetteer of India,* Karnataka State, Uttara Kannada District, p. 970.
14. Ibid., p. 929.
15. Robert L. Brown, 'Gaṇeśa in Southeast Asian Art', in Robert L. Brown, ed., op. cit., pp. 171-233. See in particular p. 177.
16. *EI,* Vol. XXXIII, No. 13, pp. 79-81.
17. *EA,* Vol. III, pp. 16-27.
18. For the dating of this and some other *Tantras* see N.N. Bhattacharya, *History of Śākta Religion,* p. 123. See also P.C. Bagchi, 'The Evolution of the Tantras' in *The Cultural Heritage of India,* IV, pp. 211-66.
19. H. Mitra, *Gaṇapati,* p. 97.
20. P.C. Bagchi, op. cit., p. 222.
21. *Śaṅkaravijaya,* p. 87.
22. *Ājitāgama,* Vol. III, Kriyāpāda, 55.1-19; *Vināyakavratakalpādi,* p. 21. The latter is quoted from the Kriyāpāda of the *Svayambhuvāgama.*
23. Christopher Wilkinson, 'The Tantric Gaṇeśa: Texts Preserved in the Tibetan Canon', in Robert Brown, ed., *Ganesh,* pp. 235-76.
24. H.Mitra, op. cit., p. 43.
25. *Ajitāgama,* Vol. III, 55.9 and 18.
26. Robert L. Brown, ed., op. cit., see 'Introduction', p. 8.
27. Ibid., fn. 24 on p. 18 of 'Introduction'.
28. Alice Getty, op. cit., pp. 68-9.
29. Christopher Wilkinson, 'The Tantric Gaṇeśa' in Robert L. Brown, ed., op. cit., pp. 235-76.
30. For the list of these texts along with the authors and translators, see Wilkinson, 'The Tantric Gaṇeśa', pp. 236-8. For the dates of these authors/translators see H. Mitra, op. cit., p. 43.
31. Christopher Wilkinson, op. cit., pp. 259, 265, 266.
32. Ibid., pp. 251, 253, 258.
33. Ibid., p. 255.
34. Ibid., p. 268.
35. The word '*maṇḍala*' literally means 'a circle' or 'centre'. In fact the *maṇḍala* consists of a series of circles drawn within a square.

The diagram is usually drawn on the ground by means of colourd threads or coloured rice powder and the various divinities of the Tantric pantheon are arranged therein. The *maṇḍala* represents a microcosm and at the same time a symbolic pantheon.

36. Ibid., p. 242.
37. Ibid., p. 251.
38. Ibid., p. 254.
39. Ibid., p. 261.
40. Ibid., p. 265.
41. Ibid., p. 268.
42. Ibid., pp. 256, 257 and 267. (The texts in question are the *Gaṇapati Sādhana Daridira Nidhiprada Nāma,* the *Śrī Ājñā Vinivarta Gaṇapati Sādhanaṃ* and the *Gaṇapati Stotra.*)
43. Ibid., p. 248.
44. Ibid., p. 256.
45. Ibid., p. 264.
46. Ibid., p. 257.
47. Ibid., p. 267.
48. *Gazetteer of Mysore State,* Kolar District, p. 532.
49. *Skanda Purāṇa,* Venkateshwar Steam Press edn., Kāśī Khaṇḍa, II.57.82.
50. ChristopherWilkinson, op. cit., p. 255.
51. *Mānava Gṛhya Sūtra,* II.14.
52. Ibid., p. 262.
53. Ibid., p. 252.
54. Ibid., pp. 252 and 259.
55. Ibid., p. 260.
56. Ibid., p. 266.
57. Ibid., p. 262.
58. Ibid., p. 262.
59. Louis Frederic, *Les Dieux du Bouddhisme,* p. 156.
60. Ibid., p. 157.
61. Ibid., pp. 267-8.
62. Alice Getty, op. cit., p. 74.
63. Christopher Wilkinson, op. cit., p. 241.
64. J.N. Banerjea, *The Development of Hindu Iconography,* p. 547.
65. B.R. Chatterjee, *Indian Cultural Influence in Cambodia,* pp. 241 and 263.
66. Alice Getty, op. cit., pp. 52 and 53.
67. Louis Frederic, op. cit., p. 153.
68. *Mṛgendrāgama,* III.36; *Somaśambhupaddhati,* Vol. II, p. 334.
69. *Mṛgendrāgama,* III.22b, p. 52; *Somaśambhupaddhati,* Vol. III, p. 632.
70. *Rauravottarāgama,* chap. IX, pp. 29-36; *Ajitāgama,* Vol. II, chap. 49.

71. Quoted from the *Svayambuvāgama* in *Ajitāgama*, Vol. III, p. 6, fn. 73.
72. *Svayambhuvāgama,* 58.4.
73. Ibid., 58.39.
74. Ibid., 58.42.
75. Ibid., 58.72.
76. Ibid., 58.75; *Vināyakavratakalpādi*, p. 21, quoted from the *Kāraṇāgama.*
77. *Svayambhuvāgama,* 58.106.
78. Ibid., 58.10. In the *Āgamas* this immersion is not permanent, as after a prescribed period, the image is taken out of the water and brought back to the temple.
79. *Vināyakavratakalpādi,* pp. 27-8. Quoted from the *Svayambhuvāgama;* See also *Ajitāgama,* Vol. III, 55.1.
80. *Ajitāgama,* Vol. III, 55.3.
81. Ibid., Vol. III, 55.6 and 10.
82. Ibid., Vol. III, 55.13.
83. *Kāraṇāgama,* I.57.58a; 60.64a. Quoted in *Ajitāgama,* Vol. II, Krīyapāda, p. 156, fn. 5.
84. *Śabdakalpadruma,* Vol. II, p. 550.
85. V.S. Apte, *The Practical Sanskrit–English Dictionary,* p. 1031.
86. *Śaṅkaravijaya,* chap. 15, pp. 87-8.
87. *Devī Rahasya,* See Pariśiṣṭas V.iii.30, p. 545.
88. *Ajitāgama,* Vol. III, 55.12.
89. Pratapaditya Pal, *Hindu Religion and Iconology,* p. 127.
90. *Ajitāgama,* Vol. III, 55.12.
91. Quoted from the *Svayambhuvāgama* in the context of *Vināyaka Sthāpanā* in *Ajitāgama,* Vol. III, p. 6, see fn.
92. *Diptāgama,* 78.40. This reference pertains to the version of the *Diptāgama* in Transcript No. 15 in the library of the FIP. At the time that I consulted it the critical edition of this text was under preparation. It has since been published by this same Institute and the reference in the published edition is I.40.
93. Mahākāla is another form of Śiva that was worshipped by the Kāpālikas. He is described as having excessively red eyes on account of heavy drinking and he sits upon a *siṃhāsana.* Cited by T.A. Gopinatha Rao, op. cit., Vol. II, Pt. I, pp. 201-2.
94. *CII,* Vol. IV, Pt. II, No. 100, pp. 533-4.
95. *Śaṅkaravijaya,* chap. 15, p. 87.
96. *Prāṇatoṣinī,* p. 611.
97. *Devī Rahasya,* Pariśiṣṭas v.iii.30, p. 545.
98. Pratapaditya Pal, op. cit., p. 7 of 'Introduction'.
99. *Prāṇatoṣinī,* p. 489.
100. V.N. Jha, 'Varṇasaṃkara in the Dharma Sūtras: Theory and Practice', *JESHO,* Vol. 13, nos. 1-3, 1970, pp. 273-88.

101. Sukumari Bhattacharji, *The Indian Theogany,* p. 184.
102. Quoted in *Ajitāgama,* Vol. III, p. 6, fn. 73.
103. *Diptāgama,* 78.38.
104. Christopher Wilkinson, op. cit., p. 243.
105. Ibid., p. 244.
106. *Īśānaśivagurudevapaddhati* , II.16.1-16.
107. Prapañcasāra Tantra, XVII.2, 8-9, 14-18.
108. *Śaṅkaravijaya,* p. 82.
109. Christopher Wilkinson, op. cit., p. 247.
110. *Śaṅkaravijaya,* pp. 82-3.
111. *Ajitāgama,* Vol. III, 55.16; *Vināyakavratakalpādi,* p. 27.
112. *Ajitāgama,* Vol. III, p. 6, fn. 73. Quoted from the *Svayambuvāgama.*
113. *Diptāgama,* 78.40.
114. *Śaṅkaravijaya,* pp. 85-7
115. *Ajitāgama,* Vol. III, 55.18.
116. *Mudgala Purāṇa,* VI.9.8; *Gaṇeśa Purāṇa,* II.125.39; II.6.24; II.31.9.
117. *Mudgala Purāṇa,* VIII.43.26-7 and *Gaṇeśa Purāṇa,* II.130.22.
118. *Ajitāgama,* Vol. III, p. 6, fn. 73. Quoted from the *Svayambhuvāgama.*
119. *Śaṅkaravijaya,* chap. 18, pp. 90-1.
120. Suvarṇa Gaṇapati's description appears in *Ajitāgama,* Vol. III, 55.14.
121. Ibid., 55.15.
122. *Śaṅkaravijaya,* p. 87.
123. Gudrun Buhnemann, *Forms of Gaṇeśa,* p. 26.
124. Told to me by the priest of the Gaṇapati temple at the Madya Kailash Temple complex, Madras. Several devotees who were present at this time also confirmed this.
125. S.K. Ramachandra Rao, ed., *Gaṇapati* (32 drawings from a nineteenth century Scroll), p. 25.
126. Gudrun Buhnemann, op. cit., pp. 18-20.
127. Ibid., p. 21.
128. Ibid., p. 29.
129. A.K. Majumdar, *Bhakti Renaissance,* p. 59.
130. *Śaṅkaravijaya,* p. 85.
131. Ibid., pp. 87 and 90.
132. *Ṛg Veda,* II.23.1. Quoted by R.C. Hazra in 'Gaṇapati-Worship and the *Upapurāṇas* Dealing with it', *JGJhRI,* Vol. 5, 1948, pp. 263-76.
133. Ibid., X.112.9. Quoted by R.C. Hazra, op. cit.
134. *Taittirīya Saṃhitā,* IV.1.2.2 and *Vājasaneyi Saṃhitā,* II.15 and 22.30. Quoted by R.C.Hazra, op. cit.
135. *Mudgala Purāṇa,* V.24.
136. V.S. Apte, *The Practical Sanskrit–English Dictionary,* p. 743.
137. *Mudgala Purāṇa,* I.20.28-30.
138. Ibid., II.33.

139. Ibid., V.11.
140. Ibid., I.43.11-12.
141. Ibid., V.19.6.
142. Ibid., III.26.27-8.
143. Ibid., II.34.1-6.
144. Ibid., I.43.38-9.
145. Ibid., II.56.38-9.
146. Ibid., III.51.25; *Gaṇeśa Purāṇa,* Krīdā Khaṇḍa, II.50.3.
147. *Mudgala Purāṇa,* I.20.4-12.
148. *Gaṇeśa Purāṇa,* Krīdā Khaṇḍa, II.1.18-21.
149. *Mudgala Purāṇa,* I.32.49; I.40.21; II.56.26; III.26.12; VIII.40.1. *Gaṇeśa Purāṇa,* Upāsanā Khaṇḍa, I.11.4; I.11.10; I.20.29; I.50.5; I.51.28.
150. *Gaṇeśa Purāṇa,* Upāsanā Khaṇḍa, I.36.19-20.
151. Ibid., I.11.3; I.12.9 and I.69.8.
152. Ibid., I.51.73.
153. Ibid., I.46.110.
154. Ibid., I.46.103.
155. *Mudgala Purāṇa,* V.45.1.
156. *Gaṇeśa Purāṇa,* Upāsanā Khaṇḍa, 1.46.
157. Ibid., Krīdā Khaṇḍa, II.138-48.
158. *Mudgala Purāṇa,* VI.9.8; *Gaṇeśa Purāṇa,* Krīdā Khaṇḍa, II.125.39; II.6.24; II.31.9. There are numerous such examples in the two Purāṇas.
159. *Mudgala Purāṇa,* VIII.43.26-7 and *Gaṇeśa Purāṇa,* Krīdā Khaṇḍa, II.130-22.
160. *Mudgala Purāṇa,* V.13.33-5.
161. Ibid., 5.15.
162. Samaresh Bandhyopadhyay, 'A Note on Gaṇapati', *JOIB,* Vol. 21, 1971-2 pp. 328-30.
163. P.K. Agrawala, 'A Note on Ardhanāri Gaṇapati' in *Studies in Indian Iconography,* pp. 155-8.
164. Samaresh Bandhyopadhyay, op. cit., pp. 328-30.
165. *Gaṇeśa Purāṇa,* Upāsanā Khaṇḍa, I.66.17, Krīdā Khaṇḍa, II.40.23; II.50.56; II.125.33. *Mudgala Purāṇa,* V.45. There are numerous such examples.
166. R.N. Nandi, *Social Roots of Religion in Ancient India,* pp. 102-4.
167. *Mudgala Purāṇa,* II.33.43.
168. Ibid., II.33.44.
169. *Gaṇesa' Purāṇa,* Upāsanā Khaṇḍa, I.50.32-3.
170. For a discussion on aspects of the philosophy of the *Mudgala Purāṇa* see Phyllis Granoff 'Gaṇeśa as Metaphor: The *Mudgala Purāṇa*', in Robert Brown, ed., *Ganesh,* pp. 85-100.

171. *Mudgala Purāṇa,* V.24.6.
172. Ibid., VI.12.
173. Ibid., VI.23.28.
174. Ibid., VI.26.2.
175. Ibid., V.23.1-4.
176. Ibid., III.21.28.
177. Ibid., IV.47.56-9.
178. *Gaṇeśa Purāṇa,* Upāsanā Khaṇḍa, I.18.2.
179. Ibid., I.82.
180. *Maharashtra State Gazetteer,* Yeotmal District, p. 703.
181. *Mudgala Purāṇa,* III.21.32.
182. G.S. Ghurye, *Gods and Men,* p. 73.
183. Kashinatha Sastri Joshi, *Sāratha Pūjā Saṃgraha,* p. 152.
184. G.S.Ghurye, op. cit., p. 73.
185. Rāmavatāra Gupta, *Gaṇeśa Mahimā,* p. 164.
187. Stewart Gordon, *The Marathas,* p. 132.

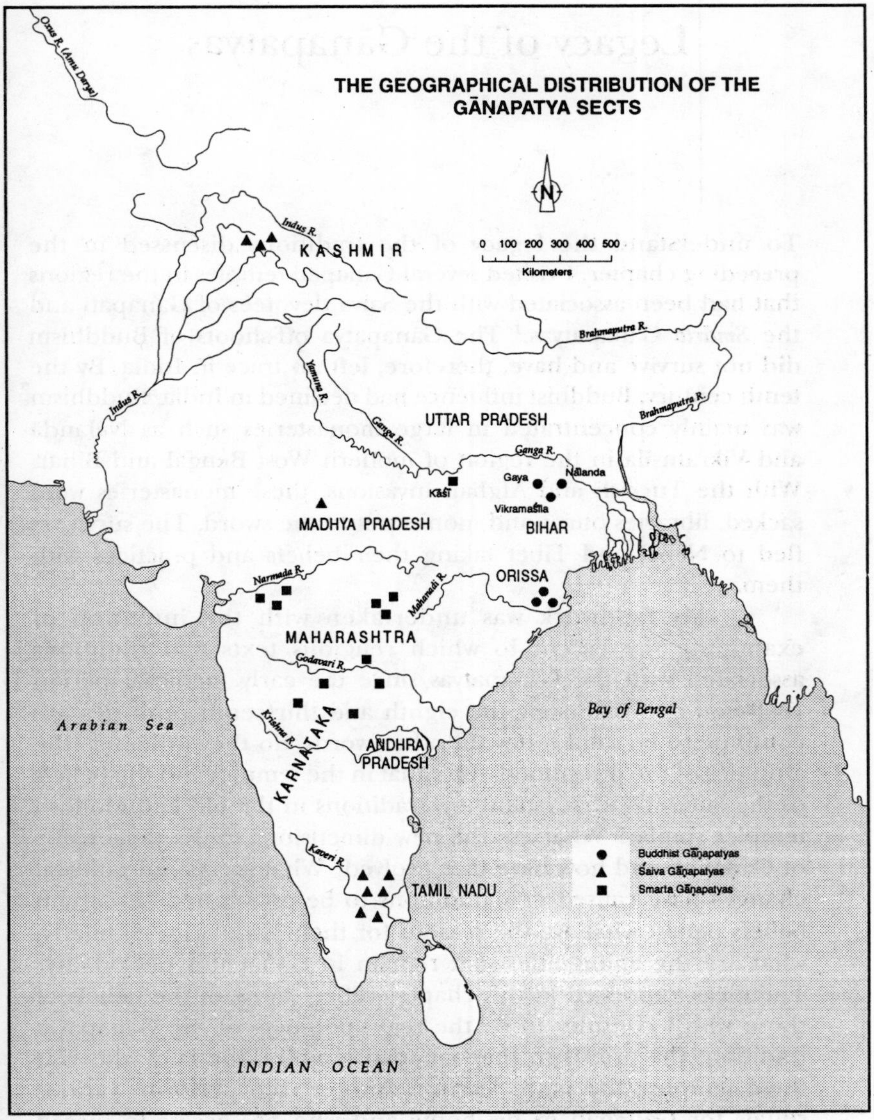

Map 3. Refers to the Sects and Subsects mentioned in Chapter VI.

CHAPTER 7

Legacy of the Gāṇapatyas

To understand the legacy of the traditions discussed in the preceding chapter, I visited several Gaṇapati temples in the regions that had been associated with the Śaiva devotees of Gaṇapati and the *Smārta* Gāṇapatyas.[1] The Gāṇapatya off-shoots of Buddhism did not survive and have, therefore, left no trace in India. By the tenth century, Buddhist influence had declined in India. Buddhism was mainly concentrated in large monasteries such as Nālandā and Vikramśīla in the region of modern West Bengal and Bihar. With the Turkish and Afghan invasions, these monasteries were sacked, libraries burnt and monks put to the sword. The survivors fled to Nepal and Tibet taking their beliefs and practices with them.

My fieldwork was undertaken with the intention of examining the extent to which religious texts and traditions associated with the Gāṇapatyas since the early medieval period (between approximately the eighth and thirteenth centuries AD) continue to be valid today. In other words, do they influence the attitudes of the priesthood, the ritual in the temples and the beliefs of the laity? To what extent are traditions in the old and modern temples similar? What are the new dimensions to the personality of Gaṇapati and how have they evolved? What social and political changes have caused new traditions to be established? If certain beliefs persist what are the reasons for their popularity? Similarly, what are the ambiguities that remain in Gaṇapati's personality? The ideas expressed in this chapter reflect some of the beliefs of those who I consider to be the real upholders of the Gāṇapatya tradition: the priests in the Gaṇapati temples; the laity who visit these temples; the more learned devotee who performs various rituals for Gaṇapati in his home and who has access to sacred texts because of his knowledge of Sanskrit and/or regional languages; and the numerous people who may not go to temples nor read any text but who are firm believers in the manifold powers of Gaṇapati.

To begin with, it is relevant to understand what the term 'Gāṇapatya' signifies today. In Maharashtra itself there are varying perceptions of the term. At Pen, an elderly resident of the village whose family has manufactured Gaṇapati statues since the 1880s, claims that a Gāṇapatya is someone who does regular *pūjā* to Gaṇapati, including *āratī* (waving of lights before the image). Most people in that respect are not Gāṇapatyas. They keep the deity's image on the family altar along with those of other deities. However special *pūjā* for him is limited to the days of the Gaṇapati festivals. These are the Vināyaka *caturthī* in the *śuklapakṣa* (the fourth day of the waxing moon) of the month of *bhādrapada* (August/September) and the Gaṇeśa *jayanti* (Gaṇeśa's birthday) celebrated on the *caturthī* of the *kṛṣṇapakṣa* (fourth day of the waning moon) in the month of *māgha* (January/February). An elderly devotee at the Daśabhuja Gaṇapati temple, Pune, felt that a Gāṇapatya was one whose *iṣṭa devatā* (personal deity) was Gaṇapati but who worshipped all the other deities as well. Others felt that a Gāṇapatya is one who worships Gaṇapati alone and does not visit the temples of other deities.

At most Gaṇapati temples today, the priests do not consider themselves to be Gāṇapatyas. In their view, a Gāṇapatya is a priest who performs the worship of Gaṇapati. He does worship other deities as well but only in the temple of Gaṇapati. In their opinion the only such Gāṇapatyas are the priests at the Gaṇapati temples at Moregaon, Cincvad, Sidhatek and Theur which are all governed by the same trust based at Cincvad, near Pune. In fact, there was a similarity of perception among the priests in these temples. At Theur, the *pramukha pujāri* felt that Gaṇapati is Śiva's son only in myth. He may have taken birth from Pārvatī, Śiva, or from both, but is not a lesser god for that. He looked upon Gaṇapati as the source of all creation. At Sidhatek, the priest believed that Gaṇapati is *Oṃ*, the symbol of the *Brahman* and source of creation. He was present even when Śiva and Pārvatī were married and is only their mind born son. At Moregaon, they accepted that Gaṇapati is Śiva's son but in only one *kalpa*. These perceptions are all based on the *Gaṇeśa* and *Mudgala Purāṇas*. In some of the *aṣṭavināyaka* shrines, such as Ojhar, where the priests' forefathers have served the temple for several generations they consider themselves Gāṇapatyas for they have never been officiants in the temple of another deity. However, in other places such as at Ranjangaon where the head priest had been appointed not too long ago, he just considered himself a Deśastha Ṛgvedi *brāhmaṇa* and had never thought about what the term Gāṇapatya signified. At Titwala, the priests and trustees considered themselves simply as Gaṇapati *pujārīs*. At the Siddhi Vināyaka temple, Bombay, the priests regarded themselves as Hindu *brāhmaṇas* who could perform *pūjā* of other deities in other temples as well. In Karnataka, Tamil Nadu, Varanasi and Kerala there is no such concept of a Gāṇapatya even though there are several temples where Gaṇapati is the principal or the only deity. However, individual priests have their own perceptions of the deity they serve. At the Śrī Vīra Gaṇapati Temple, Amdalli, Karnataka, the priest, a *Smārta*, felt that Gaṇapati is all deities rolled into one. This idea is, in fact, propounded by the Gāṇapatya Purāṇas. However, he did not consider himself a Gāṇapatya but insisted that he was a *Smārta*. What is clear is that not one person felt that a Gāṇapatya was synonymous with a *sanyāsī* which is the idea conveyed in the *Mudgala Purāṇa* and which I have discussed at length in the preceding chapter.

In Maharashtra, tradition has stressed the unity of the *aṣṭavināyaka* shrines. If a pilgrim wants the full benefit of a visit to these sacred sites he must visit them all in turn. However, it is evident that all eight are not visited equally frequently. Some like Sidhatek are remote, the road is poor and the visit entails a fairly long walk and a ferry crossing of the Bhima river. In this small village, made up mainly of poor farmers, there are days when hardly any one comes for the daily *āratī*. Others, like Moregaon, are well appointed and frequently visited. The rituals in these eight temples is also not entirely similar. This is because all the shrines are not run by the same trust. Except for Moregaon, Sidhatek and Theur which are administered by the trust based at Cincvad, the others have a separate trust each. At Lenyadri, unlike the other shrines, there is no full-time *brāhmaṇa* appointed in the temple. Consequently, some of the rituals which can only be performed by a *brāhmaṇa* such as the *abhiṣeka* (ritual bathing) and the offering of *naivedya* (food) take place only once in fifteen days when a *brāhmaṇa* specially comes for that purpose from Junnar, a few kilometres away. The laity is, therefore, attended to by a Gurav who accepts their offerings and performs the *āratī* in the morning and evening.

The Guravs rank lower than the *brāhmaṇas*. They are popularly believed to be the offspring of marriages between *brāhmaṇas* and Marathas, a caste which claims *kṣatriya* status. The Guravs were, traditionally, servants in the temples of the goddess and are found in Śaiva temples as well. They also serve at several Gaṇapati temples today. At Moregaon, there are about twenty Guravs employed whereas at Ojhar or Sidhatek there are none. The Guravs look after the cleaning, upkeep and decoration of the temple and accept the offerings brought by the laity during the day. They are not considered as *pujārīs* in most Brahmanical temples. However, in several smaller shrines devoted to Gaṇapati, where the Gurav is the sole attendant, he is commonly referred to as the *pujārī*. In these shrines there is no elaborate ritual. The Gurav usually comes once a day, does the *snāna* (bathing with water as opposed to the *abhiṣeka* performed with the *pañcāmṛtaṃ* or five nectars) of the image and performs a simple *pūjā*. At Cincvad, at the temple built over the *samādhi* of Morayā Gosāvī, a whole family of Guravs looks after the upkeep of the temple. When I visited the temple, the wife of the Gurav was accepting the offerings of the devotees from within the *garbhagṛha* (sanctum sanctorum). There was no objection to a woman entering the *garbhagṛha* and attending to the laity. At the Triśuṇḍa Gaṇapati (Gaṇapati with three trunks) temple in Pune, the priest is a Maratha who had performed *abhiṣeka* and *naivedya* and all the rituals normally associated with *brāhmaṇas* during the forty-five years that he had served the temple. He has now been replaced by a Deśastha Ṛgvedi *brāhmaṇa* because of his extreme old age. Whereas in most temples the laity is not permitted to enter the *garbhagṛha*, at Mahad the *garbhagṛha* has no enclosure and I saw devotees walk right in, make their offerings personally and touch the feet of the image. The absence of an intermediary between the devotee and the principal image in this temple enables a more intimate contact between the devotee and his god.

The *aṣṭavināyaka* shrines and the other large temples of Gaṇapati in Bombay and Pune are serviced by Deśastha Ṛgvedi *brāhmaṇas* and Konkaṇastha Ṛgvedi *brāhmaṇas*. The former are from the Deśa region, which is the heartland of Maharashtra whereas the latter are from the coastal area of the Konkan. Sometimes a third category of *brāhmaṇas* are present, the Karaḍas, who originate from Karad in Satara District, Maharashtra. They are all *Smārtas*. At most of these shrines and at the other Gaṇapati temples the priests are referred to as *pujārīs, arcakas* or, less frequently, as *kṣetra upādhyāyas*. In Maharashtra, except when the image is in white marble like in some of the newer temples, it is always coated with thick red *sindūra* and the tradition is ascribed to the myth in the *Mudgala Purāṇa* about Gaṇapati defeating the *asura* called Sindūra and then smearing himself with his red colour in order to protect the world.[2] The thick coating is prepared by mixing oil of the *bel* fruit with *sindūra* which is then pasted on the image by hand. This is usually done once a month, on the day before *saṅkaṣṭa caturthī* (the fourth day of the dark half of each month, referred to as the 'dangerous fourth'). Since it takes about four days to dry, during those days *pādapūjā* (washing the feet) of the image replaces the *abhiṣeka.* Even the images of Gaṇapati in Varanasi are coated with the same thick layers of *sindūra.* In Karnataka and Tamil Nadu the images are usually made of black stone and the only red, in most cases, is the *tilaka* on the deity's forehead. At Idagunji, however, the image of the deity is made of red sandstone and at Gokarna I saw an image in the usual black stone covered with *sindūra.* In all these places, the priests apply a *tilaka* of *sindūra* on their own foreheads as well. The Gāṇapatya Purāṇas recommend the application of red sandal paste all over the body by the Gāṇapatya. However this practice seems to have died out and it is only the deity, today, that is covered with red. The priests at the Gaṇapati temples apply *bhasma* (ash) all over the body as in the case of the Śaivas. The *Mudgala Purāṇa* states that the red stones (jasper) found in the river Narmada represent Gaṇapati.[3] This stone is the equivalent of the *śālagrāma* (ammonites) of Viṣṇu and the *liṅga* of Śiva. Devotees worship this stone as representative of the *nirākār* (formless) state of the elephant-headed deity. I have seen such stones on the family altars of several Maharashtrian *brāhmaṇa* families.

It is well known that Gaṇapati's favourite colours are red and yellow. Yet these are not the only colours in which he is dressed. At Moregaon, in the shrine over the *samādhi* (tomb) of Gosāvī, the image was dressed in purple, whereas at the main temple at Ciṅcvad the image was clothed in deep blue. The priests are also permitted to wear *dhotīs* of any colour except black. They are usually dressed in red or yellow *dhotīs* in Maharashtra and Karnataka and rarely in white. At Gokarna they were dressed in purple. In Tamil Nadu and Kerala, I often saw them dressed in white. In all cases silk *dhotīs* were considered essential for performing the *pūjā* but this, in fact, was often not the case. Priests also face financial constraints and, besides, there is often a wide gap between what is believed to be necessary and what is actually practised.

There is, by and large, a certain uniformity of worship in the Brahmanical Gaṇapati temples in Maharashtra and much of it conforms to what is prescribed in the Gāṇapatya Purāṇas. The prayers are based mainly on the *Ṛg Veda* and include the recitation of the *Puruṣa sūkta, Brahmaṇaspati sūkta* and *Śrī sūkta*. This association of Gaṇapati with Vedic hymns and ritual is because the *Smārta* Gāṇapatya sect linked the elephant-headed deity with the concept of Gaṇapati in the Vedas and thereby conferred on their chosen deity the sanctity of an ancient deity. The *Puruṣa sūkta* is recited because Gaṇapati is identified as the divine *Puruṣa,* the embodiment of the cosmos. The *Mudgala Purāṇa* states that Gaṇapati is referred to as Brahmaṇaspati and *Brahman* in the Vedas[4] and, therefore, he should be worshipped as stipulated in the Vedas and the Purāṇas.[5] At other times the text recommends that his worship must be according to the Vedas and the Āgamas.[6] In fact, in the Gaṇapati temples in Maharashtra the emphasis is mainly on the Vedas and on a few Gāṇapatya works such as the *Śrī Gaṇapati Atharvaśīrṣa* or *Gaṇapati Upaniṣad* which is regularly recited and so is the Gaṇapati *sahasranāma* which is based on the *Gaṇesa Purāṇa.*[7] The *Śrī Gaṇapati Atharvaśīrṣa* is a relatively late text (about sixteenth/seventeenth century) and is attributed to the *Atharva Veda.*[8] The *āratī,* however, is often sung in Marathi and is the composition of the seventeenth century Vaiṣṇava saint, Rāmadās. The ritual includes the *pañcāmṛtam abhiṣeka* (bathing with five nectars which include milk, curd, clarified butter, honey and sugar), *ṣodaśopacāra* (sixteen acts of homage) *naivedya* and *āratī.* On special occasions a *gaṇa homa* is performed. *Dūrvā* grass and *śamī* leaves are specially offered to the deity. They are normally put on his head. According to mythological tradition, the immortality-granting *amṛta* was spilled on the *dūrvā* grass at the time of the churning of the ocean. It is believed to be especially favoured by Gaṇapati and has its parallel in the ancient *kuśa* grass of the Vedic sacrifice. The *śamī* tree is referred to in the epics and Purāṇas as the one from whose wood the sticks for kindling the Vedic fire were made.[9]

The *Mudgala Purāṇa* recommends that all Gāṇapatyas wear a string of *śamī* seeds around the neck and, if *śamī* is not available, then seeds of the *maṇdāra* tree (the coral tree) or *vidrumā* (coral) beads.[10] It is stated that these are as important for the Gāṇapatyas as *tulsī* (basil) is to the Vaiṣṇavas. This string serves the purpose of a *japa mālā* (normally 108 beads for repeating the *mantra* of Gaṇapati). Today most priests feel that *rudrākṣa, tulsī* or even crystal beads are acceptable for doing *japa* to Gaṇapati. Very few considered that coral or coral coloured seeds were essential. However, flowers of the *mandāra* tree that are white in colour, are often offered to Gaṇapati. The image of the *mūṣaka* (mouse) is also present in these temples facing the main image. It is regularly bathed, sandal paste is applied on its forehead and it is adorned with flowers. Often, it is coated with *sindūra* like Gaṇapati. The *mūla mantra* in most of the temples is *Om Gaṃ Gaṇapataye Namaḥ.*

Further north and south of Maharashtra in the regions of Varanasi and Karnataka, the influence of the Gāṇapatya tradition decreases but does not disappear altogether. Karnātaka, according to the *Mudgala Purāṇa* was a Śaiva *kṣetra.*[11] Evidently the Gāṇapatyas in Karnataka had to compete with the older, well established Śaiva sects. According to this text it was here that Rāma worshipped Śiva when Sītā was abducted by Rāvaṇa in order to acquire the power and skill for killing the demon. He was informed by Śiva that he would have to worship Gajānana in order to succeed in his mission. By associating Gaṇapati with the well known epic *Rāmāyaṇa* and with Śiva, the Gāṇapatyas aspired to impress on the people the benefits of Gaṇapati worship. In fact, some of the old and better known Gaṇapati temples here are in the vicinity of famous Śiva temples. Others are associated with the Vaiṣṇavas.

The Gaṇapati temples in Karnataka are mainly served by *Smārta brāhmaṇas* and the influence of the traditions of Tamil Nadu and the Śaiva Āgamas is visible. The priests are referred to as *arcakas* and, less frequently, as *pujārīs.* In most of the older temples, such as at Gokarna and Idagunji, the officiants are Havig Ṛgvedi *brāhmaṇas.* At Gokarna, in addition to the Haviks, there are also Kota Ṛgvedi *brāhmaṇas.* The Haviks are descendants of *brāhmaṇas* settled by the Kadamba king Mayūravarman in the southern part of Uttara Kannada and the northern part of Dakshin

Kannada districts. The Kota *brāhmaṇas* originally came from the village Kota, about sixty miles south of Mangalore. At Bangalore several *arcakas* at the Gaṇapati temples are *Śukla Yajurvedi Smārta brāhmaṇas.* Like in Maharashtra, there are other castes who help in the upkeep of the temple and participate in the temple ritual. At Gokarna and Idagunji, the musicians who accompany the chanting of the *āratī* three times a day are Bhandaris. Below them are the low-caste Gowdas who are responsible for the cleaning of the temple. Only the *garbhagṛha* is forbidden to them and it is maintained solely by the *brāhmaṇas.* At both Gokarna and Kurudumale the head priest is an officiant at the Gaṇapati temple as well as the Śiva temple of the same village. In most of the Gaṇapati temples in Karnataka the *karmakāṇḍa* (ritual) is from the Vedas but the *mantras* and *stutis* (hymns of praise) are from the Śaiva Āgamas. In a few temples, however, the ritual is based entirely on the Śaiva Āgamas. The *Śrī Gaṇapati Atharvaśīrṣa* is recited in some temples and not in others. At Kurudumale, for example, the priest had not even heard of it. The worship of Gaṇapati at Gokarna is very similar to that of Śiva. The figure of the elephant-headed deity has an *abhiṣeka pātra* on his head. Water pours on him daylong like it does on the Śiva *liṅga.* In some of the modern Gaṇapati temples in Karnataka the *Rudracāmakam* and the *Durgā Sūkta* are also recited. Normally the *Rudracāmakam* is recited only in Śiva temples. At the Śrī Jambu Gaṇapati temple, Mallesvaram, Bangalore (so named because the temple is under an old *jamun* tree), the priest was proud of the fact that the *Rudracāmakam* was part of the daily ritual in his temple unlike in most Gaṇapati temples. At the Aneguḍḍe Śrī Vināyaka temple, Kumbhasi, where the *brāhmaṇas* are Vaiṣṇavas of the Mādhava sect the prayers are not based on the Śaiva Āgamas but include the *Śrī Gaṇapati Atharvaśīrsa* and the *Gaṇapati Sahasranāma* which are part of the *Smārta* Gāṇapatya tradition. In most of these temples the *gaṇa homa* is performed on special occasions such as the festivals of Gaṇapati or when a devotee specially requests it. At Idagunji, however, a *gaṇa homa* is performed every day. Except in the old temples where the entire ritual is in Sanskrit, the *āratī* in the modern temples is usually in Kannada.

Most of the modern Gaṇapati temples in Karnataka are *pañcāyatana* temples where Gaṇapati is the main deity. Since many of these temples are not big, the other four deities of the *pañcāyatana* do not necessarily have their own shrines around that of Gaṇapati. Often small images are placed in the four corners of the *garbagṛha* around the central large image of Gaṇapati. There are other temples such as the Śrī Vināyaka temple, R.T. Nagar, Bangalore, where there are no images of any deity other than that of Gaṇapati. The only other shrine is for the *navagrahas*. The trustees of this temple felt that it was the only way to avoid politics and anyone who came to the temple would only do so to worship Gaṇapati and not associate him with the rituals of other deities.

Like in Maharashtra, *dūrvā* grass is considered essential to Gaṇapati worship but *śamī* leaves gradually lose their importance as one goes further south. They were considered important in some temples of the Uttara Kannada district but not in others. At the Pañcamukha Heramba Gaṇapati temple, Bangalore, Gaṇapati is offered *bilva* leaves which are generally associated only with Śiva. The Heramba form of Gaṇapati has five faces and, according to the *arcaka*, the reason for this is because Gaṇapati wished to resemble his father who also has five faces. In most of these temples the exact ritual and the prayers to be recited are decided upon by the priest and not by the trustees. This accounts for much liberty in worship and for the numerous variations between temples. By and large, however, Gaṇapati in Karnataka is looked upon as an intrinsic part of Śiva's pantheon. In addition to the *bhasma* and *sindūra* worn by the temple priests in Maharashtra, those in Karnataka also use *candan* (sandal paste). The *mūla mantra* in most of the temples in Karnataka is the same as that in Maharashtra.

Many of the older temples in Karnataka are associated with their own myths. At the Vaiṣṇava Aneguḍḍe Śrī Vināyaka temple, Kumbhasi, myth has it that Bhīma, one of the Pāṇḍavas, was defeated by a *rākṣasa* named Kumbha. The latter was invincible because, as a reward for his penance to Śiva, he had attained the boon of not being destroyed by man. Kṛṣṇa advised Bhīma to propitiate Gaṇapati in the elephant form and obtain the power to destroy Kumbhāsura. Bhīma did as he was instructed and received a sword from Gaṇapati with which he was able to overcome Kumbhāsura.[12] Hence the name of the village, Kumbha + *asi* (sword). The main image of Gaṇapati is also said to be in the form of an elephant. However it is so covered with clothing and flowers that only the trunk is visible. Basically, I'm told, it is a piece of black stone.

In Gokarna which is a famous Śaiva *tīrtha*, one of the smaller Gaṇapati temples is referred to as the Ketakī Gaṇapati temple. Ketakī is a flower of the *ketaka* plant and there is a myth associating Gaṇapati with it in the *Śiva Purāṇa*. According to it, Viṣṇu and Brahmā were once engaged in an argument as to who was superior. Śiva manifested himself before them in the form of a *liṅga* and declared that whoever discovered the top or the bottom of the *liṅga* first would be considered the greatest. Viṣṇu assumed the form of a boar and descended into the earth in search of the root. Brahmā, in the form of a swan, went in search of the top. While he was flying up in the sky, he saw a *ketaka* flower falling from above. On being asked where it was falling from, the flower replied that it was from the top of the *liṅga*. Brahmā decided to take the flower and present it to Viṣṇu as proof of his having reached the top of the *liṅga*. He requested the flower to bear witness to his claim. Viṣṇu accepted defeat but Śiva overheard the conversation and cursed Brahmā for having lied, telling him that he would, as a consequence, have no temple or festival devoted to him. He also cursed the *ketaka* flower for having lied, saying that it would never be used in his worship again. Later, however, Śiva relented and agreed that it could be worn by his attendants and followers.[13] As far as I know, this is the only temple where Gaṇapati is named after this flower and it is appropriate that it should be at a place where the *liṅga* (Mahābaleśvara) is the principal object of worship. Probably, as Śiva's principal attendant Gaṇapati had the right to be worshipped with this flower. At the *aṣṭavināyaka* temple at Ojhar, Maharashtra, the priest rather vehemently said that *ketaka* flowers were never used in the worship of Gaṇapati because they were specifically associated with Śiva. Possibly, this myth originated in the region of Gokarna and is associated with Gaṇapati in only the neighbouring areas.

Both in Maharashtra and Karnataka, Mahāgaṇapati is especially popular among certain *brāhmaṇa* communities. In Karnataka he is the *kuladevatā* (family deity) of the Gauda Saraswats. The Gauda Saraswats are Mādhava Vaiṣṇavite Saraswat *brāhmaṇas* unlike the Saraswats who are *Smārtas*. Formerly they were the same community who originated in the Punjab. From there, they migrated to Kashmir, East Bihar and Goa. When Goa was taken by the Portuguese, they moved to Malabar, Cochin and Travancore.[14] In Maharashtra, Gaṇapati is the family deity of many Konkaṇastha or Citpāvan *brāhmaṇas.* Traditionally, he was the deity of the Peshwas and the Patwardhans. He is also the *grāma devatā* (guardian deity) of several villages and of cities such as Pune and Ahmedabad. Yet, among many *pujārīs* of Gaṇapati temples, their own *kuladevatā* or *iṣṭa devatā* is not Gaṇapati. At the Gaṇapati temple on Kasturba Road, Bangalore, the *pujārī's ista devatā* is Vīrabhadra (a fierce form of Śiva). At Gokarna, the *kuladevatā* of the Kota *brāhmaṇas* is Narasiṃha (half-man half-lion form of Viṣṇu). At the Mahāgaṇapati temple at Mallesvaram Circle, Bangalore, the *kuldevatā* of the *pujārī's* family is Venkateśvara of Tirupati.

In both Karnataka and Maharashtra, Gaṇapati is associated, above all else, with knowledge. His worship was popularized by *brāhmaṇas* and since the traditional primary pursuit in the life of *brāhmaṇas* was knowledge, and more specifically, spiritual knowledge, the deity became the lord of wisdom par excellence. The *Mudgala Purāṇa* repeatedly stresses this point. In two of his eight *avatāras,* those of Mahodara and Gajānana, Gaṇapati is the said to be the bestower of knowledge and success.[15] This knowledge refers to spiritual knowledge and the various *asuras* that Gaṇapati defeats in his eight different forms are essentially those shortcomings of the character that create obstacles in the path of spiritual progress and realization. Elsewhere, it is stated that Gaṇapati alone gives knowledge to achieve anything and everything.[16] The thirteenth century Maharashtrian poet-saint, Jñāneśvar, also identifies Gaṇapati, in the *Jñāneśvarī,* with the totality of the sacred texts and knowledge. This idea is present in the *Padma Purāṇa* as well, where the *modaka* is considered as the symbol of perfect knowledge. Merely by smelling it, a man can obtain immortality. He understands the meaning and essence of all sacred books and becomes adept in all sciences and arts.[17] In fact, Gaṇapati as the expounder of the *Gaṇeśa Gītā* and the central deity of the philosophical treatise, the *Mudgala Purāṇa,* naturally came to be identified with the highest form of knowledge. This idea has persisted in these regions.

At the Śrī Mahāgaṇapati temple, Bangalore, Vidyā Gaṇapati is the form of the deity which is worshipped on the *saṅkaṣṭa caturthī* in June. This is just before schools and colleges reopen after the long summer break. Devotees raise money to buy books and stationery for poor children and to pay their school fees. The image of the deity is decorated with these books and stationery items which are eventually distributed to the poor. Children in Maharashtra, and in many parts of Karnataka, begin any learning session with an invocation to Gaṇapati. The deity's role as Lord of Knowledge is also responsible for his being associated with Saraswatī the goddess of learning. Most people in Maharashtra know of Ṛddhi and Buddhi or Siddhi and Buddhi as Gaṇapati's wives. However, many still consider Saraswatī to be his wife because of his association with learning and culture. In Varanasi, like in many places of the north, although Gaṇapati is associated with knowledge he appears to be looked upon more as the remover of obstacles and the bestower of wealth and well-being. He is popular with the trading class and is, therefore, associated more frequently with Lakṣmī, the goddess of wealth and prosperity.

Inspite of being a Brahmanical deity, Gaṇapati was also traditionally popular with the lower orders of society in the regions of Maharashtra and Karnataka. According to the Gazetteer of the Bombay Presidency, Kanara District, published in 1883 (Vol. XV, Pt. I) even the Mahars, a scheduled caste considered impure by ordinary Hindus, observed *Gaṇeśa caturthī* although 'with no great care'. There is a story, popular among the Mahars, of how a fair and handsome Mahar sweeper youth named Gaṇapati used to be one of the guards at the Shaniwar Palace in Pune. One of the ladies of the palace fell in love with him. The affair was discovered and the Peshwa put the guard to death. The ghost of the dead man kept appearing to the prince in his dreams and gave him no peace until he made an effigy of the Mahar in the form of the god Gaṇapati and set him up at the eastern entrance to the palace where all would do obeisance to the Mahar's name.[18]

Bal Ganghadhar Tilak, the Maharashtrian nationalist leader, is responsible for bringing various castes together in the celebration of the *Gaṇeśa caturthī* festival. He joined with the traditional *brāhmaṇa* leaders to reshape the annual festival at the end of the last century. The purpose was to bridge the gap between *brāhmaṇas* and *non-brāhmaṇas* and between the Congress and the masses and make a united stand against British rule under the leadership of the traditional *brāhmaṇa* elites. Until Tilak's time the festival was a private and domestic affair. Tilak was the first to have large public images of the god installed in *maṇḍapas.* He established the practice of submerging collectively all the public images of the god on the tenth day. The setting up of public images was accompanied by cultural programmes and *melās* and topical political songs. This way Tilak encouraged non-*brāhmaṇas* to participate actively in the festival and thereby promoted Hindu solidarity and gave a political character to what had so far been a purely religious function.[19] Gaṇapati, as the remover of obstacles, was identified with nationalist aspirations for home rule in the early part of the twentieth century. In this process, many aspects of the Brahmanical Gaṇapati must have trickled down to the masses and some popular elements absorbed by the Brahmanical elite. Since then, *Gaṇeśa caturthī* is the most popular festival in Maharashtra. Gaṇapati has truly become a deity of all castes. At the *aṣṭavināyaka* shrines when the *pālakī* (palanquin) carrying the *utsav murti* (metal image used for festive occasions) is taken out on procession during the *caturthī* celebrations, any Hindu, whatever be his caste, is entitled to carry it part of the way. At the Siddhi Vināyaka temple in Bombay, any caste can visit it and have a *pūjā* performed. Several young priests were emphatic about the fact that because it was a Gaṇapati temple there could be no caste restrictions of any kind.

This popularisation of the cult of Gaṇapati has also resulted in a variety of images of this deity. At Pen where most of the Gaṇapati images for the *caturthī* celebrations in Maharashtra are made, I saw some very strange forms of the deity being prepared. These included Gaṇapati dressed in western clothes wearing shoes or riding a motor scooter. Rajbhau Deodhar, a *brāhmaṇa*, who has the biggest workshop and whose family has been in the business since before the time of Tilak felt that the reason for this was that Gaṇapati had become a deity of the masses. Each caste and class wanted a distinct form of its own. A group of fishermen of the koḷī caste had ordered an image of Gaṇapati seated on a fish. Today there are no kings and no royal patronage. The *brāhmaṇas* do not have the same influence they once enjoyed. Hence, people are free to worship Gaṇapati in any form they wish. None of the manufacturers at Pen base their work on any text. Their tradition has been handed down from father to son. Any image that sells well is copied by other manufacturers in the same village. The primary concern of all manufacturers is to sell the maximum number of statues and earn their living. They are willing to make Gaṇapati in any way desired by the clients. Hence some of the strange forms of Gaṇapati. This does not happen with Śiva or Viṣṇu or any of the other gods and goddesses of the Brahmanical pantheon.

The public celebration of the *Gaṇeśa caturthī* is associated with substantial proportions of a city's population or with entire villages whereas the domestic ritual consists of a *pūjā* performed by individuals in their homes. The domestic ceremony commences with the installation of a clay image of the deity on the family altar on the day of *Gaṇeśa caturthī*. The image is then invested with vital breath (*prāṇa pratiṣṭha*). Gaṇapati is worshipped and honoured as a guest in the house with a variety of offerings and with specific rituals and *mantras*. The image is kept in the house for a number of days which range from one to ten depending on the family, caste, and community. After the prescribed period has passed, a simple ritual divests the image of its special status. The patron disperses the *prāṇa* of the image which reverts back to its prior condition. The image is then immersed in water. It dissolves quickly and returns to its original formless state.

In the old temples and in some of the villages, *Gaṇeśa caturthī* is still celebrated only in the temple. The duration of festivities varies from temple to temple. At Cincvad there is no public celebration other than the one performed at the main Gaṇapati temple. The priests at Cincvad, along with thousands of devotees, go on foot from this shrine to the temple at Moregaon where Morayā Gosāvī received his visions. *Āratī* is performed there. When the procession returns another elaborate *āratī* is done at the *samādhi* temple of Morayā Gosāvī. Twenty one *stotrams*, all composed in Marathi by Gosāvī, are chanted on this occasion. At Ranjangaon and Ojhar, too, there is no public celebration. In fact, no resident of these villages generally sets up his own image at home. The temple is believed to house the Gaṇapati of every member of the village and it is there that the festival is collectively celebrated. The celebration consists of a special *pūjā* and a *yātrā*. No image is specially kept in the temple for eventual *visarjan* (immersion). At most of the *aṣṭavināyaka* shrines the *caturthī* is marked by a procession when the *utsav mūrti* is taken on a *pālakī* either around the village or in four different directions, each time starting from the centre. The procession in four different directions, like the one at Ojhar, symbolises the *puruṣārtha*—the four aims of life—*kāma, artha, dharma* and *mokṣa* (pleasure, wealth, religious merit gained through following the Sacred Law, and liberation from the cycle of birth and death). At Sidhatek, the festival is marked only by a special *pūjā* which lasts for four days ending on the *caturthī*. At the Siddhi Vināyaka temple in Bombay, on the occasion of Ganesa *caturthī*, a clay image is installed in the temple and, on the seventh day, it is immersed in the sea. The *yātrā* is reserved for *Gaṇeśa jayanti* when a procession accompanies the *utsava mūrti* carried on a *pālakī* on the *caturthī* of the *kṛṣṇapakṣa* of the month of *māgha* around the Portuguese church area. Similarly, at Titwala, the procession with the *pālakī* takes place only on *Gaṇeśa jayanti* and not on *Gaṇeśa caturthī* when only *mahāpūjā* is performed in the temple.

In most places in Karnataka where the public celebration of *Gaṇeśa caturthī* exists, it is a recent phenomenon. The domestic *pūjā* followed by the immersion of the clay image, however, is similar to that in Maharashtra. The traditional temple celebration, like in Maharashtra, also centres around a tour in a palanquin or on a *rath* (carriage) for the *utsava mūrti* of the temple. Here also, the exact duration and nature of the festivities vary among temples and between communities. At Gokarna and Idagunji, celebration consist of a *gaṇa homa* performed on *Gaṇeśa caturthī*. However, at Gokarna people worship clay images in their homes beginning on the *caturthī* and then immerse them on the eighth day. At Idagunji nobody in the village buys the individual image of Ganapati for *pūjā* and then *visarjan*. Everyone congregates at the main temple to join in the special prayers offered that day. In this village, like in some villages that house the *aṣṭvināyaka* shrines in Maharashtra, it is believed that the image in the temple belongs to everyone and, therefore, no one needs to have one in the house. At Kurudumale, a temple which dates mainly to the Vijayanagar period,[20] the annual *rath yātrā* takes place a day after the *caturthī*. At the Pañcamukha Heramba Gaṇapati temple, Bangalore, clay images of both Gaurī and Gaṇapati are kept in the temple starting from the *caturthī*. After a few days of *pūjā*, both are immersed. Here the presence of Gauri marks a departure from the practice in Maharashtra where, generally, only the image of Gaṇapati is submerged in the water.

In Varanasi the Gaṇapati temples are close to Śiva temples, for Varanasi is a traditional *kṣetra* of Śiva. The temples I visited had *Smārta brāhmaṇa* priests. They are essentially Kananjia *brāhmaṇas* who belong to the region. The Kananjias are sub-divided into various classes and the temples I visited were serviced by priests who were Dubes, Tewaris and Sarjupalli *brāhmaṇas.* In these temples the *mantras* and rituals were based mainly on the Mahāpurāṇas. One of the biggest Gaṇapati temples in Varanasi is the Baḍa *Gaṇeśa* temple. The Durgā Vināyaka temple is also well known as also the numerous small shrines to the various Vināyakas, the more famous being Dhuṇḍhīrāja Vināyaka, Sākṣī Vināyaka and Pañcāmukha Vināyaka. At the Baḍā *Gaṇeśa* temple, *Gaṇeśa* Jayanti was considered the most important festival followed by *Gaṇeśa caturthī.* However there is no public celebration on either occasion and nor does the temple organise a *rath yātrā* or *pālakī* procession. Like in Maharashtra, *dūrvā* grass and *śamī* leaves are specially offered to Gaṇapati. The *Śrī Gaṇapati Atharva-śīrṣa* is recited in addition to numerous *stotras* from various Purāṇas. *Sūktas* from the Vedas are not, as far as I know, included in the daily ritual of the temples. People merely come to the temple to make offerings and for *darśana* (a sight of the deity) and, important though the Vināyakas may be, they remain an intrinsic part of Śiva's pantheon and worship. Some of the Vināyakas such as Dhuṇḍhīrāja and Sākṣī Vināyaka have a third eye on their forehead, and Dhuṇḍhīrāja even has the crescent of the moon on his forehead. These are typical features of Śiva. According to the *Mudgala Purāṇa,* Gaṇapati became the son of Śiva by the name of Dhuṇḍīrāja in order to rid Kāśī of King Divodāsa and make it free for Śiva to reside in.[21] Kāśī and Śiva are both depicted as worshipping Gaṇapati. Śiva insists that Gaṇapati be worshipped before him. Only then will he be pleased and bestow *mukti* (liberation from rebirth) and *bhukti* (enjoyment).

According to the *Mudgala Purāṇa,* the name Dhuṇḍhīrāja was given to Gaṇapati because Śiva searched for him in all the Vedas and Śāstras in order to understand him. Gaṇapati is believed to give *dharma, kāma, artha* and *mokṣa* in this city.[22] The images of Dhuṇḍhi Gaṇapati are also found at Ranjangoan and Ojhar. None of these images appear to have any common form. Cintāmaṇi Gaṇapati is found at Gokarna, at Theur where it is the name of the *svayambhū mūrti,* and at Varanasi where he figures as one of the fifty six Vināyakas. In each place, however, the form is different and, as the name indicates, merely symbolizes Gaṇapati as the fulfiller of wishes. The *Mudgala Purāṇa* describes him as having three eyes and wearing the *cintāmaṇi* jewel in his heart.[23] What appears to have mattered was the name of the form rather than the form itself.

Both in Maharashtra and in Varanasi Gaṇapati is considered to be a *gṛhastha* (married man). In Maharashtra, because of the influence of the two Gāṇapatya Purāṇas, his wives are believed to be Siddhi and Buddhi or Ṛddhi and Siddhi although some consider Lakṣmī or Saraswatī to be his wives. However, since both Lakṣmī and Saraswatī were associated with other major gods, the Gāṇapatyas popularized Gaṇapati's association with Siddhi and Buddhi. It was essential for Gaṇapati to have his own consorts if he was to be equated with the other major deities. This permitted the deity to conform to the Brahmanical concept that a man without a wife is incomplete. Gaṇapati is not the only deity to have two wives and nor is he the only deity who is looked upon as the husband of various goddesses. Śiva and Viṣṇu are both sometimes described with more than one wife. Gaṅgā and Kāśī are sometimes referred to as Śiva's wives in addition to Ūmā, Pārvatī, Durgā or Satī. Similarly, Viṣṇu is sometimes flanked by Bhūdevī and Śrīdevī. Brahmā, likewise, is described with his two wives, Gāyatrī and Saraswatī. The names of Gaṇapati's consorts are such that they can be interpreted as the very gifts that his worship bestows and which are essential for a successful life. In that way Gaṇapati can be conceived of both as a *brahmacārin* and as a *gṛhastha* at the same time. Also, that way Siddhi and Buddhi become acceptable even to those who prefer to consider Lakṣmī or Saraswatī as his wife. In Varanasi, where the recently established cult of Santoṣī Mā has become very popular, Gaṇapati is considered both a husband and a father. At the Baḍā *Gaṇeśa* temple he is depicted with Ṛddhi and Siddhi along with their sons referred to as Śubha and Lābha. There is even a shrine for Santoṣī Mā. Reference to Gaṇapati's sons occurs only in the *Śiva Purāṇa* where they are referred to as Kṣema and Lābha.[24] They are not mentioned in the Gāṇapatya texts and this aspect of Gaṇapati's personality was only recently popularised by the creation of the goddess Santoṣī Mā in north India. It is, however, not accepted in the traditional Gaṇapati temples of Maharashtra and Karnataka, where, inspite of the popularity of the film *Jai Santoshi Ma,* the majority of the people I spoke to were not aware that Gaṇapati had any sons. The Gaṇapati temple at Titwala was the only temple that

I visited in Maharshtra which had images representing his two sons (along with their mothers) beside the principal image of Gaṇapati.

The relevance of the *Gaṇesa* and *Mudgala Purāṇas* also varies from place to place. The *Gaṇeśa Purāṇa* has been published in Sanskrit with a Marathi translation and the *Mudgala Purāṇa* is available in Sanskrit. I do not know of any Marathi translation of the latter although abridged translations in Marathi of some portions exist. Obviously then, these texts have some relevance today. At Moregaon a *brāhmaṇa* resident of the village reads excerpts from the *Mudgala Purāṇa* in the temple at the request of devotees. Such sessions last from three days to a month. The sixth *khaṇḍa* of the *Mudgala Purāṇa* is especially popular as it deals with this particular sacred site. Portions of the *Gaṇeśa Purāṇa* are also read. However, the *Gaṇeśa Gītā* which forms part of the *Gaṇeśa Purāṇa* is unknown to most people and, I am told, is never recited. At Ojhar, almost throughout the year, at around 8.00 a.m. some part of the *Gaṇeśa* or *Mudgala Purāṇa* is read within the precincts of the temple. The Maratha who reads it lives in the village but is not part of the temple. He knows Sanskrit and is able to translate what he reads into Marathi. The audience consists mainly of the residents of the village. At Theur and Sidhatek these texts are not read. The reason given at Sidhatek was that the village was too small. The majority of the population consisted of farmers who spent most of the day in the fields and who only came to the temple for *darśana.* In none of the other temples that I visited in Maharashtra were these texts ever referred to. In Karnataka, at the Gaṇapati temple on Kasturba Road, Bangalore, on important occasions such as the twenty days celebrations for the *Gaṇeśa caturthī,* lectures (basically stories) based on the *Gaṇeśa Purāṇa* are sometimes organized but none from the *Mudgala Purāṇa.* At Gokarna, the *pramukha pujārī* was familiar with the *Gaṇeśa* and *Mudgal Purāṇas* but the texts were never read in the village. At Idagunji no one had even heard of them. At the Badā *Gaṇeśa* temple at Varanasi, the priest whose family has served in the temple since four generations had heard of the *Gaṇeśa* and *Mudgala Purāṇas.* However, he had never seen the texts and did not even know if they were available. Essentially, the public is familiar with those myths of Gaṇapati which are described in the Śaiva Purāṇas.

So, in the final analysis, who are the texts relevant to

today? Probably they have become a part of the religious heritage of the region and only very few scholars read them. Portions of them are also read by interested lay persons and devotees. They are also relevant to a few residents in those villages with *aṣṭavināyaka* shrines where limited portions of these texts are sometimes read. However, it is certain that only a very small number of myths from these Purāṇas are known. This is the case with most of the sacred texts today. Take for instance the Āgamas. These texts are acknowledged as being authoritative in many temples of Tamil Nadu. Yet, there is hardly anyone who really knows them. Many of them are not even known to exist any more. Most priests are familiar with some of the rituals prescribed in them and these rituals are preserved by the principle of heredity and not by the study of texts.

Further south, in Tamil Nadu, the priests in the more important Gaṇapati temples are mainly *Yajurvedi Smārtas.* Whereas the Gaṇapati *homa, pañcāmṛtam abhiṣeka* and the *Sahasranāma* are common to these different regions, the *Śrī Atharvaśīrṣa* was not included in the ritual of the temples I visited. In some temples the Rudracāmakam is also recited daily. *Gaṇeśa caturthī* is celebrated with a *homa* and the distribution of *prasād.* In some temples the *utsava mūrti* is taken on a *pālakī* around the temple and the streets of the neighbourhood and then returned to the temple. Where there is public celebration it is a more recent phenomena although the domestic celebration is the same as in Karnataka and Maharashtra in that clay images are installed in individual homes, worshipped, and then immersed in the sea, river or tank. As in the case of Śiva temples in Tamil Nadu, the priests in the Gaṇapati temples are referred to as *gurukkals* whereas the term *arcaka* is usually used for priests in Viṣṇu temples. The *gurukkals* are not recognised as regular *brāhmaṇas.* They are Saivites to a greater extent than the *Smārtas.* In fact, in most of the smaller temples, the priests are Śaivas rather than *Smārtas.* At the Ālavṛkṣa Eyarkai Temple (Banyan tree natural Vināyaka) in the Government Estate, Madras, the *gurukkal* said that he served as an officiant only in temples of Śiva or Gaṇapati. At some of the smaller shrines such as the Śakti Vināyaka temple, opposite Adyar Park Sheraton hotel, the temple priest is a Mudaliar. The Mudaliars were originally an artisan caste and they are generally Saiva by religion. In this particular temple all the *pūjā* is in Tamil. The ritual is also very simple—*snāna, naivedya* and *āratī*. At a small roadside shrine on TTK road, Madras, there is a temple called the Golden Vināyaka. Here the priest calls himself a Śivācārya and said that he based his *pūjā* entirely on the *Kāmikāgama*. The officiants in the temples I visited were not familiar with the *Gaṇeśa* and *Mudgala Purāṇas* even though there is a south Indian version of the *Gaṇeśa Purāṇa* called the *Vināyaka Purāṇa*. In all the temples the priests believed that Gaṇapati is not equal to Śiva. Neither is he an independent deity. He is only the son of Śiva and, therefore, important though he may be, he can never be as great as his father. However, being an important member of the family, he is entitled to his own temples and rituals.The forms of Gaṇapati in some of the temples recall the forms mentioned in the *Śaṅkaravijaya*. The Golden Vināyaka temple recalls the Suvarṇa Gaṇapati of the *Śaṅkaravijaya*. Another, the Śakti Vināyaka, recalls the Sakti Vināyaka of the *Ajitāgama*.[25] However, in this particular temple, Gaṇapati is not depicted with any *śakti* and is represented alone.

In Tamil Nadu the difference between the Vaiṣṇavas, the *Smārtas* and the Śaivas has been more marked than in other regions. However, most non-*brāhmaṇa* Tamilians maintain multiple sectarian affiliations, seldom shifting from one to another, but more often adding to their affiliational connections through time. Today there are syncretic tendencies but these appear in the *Smārta* context. A case in point is the Śrī Ānanda Vināyaka temple, Madras. It is a *pañcāyatana* temple where Gaṇapati is the principal deity and is looked upon as an *avatāra* of Lord Venkateśvara by the priests because the idol was gifted by the Tirupati temple where Lord Venkateśvara, a form of Viṣṇu, is the principal deity. The priest is an Iyer but he wears the *tilaka* of the Vaiṣṇavas as does the deity he serves. The Gaṇesa *caturthī pūjā* is performed with 1008 *śankhas* and chanting from the *Kṛṣṇa Yajur Veda*. The *śankha* is an attribute of Viṣṇu and, in this case, because Gaṇapati is looked upon as an incarnation of a form of Viṣṇu, he is associated with it. Hence, Gaṇapati is the link between various castes in Maharashtra and various sects in Tamil Nadu, even as he was the bridge between Śivaism and Buddhism in the early medieval period.

Dūrvā grass is important for Gaṇapati worship in Tamil Nadu, but not so, *śamī*. The *arka* (*Calotropis gigantea*) root and *arka* flowers are also specifically associated with Gaṇapati in this region. The *arka* plant is associated with Gaṇapati in some Mahapurāṇas and Śaiva Āgamas and, therefore, some of the temples in Karnataka where the influence of the Śaiva Āgamas exists *arka* flowers are used in the worship of the deity. According to the *Svayambhuvāgama,* the *bali* to Gaṇapati consists of, among other things, *arka* flowers.[26] According to the *Agni Purāṇa,* oblations done to Gaṇapati with the root of white *arka,* are believed to result in the fulfilment of all wishes of the worshipper.[27]

In contrast to Tamil Nadu where Gaṇapati worship is based on the Śaiva Āgamas, in Kerala, in the temples I visited, it is based on the Vedas. This is not taking into consideration temples which have been set up by other communities and where the ritual conforms to the regions where the communities come from. Like Maharashtra, Kerala too had a royal family, albeit a small one, that considered Gaṇapati as its family deity—that of the Rājās of Edapilli. Edapilli was a tiny state in the Malabar which was ruled by rājās belonging to the Namboodiri caste of *brāhmaṇas.* The dynasty claimed its origin from the days of Paraśurāma (looked upon as one of the ten incarnations of Viṣṇu). Information about Edapilli is available mainly from Portuguese and Dutch sources. The state and the ruling dynasty existed from at least before the arrival of the Portuguese. This state, which was originally independent, came under the suzerainty, at one time or another, of Travancore and Cochin. The would-be-Raja and his family still live at the Edapilli palace in Cochin. Gaṇapati is their family deity and an image of a ten-armed Gaṇapati made of *pañcalohā* (five metals) is now worshipped in the *pūjā* room of the palace. At certain times of the day this *pūjā* is open to the public. However, since very few people know about this temple there are not many visitors. Vāsudeva Rājā, the brother of the would-have-been Rājā, said the image had been around all his life (he is about fifty years of age) and his parents' life. He maintained that Gaṇapati had been the family deity for generations but could not say for how many generations. The image housed at the Edapilli palace had formerly been the *utsava mūrti* at the temple of Gaṇapati at Panangad (on the outskirts of Cochin) which once belonged to the royal family. The temple at Panangad has an image that is believed to be *svayambhū.* When the Rājā lost his land after his state was abolished he was obliged to give up this temple. Since the *svayambhū mūrti* could not be moved, he only took away the *utsav mūrti* and entrusted the temple to the care of the forty odd families residing in Panangad. There is no other image in the temple at Panangad. There are two smaller shrines in the large compound, one for the *nāgas* and the other for Śiva. This Gaṇapati temple is believed to be at least two hundred years old although there were some trustees who said that tradition had it that it was about six hundred years old.

The priests at this temple at Panangad are Embrandri *brāhmaṇas*. The Embrandris are a *brāhmaṇa* caste who immigrated from the South Kannada District of Karnataka. They are not as high a caste as the Namboodiris but some families have intermarried with the Namboodiris. The *mūla mantra* in this temple is *Gaṃ namaḥ*. The celebration of *Gaṇeśa caturthī* at Panangad includes a special *homa* with the offering of 1008 coconuts and other items like rice and sugar cane. The festivities do not include a *yātrā* nor the immersion of a clay image of the deity. The prayers include the Puruṣa Sūkta and the *gāyatrī mantra*, The *Śrī Gaṇapati Atharvaśīrṣa* is not recited and no one had heard of the *Gaṇeśa* and *Mudgal Purāṇas*.

Some of the better known temples dedicated to Gaṇapati in Kerala are the Madhura Gaṇapati in Kasargod, the Mahāgaṇapati temple in Calicut and the Gaṇapati temple in Trivandrum. The temple priests in Kerala are referred to as *tantri*. What is common to Tamil Nadu and Kerala is the representation of Gaṇapati with the trunk turning right holding the *amṛta kalaśa* (jar of ambrosia). This form appears to be special to these two regions and gives Gaṇapati another dimension to his personality—the giver of immortality.

What appears common in Varanasi, Maharashtra, Karnataka and Tamil Nadu is the association between Hanumān and Ganapati. The popularisation of the cult of Hanumān in the region of Maharashtra is largely due to the seventeenth century saint, Rāmadās. The latter worked towards a spiritual regeneration of society and established a chain of monasteries throughout the Maratha state where physical education was imparted with special attention to the formation of bodily strength and character. The presiding deity in these *maṭhas* was Hanumān.[28] Hanumān was a symbol of strength and his role in the *Rāmāyana* is believed to have inspired Śivājī and the Marathas to fight against Mughal domination. The images of both Gaṇapati and Hanumān are smeared with thick coats of *sindūra*. Whereas one represents wisdom and knowledge, the other represents physical might, both necessary qualities for a successful life. In Maharashtra what is striking is the presence of an image of Hanumān in virtually all the Gaṇapati temples and shrines, old and new. Probably it was during Rāmdās' time or shortly thereafter that many Gaṇapati temples acquired a shrine to Hanumān, popularly known as Māruti or as Āñjaneya in the south. In Ahmadnagar both the deities are looked upon as *grama devatās* of the city. Hanumān guards the northern gate of the old city wall and Gaṇapati is the guardian of the southern gate. Both have temples in these locations.[29] At Sidhatek the *gramadevatā* is Hanumān. One difference between the two, however, is that Gaṇapati in Maharashtra and Varanasi is considered to be a *gṛhastha* whereas Hanumān is a *brahmacārin.* In Karnataka and Tamil Nadu both are *brahmacārins.* Hanumān is also present in many Gaṇapati temples in Karnataka and Tamil Nadu. At Varanasi there were many small shrines under trees where images of both deities are placed. In Pune, in a small shrine not far from the Kasbah Gaṇapati temple, I came accross a tall (about 6 ft.) and powerful looking statue of Gaṇapati where he resembles the figure of Hanumān. His belly protrudes only slightly and thus he does not look stocky. In one of his hands he bears a mace which is an attribute of Hanumān. The other hands bear no attributes. This process of syncretism finds its culmination at the Śrī Ānanda Vināyaka temple in Madras where there is a syncretistic deity who is half Hanumān and half Gaṇapati (plate 4). He is referred to as *Ādianta Prabhū* (eternal lord). The left side is Hanumān and the right is Gaṇapati. The image stands on a lotus. At Varanasi one of the popular prayers to Gaṇapati is the Gaṇesa *cālīsā* which has its counterpart in the Hanumān *cālīsā.*

How the priests view themselves also differs in temples. Whereas most priests, including the ones at the *aṣṭavināyaka* shrines, consider themselves as the *sevaks* or servants of the lord, three priests, one at the Gaṇapati temple on Kasturba Road, Bangalore, another at Kurudumale, also in Karnataka, and the third at the Golden Vināyaka temple, Madras, considered themselves as *pratinidhis* or representatives of the lord. Their claims to be representatives of the deity they serve can be understood in the context of the *Āgamas* on which they base their worship. One of the Āgamic precepts is that 'one must become Śiva to worship Śiva' and that 'only Śiva can worship Śiva'.[30] Fuller describes how, among the Mīnākṣī temple priests (Madurai, Tamil Nadu), the Āgamic precepts are taken to mean that a priest must become a form of Śiva before he can worship him. This transformation is first achieved when a priest is initiated and consecrated by his *guru,* and it is repeated thereafter when the priest invokes Śiva in himself before commencing a ritual. Similarly, by extension of that precept, these priests in the Gaṇapati temple felt that they were representatives of Gaṇapati by reason of their *dīkṣā* (initiation) and consecration. The priest at Kurudumale performed *pūjā* at both the Śiva and the Gaṇapati temple. He considered the laity to be the *sevaks* whereas, being the intermediary between them and the deity and since he prayed on their behalf, he was the *pratinidhi.* The priest at the Pancamukha Heramba Gaṇapati temple, Mahālakṣmī layout, Bangalore, considers himself a messenger between the laity and the god. Without using the word *pratinidhi* he insisted that he was a part of the deity, in this case, Śiva, because he looked upon Gaṇapati as an *avatāra* of Śiva.

There is a popular belief about Gaṇapati which does not find mention in the Gāṇapatya or other texts dealing with Gaṇapati. In Maharashtra, the image of the deity with the trunk turning right is known as Siddhi Vināyaka and it is commonly believed that this form has a special significance. It requires special *pūjā* and, when not worshipped according to strictly defined procedures, it can be unlucky. Therefore, it is not recommended for homes but is usually housed in a temple. A friend told me how her father had presented an antique bronze image of Gaṇapati with the trunk turned right to neighbours in Bombay. He discovered, subsequently, to his horror, that the antique had been thrown into the sea because the neighbours feared it would bring bad luck.[31] The biggest temples to Siddhi-Vināyaka are in Bombay and Pune. It is believed that the worship of Siddhi Vināyaka ensures *siddhi,* or success, quickly. According to members of a family I met in Pen, their *guru* was regarded by his devotees as an incarnation of Gaṇapati with his trunk to the right. This family believed that Gaṇapati with the trunk to the left signified Śiva's son whereas Gaṇapati with the trunk to the right symbolised the deity in his capacity as the source of all creation. The *guru* in India is traditionally looked upon and worshipped as God. He is the representative of Brahma, Viṣṇu or Śiva because by showing the devotee the path to realization he becomes the creator of a new, more evolved human being. Many devotees of the late Swāmī Chinmāyānanda looked upon him as an incarnation of Ādi Śaṅkara who, in turn, was considered to be an incarnation of Śiva. If some people in Maharashtra look upon their *guru* as an incarnation of Gaṇapati, it is understandable since Gosāvī and his seven descendants established a tradition of Gaṇapati incarnating in human form in this region.

In Karnataka, Tamil Naḍu and Kerala there were many images of Gaṇapati with the trunk turning right but each time I was told that it did not have any special significance. In Karnataka and Tamil Nadu such an image is referred to simply as *balamuri* Gaṇapati and *valamburi* Gaṇapati respectively. In Karnataka some priests considered that Gaṇapati with his trunk to the right represented the *tejas* (brilliant or fierce) aspect of the deity whereas the image with the trunk to the left represented the *saumya* (mild) aspect. At Idagunji the image with the trunk turning right is referred to as Ugra (fierce) Gaṇapati. At other places the trunk turning left was considered *sātvic* (endowed with the quality of *sattva* or goodness), the straight, *rājasic* (endowed with the quality of *rajas* or passion), and the right, *tamasic* (endowed with the quality of *tamas* or darkness/ignorance). In Kerala, at the Guruvayoor temple, there is a Gaṇapati shrine where the trunk of the image turns right. I was told that it had no particular significance and that it made no difference whether the trunk turned to the right or the left. This tradition of Siddhi-Vināyaka with the trunk to the right does not find mention in the Gāṇapatya texts which, on the contrary, refer to Gaṇapati with the straight trunk. It was probably started by some temple priests in order to attract a greater number of followers and gradually became established. Even in some of the small temples in Pune the image of a Gaṇapati with trunk turning right is installed since it is associated with greater power and, thereby ensures a greater clientele. Images of Gaṇapati with the trunk turned to the right appear as early as the seventh century (plate 5) but the Purānas and Āgamas make no mention of whether the trunk should turn left of right. It is possible that these variations existed because of different artisans who produced the images and, much later, the idea of their having a special significance was popularized.

Inspite of the several perceptions of Gaṇapati's civil status in different regions what is evident everywhere is that the link between him and the goddess remains constant. She may be Lakṣmī, Saraswatī, Sakti, Siddhi and Buddhi, Ṛddhi and Siddhi, Vallabhā or Santośī Mā. The goddess is mother, wife, female counterpart, half of him (*ardhanārī*), symbol of his attributes or powers, his sister or daughter. The latter is the most recent addition to Gaṇapati's pantheon. As the *pujārī* at the Daśabhuja Gaṇapati temple in Pune said, the name of the *devī* on Gaṇapati's lap does not really matter. The *devī* has many forms and what is significant is that Gaṇapati is associated with her regardless of whether she is in the form of mother, wife, sister or daughter. Since the Gāṇapatyas considered Gaṇapati to be synonymous with *Brahman*, and all the other deities as aspects of the *Brahman*, Gaṇapati accompanied by Lakṣmī or Saraswatī is acceptable in that Viṣṇu or Brahmā are merely aspects of Gaṇapati. Similarly, although Gaṇapati is popularly accepted as Pārvatī's son, it is he and not Śiva who is closely associated with rites celebrating the Durgā festival. Similarly, the harvest festival in which Gaṇapati worship is an important component is eloquent of his role vis a vis the goddess.

The *vratas* of Gaṇapati are performed on the *caturthī*. However, the *caturthī* is also associated with many *vratas* of the Goddess and, more often than not, these are undertaken for the attainment of conjugal happiness. That of the month of *jyeṣṭha* is celebrated as the *sativrata*. By performance of this rite, the devotee is said to rejoice in the world of the mother of Gaṇapati, at par with him.[32] *Gaurīvrata* is observed on the fourth day in the bright half of the month of *māgha*. This *vrata* is said to increase conjugal blessedness and its observance is recommended annually for both men and women.[33] It is especially auspicious for unmarried girls desirous of a bridgroom or by a women seeking matrimonial bliss and good fortune for their husbands and sons.[34] Sometimes the worship of Ūmā is specially recommended on the *caturthīs* of the bright halves of *māgha, āśvayuj* and *jyeṣṭha*.[35]

In Maharashtra, at Cincvad and Ojhar, it is generally believed that Gaṇapati has a sister in each of the four directions and he goes to meet her annually on the occasion of *Gaṇeśa caturthī*. This represents the traditional celebration of the festival and not the public celebration introduced by Tilak. At Ojhar, for instance, the *pālakī* of Gaṇapati with Siddhi and Buddhi is first taken to a village five kilometres east of Johar to the temple of

Ambikā. The goddess is worshipped and the *pālakī* with Gaṇapati returns to Ojhar. Next, the procession proceeds south, west and north of Ojhar where, each time, it visits the local goddess's shrine. It would be difficult to explain the constant association with the goddess if in folk memory Gaṇapati is not a part of her. The close association between the goddess and Gaṇapati is further evident in the rite of immersion of the idol of Gaṇapati in water after celebration of *Vināyaka caturthī*. This practice does not occur with the images of Śiva, Viṣṇu, Rāma, Kṛṣṇa or the other deities. It is otherwise associated only with the Goddess as on the occasion of Durgā *pūjā*.

Since Pārvatī absorbed within her all the numerous village and tribal goddeses, she became representative of the universal *Śakti*. However, because of her role as the consort of Śiva, her relationship with Gaṇapati remains ambiguous. Although commonly represented as the mother of Gaṇapati, it is clear that she is also his consort. In Bengal, Gaṇapati is married to the banana tree, the 'Kala Bau' during Durgā *pūjā* which is none other than Durgā herself ritually transformed during the festival. At other times, however, Gaṇapati is conceptualised as the son of Durgā and brother of Lakṣmī and Saraswatī. Take, again, the worship of Gaṇapati with Gaurī at the harvest festivals where ritual motifs of menstruation and rebirth are integral. This idea was neatly summed up by Nārāyaṇa Upādhyāya the *pramukha pujārī* at Gokarna. He said that Pārvatī is the symbol of the earth and so Gaṇapati, as the son of the earth, is also symbol of the earth. The *gaṃ* in the *mūla mantra* of Gaṇapati signifies the earth. We get everything from the earth. Since Gaṇapati is so closely associated with the earth which itself is endangered in the *Kali yuga*, Gaṇapati worship becomes of primordial importance in this age. Naturally his worship is intrinsically associated with that of the *devī*: the Earth Mother and her consort-cum-son.

Even the mouse that Gaṇapati rides on is associated with the earth. According to the *Brahmavaivarta Purāṇa*, when all the gods offered Gaṇapati presents after the name-giving ceremony, the Earth gave him a rat to serve as his vehicle.[36] According to the *Ṛgvidhāna*,[37] rats, mice and moles must be propitiated with sacrificial offerings of boiled rice placed on a mole-hill. Moles were believed to know the very essence of the earth, and the mounds thrown up by them represented this essence and brought about good fortune.[38] The underworld which the mouse inhabits is the world of the dead and the womb of the earth from where regeneration occurs. This theme of death by sacrifice and regeneration is itself intrinsic to the fertility rites associated with agriculture and which appear to be associated with the earliest stages of this deity's origin. The red *sindūra* coating on the images of Gaṇapati and the elephant head on a human body evoke the concept of blood sacrifice. Gaṇapati's *sindūra* coated image recalls the *sindūra* associated with the goddess. The Goddess Lalitā (a form of Pāvatī) is described as being of red-complexion.[39] Similarly Bhadrakālī is described as being dressed in red and smeared with red unguents.[40] Even the *arka* leaves and flowers with which Gaṇapati is worshipped, specially in Karnataka and Tamil Nadu, are associated with the goddess and appear to be symbolic of fertility. In the context of *devī* worship, the *Nārada Purāṇa* prescribes that a thousand flowers of the *arka* be offered to the goddess.[41] A hymn in the *Atharva Veda*[42] refers to the *arka* wood amulet which is prescribed for making the devotee's penis as large and virile as that of the elephant, ass and horse. The *arka* wood is the giver of virility to men and has a definite sexual connotation. Among the *brāhmaṇas* there has been a tradition, whereby, if a man wanted to marry a third time, he was first symbolically married to the *arka* plant. After the ceremony the plant was cut down.[43] The significance of this ritual is that the third time is unlucky. Therefore, the *arka* takes on the ill-luck and leaves the man free to marry a fourth time without fear. According to an old tradition, leaves of the *arka* plant were used to garland adulterers and publicly disgrace them.[44]

Gaṇapati's civil status remains ambiguous not only in the region under discussion but in the whole country. This is because of the process of Brahmanization that the deity has undergone. It is within the Brahmanical context that he becomes Śiva's son. To rule out all possibility of ambiguity in his relationship with Pārvatī he was made into a *brahmacārin.* Within the Śaiva context, Gaṇapati and Kārtikkeya represent the ideal sons. There is no further need for them to have families because Śiva's family symbolises all aspects of the human condition. Yet, folk tradition and folk memory have continued to associate the deity with the Goddess, for Gaṇapati existed before his induction into the Śaiva pantheon and his rituals were closely linked to those of the Goddess. Finally, this association manifests itself in a variety of ways in the Brahmanical context where he is associated with numerous goddesses. Gaṇapati with Lakṣmī symbolises Gaṇapati as the harbinger of wealth since Lakṣmī symbolises wealth. She initially represented agricultural prosperity and, later, commercial prosperity. As the goddess of wealth she was first linked to Kubera and then to Gaṇapati. The *Mudgala Purāṇa* found the ideal explanation for this association which would remove all amibiguities in the eyes of the Gāṇapatyas. According to the text, since Viṣṇu is born of Gaṇapati and, therefore, is a form of Gaṇapati, Lakṣmī being depicted with either of them makes sense.[45] Therefore, Gaṇapati is referred to as *Lakṣmīpati*[46] (lord of Lakṣmī). The distinctions that we perceive are all the result of *māyā*. With Saraswatī, Gaṇapati symbolises the harbinger of wisdom and knowledge since Saraswatī is the goddess of learning. This association was subsequent to his association with Pārvatī and Lakṣmī and carries no echoes of Gaṇapati's elephant past. His role of the deity of knowledge derives purely from within the Brahmanical context.

The most recent goddess with whom Gaṇapati is associated is Santośī Mā. Her cult is especially important in the urban areas of north India although her popularity has spread even to some rural areas. Her worship necessitates no knowledge of traditional rituals and prayers. It is simple and does not require the mediation of a priest. Santosī Mā, who is gentle and benevolent, is the new saviour of the harassed modern woman. The 'demons' today are ill-treatment of women by in-laws, female infanticide, bride burning and other tensions associated with modern life. Since Gaṇapati is the remover of obstacles, it is possible that in the popular mind his daughter, too, partakes of his special powers. Each time Gaṇapati is associated with a goddess whether as a son, husband or male counterpart, he shares her powers and functions. As the son of Pārvatī he is invincible before the power of Śiva. Or, he is the deity with chothonic powers even as Pārvatī represents the earth. With Lakṣmī, he is the giver of wealth and with Saraswatī, knowledge. Siddhi and Buddhi are an intrinsic part of him and have no independent existence. It is, therefore, appropriate that Santośī Mā appears through the intermediary of a deity who is benevolent and who grants success to his devotees. She is gentle and powerful like her father. Besides, it is not possible for modern families to identify themselves with the family of Śiva, nor with those of Rāma and Kṛṣṇa beyond a point. In the case of Gaṇapati, however, the film depicts him with two sons who desire a sister on whose hand they can tie a *rākhī*—a situation prevalent in numerous Indian families. So Gaṇapati, on being persuaded by his wives, sister and sons, creates his mind-born daughter, Santośī Mā. The creation of Santośi Mā suggests the importance of a daughter and Gaṇapati becomes the first Hindu deity to have a daughter who becomes as important as the sons of Śiva. It is easy to create family situations involving Gaṇapati since the sacred texts provide little information on this subject. The personality and traits of this daughter mirror some of the modern perceptions of Gaṇapati himself.

Finally, the Gāṇapatyas have, indeed, left a substantial legacy. The *Smārta* Gāṇapatyas succeeded in making Gaṇapati a major Brahmanical deity and, in some cases, as popular as Śiva, Viṣṇu or the goddess. The regions where they flourished continue to be the regions where the deity has the most numerous temples dedicated to him and where he is one of the favourite deities. Like Śiva and Viṣṇu who are believed to have incarnated in the form of several historical figures such as Lakulīśa, Śaṅkarācārya, Kṛṣṇa and the Buddha (the latter in some Vaiṣṇava texts is accepted as an incarnation of Viṣṇu), Gaṇapati, too, is believed to have incarnated in the person of Morayā Gosāvī and his seven descendants. This is, perhaps, one of the main reasons why Maharashtra, specially the region around Pune, became and has remained the stronghold of the Gāṇapatya tradition. In Karnataka, Varanasi and Tamil Nadu, although there are several Gaṇapati temples he remains second to Śiva. Certain common features prevail in these areas. The way of bowing and paying obeisance to Gaṇapati appears to be the same in the regions where the *Smārta* Gāṇapatyas and the Gāṇapatyas off-shoots of the Śaivas flourished. Some of the forms popularized in the *Āgamas* continue to be popular such as Mahāgaṇapati, Nṛtya Gaṇapati, Heramba Gaṇapati, Vīra Gaṇapati, Prasanna Gaṇapati and, to a lesser extent, Suvarṇa Gaṇapati. The Gāṇapatya Purāṇas introduced numerous myths identifying Gaṇapati with various older divinities. This has resulted in him being worshipped by *Smārtas*, Śaivas and Vaiṣṇavas alike in temples where he is the principal, and often the only, deity and where he is sometimes identified with Viṣṇu or Śiva. The Gāṇapatyas established a tradition which has become a part of the religious life not only of the regions where they flourished but in other parts of the country as well. In New Delhi, for example, there are at least three Gaṇapati temples where the ritual is the same as in the temples of Tamil Nadu. The priests are Iyers (*Smārta brāhmaṇas*) and the patrons are largely members of the South Indian community, although, increasingly, other residents living in the areas also frequent the temples. *Gaṇeśa caturthī* is becoming an increasingly popular festival with public celebrations in a greater number of regions. Similarly, in other parts of India as well, where Gaṇapati was traditionally a part of the temples of other deities, he now has temples devoted to him alone. Judging by the number of mediums in which Gaṇapati is portrayed—metal, ceramic, terracotta, stone, cloth, glass, shell, *arka* root, coral, mud, etc.,—and the numerous homes where he adorns not only the family shrine but also the living room or the garden, this deity is, indeed, the most popular Hindu deity today. Having a Gaṇapati as a decorative piece is in fashion and one has to only visit the Government Emporia, *melas*, craft bazaars and exhibitions of paintings and handicrafts to realize the extent to which Gaṇapati inspires artistic expression in India.

NOTES

1. Details regarding the temples I visited are given in Chapter I under the subheading 'Sources'.
2. *Mudgala Purāṇa*, IV.48.19-20.
3. Ibid., IV.47.61
4. Ibid., 8.42.4-5.
5. Ibid., 6.9.8.
6. Ibid., V.24.10.
7. *Gaṇesa' Purāṇa*, Upāsanā Khaṇḍa, I.46.
8. For a translation of the text see 'Appendix' of Paul B. Courtright's *Gaṇeśa: Lord of Obstacles, Lord of Beginnings*, pp. 252-4.
9. Ibid., p. 208.
10. *Mudgala Purāṇa*, V.24.21-4.
11. Ibid., III.26.44.
12. Told to me by Śrī Sūrya Narain Upādhyāya, the head priest at this temple.
13. *Śiva Purāṇa*, Vidyeśvarasaṃhita, I.7 and 8.
14. *Gazetteer of Karnataka*, South Kannad District, p. 110.
15. *Mudgala Purāṇa*, I.20.7-8.
16. Ibid., VI.7.15.

17. *Padma Purāṇa*, II.i.63.8-9.
18. Quoted by Paul B. Courtright, op. cit., p. 150.
19. Richard Cashman, 'The Political Recruitment of the God Ganapathi' in Robin Jeffrey *et al.*, eds., *India: Rebellion to Republic*, pp. 37-63.
20. *Gazetteer of India*, Mysore State, Kolar District, p. 82.
21. *Mudgala Purāṇa*, I.39.49. For an older version of the myth see *Vāyu Purāṇa*, II.30.
22. Ibid., I. 52.4-16.
23. Ibid., I.20.35.
24. *Śiva Purāṇa*, II.iv.20.8.
25. *Ajitāgama*, Vol. III, 55.6.
26. *Svayambhuvāgama*, 58.106, p. 292.
27. *Agni Purāṇa*, II.i.301.7.
28. G.S. Sardesai, *New History of the Marathas*, Vol. I, p. 275.
29. Paul B. Courtright, op. cit., p. 109.
30. C.J. Fuller, ' "Only Śiva can worship Śiva": Ritual mistakes and their Correction in a South Indian temple', *Contributions to Indian Sociology* (NS), Vol. 27, 2, 1993, pp. 169-89.
31. Told to me by Shereen Ratnagar.
32. *Nārada Purāṇa*, IV.113.90-1.
33. Ibid.
34. Ibid., IV.112.2-7.
35. *Nīlmata Purāṇa*, 511-14.
36. *Brahmavaivarta Purāṇa*, 3.13.12cf.
37. *Ṛgvidhāna*, II.14.5. Quoted by Margaret Stutley, *Ancient Indian Magic and Folklore*, p. 120.
38. *Śatapatha Brāhmana*, II.i.17. Quoted by Margaret Stutley, op. cit.
39. *Nārada Purāṇa*, III.88.35-7
40. *Śiva Purāṇa*, II.v.36-7.
41. *Nārada Purāṇa*, III.i.67.60.
42. *Atharva Veda*, VI.72.
43. E. Thurston, *Castes and Tribes of Southern India*, Vol. I, A and B, pp. 295-6.
44. Ibid., p. 296.
45. *Mudgala Purāṇa*, VII.11.
46. Ibid., VII.11.25.

CHAPTER 8

Conclusion

Gaṇapati, as we know him, is the creation of *brāhmaṇas.* He represents a syncretism of different traditions which converge to form a composite deity around the fourth century of the Christian era. However, one aspect of Gaṇapati's antecedents, namely the concept of a sacred elephant, reaches back to the early stages of civilisation in the subcontinent. The first evidence of the elephant having some sacred significance comes from a few Harappan sites. The elephant motif appears on seals, amulets and terracotta art in the Mature Indus period. The symbol of the elephant possibly originated as a totem of a descent group which came into prominence during this period. Although many of the seals on which it is depicted had a secular function, it is generally accepted that the motifs themselves had a magico-religious significance.

Between the Harappan period and about 600 BC there is a blank in the availability of data on the elephant. Thereafter, there is evidence of people and places named after it and the motif reappears on coins and sculpture. There are literary references to the worship of the elephant deity and to rituals of a religious nature associated with the animal. Much of this evidence highlights the existence of a tradition where the elephant was venerated by some categories of people in and around the zone where the ancient Harappan culture had flourished. By the mid-first millennium BC, the elephant had also become the mount for kings. It was associated with royalty because of its size and majestic appearance. It symbolised nobility of character, grandeur and strength. This link with kingship and divinity determined the nature of the role it was to play in the different religions which evolved in north India from about 600 BC. The worship of the elephant and associated rituals did not form part of the Vedic tradition. However, the elephant symbol was eventually adopted by the three major religions of ancient India—Brahmanism, Buddhism and Jainism—

and was adapted to suit the needs of each. In Buddhism and Jainism it became the symbol of the divine conception of the Buddha and Mahāvīra, respectively. In the Brahmanical context it became, Airāvata, the elephant mount of Indra. At a later stage, when Indra declined in importance and Śiva rose to prominence, the elephant was converted into the therianthropic son of Śiva. Some Puranic myths highlight the continuity of tradition by describing how the head of Airāvata was cut off and transferred onto the headless torso of Gaṇapati. This close association of the elephant with the Buddha, Mahāvīra and Śiva is one reason why the elephant-headed deity eventually became a major god in the pantheons of these religions whereas the other animals such as the bull, the ram or the lion/tiger, which also appear in a divine context from Harappan times, remained at the level of sacred animals.

This does not imply that the significance of the elephant continued unchanged from Harappan times until the dawn of the Christian era. In the long span of nearly two thousand years the motif must have come to represent changing ideas and concepts. If no evidence of this evolution remains, it may be because of the use of perishable mediums such as wood or clay and the lack of any textual reference. The apparently sudden reappearance of the elephant motif after 600 BC can hardly be considered as a new development for nothing happens all of a sudden. Only the mediums were new (stone for the Aśokan inscriptions and the early Buddhist *stūpas* and metal for coins). The motifs must have been those that the artisans were familiar with. In fact, art motifs survive the ideas which they express and are capable of assuming, from one period and from one religion to another, more than one signification. The tree, for example, had a sacred significance in Harappan culture. Later, it was associated with the *kevalas* or *caityas* of the Jaina Tīrthaṅkaras. It became the sacred Bodhi tree under which the Buddha achieved enlightenment. It became the *pipal* tree (*ficus religiosa*) associated with Śiva, the *tulsī* plant (basil) which is married to Viṣṇu in the Vaiṣṇava context and the banana tree which is married to Gaṇapati,[1] as part of the celebrations of the festival of the goddess Durgā in Bengal. Similarly, the wheel representing the sun or the cycle of nature became the wheel of Dharma in the Buddhist context. In each case the context changed but the sacred connotation of the motif remained.

Similarly, the practice of ritual processions, which constitute part of religious celebrations in the modern context, seem to have their origin in Harappan religion. In the mid-second millennium BC (post Harappan period) an image of the elephant with provision for wheels has been found which suggests that it was used in processions. The elephant festival in the early centuries of the Christian era also included a ceremonial procession. Such processions eventually became a part of the ritual of various religious sects. Fa-hien, a Chinese Buddhist monk who visited India in the fourth century AD, mentions a car-procession at Pāṭaliputra where an icon of the Buddha was taken out in procession.[2] In the early medieval period this ritual was connected with almost all the major gods and goddesses. Undoubtedly, the ritual evolved over the centuries in nature and significance. In the early medieval period the divinity, in human form, was usually carried in a chariot drawn either by a horse or an elephant whereas in the Harappan culture the animal emblem was carried on poles or mounted on wheels. Whereas in the early medieval period the gods were treated as the divine counterparts of the king who had to be bathed, fed, clothed and entertained in a manner similar to that of the king, in the Harappan period the animal emblems may have represented animal spirits or the mythical ancestors of the rulers. For these reasons, even if there is a blank in the availability of data on the elephant between the Harappan period and the early historical period, from the evidence that suddenly becomes available in the post 600 BC period, it is possible to infer that the elephant did, indeed, continue to be an object of veneration throughout the centuries, although perceptions of its character and role, as also the exact nature of its worship, evolved to suit changing material conditions and the religious needs of new social groups.

In the early historical period, the elephant was associated with a goddess in some regions such as Kapīśa in modern Afghanistan. Even this association appears to reach back further into time and continues to exist in some folk rituals today. Whereas the Brahmanical Gaṇapati branched off along a path newly created for him by the Brahmanical religion, the older rituals associated with the sacred elephant must have persisted outside the Brahmanical framework. Some of these can be gleaned from existing folk rituals. These are often not described in any text and they generally evolve more slowly than those of the 'high' tradition.

Besides, they are usually restricted to a few places, normally in regions where material conditions have not been radically transformed. Goddess cults often center around fertility rites and imply human or animal sacrifice. The best known of such cults today is that of Durgā associated with the buffalo sacrifice. In certain villages in Andhra Pradesh, where buffalos are sacrificed to the goddess on her festival, a woman from one of the Untouchable communities, referred to as Mātaṅgī, is considered to be the special representative or manifestation of the goddess and is associated with the buffalo sacrifice. Mātaṅgī is also the name of a minor goddess in the Purāṇas and the term is understood as 'elephant goddess' since the term 'mātaṅga' signifies elephant. I wonder how this specific epithet came to be associated with the goddess Durgā unless, in the distant past, a counterpart of Durgā did not play a similar role in the context of elephant sacrifice. Durgā and Mahiṣāsura, the buffalo demon that she kills, (only in the Brahmanical context is the slayed animal referred to as an *asura*), appear to have had a parallel in a goddess who killed the elephant demon. In other words, the sacrificed animal was originally looked upon as the consort of the goddess, as is the case even today in certain folk traditions, and it replaced what, in the earlier stages, must have been a human consort. Mahiṣa has a counterpart in the Heramba form of Gaṇapati. Heramba signifies 'buffalo' and I wonder how the elephant-headed deity is even remotely connected with the buffalo. Besides, this form of Gaṇapati has five heads, like Śiva, and rides a lion like Durgā. Evidently, the elephant had been closely associated with the goddess and had played the same role as the buffalo or as Śiva, vis-a-vis her. If Mātaṅgī (elephant goddess) is the representative of Durgā then Heramba Ganapati (buffalo-Gaṇapati) is the counterpart of mahiṣa. Even the myths of Gaṇapati's beheading and the tradition of applying *sindūra* on his images retain the idea of sacrifice.

In certain parts of Bihar terracotta elephants are associated with the marriage ceremonies on the bride's side.[3] They are installed in a specially made *maṇḍapa* in the courtyard of the house. Votive elephants are also offered to the village goddesses in some parts of Uttar Pradesh, mainly in the districts of Gorakhpur, Deoria and Azamgarh. The sacred spots of the goddesses are usually below *neem, pipal* or palm trees. Clusters of terracotta elephants are found in practically every settlement of these three districts.[4]

There is even a goddess known as Hāthī Māī (elephant mother) in Gorakhpur town. Folk memory has retained the association between the elephant and the goddess. There are other rituals where women are closely associated with the elephant just as they were in the case of the ancient elephant festival described in Chapter II. One such example is the *chaṭha* (the sixth) festival—so called because it takes place six days after *Dīpāvalī* (festival of lights)—which is celebrated primarily in Bihar and the adjacent parts of eastern Uttar Pradesh. It is a festival in honour of the Sun god. One of the important rituals of this festival is the setting up of a *manḍapa* in which is installed one or more terracotta elephants facing the west, the direction of the setting sun and the rising moon. The elephants are then painted with *sindūra* and riceflour paste and a water jar (*ghaḍā*) is placed above them. An earthern bowl attached to each votive figure is filled with fruit and sweetened wheat-cakes which are offered to the setting sun. Throughout the performance of this ritual, folk-songs are sung by women. The next morning the *manḍapa* with its votive contents are shifted to the waterside. The rising sun is worshipped and the terracotta elephants are immersed in the water marking the end of the ceremony.[5] The association of the elephant with the sun goes back several centuries. I have referred to the elephant, kept in the Sun Temple at Taxila before the turn of the Christian era, in Chapter II. Even the association of the votive elephant with the bowl of water, and finally its immersion in water speak of age-old associations which have continued in the case of Gaṇapati, regardless of the fact that within the Brahmanical framework he acquired a new identity and a different set of rituals.

The concept that creation starts from water is an ancient one and the elephant's close association with water derives from its early role as the consort of the goddess in her form as Earth Mother, or as the mythological ancestor of a lineage. Because of its role, vis-a-vis the goddess, the elephant came to be used as a metaphor for rain clouds, the harbingers of fertility to the earth and prosperity to mankind. This role is modified in the Brahmanical context, where Gaṇapati becomes the son of Śiva and, thereby, assumes the role of son of the goddess Pārvatī. This situation creates tension in his relationship with Śiva and ambiguity about his role, vis-a-vis the goddess in general. He is made into a *brahmacārin* (celibate) and even in those regions where the

Brahmanical *Gaṇapati* is looked upon as a *gṛhastha* (married) there is ambiguity about his exact civil status. This is the result of the Brahmanisation of a deity who had, in the process, to be accomodated into an established framework which forced upon him certain constraints that were in contradiction to his original character. This original character was retained in folk rituals. It has also persisted, in a subtle manner, in the Brahmanical context, because of Gaṇapati's constant association with various goddesses whether it is Lakṣmī, Saraswatī, Gaurī, Durgā, Siddhi and Buddhi or Santośī Mā.

It is unlikely that there was ever one single sacred elephant. It is more likely that the elephant was worshipped, in the pre-Christian era, in a manner similar to that of the *nāgas* (serpents). Snakes in general were venerated. In addition, there were shrines for particular snake deities (such as Maṇināga in Rājagṛha) who were known by various names in different regions. While some shrines had the image of a snake, others consisted merely of stones daubed with red paint. Elephant worship must have been similar to snake worship for in the latter half of the first millennium BC, the term *nāga* became a synonym for the elephant and many famous *nāgas* were represented in both serpent and elephant form.

The elephant deity first acquired a therianthropic form in the Buddhist context. Buddhism absorbed many minor cults in the regions where it gained a stronghold. The elephant deity was one such cult and it is first depicted in the form of an elephant-headed *yakṣa* in the Buddhist *stūpa* at Amarāvatī in the second century AD. This form enables it to be distinguished from the elephant symbol of the Buddha's conception or from the purely decorative motif of the elephant. In the Buddhist perspective only the Buddha could have a perfect physical form. All other cults, in form and attitude, had to be shown as inferior to the Buddha. The rotund and stunted physique of the various *yakṣas* presents a contrast to the noble physique of the Buddha. This form became the basis for the iconography of the syncretic deity, Gaṇapati-Vināyaka.

The popularity of Buddhism and the impetus it received from the time of Aśoka in the third century BC posed a threat to the social order propounded by the older Vedic religion. The antagonism of the latter is expressed in the creation of the demonic Vināyakas. Although these demons represent age-old evil forces, in fact, they personify popular cults that had become a part and parcel of Buddhism. Special rites are elaborated for warding off the evils of the Vināyakas which are stated to affect every age group and category of society and these are included in the domestic manuals of the *brāhmaṇas*. They are made an integral part of domestic rites and, thereby, local superstitions and rituals are recognized by Brahmanism and a clientele requiring their performance is ensured. Many syncretic Hindu cults have developed as a result of challenges posed to the Hindu social order in the course of the centuries by Buddhism, Islam and Christianity and this shows the remarkable capacity of Hinduism for self-renewal.

At the turn of the Christian era, Śiva and Viṣṇu rose in importance and took the place of the older Vedic divinities. These gods represented the needs of a changing social order. It is with the rise of Śiva that the elephant deity finally finds mention in Brahmanical texts as part of Śiva's entourage. Simultaneously, in the same region, the Vināyakas gradually evolved into one single Vināyaka whose worship became an established part of the Brahmanical faith. No longer totally maleficient, the single Vināyaka lacked an iconographical form. Certain similarities of concept and function lead to Vināyaka being identified with the elephant deity around the fourth century AD. The Buddhist iconographic form of the elephant-headed *yakṣa* was adopted for the new Brahmanical deity.

After about AD 400, images of Gaṇapati-Vināyaka proliferate. The cult spreads to all the regions of the sub-continent and grows more complex. In each region it acquires a special flavour of its own, determined by the ecology, past and existing religious beliefs, inclination of the rulers, and so on. Between the sixth and twelfth centuries of the Christian era several developments take place. On the one hand, Gaṇapati develops as a part of the Puranic Śiva's pantheon. He evolves from an ordinary *gaṇa* of Śiva to the position of his younger son, eventually replaces Skanda as the older son and, finally, becomes worthy of worship as a deity in his own right. By the eighth century, he is acknowledged as a part of the Śaiva pantheon all over the country. From the ninth/tenth century, temples are constructed for him, land grants are made for their maintenance and he is invoked in the epigraphs of kings and ministers. Simultaneously, in the context of certain esoteric Buddhist sects, he comes to symbolise the union of Buddhism and Brahmanism and is depicted with attributes of both the Buddha and Śiva, or of Śiva and the Boddhisattva Avalokiteśvara.

While Gaṇapati evolves along different lines among various religious comunities he also acquires a particular significance for certain categories of society such as the traders. His role as an important deity of the trading class appears to manifest itself first in Rajasthan amongst the Jaina mercantile community from about the seventh century AD. He is initially worshipped not as a giver of wealth, but as the remover of obstacles for the acquisition of wealth. Eventually, invocation to him alone is deemed sufficient to ensure success in business matters. After a couple of centuries, this role is acknowledged in Brahmanical texts. As Gaṇapati becomes popular with the traders in south India, he acquires special forms specifically associated with this community.

The rise of the Brahmanial Gaṇapati from about the fourth-fifth century AD is closely associated to certain social and economic changes that take place during this period. These centuries correspond to a period which some historians[6] have characterised as one of urban decay marked by the decline of long-distance trade and the ruralization of economy over a greater part of the subcontinent. The Purāṇas reflect Brahmanical reaction to the loss of urban householder clients and to other stressful socio-economic changes resulting from the decline of urban life and the development of an increasingly village-based subsistence economy. These developments forced many urban *brāhmaṇas* to search for an alternative means of livelihood. The changing environment is reflected in Brahmanical texts which stress the virtue of making land grants to *brāhmaṇas*, a practice that became an increasingly important element in the rural economy from the fifth century onward. Brahmanical social attitudes towards certain occupations undergoes a change. Agriculture, until now only associated with the *vaiśya* caste, is prescribed for *brāhmaṇas* even if only in a managerial capacity.[7]

It is in this period and against this background that Gaṇapati rises in popularity. Śivaism is gaining in importance but this particular deity suddenly becomes popular and it is insisted that his worship be performed first. Even though he is not given the same importance as Śiva or Viṣṇu, he is associated with all forms of worship. He is made a part of the Brahmanical pantheon even though his form and figure present a stark contrast to the forms of other Brahmanical deities. An agricultural and village deity, associated with fertility and well-being, becomes a Brahmanical deity responsible for the removal of obstacles, for conferring knowledge and for granting wealth and prosperity at all levels. It is precisely in the region where trade continues to prosper that Gaṇapati is first identified with the prospering mercantile community. Later, his popularity with the merchant community spreads to the south among agriculturists turned traders.

As Gaṇapati rises in importance some people choose to worship him exclusively. The early Gāṇapatyas appear to have been sub-sects of the Buddhists and the Śaivas and these five or six sects appeared around the ninth century AD. Each sect worshipped a particular form of Gaṇapati and members of the sect were identified by a particular sign branded on the shoulder. However, none of these sects appear to have had any specific doctrine nor an exclusive laity. They were distinct from the *Smārta* Gāṇapatyas who emerged in the region of Maharasthra, Karnataka, some parts of Andhra Pradesh and in Varanasi around the twelfth century. The *Smārta* Gāṇapatyas considered Gaṇapati as the greatest god. They acknowledged the other deities of the *pañcāyatana*, but considered them to be emanations of Gaṇapati. They established a theology in line with traditional Brahmanical beliefs and practices and were responsible for establishing Gaṇapati as a major Brahmanical deity. The region in which this sect evolved is the very region where Gaṇapati continues to be one of the most popular deities and where he has several important temples and pilgrimage sites.

Many of the existing perceptions of Gaṇapati belong to the realm of oral tradition and it would be difficult to exaggerate the importance of this tradition as a medium for the dissemination of ideas and attitudes in India. One such example is the belief that Gaṇapati with the trunk turning to the right requires special worship. This belief is not reflected, as far as I know, in sacred literature. It would, therefore, be worthwhile to enquire into other traditions of this nature, existing in different regions. A detailed study of Gaṇapati worship by occupational groups within a particular region would also help deepen our understanding of some of the varying perceptions of the deity in the contemporary context. In this study I have focussed on one occupational group, the traders. Gaṇapati represents what is true of so much else in Indian culture. Nothing emerges suddenly. Nor do new beliefs and concepts completely wipe out older ones. They only modify them. This process of evolution is a continuing one and, therefore, contemporary studies on Gaṇapati become all the more important.

NOTES

1. This is a tradition associated essentially with the celebration of Durgā *pūjā* in Bengal where the banana tree 'Kala Bau' is ritually transformed into the Goddess during the festival.
2. Quoted in R.N. Nandi, *Religious Institutions and Cults in the Deccan* (*c.* AD 600-1000), p. 30.
3. Ibid., p. 31.
4. Ibid., p. 34.
5. Vidula Jayaswal and Kalyan Krishna, *An Ethno-Archaeological View of Indian Terracottas,* pp. 27-8.
6. R.S. Sharma, *Indian Feudalism, c. 300-1200; Social Changes in Early Medieval India (c.* AD *500-1200); Urban Decay in India, c.300- c.1000*; R.S. Sharma and D.N. Jha, 'The Economic History of India upto AD 1200: Trends and Prospects', *JESHO,* Vol. 17, No.1, 1974, pp. 48-80; For the impact on religious life of these changes see R.N. Nandi, *Social Roots of Religion in Ancient India.*
7. R.N. Nandi, op. cit., p. 16.

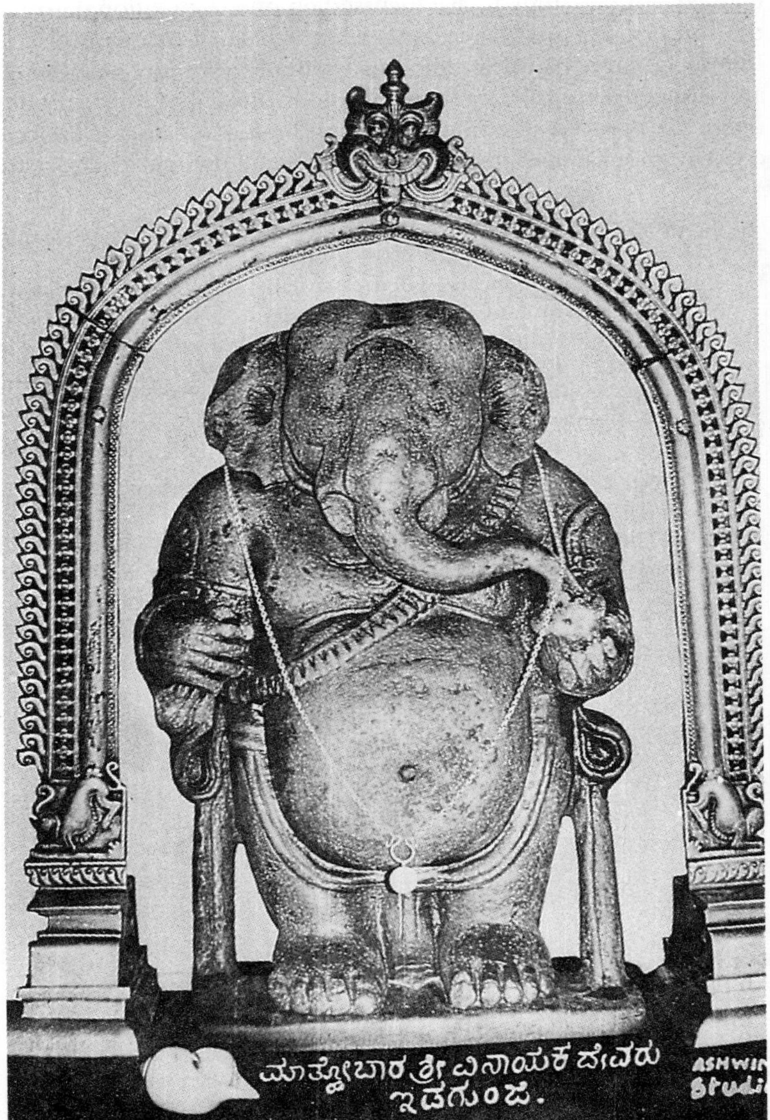

Plate 1. The principal image of Gaṇapati at the Śrī Mahāgaṇapati temple at Idagunji, Karnataka. Photo courtesy: the trustees.

Plate 2. Siṃha Gaṇapati in the *Utsava* Hall of the Śrī Siddhi-Buddhi Vināyaka Mandir, New Delhi. Author's photo.

Plate 3. Vaiṣṇava Gaṇapati, *Utsava* Hall of the Śrī Siddhi-Buddhi Vināyaka Mandir, New Delhi. Author's photo.

Plate 4. Ādianta Prabhū showing a syncretism between Gaṇapati and Hanumān. Madhya Kailash Temple Complex, Adyar, Madras. Author's photo.

Plate 5. Gaṇeśa, *c.* seventh-eighth century. Vijayawada, Andhra Pradesh. Madras Museum No. 89/38. Photo courtesy: American Institute of Indian Studies, Varanasi.

Plate 6. Painting of Heramba Gaṇapati, *c.* eighteenth century. Allahabad Museum. Photo courtesy: American Institute of Indian Studies, Varanasi.

Bibliography

PRIMARY SOURCES

1. LITERATURE

Agni Purāṇa, ed., J.L. Shastri, trans., N. Gangadharan, Ancient Indian Tradition and Mythology series, Vols. 27-30, Motilal Banarsidass, Delhi, 1984-7.

Ajitāgama, cri. edn., N.R. Bhatt, 3 vols., Publication de l'Institut Français d'Indologie, No. 24. I, II and III, Institut Français d'Indologie, Pondicherry, Vol. I - 1964, Vol. II - 1967 and Vol. III - 1991.

Amarakośa, With Unpublished South Indian Commentaries, ed., A.A. Ramanathan, Madras, 1983.

Arthaśāstra of Kautilya, trans., R. Shamasastry with an 'Introductory Note' by J.F. Fleet, Mysore, 1960; *The Kautilya Arthaśāstra*, cri. edn., trans. and Commented upon by R.P. Kangle, 3 vols., 2nd edn., 1969, rpt, Motilal Banarsidass, Delhi, 1988.

Atharva-Veda, Sanskrit text with English translation by William Dwight Whitney, revised and edited by Nag Sharan Singh, 2 vols., Nag Publishers, Delhi, 1987. *Hymns of the Atharvaveda,* trans., Ralph T.H. Griffith, 2 vols., rpt, Munshiram Manoharlal, New Delhi, 1985.

Baudhayana Dharma Sūtra, trans., G. Buhler, Sacred Books of the East, Vol. XIV, 1st edn. Oxford University Press, 1882, rpt, Motilal Banarsidass, Delhi, 1991.

Bhagavata Purāṇa, ed., J.L. Shastri, trans., Board of Scholars, Ancient Indian Tradition and Mythology, Vols. 7-11, Motilal Banarsidass, Delhi, 1976-8.

Bhaviṣya Purāṇa, Geeta Press, Gorakhpur; ed., Rajendra Nath Sharma, Nag Publishers, Delhi, 1984.

Brahma Purāṇa, ed., J.L. Shastri and G.P. Bhatt, trans., Board of Scholars, Ancient Indian Tradition and Mythology series, Vols. 33-6, Motilal Banarsidass, Delhi, 1985-6.

Brahmāṇḍa Purāṇa, ed., J.L. Shastri, trans., Ganesh Vasudeo Tagare, Ancient Indian Tradition and Mythology series, Vols. 22-6, Motilal Banarsidass, Delhi, 1983-4.

Brahmavaivarta Purāṇa, Text with Hindi trans., Tarinish Jha, Hindi Sahitya Sammelan, Prayag, Sak. 1903, San. 1982.

Bṛhadāraṇyaka Upaniṣad, in S. Radhakrishnan's *The Principal Upaniṣads*, 1st edn. 1953, centenary edn, Oxford University Press, New Delhi, 1991, pp.149-333.

Bṛhaddharma Purāṇa, ed., M.M. Haraprasad Sastri, Chaukhambha Amarbharati Prakashan, Varanasi.

Buddhacarita of Aśvaghosa, trans., E.B. Cowell, Sacred Books of the East, Vol. 49, Pt. I, 1st edn. Oxford University Press, 1894, rpt, Motilal Banarsidass, Delhi, 1965.

Daśōpaniṣads (With Commentary of Śrī Upaniṣad Brahma Yogin), Vol. II, Sanskrit text with introduction in English, eds., Pandits of Adyar Library under the supervision of Prof. C. Kunhan Raja, Adyar Library Series no. 15, Madras, 1936.

Devī Rahasya with Pariśiṣtas, eds., Ram Chandra Kak, Harabhatta Shastri, Butala Publications, Delhi, 1985.

Dhammapada, ed., and trans., F. Max Muller, Sacred Books of the East, Vol. 10, 1st edn. Oxford University Press, 1881, rpt by Motilal Banarsidass, Delhi, 1965.

Diptāgama, transcript No. 15 in library of the French Institute of Pondicherry.

Gaṇeśa Purāṇa, Shri Yogindra Matha, Moregaon, Pune, Upāsanā Khaṇḍa in 1979 and Krīḍā Khaṇḍa in 1985.

Garuḍa Purāṇa, ed., J.L. Shastri, trans., Board of Scholars, Ancient Indian Tradition and Mythology series, Vols. 12-24, Motilal Banarsidass, Delhi, 1978-80.

Gāthāsaptaśati of Hala, ed., S.A. Joglekar, Sanskrit text with translation in Marathi, Pune, 1956.

Guhyasamāja Tantra, ed., Sridhar Tripathi, Buddhist Sanskrit Texts, No. 9, Mithila Institute of Post Graduate Studies and Research in Sanskrit Learning, Darbhanga, 1988.

Hevajra Tantra: A Critical Study, trans., D.L. Snellgrove, in 2 Parts, Oxford University Press, London, 1959.

Īśānaśivagurudevapaddhati of Īśānaśiva, ed., T. Ganapati Sastri, 4 vols., Trivandrum Sanskrit Series, Vols. 69, 72, 77 and 83, Trivandrum, 1922-5.

Jātakas, ed., E.B. Cowell, trans., various scholars, 6 vols., rpt by Cosmo Publications, Delhi, 1973-9.

Jñāneshwarī, (Śrī Jñāndeva's Bhāvartha Dīpikā otherwise known as Jñāneshwarī), trans. from Marathi by Ramachandra Keshav Bhagwat, Samata Books, Madras, 1979. *Jñāneshwarī by Śrī Jnyandev*, trans., R.K. Bhagat, revd by V.V. Dixit, 2 vols., Poona, 1954.

Kathāsaritsāgara by Somadeva, trans., C.H. Tawney, 2 vols., Calcutta, 1880-4;

trans., C.H. Tawney, ed. with notes by N.M. Penzer, 10 vols., 1st edn. London, 1924-8, rpt by Motilal Banarsidass, Delhi, 1968.

Kūrma Purāṇa, ed., J.L. Shastri, trans., Ganesh Vasudeo Tagare, Ancient Indian Tradition and Mythology series, Vols. 20 and 21, Motilal Banarsidass, Delhi, 1981-2.

Lakṣmī Tantra, trans. and notes by Sanjukta Gupta, E.J. Brill, Leiden, 1972.

Lalitavistara Sūtra (The Voice of the Buddha), trans. into English from the French by Gwendolyn Bays, 2 vols., Dharma Publishing, Berkeley, California, 1983.

Liṅga Purāṇa, ed., J.L. Shastri, trans., Board of Scholars, Ancient Indian Tradition and Mythology series, Vols. 5 and 6, Motilal Banarsidass, Delhi, 1973.

Mahābhārata, cri. edn., various scholars, Poona, 1927-66; Geeta Press, 7th edn., Gorakhpur; trans., J.A.B. Van Buitenen, 3 vols., Chicago University Press, Chicago/London, 1973, 1975 and 1978.

Mahānirvāṇatantra (Tantra of the Great Liberation), ed., Arthur Avalon, 1st edn. 1913, 4th edn., Ganesh and Co., Madras, 1963.

Mahā-Parinibbāna-Sutta, in *Buddhist Suttas*, trans., T.W. Rhys Davids, Sacred Books of the East, Vol. XI, 1st edn. Oxford University Press, 1881, rpt by Motilal Banarsidass, Delhi, 1989.

Mahavairocana-Sūtra, trans. from the Chinese version of Śubhakārasiṃha and I-hsing (AD 725) by Chikyo Yamamota of Koyasan University, Japan, International Academy of Indian Culture and Aditya Prakashan, New Delhi, 1990.

Maitrāyanī Saṃhitā, ed., D. Satvalekar, Svadhyaya Mandal, Oudh, Vik. Sam., 1998.

Mānavagṛhyasūtra of the Maitrāyaṇīya Śākhā With Commentary of Aṣṭāvakra, ed., Ramakrishna Harshaji Sastri, Panini, Delhi, 1982.

Manu Smṛti (The Laws of Manu), ed. F. Max Muller, Sacred Books of the East, Vol. XXV, 1st edn. Oxford University Press, 1886, rpt by Motilal Banarsidass, Delhi, 1987. *Manusmṛti, With the Sanskrit Commentary Mānvarthamuktāvali of Kulluka Bhaṭṭa*, ed., J.L. Shastri, 1st edn. 1983, rpt by Motilal Banarsidass, Delhi, 1990.

Mārkaṇḍeya Purāṇa, trans. with notes by F. Eden Pargiter, rpt, Indological Book House, Delhi/Varanasi, 1969.

Mātaṅgalīlā of Nīlakaṇṭha, ed. with notes by T. Ganapati Sastri, Trivandrum Sanskrit Series, No.X, Trivandrum, 1910. *The Elephant Lore of the Hindus. The Elephant Sport (Mātaṅgalīlā) of Nīlakaṇṭha*, trans. into English by Franklin Edgerton, New Haven, Connecticut, 1931.

Matsya Mahāpurāṇa, Sanskrit text with trans. arranged by Nag Sharan Singh, Nag Publishers, Delhi, 1983.

Mayamata, cri. edn. and trans. into French by Bruno Dagens, 2 vols.,

Publication de l'Institut Français d'Indologie, No. 40, Pondicherry, Vol. I, 1970 and Vol. II, 1976. *Mayamata: An Indian Treatise on Housing Architecture and Iconography,* trans. into English by Bruno Dagens, Sitaram Bhartia Institute of Scientific Research, New Dẹlhi, 1985.

Milindapañha, original text with Hindi translation, ed. and trans., Swami Dwarikadas Shastri, Bauddhabharati, Varanasi, 1990.

Mṛgendrāgama (Kriyāpāda and Caryāpāda) with the commentary of Bhaṭṭa Nārāyaṇakaṇṭha, cri. edn., N.R. Bhatt, Publications de l'Institut Français d'Indologie, No. 23, Pondicherry, 1962. *Mṛgendrāgama (Section de la Doctrine et du Yoga) avec la vṛtti de Bhaṭṭanārāyaṇakaṇṭha et la dīpikā d'Agoraśivācārya,* trans. into French with introduction and notes by Michel Hulin, Publications de l'Institut Français d'Indologie, No. 63, Pondicherry, 1980. *Mṛgendrāgama (Section des Rites et Section du Comportement) avec la vṛtti de Bhaṭṭa Nārāyaṇakaṇṭha,* trans. into French with Introduction and Notes by Hélène Brunner-Lachaux, Publications de l'Institut Français de Pondicherry, No. 69, Pondicherry, 1985.

Mudgala Purāṇa, Sri Mudgala Prakashan Mandalam, Bombay, October, 1976.

Nārada Purāṇa, ed., J.L. Shastri, trans., Ganesh Vasudeo Tagare and Hemendra Nath Chakravorty, Ancient Indian Tradition and Mythology series, Vols. 15-19, Motilal Banarsidass, Delhi, 1980-2.

Narasiṃha Purāṇa, text with Eng. trans. and notes by Siddheswar Jena, Nag Publishers, Delhi, 1987.

Nīlamata Purāṇa, cri. edn. and trans., Ved. Kumari, 2 vols, J & K Academy of Art, Culture and Languages, Srinagar, 1968.

Padma Mahāpurāṇa, ed., Nag Sharan Singh, 4 vols., rpt of the Venkateshwar Steam Press edn., Bombay, Nag Publishers, Delhi 1984-5. *Padma Purāṇa,* ed., J.L. Shastri, trans., N.A. Deshpande, Ancient Indian Tradition and Mythology series, Vols. 39-48, Motilal Banarsidass, Delhi, 1988-90.

Prāṇatoṣinī (tantra) by Rāmatoṣaṇa Vidyālamkāra, ed., J. Vidyasagar, Calcutta, 1898.

Prapañcasāra Tantra, ascribed to Śaṅkarācārya, revd and documented with exhaustive introduction by Arthur Avalon and ed. by Atalananda Sarasvati, 1st edn. 1935, 3rd edn. by Motilal Banarsidass, Delhi, 1989.

Rājataraṅgiṇī of Kalhaṇa, trans. with an introduction, commentary and appendices by M.A. Stein, 2 vols., 1st edn. 1900, rpt by Motilal Banarsidass, Delhi, 1989.

Rāmāyaṇa, 8th edn, Geeta Press, Gorakhpur.

Rauravāgama, cri. edn., N.R. Bhatt, Vol. I, Publications de l'Institut Français d'Indologie No. 18, Pondicherry, 1961-72.

Rauravottarāgama, cri. ed., N.R. Bhatt with introduction and notes, Publications de l'Institut Français d'Indologie, No. 66, Pondicherry, 1983.

Śaiva Upanisads, trans. into English by T.R. Srinavasa Ayyangar and ed., G. Srinivasa Murti, Adyar Library, Madras, 1953.

Sāmaveda, ed. with trans. in Hindi by D. Satvalekar, Pardi. *The Sāma-Veda Saṃhitā*, text with English trans by Ralph T.H. Griffith, 2 vols. Nag Publishers, Delhi, 1991 (based on Griffith's trans publ in 1893).

Sāmavidhāna Brāhmaṇa (with Vedarthaprakāśa of Sāyana and Padarthamātṛavivṛti of Bharatsvāmin), ed., B.R. Sharma, Kendriya Sanskrit Vidyapeetha Series, No.1, Tirupati, 1964.

Samyutta-Nikāya (The Book of the Kindred Sayings), trans., Mrs. Rhys Davids, Pt. I, Luzac and Company Ltd., London, 1950.

Śaṅkaravijaya of Ānandagiri, ed., Pt. Jibananda Vidyasagara, Calcutta, 1881. *Śrī Śaṅkaravijaya of Ānantānandagiri*, ed., N. Veezhinathan, Madras University Philosophical Series, No. 16, Madras, 1971.

Skanda Mahāpurāṇam, Sri Venkateshwara (Steam) Press, 7 vols., Bombay, Samvat 1966. *Skanda Purāṇa*, 7 vols., rpt of the above edn, Nag Publishers, Delhi, 1986; ed., G.P. Bhatt, trans., G.V. Tagare, Ancient Indian Tradition and Mythology series, Vols. 49-54, Motilal Banarsidass, Delhi, 1992-4.

Śiva Purāṇa, eds., Arnold Kunst and J.L. Sastri, trans., Board of Scholars, Ancient Indian Tradition and Mythology series, Vols. 1-4, Motilal Banarsidass, Delhi, 1969-70.

Somaśambhupaddhati, text with translation into French and notes by Helene Brunner-Lachaux, 3 vols., Publications de l'Institut Français d'Indologie, No. 25, I, II and III, Pondicherry, 1963, 1968 and 1977.

Śrī Gaṇeśa Kośa (in Marathi), ed., Amarendra Gadgil, 2nd edn., Sriram Baku Agency, Pune, 1981.

Śrī Gaṇeśatharvaśīrṣam Sabhāṣyam, ed., Vamana Sastri Islampurkar, Anand Ashram Press, Poona, 1919.

Śrī Ucchiṣṭa Gaṇapati Stotra Satanāmāvalī, Pub. by T.S. Sundaresa Sharma, Tanjore, 1959.

Sutta-Nipāta, ed., F. Max Muller, trans., various scholars, Sacred Books of the East, Vol. X, Part II, 1st edn. Oxford University Press, 1881, rpt by Motilal Banarsidass, Delhi, 1965.

Svayambhuvāgama, chap. 58, Transcript No. 39 in the library of the French Institute of Pondicherry.

Taittirīya Āraṇyaka, Pt. II (With Commentary of Sāyaṇa) Ananda Ashram Press, Poona, 1925.

Unpublished Upaniṣads, eds., Pandits of Adyar Library under the supervision of Dr. C. Kunhan Raja, Sanskrit text with introduction in English, Adyar Library Series-14, Madras, 1933,

Vāmana Purāṇa, text with Hindi trans. by a group of scholars, ed., Anandswaroop Gupta, All India Kashiraj Trust, Varanasi, Vik. Sam. 2025.

Varāha Gṛhyasūtra, (with short extracts from the Paddhatis of Gaṅgādhara and Viśiṣṭha), Cri. edn., Raghu Vira, Panini, New Delhi, 1982.

Varāha Purāṇa, ed., J.L. Shastri, trans., S. Venkitasubramania Iyer, Ancient Indian Tradition and Mythology series, Vols. 31 and 32, Motilal Banarsidass, Delhi, 1985.

Vāyu Purāṇa, ed., G.P. Bhatt, trans. and annotated, G.V. Tagare, Ancient Indian Tradition and Mythology series, Vols. 37 and 38, Motilal Banarsidass, Delhi, 1987-8.

Vijñānabhairavatantra, ed. with French trans., L. Silburn, Publications de l'Institut de Civilisation Indienne, series in-8, fasc. 15, Paris, 1961.

Vināyakavratakalpādi, Transcript No. 1001 copied from Manuscript No. 43428, both in the library of the French Institute of Pondicherry.

Viṣṇudharmottarapurāṇam, ed., Charudev Shastri, 2 vols., rptd from the Venkateshwar Steam Press edn, Bombay, Nag Publishers, Delhi, 1985.

Viṣṇu Purāṇa, trans., H.H. Wilson, ed., F. Hall, 7 vols., London, 1966.

Yājñavalkya Smṛti, Vol. I, (With the Commentary of Vijñāneśvara called the Mitaksara), trans., Rai Bahadur Sirsa Chandra Vidyarnava, Allahabad, 1918. *The Yājñavalkya Smṛti*, Trivandrum Sanskrit Series, Trivandrum, 1922.

2. EPIGRAPHY

Brahmi Inscriptions from Bharhut, ed., H. Luders, *CII*, Vol. II, revised and supplemented by E. Waldschmidt, M.A. Mehendale, Ootacamund, 1963.

Epigraphia Andhrica, eds., N. Venkataramanayya and P.V. Parabrahma Sastry, Vols. I-IV, Hyderabad, 1969, 74 and 75.

Epigraphia Carnatica, eds., B.R. Gopal *et al.*, 9 vols, Institute of Kannada Studies, University of Mysore, 1972-90.

Epigraphia Indica, Various Editors, 42 vols., Calcutta and Delhi, 1892 (in progress).

Inscriptions of Bengal, ed., N.G. Majumdar, Vol. III, Varendra Research Society, Bengal, 1929.

Inscriptions of the Kalachuri-Cedi Era, ed., V.V. Mirashi, *CII*, Vol. IV, Pt. I and II, Ootacamund, 1955.

Inscriptions of Orissa (c. AD 600-1100), ed., Sri Satyanarayan Rajaguru, Government of Orissa, Bhubaneshwar, 1960.

Inscriptions of the Seleucid and Parthian Period and of Eastern Iran and Central Asia, ed., H.W. Bailey, *Corpus Inscriptionum Iranicarum*, Pt. II, Vol. V (Saka), Percy Lund, Humphries and Co. Ltd., London, 1968.

Inscriptions of the Śilāhāras, ed., V.V. Mirashi, *CII*, Vol. VI, Archaeological Survey of India, New Delhi, 1977.

Inscriptions of the Vakatakas, ed., V.V. Mirashi, *CII*, Vol. V, Archaeological Survey of India, Ootacamund, 1963.

Kharoshthi Inscriptions (With the exception of those of Aśoka), ed., Sten Konow, *CII*, Vol. II, Pt. I, Calcutta, 1929.

Maity, S.K. and R.R. Mukherjee, *Corpus of Bengal Inscriptions*, Firma K.L. Mukhopadhyay, Calcutta, 1967.

Sharma, Mukunda Madhava, *Inscriptions of Ancient Assam*, Gauhati University, Assam, 1978.

Sircar, D.C., *Some Epigraphical Records of the Medieval Period from Eastern India*, Abhinav Publications, New Delhi, 1979.

——— *Select Inscriptions*, 2 Vols., Calcutta, 1965.

——— 'Two Brahmi Inscriptions', *JBRS*, Vol. XXXIX, Pts. 1-2, pp. 41-8.

South Indian Inscriptions, ed. and trans., E. Hultzch, Vol. II, Pts. 1 and 2, Madras, 1891 and 1892.

SECONDARY SOURCES

Abraham, Meera, *Two Medieval Merchant Guilds of South India*, Manohar Publications, Delhi, 1988.

Acharya, G.V., 'Gala Inscription of Siddharājā Jayasiṃha, (Vikrama) Samvat 1193', *JBBRAS*, Vol. 25, No. 2, 1918-19, pp. 322-4.

Agrawala, P.K., 'The Kumbhāṇḍa Figures in Sanchi Sculpture', *EW*, Vol. 37, Nos. 1-4, Dec. 1987, pp. 179-89.

——— 'A Pañca-Gaṇeśa Panel from Varanasi', *JOIB*, Vol. 25, pp. 71-3.

——— 'The Kumbhāṇḍa Overlord Virūḍhaka', pp. 67-74 in Devendra Handa and Ashvini Agrawal, ed., *Ratna-Chandrika: Panorama of Oriental Studies*, (Shri R.C. Agrawala Festschrift), Harman Publishing House, New Delhi, 1989.

——— *Goddess Vināyakī*, Prithvi Prakashan, Varanasi, 1978.

——— *Goddesses in Ancient India*, Abhinav Publications, Delhi, 1984.

——— 'A Note on Ardhanārī Gaṇapati' in *Studies in Indian Iconography*, pp. 155-8.

Agrawala, R.C., 'Some Interesting Sculptures of Yakṣas and Kubera from Rajasthan', *IHQ*, Sep. 1957, pp. 201-7.

——— 'Unusual Icons of Vaikuṇṭha Viṣṇu with Aśvamukha', *JOIB*, Vol. 25, pp. 387-9.

——— 'Some More Unpublished Sculptures from Rajasthan', *Lalit Kala*, Vol. 10, 1961, pp. 31-3.

——— 'Sculptures from Abaneri, Rajasthan', *Lalit Kala*, Vol. Nos. 1-2, 1955-6, pp. 130-5.

——— 'Ūrdhvaretas Gaṇeśa from Afghanistan' in *EW* (NS), Vol. 18,

Nos. 1-2, Mar-Jun. 1968, pp. 166-8.
——— 'The Aṣṭamātṛkas of Marwar', *IHQ*, Vol. 29, 1953, pp. 393-5.
——— 'Some Interesting Sculptures from Devangana, Rajasthan', *Lalit Kala*, Vol. 8, 1960, pp. 69-71.
——— 'Skanda-Kārttikeya in Sculptures from Rajasthan', *Lalit Kala*, Nos. 3-4, 1956-7, pp. 109-11.
——— 'Some More Unpublished Sculptures from Rajasthan', *Lalit Kala*, Vol. 10, 1961, pp. 31-3.
——— 'Yakṣa Torso from Bharatpur Region', *JOIB*, Vol. 17, Nos. 1-4, 1967-8, pp. 64-5.
Agrawala, V.S., *Śiva-Mahādeva - the Great God*, Varanasi, 1966.
——— *India as Known to Pāṇini (Aśṭadhyāyī)* Banaras Hindu University, 1st edn. 1953, rpt, Varanasi, 1963.
——— *Devī-Mahātmyam. The Glorification of the Great Goddess*, All India Kashiraj Trust, Varanasi, 1963.
——— 'Geographical Data in Pāṇini', *IHQ*, Vol. 29, 1953, pp. 1-34.
——— 'Images of Brahmā, Vishnu and Śiva, etc.', Catalogue of the Mathura Museum 2, *JUPHS*, Vol. 22, 1949, pp. 102-220.
——— *Ancient Indian Folk Cults*, Prithvi Prakashan, Varanasi, 1970.
——— 'Meaning of Gaṇapati', *JOIB*, Vol. 13, 1963, pp. 1-4.
——— 'Miscellaneous Architectural Sculptures: Buddhist', *JUPHS*, Vols. 24-5, 1951-2, pp. 77-118.
Allan, John, *Catalogue of the Coins of Ancient India*, 1st edn. London, 1936, rpt, Munshiram Manoharlal, New Delhi, 1975.
Allchin, Bridget and Raymond, *The Rise of Civilization in India and Pakistan*, Select Book Service Syndicate, New Delhi, 1989.
Allchin, F.R., 'The Legacy of the Indus Civilization' in Gregory L. Possehl, ed., *Harappan Civilization*, 2nd revd edn., American Institute of Indian Studies, Oxford and IBH Publishing Co. Pvt. Ltd., New Delhi, 1993.
Apte, V.M., *Social and Religious Life in the Gṛhya Sūtras*, The Popular Book Depot, Bombay, 1954.
Apte, V.S., *The Practical Sanskrit - English Dictionary*, 4th revd and enlarged edn., Delhi 1965, rpt, Motilal Banarsidass, Delhi, 1978.
Aravamuthan, T.G., 'Ganesa: Clue to a Cult and a Culture', *Journal of Oriental Research*, Madras, Vol. 18, 1949, pp. 221-45.
Ardeleanu-Jansen, Alexandra, 'The Terracotta Figurines from Mohenjo-daro: Considerations on Tradition Craft and Ideology in the Harappa Culture (CA. 2400-1800 BC)', *Lahore Museum Bulletin*, Vol. I, No. 2, July-Dec. 1988, pp. 9-28.
Atre, Shubhangana, *The Archetypal Mother: A Systemic Approach to Harappan Religion*, Ravish Publishers, Pune, 1987.
Ayyar, P.V. Jagadha, *South Indian Shrines*, Asian Educational Services, New Delhi, 1982.

Bagchi, P.C., 'The Cult of the Buddhist Siddhācāryas', *Cultural Heritage of India,* Vol. IV, Calcutta, 1956, pp. 273-9.

——— 'Evolution of the Tantras', *Cultural Heritage of India,* Vol. IV, Calcutta, 1956, pp. 211-16.

Bandyopadhyay, Samaresh, 'A Note on Ganapati', *JOIB,* Vol. 21, 1971-2, pp. 328-30.

Banerjea, J.N., *The Development of Hindu Iconography,* 4th edn., rpted from second rev edn. of 1956, Munshiram Manoharlal, New Delhi, 1974.

Banerjee, Priyatosh, 'A Note on the Worship of Images in Jainism (*c.* 200 BC - 200 AD)', *JBRS,* Vol. 36, Pts. 1-2, Sep.-Dec. 1950, pp. 57-65.

Banerji, Adris, 'Further Unpublished Sculptures from Mewar', *Lalit Kala,* No. 10, Oct. 1961, pp. 18-20.

Banerji, R.D., *The Temple of Śiva at Bhūmāra,* Memoirs of the Archaeological Survey of India, No. 16, 1924.

——— *Bas Reliefs of Badami,* Memoirs of the Archaeological Survey of India, No. 25, 1928.

Barua, Benimadhab, *Gaya and Buddha-Gaya,* Bhartiya Publishing House, Varanasi, 1975.

——— *Bharhut,* Indological Book Corporation, Patna, 1979.

Basham, A.L., *The Wonder that was India,* 1st edn., London, 1954, rpt in paperback of 3rd revd edn., 1967, Sidgwick and Jackson, London, 1988.

Bedekar, V.M. 'Kubera in Sanskrit Literature with special reference to the Mahābhārata', *JGJhRI,* Vol. 25, 1969, pp. 425-51.

Bhandarkar, R.G., *Vaishnavism, Saivism and Minor Religious Systems,* rpt of 1913 edition, Indological Book House, Varanasi, 1965.

Bharati, A., *The Tantric Tradition,* Rider and Company, London, 1965.

Bhattacharji, Sukumari, *Literature in the Vedic Age,* Vol.II, K.P. Bagchi and Co., Calcutta, 1986.

——— *The Indian Theogony,* Cambridge University Press, London, 1970.

Bhattacharya, B.C., *The History of Sarnath or the Cradle of Buddhism,* Benares, 1924.

——— *The Jaina Iconography,* revd edn., Motilal Banarsidass, Delhi, 1974.

Bhattacharyya, Benoytosh, *Indian Buddhist Iconography,* 2nd ed., Calcutta, 1958.

——— 'Tantrika Culture Among the Buddhists', *Cultural Heritage of India,* Vol. IV, Calcutta, 1956, pp. 260-72.

Bhattacharyya, N.N., *History of the Tāntric Religion,* Manohar, New Delhi, 1982.

——— *Ancient Indian Rituals and their Social Content,* Curzon Press, London, 1975, and Rowman & Littlefield, Totowa, USA, 1975.

——— *History of Sākta Religion,* Munshiram Manoharlal, New Delhi, 1974.

Biardeau, Madeleine, 'The Śamī Tree and the Sacrificial Buffalo', *Contributions to Indian Sociology* (NS), Vol. 18, No. 1, 1984, pp. 1-23.

Bolon, Carol Radcliffe, 'Two Chalukya Queens and their Commemorative Temples' in Vidya Dehejia, ed., *Royal Patrons and Great Temple Art,* Marg Publications, Bombay, 1988, pp. 61-76.

Bopearachchi, Osmund, 'On the So-Called Earliest Representation of Gaṇeśa', in Marie-Françoise Boussac and Jean-Francois Salles, eds., *Athens, Aden, Arikamedu,* Manohar Publishers and Centre des Sciences Humaines, New Delhi, 1995.

Brown, Robert L., ed., *Ganesh: Studies of an Asian God,* State University of New York Press, Albany, 1991.

——— 'Gaṇeśa in Southeast Asian Art: Indian Connections and Indigenous Developments', in Robert L. Brown, ed., *Ganesh: Studies of an Asian God,* State University of New York Press, Albany, 1991, pp. 171-234.

Brubaker, Richard L., 'Barbers, Washermen and Other Priests: Servants of the South Indian Village and its Goddess', *History of Religions,* Vol. 19, No. 2, Nov. 1979, pp. 128-52.

Buhnemann, Gudrun, *The Worship of Mahāgaṇapati According to the Nityollāsa,* Institut fur Indologie, Wichtrach (Switzerland), 1988.

——— *Forms of Gaṇeśa,* Institut fur Indologie, Wichtrach, Switzerland, 1989.

Burnouf, E., *Introduction a l'Histoire du Buddhisme Indien,* Paris, 1876.

Cashman, Richard, 'The Political Recruitment of the God Ganapathi' in Robin Jeffrey *et al.*, eds., *India: Rebellion to Republic (Selected Writings, 1857-1990),* Sterling Publishers, 1990.

Chakravarti, Chintaharan, 'Tradition about Vānaras and Rākṣasas', *IHQ,* Vol. 1, Pts. 3-4, pp. 779-81.

Chakravarti, Uma, 'Women, men and beasts: The Jātaka as popular tradition', *Studies in History,* Vol. 9, No.1, NS, Jan.-Jun. 1993, pp. 43-70.

Champakalakshmi, R., 'State and Economy: South India, *circa* AD 400-1300' in Romila Thapar, ed., *Recent Perspectives of Early Indian History,* Oxford University Press, New Delhi, 1993, pp. 266-308.

——— 'Ideology and the State in South India', Mamidipudi Venkatarangaiah Memorial Lecture -1, *Andhra Pradesh History Congress,* Srisailam, 1989.

Chanda, Ramaprasad, *The Beginnings of Art in Eastern India with Special Reference to Sculptures in the Indian Museum, Calcutta,* Memoirs of the Archaeological Survey of India, No. 30, 1927.

——— *Exploration in Orissa,* Memoirs of the Archaeological Survey of India, No. 44, 1930.

——— 'Nidhiśṛnga (Cornucopia): A Study in Symbolism', *Prince of Wales Museum Bulletin,* No. 9, 1964-6, pp. 1-33.

Chandra, Moti, 'The White Elephant', *Lalit Kala,* Nos. 1-2, 1955-6, p. 96.

Chandra, Pramod, *The Sculpture of India, (3000 BC–1300 AD),* National Gallery of Art, Washington, 1985.

Chandra, Rai Govind, 'Problem of Yakṣas', *JGJhRI*, Vol. 28, Jan-Apr. 1972, Pts. 1-2, pp. 499-521.

Chatterjee, Asim Kumar, *The Cult of Skanda-Kārttikeya in Ancient India*, Punthi Pustak, Calcutta, 1970.

Chatterji, B.R., *Indian Cultural Influence in Cambodia*, University of Calcutta, 1928.

Chatterjee, J.C., *Kashmir Shaivism*, 1st edn. 1914, rpt, Indological Book Corporation, Patna, 1978.

Chattopadhyaya, B.D., 'Origin of the Rajputs: The Political, Economic and Social Processes in Early Medieval Rajasthan', *Indian Historical Review*, Vol. III, No.1, pp. 59-82.

Chattopadhyaya, Debiprasad, *Lokāyata: A Study in Ancient Indian Materialism*, People's Publishing House, New Delhi, July, 1959.

Chattopadhyaya, Sudhakar, *Reflections on the Tantras*, Motilal Banarsidass, Delhi, 1978.

——— *Evolution of Hindu Sects*, Munshiram Manoharlal, New Delhi, 1970.

Chavannes, E., 'Une Sculpture Bouddhique de l'Annee 543 p.c.', *Ars Asiatica*, Vol. 2, 1914, pp. 13-19.

Cohen, Lawrence, 'The Wives of Gaṇeśa' in Robert L. Brown, ed., *Ganesh: Studies of an Asian God*, State University of New York Press, Albany, 1991, pp. 115-40.

Coomaraswamy, A.K., *Yaksas* (2 parts), rpt, Munshiram Manoharlal, New Delhi, 1971.

——— 'Ganesha', *BMFA* (Boston), Vol. 26, April 1928, pp. 30-1.

——— *History of Indian and Indonesian Art*, 1st edn. 1927, republication, Dover Publications, New York, 1965.

Courtright, Paul B., *Gaṇeśa: Lord of Obstacles, Lord of Beginnings*, Oxford University Press, New York and Oxford, 1985.

——— 'The Beheading of Gaṇeśa', *Purāṇa*, Vol. 22, No. 1, pp. 67-80.

Cousens, H., *The Chalukyan Architecture of the Kanarese District*, Central Publication Branch, Calcutta, 1926.

Crooke, William, *The Tribes and Castes of North Western India*, Vol. IV, rpt, Cosmo Publications, Delhi, 1975.

Dagens, Bruno, *Les Enseignements Architecturaux de l'Ajitāgama et du Rauravāgama*, Publications de l'Institut Français d'Indologie, No. 57, Pondicherry, 1977.

Dandekar, R.N., *Vedic Mythological Tracts*, Ajanta Publications, Delhi, 1979.

Das, D.N., 'Serpent Worship in Ancient Kalinga', *PIHC*, 1965, pp. 43-4.

Das, Veena, 'The Mythological Film and its Framework of Meaning: An Analysis of Jai Santoshi Ma', *India International Centre Quarterly*, Vol. 8, No. 1, Mar. 1980, pp. 43-56.

Dasgupta, K.K., *The Audumbaras*, Calcutta, 1965.

——— *A Tribal History of Ancient India - A Numismatic Approach*, Nababharat Publishers, Calcutta, 1974.

Dasgupta, Shashi Bhusan, *An Introduction to Tantric Buddhism,* University of Calcutta, 1950.

Dehejia, Vidya, *Slaves of the Lord,* Munshiram Manoharlal, New Delhi, 1988.

Deva, Raja Radha Kanta, *Śabdakalpadruma,* 5 vols., 1st edn. Saka era 1808 by Baptist Mission Press, Calcutta, rpt, Chowkhamba Sanskrit Series Office, Varanasi, 1961, 1967

Dhavalikar, M.K., 'A Note on Two Gaṇeśa Statues from Afghanistan', *EW* (NS), Vol. 21, nos. 3-4, 1971, pp. 331-6.

——— 'Daimabad Bronzes' in Gregory L. Possehl, ed., *Harappan Civilization,* 2nd revd edn., American Institute of Indian Studies, Oxford and IBH Publishing Co. Pvt. Ltd., New Delhi, 1993, pp. 421-6.

——— 'Gaṇeśa: Myth and Reality' in Robert L. Brown, ed., *Ganesh: Studies of an Asian God,* State University of New York Press, Albany, 1991, pp. 49-68.

Diskalkar, D.B., 'Gaṇeśar Inscription of V.S. 1291 (A.D. 1235)', *ABORI,* Vol. 9, Pts. 1-4, 1927-8, pp. 179-81.

——— 'Some Unpublished Inscriptions of Vastupāla', *ABORI,* Vol. 9, Pts. 1-4, 1927-8, pp. 179-81.

Drabu, V.N., *Saivāgamas. A Study in the Socio-Economic Ideas and Institutions of Kashmir (200 BC- AD 700),* Indus Publishing Company, New Delhi, 1990.

Drury, Nevill, *Shamanism,* Element Books Ltd., Brisbane, 1992.

During Caspers, E.C.L., 'Some Thoughts on the Indus Script' in Ellen M. Raven and Karel T. Van Kooij, eds., *Indian Art and Archaeology,* E.J. Brill, Ledien, 1992, pp. 54-67.

——— 'Magic Hunting Practices in Harappan Times' in K. Friefelt and S. Sprensen, eds., *The Indus Civilization,* South Asian Archaeology, Curzon Press, London, 1985, pp. 227-36.

Eliade, Mircea, ed., *The Encyclopaedia of Religion,* Macmillan Publishing Company, New York, and Collier Macmillan Publishers, London, 1987.

——— *Patterns in Comparative Religion,* Sheed and Ward, Inc., New York, 1958.

Farquhar, J.N., *An Outline of the Religious Literature of India,* rpt, Motilal Banarsidass, Delhi, 1967.

Ferreira, John V., *Totemism in India,* Oxford University Press, Bombay, 1965.

Foucher, A., *The Beginnings of Buddhist Art,* rpt, Varanasi, 1972.

——— *Etudes sur l'Art Bouddhique de l'Inde,* Tokyo, 1922.

——— *On The Iconography of the Buddha's Nativity,* Memoirs of the Archaeological Survey of India, No. 46, 1934.

Frankfort, H., *Cylinder Seals,* Macmillan & Co., London, 1939.

Frederic, Louis, *Les Dieux du Bouddhisme. Guide Iconographique,* Flammarion, Paris, 1992.

Fuller, C.J., 'Only Śiva can worship Śiva: Ritual Mistakes and their Correction in a South Indian Temple', *Contributions to Indian Sociology,* (NS), Vol. 27, No. 2, 1993, pp. 169-89.

Garde, M.B., 'The Site of Padmavati', *ASIAR,* 1915-16, Calcutta, 1918, pp. 101-[illegible].

Gazetteer of India, Karnataka State, Uttara Kannada District, Bangalore, 1985.

Gazetteer of India, Karnataka State, South Kanara District, Bangalore, 1973.

Gazetteer of India, Kerala, Trichur, Kerala, 1962.

Gazetteer of India, Mysore State, Kolar District, Bangalore, 1968.

Gazetteer of Kashmir and Ladakh, Vivek Publishing House, Delhi, 1974.

Geiger, W., *Pali Literature and Language,* trans., Balakrishna Ghosah, 2nd edn., Oriental Books Rpt Corporation, Delhi, 1968.

Getty, Alice, *Gaṇeśa,* 1st edn. Clarendon Press Oxford, 1936, 2nd edn., Munshiram Manoharlal, New Delhi, 1971.

Ghurye, G.S., *Gods and Men,* Popular Book Depot, Bombay, 1962.

——— *Vedic India,* Popular Prakashan, Bombay, 1979.

Gonda, J., *The Ritual Sūtras,* (J. Gonda, ed., *A History of Indian Literature,* Vol. I, Fasc. 2), Otto Harrassowitz, Weisbaden, 1977.

——— *Medieval Religious Literature in Sanskrit,* (J. Gonda, ed. *A History of Indian Literature,* Vol. II, Fasc. 1), Otto Harrassowitz, Wiesbaden, 1977.

——— *Viṣṇuism and Śivaism,* 1st edn. London, 1970, 1st Indian edn., Munshiram Manoharlal, New Delhi, 1976.

——— *Aspects of Early Viṣṇuism,* Utrecht, 1954.

Gopalachari, K., *Early History of the Andhra Country,* University of Madras, 1941.

Gopalan, R., *History of the Pallavas of Kanchi,* University of Madras, 1928.

Gordon, Stewart, *The Marathas (1600-1818),* The New Cambridge History of India, Vol. II. 4, Cambridge University Press and Foundation Books, New Delhi, 1993.

Granoff, Phyllis, 'Gaṇeśa as a Metaphor: The Mudgala Purāṇa' in Robert L. Brown, ed., *Ganesh: Studies of an Asian God,* State University of New York Press, Albany, 1991, pp. 85-99.

Graves, Robert, *Greek Myths,* Cassell and Co. Ltd., London, Graves, Robert, *Greek Myths,* Cassell and Co. Ltd., London, 1958.

Gupta, Rāmavatāra, *Gaṇeśa Mahimā,* Pustak Mahal, Delhi.

Gupta, Sanjukta, Dirk Jan Hoens and Teun Goudriaan, *Hindu Tantrism,* E.J. Brill, Leiden, 1979.

Gupte, B.A., 'Harvest Festivals of Gauri and Ganesh', *Indian Antiquary,* Vol. 35, Nov. 1906, pp. 60-4.

Guseva, N.R., *Jainism,* trans. from the Russian by Y.S.Pedkar, Sindhu Publications, Bombay, 1971.

Haldar, J.R., *Early Buddhist Mythology,* New Delhi, 1977.

Harle, J.C., *The Art and Architecture of the Indian Subcontinent,* Penguin Books, England, 1986.

——— 'Towards Understanding Gupta Sculpture' in Kal Khandalavala, ed., *The Golden Age,* Marg Publications, Bombay, 1991, pp. 7-14.

Hazra, R.C., 'The Gaṇeśa Purāṇa', *JGJhRI,* Vol. 9, 1951, pp. 79-99.

——— 'Gaṇapati-Worship and the Upapurāṇas Dealing with it', *JGJhRI,* Vol. 5, Pt.4, 1948, pp. 263-76.

——— *Studies in the Puranic Records on Hindu Rites and Customs,* rpt, Motilal Banarsidass, Delhi, 1987.

Heras, H., *The Problem of Gaṇapati,* Indological Book House, Delhi, 1972.

Hiltebeitel, Alf, 'The Indus Valley "Proto-Śiva", Reexamined through Reflections on the Goddess, the Buffalo and the Symbolism of *vāhanas', Anthropos,* Vol. 73, 1978, pp. 767-97.

——— 'Rāma and Gilgamesh: The Sacrifices of the Water Buffalo and the Bull of Heaven', *History of Religions,* Vol. 19, No. 3, Feb. 1980, pp. 187-223.

Hingorani, R.P. *Jaina Iconography in Rūpamaṇḍana,* Kishor Vidya Niketan, Varanasi, 1978.

Jaiswal, Suvira, *The Origin and Development of Vaiṣṇavism,* 2nd ed., Munshiram Manoharlal, New Delhi, 1981.

James, E.O., *The Cult of the Mother Goddess,* Thames and Hudson, London, 1959.

Jash, P., *History of Śaivism,* Calcutta, 1974.

Jayakar, Pupul, *The Earth Mother,* first published *as The Earthen Drum* by the National Museum, 1980, revd and updated edn., Penguin Books, New Delhi, 1989.

Jayaswal, Vidula and Kalyan Krishna, *An Ethno-Archaeological View of Indian Terracottas,* Agam Kala Prakashan, New Delhi, 1986.

Jha, D.N., ed., *Feudal Social Formation in Early India,* Chanakya Publications, Delhi, 1987.

Jha, V.N., 'Varṇasaṃkara in the Dharma Sūtras: Theory and Practice', in *JESHO,* Vol. 13, Nos. 1-3, 1970, pp. 273-88.

Joshi, Kashinatha Sastri, *Sāratha Pūjā Saṃgraha,* Chitralekha Agency, Pune.

Joshi, M.C. and K.S. Ramachandran, 'A Rare Wooden Sculpture of Five Faced Gaṇeśa', *EW*(NS), Vol. 21, Nos. 3-4, Sep.-Dec. 1971, pp. 337-40.

Kakar, Sudhir, *Shamans, Mystics and Doctors,* 2nd impression, Oxford Indian Paperbacks, New Delhi, 1992.

Kane, P.V., *History of Dharmaśāstra,* 5 vols., Govt. Oriental Series, Class B, No. 6, Bhandarkar Oriental Research Institute, Poona, 2nd edn., 1968-74.

Keith, A.B., *A History of Sanskrit Literature,* rpt, Oxford University Press, Delhi, 1973.

Kenneth, K.S. Ch'en, *Buddhism in China* (A Historical Survey), Princeton University Press, New Jersey, 1964.

Kern, H., *Histoire du Bouddhisme dans l'Inde,* Vol. 2, Leipzig, 1884.

Klingender, Francis, *Animals in Art and Thought,* Routledge and Kegan Paul, London, 1971.

Kosambi, D.D., *Myth and Reality,* Popular Prakashan, Bombay, 1962.

Lahiri, A.N., *Corpus of Indo-Greek Coins,* Poddar Publications, Calcutta, 1965.

Lal, B.B., 'Excavation at Hastinapura and other Explorations in the Upper Ganga and Sutlej Basins, 1950-52', *Ancient India,* Nos. 10 and 11, 1954 and 1955, pp. 5-151.

Lal, B.B. and S.P. Gupta, *Frontiers of the Indus Civilization,* (Sir Mortimer Wheeler Commemoration Volume), Books & Books, New Delhi, 1984.

Lanius, M.C., 'Rajasthani Sculpture of the Ninth and Tenth Centuries', pp. 78-84 in Pratapaditya Pal, ed., *Aspects of Indian Art,* E.J. Brill, Leiden, 1972.

Law, B.C., *A History of Pali Literature,* Vol. I, 1st edn., 1933, rpt, Bhartiya Publishing House, Varanasi, 1974.

——— *Kauśāmbī in Ancient Literature,* Memoirs of the Archaeological Survey of India, No. 60, 1939.

——— *Rājagriha in Ancient Literature,* Memoirs of Archaeological Survey of India, No. 58, 1938.

Levi-Strauss, Claude, *Totemism,* Penguin Books, 1973.

Lippe, Aschwin de, *Indian Mediaeval Sculpture,* North Holland Publishing Company, Amsterdam, 1978.

Lohuizen-de Leeuw, J.E. Van, 'Gandhara and Mathura: Their Cultural Relationship', pp. 27-43 in Pratapaditya Pal, ed., *Aspects of Indian Art,* E.J. Brill, Leiden, 1972.

Longhurst, A.H., *Pallava Architecture,* 2 vols., Cosmo Publications, New Delhi, 1982.

Lorenzen, David, *The Kāpālikas and Kālāmukhas: Two Lost Saivite Sects,* Motilal Banarsidass, New Delhi, 1972.

Macdonell, Arthur A., *A History of Sanskrit Literature,* rpt, Motilal Banarsidass, Delhi, 1990.

Mackay, Ernest, *Early Indus Civilization,* revd and enlarged edn. by Dorothy Mackay, Indological Book Corporation, New Delhi, 1976.

——— *Further Excavations at Mohenjo-Daro,* Vol. I., rpt, Indological Book Corporation, New Delhi, 1976.

Mahadevan, T.M.P., 'Saivism and the Indus Civilisation', *JGJhRI,* Vol. 4, Nov. 1946, pp. 1-10.

Maharashtra State Gazetteer, Yeotmal District, 1st edn. 1908, revd edn., Bombay, 1974.

Majumdar, A.K., *Bhakti Renaissance,* 2nd edn., Bharatiya Vidya Bhavan, Bombay, 1979.

Marshall, Sir John and Alfred Foucher, *The Monuments of Sanchi,* rpt, Swati Publications, New Delhi, 1982.

Meadow, Richard, 'Animal Domestication in the Middle East' in Gregory Possehl, ed., *Harappan Civilization,* 2nd revised edn., American Institute of Indian Studies, Oxford and IBH Publishing Co. Pvt. Ltd., New Delhi, 1993.

Misra, O.P. *Iconography of the Saptamātṛkas,* Agam Kala Prakashan, Delhi, 1989.

Misra, R.N., *Yaksha Cult and Iconography,* Mushiram Manoharlal, New Delhi, 1981.

Mitra, Haridas, *Gaṇāpati,* Visva-Bharati, Santiniketan, 1959.

Modhey, S.G., 'God Kubera in the Rāmāyaṇa', *JOIB,* Vol. 21, 1971-2, pp. 299-306.

Moor, Captain Edward, 'Account of an Hereditary living Deity to whom Devotion is paid by the Bramins of Poona and its Neighbourhood', *Asiatick Researches,* Vol. 7, 1801, pp.383-97.

Mukherjee, A.N., *Origin and History of Pāla Sena Sculpture,* Ashutosh Museum, Calcutta, 1966.

Munshi, K.M., ed., *The Glory that was Gurjaradeśa,* AD *550-1300,* Pt. 1, Bombay, 1955.

Nagarch, B.L., 'Śiva Temples - Gandai', G. Kuppuram and K, Kumudamani, eds., *History, Archaeology, Art and Religion* (Prof. Upendra Thakur Felicitation Volume), Vol. I, pp. 93-199, Sundeep Prakashan, Delhi, 1990.

Nagaswamy, R., *Masterpieces of Early South Indian Bronzes,* National Museum, New Delhi, 1983.

——— *Śiva Bhakti,* Navrang, New Delhi, 1989.

Nandi, R.N., *Social Roots of Religion in Ancient India,* K.P. Bagchi and Company, New Delhi, 1986.

——— *Religious Institutions and Cults in the Deccan,* Motilal Baṇarsidass, Delhi, 1973.

Narain, A.K., *The Indo-Greeks,* Oxford University Press, Delhi, 1980.

——— 'On the Earliest Gaṇeśa', pp. 142-4 in J.E. Van Lohuizen De Leeuw, ed., *Studies in South Asian Culture,* Vol. 7, (Senarat Paranavitana Commemoration Volume), E. J. Brill, Leiden, 1978.

——— 'Gaṇeśa: A Protohistory of the Idea and the Icon' in Robert L. Brown, ed., *Ganesh: Studies of an Asian God,* State University of New York Press, Albany, 1991, pp. 19-48.

Nath, Amarendra, 'Gaṇeśa in Central Asian Art: An Identification', *Journal of Indian Society of Oriental Art* (NS), Vol. 6, 1974-5, pp.1-4.

Nilkanta Sastri, K.A., *A History of South India,* 7th impression, Oxford University Press, 1987.

Norman, K.R., *Pali Literature,* (J. Gonda, ed. *A History of Indian Literature,* Vol. 7, Fasc. 2), Otto Harrassowitz, Wiesbaden, 1983.

Obeyesekere, Gananath, *The Cult of the Goddess Pattini,* University of Chicago, Chicago, 1984.

O'Flaherty, W.D., *Asceticism and Eroticism in the Mythology of Śiva,* Indian edn., Oxford University Press, Delhi, 1975.

——— *Sexual Metaphors and Animal Symbols in Indian Mythology,* rpt, Motilal Banarsidass, Delhi, 1981.

Pal, Pratapaditya, *Bronzes of Kashmir,* Graz, New York, 1975.

——— *The Ideal Image: The Gupta Sculptural Tradition and its Influence,* The Asia Society, New York, 1978.

——— *Hindu Religion and Iconology (According to the Tantrasāra),* Vichitra Press, Los Angeles, 1981.

Pandey, Rajendra, *Kāśī Through the Ages,* Sundeep Prakashan, Delhi, 1979.

Panigrahi, K.C., *Archaeological Remains at Bhubaneswar,* Orient Longmans, Delhi, 1961.

Parekh, V.S., 'An Image of Double-Faced Gaṇeśa from Junagadh', *JOIB,* Vol. 27, pp. 40-2.

Peterson, Indira Viswanathan, *Poems to Śiva,* Motilal Banarsidass, Delhi, 1991.

Possehl, Gregory L., ed., *Harappan Civilization,* 2nd revd edn., American Institute of Indian Studies, Oxford and IBH Publishing Col. Pvt. Ltd., New Delhi, 1993.

Preston, Lawrence, W., 'Subregional Religious Centres in the History of Maharashtra: The Sites Sacred to Gaṇeśa', in N.K. Wagle, ed., *Images of Maharashtra: A Regional Profile of India,* Asia Publishing House, Bombay, 1980.

Radhakrishnan, S., *Indian Philosophy,* Vol. I, Centenary edn, Oxford University Press, 1990.

Raja-Manikam, *The Development of Saivism in South India Under the Pallavas of Kanci and the Imperial Colas (AD 300-1300),* University of Madras, 1951.

Ramasubramaniam, V., 'The Gaṇapati-Vināyaka-Gajānana Worship: Analysis of an Integrated Cult', *Bulletin of the Institute of Traditional Cultures,* Madras, 1971, pp. 110-46.

Rao, S.K. Ramachandra, ed., *Gaṇapati (32 Drawings from a 19th Century Scroll),* Karnataka Chitrakala Parishath, Bangalore, 1989.

Rao, T.A.G., *Elements of Hindu Iconography,* 2 vols., 4 pts., rpt of 1914 Madras edn., Motilal Banarsidass, Delhi, 1985.

Rao, U. Venkatakrishna, 'The Gaṇapaty Cult', *Quarterly Journal of the Mythic Society,* Vol. 41, July 1950, pp. 92-9.

Ratnagar, Shereen, *Enquiries into the Political Organization of Harappan Society,* Ravish Publishers, Pune, 1991.

Ray, Nihar Ranjan, *Maurya and Sunga Art,* Calcutta, 1965.

Riviere, Juan Roger, 'The Problem of Gaṇeśa in the Purāṇas', *Purāṇa,* Vol. 4, 1962, pp. 96-102.

Sahu, B.P., *From Hunters to Breeders,* Anamika Prakashan, New Delhi, 1988.

Samaddar, J.N., 'Industrial and Trading Organisation in Ancient India', *JBORS,* Vol.7, Pt. 4, 1921, pp. 35-54.

Saraswati, Baidyanath, *Kāśī: Myth and Reality,* Indian Institute of Advanced Study, Simla, 1975.

Sardesai, G.S., *New History of the Marathas,* Vol. I, 1st edn., 1946, rpt, Bombay, 1957.

Schastok, Sara L., *The Śāmalājī Sculptures and 6th Century Art in Western India,* E.J. Brill, Leiden, 1985.

Shah, U.P., *Jaina-Rūpa-Maṇḍana (Jaina Iconography),* Vol. I, Abhinav Publications, New Delhi, 1987.

——— 'Minor Jaina Deities', *JOIB,* Vol. 32, pp. 82-98.

——— 'Ancient Sculptures from Gujarat and Saurashtra', *Journal of Indian Museums,* Vol. 8, 1952, pp. 49-57.

——— 'Some Early Sculptures from Ābu and Bhinmal', *BBMPG,* Vol. 12, 1955-6, pp. 43-56.

——— *Sculptures from Śāmalājī and Roda (North Gujarat) in the Baroda Museum,* Baroda, 1960.

——— 'Western Indian Sculpture and the So-called Gupta Influence', pp. 44-8 in Pratapaditya Pal, ed., *Aspects of Indian Art,* E.J. Brill, Leiden, 1972.

Sharma, B.N., *Iconography of Vaināyakī,* Abhinav Publications, Delhi, 1979.

——— 'Abhiśeka in Indian Art', *JOIB,* Vol. 21, 1971-72, pp. 108-13.

Sharma, R.S., *Material Culture and Social Formations in Ancient India,* MacMillan India Ltd., Delhi, 1983.

——— *Indian Feudalism, c. 300-1200,* University of Calcutta, 1965, 2nd edn, MacMillan, Delhi, 1980.

——— Social Changes in Early Medieval India (*c.* AD 500-1200), Delhi, 1969.

Sharma, R.S. and D.N. Jha, 'The Economic History of India upto AD 1200: Trends and Prospects', *JESHO,* Vol. 17, No. 1, 1974, pp. 48-80.

Shrimali, K.M., *History of Pañcāla,* 2 vols., Munshiram Manoharlal, New Delhi, 1983, 1985.

Shrivastava, M.C.P., 'Gaṇeśa and Jyeṣṭhā: A Comparative Study', *JBRS,* Vol. LVIII, Pts. 1-4, 1972, pp. 165-70.

Sills, David, L., *International Encyclopedia of the Social Sciences,* Vol. 10, Macmillan Co. and the Free Press, 1968.

Singh, Harihar, *Jaina Temples of Western India,* ParshvanathVidhyashram Research Institute, Varanasi, 1982.

Singh, R.B.P., *Jainism in Early Medieval Karnataka, (A.D. 500-1200),* Motilal Banarsidass, Delhi, 1975.

Singh, Sarva Daman, 'The Elephant and the Aryans', *JRAS,* 1963, pp. 1-6.

Sircar, D.C., *Studies in the Religious Life of Ancient and Medieval India,* Motilal Banarsidass, Delhi, 1971.

——— *Studies in the Geography of Ancient and Medieval India,* 2nd edn., Motilal Banarsidass, Delhi, 1971.

——— 'Mahāmāyūrī: List of Yakṣas', *Journal of Ancient Indian History,* Vol. 5, Pts. 1-2, 1971-2.

Śivaramamurti, C., 'Early Eastern Chalukya Sculpture', *Bulletin of the Madras Government Museum,* (New Series - General Section), Vol. 7, No. 2, Madras, 1957.

——— 'Geographical and Chronological Factors in Indian Iconography', *Ancient India,* No. 6, New Delhi, 1950, pp. 21-63.

——— *South Indian Bronzes,* New Delhi, 1963.

Smith, Vincent A., *The Jain Stupa and Other Antiquities of Mathura,* Archaeological Survey of India (New Imperial Series), Vol. 20, 1901.

Snellgrove, D.L., *The Hevajra Tantra. A Critical Study,* 2 Parts (London Oriental Series, Vol. 6), London, 1959.

Snodgrass, Adrian, *The Matrix and Diamond World Maṇḍalas in Shingon Buddhism,* 2 vols. Sata-Pitaka Series, Indo-Asian Literatures, Vol. 354, Aditya Prakashan, New Delhi, 1988.

Sompura, Kantilal F., *The Structural Temples of Gujarat,* Gujarat University Theses Publication Series - 4, Ahmedabad, 1968.

Soundara Rajan, K.V., *Cave Temples of the Deccan,* Archaelogical Survey of India, New Delhi, 1981.

Sorensen, S., *An Index to the Names of the Mahābhārata,* rpt, Motilal Banarsidass, Delhi, 1963.

Srinivasan, C.R., 'Saptamātṛkas', *JOIB,* Vol. 24, 1974, Nos. 1-2, pp. 428-35.

Srinivasan, K.R., *Cave Temples of the Pallavas,* Archaeological Survey of India, 1st edn. 1964, rpt, New Delhi, 1993.

Stein, Aurel, *An Archaeological Tour in Upper Swat and Adjacent Hill Tracts,* Memoirs of the Archaeological Survey of India, No. 42, Calcutta, 1930.

Stutley, Margaret, *Ancient Indian Magic and Folklore,* Routledge and Kegan Paul, London, 1980.

Subbarayalu, Y., 'The Cola State', *Studies in History,* Vol. IV, No. 2, 1982, pp. 265-306.

Subrahmanian, N.S., ed., *Encyclopaedia of the Upaniṣads,* Oriental University Press, London, 1986.

Sukul, Kubernath, *Varanasi Down the Ages,* Patna, 1974.

Tarn, W.W., *The Greeks in Bactria and India,* Cambridge, 1938 and 1951.

Thapar, Romila, *Aśoka and the Decline of the Mauryas,* OUP, London, 1961.

——— 'Origin Myths and Historical Tradition', *Ancient Indian Social History,*

1st edn. 1978, rpt of 1984 edn., Orient Longman, New Delhi, 1990, pp. 294-325.

Thurston, E., *Castes and Tribes of Southern India,* 1st edn., Madras, 1909, rpt, Johnson Reprint Corporation, USA, 1965.

Tiwari, J.N., *Goddess Cults in Ancient India (With special Reference to the First Seven Centuries AD),* Sundeep Prakashan, Delhi, 1985.

Tiwari, Maruti Nandan and Kamal Giri, 'Images of Gaṇeśa in Jainism' in Robert L. Brown, ed., *Ganesh: Studies of an Asian God,* State University of New York Press, Albany, 1991, pp. 101-14.

Tucci, Guiseppe, 'Preliminary Report on an Archaeological Survey in Swat', *EW,* Vol. 9, 1958, pp. 279-328.

Upadhye, A.N. 'Paiśāci Language and Literature', *ABORI,* Vol. 21, 1940, pp. 1-37.

Virji, K.K., *Ancient History of Saurashtra,* Konkan Institute of Arts and Sciences, Bombay, 1955.

Vogel, J. Ph., *Indian Serpent Lore,* 1st edn. London, 1926, rptd by Indological Book House, Varanasi and Delhi, 1972.

Warder, A.K., *Indian Buddhism,* 1st edn. Delhi, 1970, rpt of 2nd revd edn, 1980, Motilal Banarsidass, Delhi, 1991.

Watters, Thomas, *On Yuan Chwang's Travels in India, (AD 629-645),* 1st edn. London, 1904-5, 2nd Indian edn., Munshiram Manoharlal, New Delhi, 1973.

Wayman, A., *The Buddhist Tantras: Light on Indo-Tibetan Esotericism,* New York, 1973.

Weiner, Sheila L., *From Gupta to Pāla Sculpture,* rptd from *Artibus Asiae,* Vol. 25, pp. 167-82, Ascona, Switzerland.

Wilkinson, Christopher, 'The Tantric Gaṇeśa: Texts Preserved in the Tibetan Canon' in Robert L. Brown, ed., *Ganesh: Studies of an Asian God,* State University of New York Press, Albany, 1991, pp. 235-76.

Winternitz, Maurice, *A History of Indian Literature,* 3 vols., 1st edn., Delhi, 1981, rpt, Motilal Banarsidass, Delhi, 1988.

——— 'Gaṇeśa in the Mahābhārata', *JRAS,* 1898, No. 3, pp. 380-4.

——— 'Notes on the GuhyasamājaTantra and the Age of Tantras', *IHQ,* Vol. 9, No. 1, Mar. 1933, pp. 1-10.

Woodcock, George, *The Greeks in India,* Faber and Faber, London, 1966.

Zeuner, Frederick E., *A History of Domesticated Animals,* London, 1963.

Zimmer, Heinrich, *Myths and Symbols in Indian Art and Civilization,* Pantheon Books, New York, 1962.

——— *The Art of Indian Asia,* 2 vols., New York, 1955.

Zvelebil, K.V., *Tamil Traditions on Subrahmaṇya-Murugan,* Institute of Asian Studies, Madras, 1991.

Index